NED SHERRIN

NED SHERRIN

The Autobiography

NED SHERRIN

LITTLE, BROWN

LITTLE, BROWN

First published in Great Britain in August 2005 by Little, Brown

The publishers are grateful for permission to reproduce extracts from the
following: 'I wonder what happened to him' by Noël Coward, courtesy Methuen
Publishing Limited; *Facing the Nation: Television and Politics, 1936–1976* by
Grace Wyndham Goldie, published by Bodley Head, courtesy David Higham
Associates; from article written in *The Times* in 1963 and from sketch written for
That Was The Week That Was, both by Bernard Levin, by permission of Curtis
Brown Group Ltd on behalf of the Estate of Bernard Levin © Bernard Levin
1963; for the *BBC-3* sketch material written by Alan Bennett in 1965, courtesy
PFD; *From Congregations to Audiences Part One* by David Frost © David Frost,
permission granted by Curtis Brown Group Ltd; from sketch written by Dennis
Potter © Dennis Potter, 1963, all rights reserved; *Jeffrey Bernard is Unwell* by
Keith Waterhouse, and *TW3* sketches by Keith Waterhouse and Willis Hall ©
Willis Hall and Keith Waterhouse 1963, all by permission The Agency (London)
Ltd, all rights reserved; *Streets Ahead* by Keith Waterhouse by permission
Hodder and Stoughton Ltd; *Damn You, England: Collected Prose* by
John Osborne, courtesy Faber & Faber Ltd.

A CIP catalogue record for this book is available from the British Library.

ISBN 0 316 72499 8

Typeset in Sabon by M Rules
Printed and bound in Great Britain by
Clays Ltd, St Ives plc

Little, Brown
An imprint of
Time Warner Bool̶ ̶ ̶ ̶ ̶ ̶ ̶ ̶ ̶ UK
Brettenham
Lancaster
London WC
www.twbg

CONTENTS

FOREPIECE

I was born between the villages of High and Low Ham in the county of Somerset. For a long time I thought how neat it would be to go to the House of Lords as Lord Sherrin of High and Low Ham – the perfect theatrical title; but no call came.

Then I pondered using it as a title for this book. Finally I am persuaded that the words 'The Autobiography' will do as well as any, for that is what it is.

CHAPTER 1

I've Just Come up from Somerset Where the Cider Apples Grow . . .

This is not the time nor the place for me to draw on my diary records of my drug-fuelled, three-in-a-bed romps with Dame Sybil Thorndike and Dame Edith Evans in those permissive 1960s.

No, to begin we must go back another hundred years.

High Ham, Fearful Death. On Friday (yesterday) a fearful death from burning occurred in this village to the wife of Mr John Couzins. It appears that the poor woman's husband, who is partially blind, left the house for a few minutes after eleven in the morning to draw some cider, and was gone about a quarter of an hour. When he returned, to his great dismay he discovered that his wife was nearly burnt to death, her clothes being literally burnt off her body and her hair quite destroyed. Mr Couzins immediately called assistance, when a man named Samuel Sweet ran in with a bucket of water, but he arrived too late to be of any service in saving the woman's life. The leaf of the table, about a foot and a half square, against which she was sitting, was charred quite black. It is thought her clothes must have caught fire immediately after her husband went out, and that she must have gone back to the table and sat down, where she was found. The actual cause of death is supposed to be suffocation from the smoke. The deceased was 78 years old and nearly helpless. The old man feels the shock very acutely.

Poor Jane was one of my great-great-grandmothers on my father's side. The report is from the *Langport Herald*, 30 April 1864. Twenty-four years later in 1888 my father was born. It is strange that no memory of this horrific accident has found a place in family lore. Surely it cannot have faded before my father's birth, or his sister's two years earlier in 1886, especially as my grandmother was given the name of Jane. Was it considered too embarrassing, or simply too tragic?

On the whole Sherrins appear to have lived quiet lives, close to their native soil – farmers, butchers, millers. The exceptions are those who, perhaps as the youngest members of large families, sought a future elsewhere and chose to emigrate – and me.

Sherrin roots are in and around Sedgemoor in the Somerset Levels – the wetlands, the King Alfred's cake-burning country. Most of the High Ham Sherrins can be traced back to three brothers, John, Philip and Adam, born in the mid-1700s.

Over a hundred years later two lines of distant cousins merged in 1886 when my grandfather, Alfred Sherrin, married my grandmother, Jane Sherrin (née Sherrin). In between are innumerable Sherrin broods with up to nine children each. Homes and birthplaces are scattered around Sedgemoor. High Ham, Bridgewater, Martock, Shapwick, Ashcott and Glastonbury all feature. The census in 1881 reveals farmers varying from Philip Sherrin, farmer of twenty-five acres employing one man, to Adam Sherrin, 'Farmer 200 acres employing 6 men and 3 boys.' Scattered through the records are 'Dairy servant (Ag)'; 'Farm servant (Indoor)'; Farmer's wife'; 'General servant (Domestic)'. There is a 'Farmer's assistant, Stowell Sherrin'; a butcher and a boot- and shoe-maker. The Christian names have a biblical, antique ring: Josiah, Job, Tryphena, Wesley, Betsy, Bessie, Eliza, Samuel, Amelia, Minnie, Lily, Nellie, Louisa, Sophia, Ada, Martha, Cornelius, Adam Vile – even a Marlyn.

Somewhere during the nineteenth century a 'base born' son was delivered to a Couzins before she married a Sherrin. 'Base born' was a new phrase to me but there it is in the census for 1851.

My immediate family of Sherrins have never been curious about the family tree. My father poo-pooed any interest in a Sherrin diaspora. Perhaps he imagined distant relatives returning from outposts of Empire to invade his birthright.

I owe this information to two Australian Sherrins. When I was directing *Jeffrey Bernard Is Unwell* in Perth I found myself at a dinner party sitting next to an attractive young woman whose name was Sherrin Ayre. Her Sherrin ancestors, John and Elizabeth Sherrin, emigrated to Queensland from High Ham on the *Combodia* in 1855. I can only speculate on their reasons for leaving the village. Was he a youngest son given a few sheep and a couple of tickets to a new life?

Sherrin Ayre's sister Desley Hardy is the devoted family archivist. Her researches go back to the 1600s. Her diligence also revealed an 1881 census reference to my great-grandfather on my mother's side, William Drewett, a 'domestic coachman' in Frenchay, near Bristol. He had six children. My grandfather, Richard Blackmore, was the third, born in 1867. In the census he is described as an 'office boy'. He came to Castle Cary soon afterwards as a solicitor's clerk. His children revered his achievement. His self-made rise from office boy to stern Victorian patriarch, solicitor and county councillor was marvelled at. Long before his death he added his name to the writing paper of his firm, Woodforde and Drewett. Woodforde makes a link with the celebrated, heavy-eating, eighteenth-century parson–diarist. Parson Woodforde's rectory was for a time a couple of miles down the road at Alford, a living he combined with Castle

Cary before he moved to Norfolk. Two Miss Woodfordes survived in Cary until the 1950s.

My father, Thomas Adam Sherrin, was a country character; an hour-over-a-five-bar-gate conversationalist. The gate could serve to pass the time of day or it could be the setting for a deal in pounds, acres or animal flesh. He liked to string a negotiation out. He lived for a bargain. He was a wag who, once he found a joke on someone, worried it mercilessly. Short and paunchy with a Mr Punch nose and a crafty glint in his eye, he was slow to see a joke against himself.

His life had not been easy. His father died in 1903 when he was fifteen. He was removed from Langport Grammar School to run the farm for his mother, Jane, and his two cottage-loaf sisters, Lou and Em. Years later he would talk of playing the violin. I never saw one; but 'fiddle' and 'bass viol' were words he used easily, and the late years of the nineteenth century and the early years of the last century were times in which village people made their own music.

The family unit remained undisturbed for nearly a quarter of a century. My father farmed the smallholding. Aunt Lou taught generations at the village school. Aunt Em and her mother ran the farmhouse. In the late twenties it all changed.

A new teacher, Frances Drewett, arrived from Castle Cary to teach at High Ham School. She lodged with the Sherrins and my father married her younger sister, Dorothy, known as Dolly. He was approaching forty. My mother was in her thirties. They honeymooned briefly in Torquay, the farthest my father had been from home. In March 1928 my brother Alfred was born just in time to be photographed in his grandmother's arms. She died a month later. I was delivered nearly three years afterwards on 18 February 1931.

I cannot be sure of the exact date. My brother's arrival had been an event, recorded to the minute. As a second coming my birth was of less moment. The certificate says '18 Feb'. At least one family bible suggests a day later. No one remembered clearly at what time of the day or night I appeared. No astrologer can produce an accurate chart for me – if such a thing is feasible. My father felt cheated, I suspect. With a son to help him on the farm what he had applied for was a daughter to help his wife around the house. Now he had to hire a maidservant.

We left Ham in 1934 when I was three. I do not remember Gawler's farm. (Why Gawler's? Who were the Gawlers? They do not appear in the family tree or the nineteenth-century census.) We landed some six or seven miles away in the village of Kingweston. Kingweston as I became aware of it was feudally organised. The squire, known as 'The Squire', was Capt. W. F. Dickinson, OBE. "Ee be OBE, 'ee be' was whispered in the village. Trained as an architect, he was, as far as I could see, entirely occupied with watercolour painting, amateur theatricals and fierce readings of the First Lesson in church on Sundays. He had scant regard for punctuation and little patience with difficult Old Testament names. His spindly frame was in sharp contrast to Mrs Dickinson's ample figure, cloaked, in my memory, in long, businesslike but flowing suits of blue or brown. There were two children, Joy, a tall, shy girl, and the son and heir, Caleb, handsome, charming, fair and fresh-faced, chafing perhaps at the limitations of village life.

Kingweston is strung out along one street. Half a dozen cottages, a tiny post office and Lower Farm, in which we lived, border the main road. Two more farms, the Dower House and some twenty more cottages straggle up towards the 'Big House' and the church.

Home Farm was the home to old Mr Mauder, a stalwart Devonian, a martyr to gout. At Middle Farm were the Sawtells. Mr Sawtell, a 'gentleman farmer', tall and droll; Mrs Sawtell, inquisitive, pious, organising and the village organist. They had two daughters – Helen, dashing; Mary, studious. They were a few years older than my brother and me. We saw them as dauntingly worldly and sophisticated.

During the war the Sawtells inaugurated a triangle of dinner parties. These exchange visits were roundly condemned by my father who preferred to sit at home with his mug of cider and plate of cheese or ham; but hospitality had to be returned and so it was until the practice petered out. My brother and I alone looked forward to the luxury of a large, three-course hot meal instead of our usual frugal supper. I relished the moment after the meal when the women retired to the drawing room and the men and boys stepped out on to darkened lawns. Here we stood around relieving ourselves on the grass with cries of 'Oi'm 'yer!', 'Oi'm 'yer!' to avoid damp disasters.

The move from Ham to Kingweston meant that my father was exchanging the stewardship of his own smallholding for a role as tenant farmer on a much larger spread. He was ambitious and it was a challenge. Home life was the farm. My father had no other interests. He got up at six o'clock to administer it and to start milking. In the late thirties he bought a milking machine, the second for miles around. He was always cannily careful to be second with innovations – electric light, Fordson tractor, combine harvester. He liked to assess how new equipment suited a neighbour. The drama of the milking machine almost defeated him. On their first introduction to it the cows could hardly be coaxed or cajoled or driven into the stalls. Hours were spent on pushing and persuading. Not all had been serviced when the time for afternoon milking came around. The village sniggered. My father fumed. My brother and I held our peace. By the next day progress had been achieved. Soon the machine was indispensable.

For a child a major task was collecting eggs. Free range chickens are wilful. They lay behind stinging nettles, under haystacks and in the far corners of barns. There were hens to be fed, necks to be rung, ducks whose throats had to be slit. There were sheep to be moved. Every summer my brother and I drove the cows seven or so miles to moorland under Glastonbury Tor. When autumn came we drove them back again. Haymaking I hated, dusty and depressing, but it usually happened in term-time. Harvest I tolerated for the orgy of rabbit-catching as the binder closed in on the few remaining square yards of corn. Acres of wheat or barley or oats had to be stooked (we called it 'stitched') in groups of a dozen or so sheaves.

As evenings darkened I used to look enviously across the cleared corn-stubble of Big Common, Long Common, Stockwell, Plough Meads, Copythorn, or the field more romantically named Larkswhistle, to the railway line along which the Great Western Railway's Torbay Express or Cornish Riviera carried passengers to seaside resorts or back again to urban destinations. Pink lights lit the diners in the restaurant cars. The soup they were drinking may have been Brown Windsor; but I marvelled at this promise that there was a more glamorous life elsewhere. I already wanted some of it.

Recalled from an evening dream of faraway places, I helped to pitchfork the sheaves on to wagons expertly crafted by Lamperts of Catsgore, prettily painted in blues and pinks, labelled with the names of the owner and the wagon maker.

They were pulled by solid carthorses, Captain (white) or Jolly (chestnut) or Bonnie (speckled) or Blackbird (black), or Prince, a bay. The thirty or so cows all had names, too. We started with mixed shorthorns and finished with Ayrshires. The only name I can remember is Primrose, a shorthorn with a Jersey colouring.

The cowman was Albion Henry Small. 'Old Henny' was solid, placid and patient. He doubled as kitchen gardener. In later years I regretted the destruction of an asparagus bed which the Wyatts, the previous tenants, had cultivated. My father had no time for asparagus and I was unaware of its delights. Henny and his wife Florrie, who came in on Tuesdays to stir the wash in a huge copper built into the stonework, had migrated from High Ham with us. With them came their son Roy, then a village Romeo and a natural for the up-to-date job of tractor driver when the first Fordson arrived. The carter was Herbie Bown.

Those were the days of polished horse brasses and ploughing matches with red, white and blue rosettes as the prizes. A wizened little man with a large, silent wife, Herbie was one of my favourites. He had exciting, sometimes lurid traveller's tales of early life in Canada – camp fires and logging. His speech oddities included pronouncing 'cartridges' as 'kidderidges' and 'partridges' as 'pidderidges'. His favourite saw, when offered a half pint was, 'The Lord never made halves, he made whole ones.' He and his son Arnold, second tractor driver, encouraged me to swig the sharp cider from their stone flasks.

At the end of every summer we collected apples from our two orchards. We despised the big yellow Morgan Sweets, insipid as Golden Delicious today. We plumped for small red Kingston Blacks and Russett cider apples. Layer after layer of straw and fruit was piled on the cider press, flattened with creaking machinery and squashed into a monstrous straw 'n' apple cake. This, the 'cheese', yielded up sweet apple juice which my brother and I downed thirstily before it could be transferred to huge barrels in the cellar where it matured.

Every day 'the men' – there was also the shepherd, Arthur Callow – filled their stone jars and took them to the fields. At midday and in the evening they were refilled. Years later the jars were replaced by thermos flasks of tea or coffee. Fashions had changed; it was a quiet revolution, gradually achieved.

During haymaking and harvest my mother cooked huge hot meals and drove them out to the fields along with more stone jars of tea, doorsteps of fresh bread and butter, jam or cheese. Extra hands were co-opted for these seasonal bouts. She spent days cutting and cooking and spreading and packing.

Lower Farm, an ancient coaching inn, was large, rambling and draughty. The arrival of electricity in the late thirties freed us from the paraphernalia of candles and Aladdin paraffin lamps. In later years my brother did a deal with R. J. O. Meyer, cavalier cricketer, gambler and founder and headmaster of Millfield

School. Millfield spread its pupils in large houses around Glastonbury. Already it occupied Kingweston House. The Dickinsons had decamped to the Dower House. Later my brother accommodated half a dozen boys in one unused wing of Lower Farm in return for his son Richard's education at Millfield.

In my childhood the floors of the corridors and practical rooms downstairs were flagged and freezing. The dining and drawing rooms were carpeted, the hall tiled. Up a small flight of steps was 'the morning room', a title inherited from the Wyatts though we never used it morning, noon or night, except as a retreat for my brother and, increasingly, for me. It gave on to the 'toy room' – Hornby and Meccano. For some inexplicable reason the old wall telephone with its fixed speaker and detachable earpiece stayed in the morning room for inconvenient years.

Pre-war memories jostle, a kaleidoscope of images, treats and disappointments. Summer fortnights in a boarding house, 'a stone's throw from the front', at Burnham-on-Sea. Knickerbocker Glories and North Poles at the ice-cream parlour overlooking a miniature railway which had disappeared when we went back for a second year. We were told that it had been bought up by a 'rich man' who removed it to the grounds of his stately home so that only privileged children might ride in it. I narrowly escaped a conversion to socialism. When I mentioned this in an article in the late 1980s I was promptly told that it had in fact gone bust and was only preserved elsewhere thanks to genuine altruism on someone's part. This corrective information came too late for Ms Thelma Lambert, who was so moved by my story that she based a children's novel on it, *No Train for Sam*.

Pre-war bananas. Pre-war lights on the way home from Sunday mystery tours in the Austin Seven, AYA 422. Mystery tours might dwindle into a visit to check on cattle on Butleigh Moor or flower into summer visits to the strawberry fields of Cheddar or expeditions as far as Minehead and Dunster. Here an exotic polo match might be thrown in for excitement or a boiling radiator on Porlock Hill for exasperation. Smashing small crabs on the muddy beach at Blue Anchor. Wool sales at Dorchester. Sorties deeper into Hardy country and on to Weymouth. White Horse spotting on Salisbury Plain, Mars Bars and Milky Ways soon to be banished with bananas 'for the duration'. Sleepily scanning the lights of towns on the low, undulating hillsides, a memory cherished through years of blackout and bicycling.

The village school was the neighbouring Barton St David C of E. On my first day in 1935 my brother pushed me into Miss Barrington's infants' class from which he had just graduated. Cyril Bailey, starting at the same time, cried all morning. They had to send for his mother. I stayed dry-eyed and pleased with myself.

Furtive first essays in sexual curiosity took place in the boys' lavatory behind the school. 'I'll show you mine if you show me yours.' I showed him mine and he ran away. My mother drove us to school most mornings. At the end of the day we walked the mile and a half home in all weathers.

A happy time yielded some grievances. A new teacher, Miss Williams, gave my drawing of her fewer marks than the one drawn by the boy at the next desk. What explanation could there be other than that I had put (accurately but unflatteringly) a network of lines across her face and he drew none. We collected things: cigarette cards, stamps, tadpoles, flowers. Another injustice. I amassed hundreds more flowers than anyone else and pressed them devotedly. And I labelled them accurately. But I lost – too many ink blots.

I gave my first public performance in a non-speaking role in an Empire Day pageant drilled on the school playground. In a makeshift smock I was a New Zealand sheep farmer.

More exciting was pre-war county cricket. It was a vintage, cavalier period for Somerset. My father drove us to see Constantine and the West Indies at Taunton – languishing near the bottom of the table Somerset had a reputation as giant killers.

We cycled to Wells to see Arthur Wellard (along with Harold Gimblett one of my two heroes) hit five sixes in one over off a heavyset, old gentleman from Kent of whose reputation I was unaware. It was the great Frank Woolley in his last season. I lay in bed with measles in 1938 as the BBC's cricket commentator, Howard Marshall, warmly commended 'Young Hutton' who reached his record Test score against Australia at the Oval.

The year before there was a visit to London to stay with an aunt and uncle the week after the Coronation in May. This was a revelation.

We stood, two feet high, submerged among the masses on the platform of Paddington Station, lost, until the crowds dissolved and my aunt's breeched and booted chauffeur loomed over us and led us to my aunt. Safe in the car we drove to Piccadilly Circus where we were decanted into the Underground and my first moving staircase. The excitement of the journey from Piccadilly Circus to Leicester Square was short-lived; but when we had conquered the up-escalator there was the car ready to take us on to Upminster.

I have no memories of Upminster but, dimly, I recall the pier at Southend; being photographed riding a Shetland pony at London Zoo (Alfred bravely made friends with a small gorilla); and especially the Mall with the decorations from the Coronation a week earlier on our way to see *Tarzan and the Green Goddess* at the Odeon, Leicester Square.

The changes brought about by the advent of war were not as dramatic deep in Somerset as in the capital; but I remember its declaration vividly. I was recovering from whooping cough when Neville Chamberlain announced that we were 'at war with Nazi Germany'. The moment is fixed in my memory. I had just been sick under a large yew tree in the garden and was re-entering the dining room through the French windows as the broadcast began.

Kingweston was soon threatened with evacuees. Eventually a bus turned up on the main road outside our farm. My brother and I eavesdropped behind a privet hedge. A few figures dismounted and surveyed the village. We heard one say, 'No pub, no pictures, no fish and chips – get back in the bus.' With that they disappeared.

Caleb Dickinson, who had served a short, enjoyable farming apprenticeship with my father, realised his ambition to join the Air Force and was reported missing, presumed lost, on his first active service flight. His picture, with his delicate features, looked out dreamily from our few family photographs, stuck on a drawing-room table; inside the glass a pair of his Air Force wings.

During the war, with little petrol, Sunday nights saw our convoy of four pedalling the pilgrimage to Castle Cary to visit my grandparents. Alfred and I were on our best behaviour. I holed up in the library reading bits of Dickens and Thackeray from the rows of bound collected works. We both caught up on the 'Garth' and 'Jane' strips in the *Daily Mirror* to which my grandfather unaccountably subscribed. I think for my more simple grandmother.

My father joined the War Agricultural Committee devoted to 'ploughing up' as the countryside began to 'Dig for Victory'. Occasionally he brought colleagues back for a meal. One dignified old gentleman, the chairman, was my first drunk. He had taken a good deal of whisky on board before trying to spear elusive lettuce leaves with his fork. Having finally succeeded he couldn't find his mouth and the forkful jabbed either side of his flushed face. At the far end of the table Alfred and I struggled not to giggle. I remember whispering, 'Is he blind?' 'No,' hissed Alfred. 'He's drunk!'

More and more land was cultivated. More harvesting. High in the sky above, plane-spotting became more thrilling on hot summer days as swastikas appeared on some of the aeroplanes. We learned from our cigarette-card identification kits to spot a Heinkel or a Messerschmitt. We stood riveted by the dog-fights or plunged for cover under the stooks of corn if the planes dived too low. Bristol was bombed and we stood outside the front door in the cold night air, looked north and watched the pink glow over the Mendips as it burned.

A great-uncle and -aunt evacuated themselves from Bristol. Uncle Ted, Grandfather Drewett's younger brother, who had also done well, if not as well as his sibling, had been the village grocer at Badminton. On one of our more ambitious sorties before the war my brother and I visited him. With a great sense of importance he beckoned us to stand very near the telephone and keep quiet. 'I am calling the Duke of Beaufort,' he said. 'If you listen carefully you will hear, possibly for the only time in your life, the voice of a real life duke . . . Good evening, your Grace . . .' I seem to remember it was an order for several bottles of whisky.

Uncle and Aunt had barely arrived in Kingweston – indeed it was their first night under our roof – when, sitting at supper, we heard a whine and a series of cracks. The family had no idea what was happening. The evacuees did and dived under the dining-room table. We watched transfixed. A hastening-home German bomber had jettisoned a stick of nine bombs mostly across our Home field some hundred yards away from the house. We had our village Local Defence Volunteers (LDV) and, perhaps, by then, our Home Guard. They didn't know what to do about it. We collected shrapnel and the craters were filled in.

When they settled down, Uncle Ted imported tins of Heinz chicken and tomato soup for his supper which he slurped down enthusiastically as my brother and I, confined to our good bread and cheese or cold meat, watched open-eyed with envy.

Breakfast was large and traditional. Lunch was called dinner and was a substantial meat and pudding affair. Tea was solid bread and cake. Supper was cold. Ration books were a nuisance, but living on a farm meant poultry and eggs in easy supply and there were permits to kill two pigs a year. My father preserved the main pieces in a large lead-lined salter, while producing a wealth of chitterlings and brawn and other good-ies for consumption immediately after the slaughter. Hams and a variety of joints emerged over the next six months. So did large chunks of beef from some deal my father must have made with a friendly butcher. I'm not sure if this was an illegal manoeuvre or not – as it usually meant journeys after dark I suspect it was.

Millfield had not yet annexed the Big House. It became the headquarters of a searchlight battery. Officers, soldiers and WRACs masterminded the fight against the Germans from the top of the drive.

Here I had been privileged to see one of the Dickinson's pre-war theatrical performances. The highlight of a village fête held in the grounds, it was a one-act sketch called *Brought Home by Broadcast*. For a long time my ideas of theatre were conditioned by it. Curtains were drawn back at the end of one of the large rooms to reveal Capt. Dickinson in drag as a cantankerous old lady, sitting in an armchair beside a large Bush wireless. From his/her opening soliloquy we gathered that his/her daughter had disappeared. He/she looked at a watch, moved to the wireless and switched it on. We had heard a rustling as the formidable figure of Mrs Dickinson made her way as discreetly as possible to take up a position behind the set. In clear (and unmistakable) tones she read a BBC SOS: '. . . last heard of in . . . seriously ill . . . please get in touch with . . .' With a look of satisfaction the old lady (Squire) switched off the wireless and returned to his/her chair. Simultaneously and more noisily Mrs Dickinson returned to her prompter's stool. After a very short second monologue a door, or rather a curtain, burst open and in bounced Joy Dickinson as the prodigal daughter. Her mother/father feigned ill-ness for a few moments and then revealed that the SOS was a ruse to bring the erring girl home. She, in turn, confessed that she had been lying low down the road all the time. This swift exchange of plot and counterplot brought the entertainment to a close. They took a couple of curtain calls and I rather think Mrs Dickinson's Wireless Announcer took one too.

Brought Home by Broadcast, my second toy theatre, a blue and cream Christmas present (the first was concocted out of cornflake packets), a pantomime – *Cinderella* at the Playhouse, Street; these were my first live theatrical experiences. By now I was eight. *Cinderella* was a big disappointment. I was depending on the transformation scene – pumpkin to gilded coach – to be magical. Instead the curtains closed on the pumpkin and a cage of mice. Dandini came out and did her paper-tearing act, the curtains parted again revealing a coach drawn by four Shetland ponies. Not much magic.

The next autumn, 1939, we went to the Playhouse to book tickets for that year's panto. The Austin Seven driven by my mother was overturned by the larger car of a friend of my father. My brother and I were uninjured, my mother had a few days in bed and I was alarmed that we might miss the panto. We did. War broke out and there was no show.

During the war we made occasional visits to 'the pictures' at Glastonbury or Street or, as our cycling grew more ambitious, to Yeovil. My first movie was a surprise on a 'mystery tour'. We reached Wells and saw Sonja Henie in a skiing and skating vehicle. At about the same time my brother and I were taken to a film demonstration of tractors, balers and combine harvesters at Yeovil. A screen was lowered. Fields of corn swayed before our eyes and an insistent commentary accompanied the pictures. For one of my father's older farmer friends this was a first. 'Tom! Tom!' he hissed to my father. 'Where's thick feller talking from?' My brother and I felt very knowledgeable in face of this adult naivety.

Wireless was a different matter. Alfred had played with a primitive crystal set but I only heard a few unintelligible squeaks from it. Towards the end of the thirties my father came home bearing a large Bush radio. He always wore a sheepish look when he bought something new – tractor, combine, wireless, milking machine, eventually, in the fifties, television. He was defensively prepared for ridicule and reluctant to betray pride in his purchase. This was achieved, in the case of wireless and television sets, after a long haggle with a local garage owner at Charlton Mackerell over a second-hand set.

He had very definite wireless favourites and no-go areas. *Band Wagon* was 'not funny'. *ITMA*, with Tommy Handley as 'It's That Man Again', was 'a lot of rot'. Will Fyfe and Harry Lauder were always welcome. Gracie Fields was an event; however, sometimes 'she made a fool of herself'. *Garrison Theatre* with Charlie Shadwell, Jack Warner and Joy Standing with their catchphrases, 'Blue pencil', 'Mind my bike', and 'Programmes, choclits, cigarettes', was usually acceptable. Some guests were not. Margaret Eaves' powerful soprano took her into a despised class of 'screechers'. Crooners, on the other hand, 'bawled'. Count John McCormack was above reproach. The Western Brothers, Kenneth and George, were 'clever'. Murgatroyd and Winterbottom – Tommy Handley and Ronald Frankau – 'daft'.

Hymns were good listening. At the beginning of the war, when they played the national anthems of all the Allied nations before Sunday's nine o'clock news, the family stood to attention for some fifteen or twenty minutes. Very soon we reached a satisfactory compromise, not standing until God Save the King, which was always top of the bill.

A half-hour classic serial preceded the anthems. It was touch and go if it was Dickens – 'Too many people. Can't make out the story.' Trollope was simpler and fared better. H. Seton Merriman's *Barlasch of the Guard* is the first I can remember hearing in full, having spent months switching on earlier and earlier for the anthems in the hope of getting my father hooked on the serial. The names of the members of the BBC Repertory Company come back as familiarly as the initials of Somerset cricketers. Gladys Young, Carleton Hobbs, Mary O'Farrell, Laidman Browne, James McKechnie, Frederick Lloyd, Marjorie

Westbury, Belle Crystal were the stars and the most vivid memory of all is the acute family embarrassment around the supper table as Grizelda Hervey's Irene repeated her lament, 'Rape, rape, rape', as she fled from her husband Soames Forsyte (Ronald Simpson) in *The Forsyte Saga*. We stared hard at our plates of bread and cheese.

L. Du Garde Peach's Sunday serials, which had some historical interest, were passed fit for listening, especially if Richard Goolden was appearing. *Toy Town* was 'silly', J. B. Priestley's wartime epilogues after the news were immediately switched off. My father did not like his accent and mistrusted him. Years later I heard that Sir Edward Boyle's father couldn't stand him either: 'Sounds like the sort of feller who'd make off with your spoons!'

It was an age of catchphrases. The relentless weekly visits to the living room by radio series made familiarity breed respect and laughter. It was lazy writing – but effective. Even if you only heard snatches of *ITMA* you soon cottoned on to 'TTFN', 'Can I do yer now, sir?' 'After you, Claude', 'No, after you, Cecil.' 'Don't forget the diver.' 'This is Funf speaking.' 'I don't mind if I do, sir!' – all from *ITMA*. Other shows followed: 'Large lumps, they're lovely', 'Sarsparilla!', 'Hello, playmates', 'In our shed'; and then there was a new crop from the later wartime series, *Stand Easy* (Army) and *Much Binding in the Marsh* (Air Force).

The catchphrase has had a renaissance recently with Harry Enfield's 'Loadsamoney', and in *The Fast Show* with 'Where's me washboard?' and 'This year, I shall mostly be wearing . . .' It has gone mad in *Little Britain*: 'I'm the only gay in the village', 'Yeah but no but yeah . . .' and 'I'm a lady – in lady's clothes'. But these series do cushion their catchphrases with a deal more characterisation than they bothered with in *ITMA*.

The searchlight headquarters at the Big House also brought live entertainment to the village. Occasionally officers and their wives were billeted on us at Lower Farm and when ENSA

(Entertainments National Service Association, often recast as Every Night Something Awful) parties came to entertain the troops Alfred and I might be squeezed in to share the 'fun'. Eventually this got out of hand. At the last I attended the audience consisted entirely of village children. The gallant entertainers had come from Wells, some ten miles away, to entertain the brave fighting boys. They made no secret of their displeasure. The soldiers knew what to avoid.

Some time later the village farmers were all invited to a cocktail party at the officers' mess. My father 'didn't hold with that nonsense', so he and my mother did not go, but Alfred and I turned up.

Clutching my orangeade and picking my way waist-high through various condescending officers' wives, I heard my first piece of theatrical gossip. 'I loved Owen Nares,' said one woman. 'So did I,' said another. 'I'm told that Ivor Novello has inherited his mantle,' said the first. I glowed at the idea of having such an important gobbet of information in my possession, but as the days went by I could find no one in Kingweston who would have made head or tail of the information that 'Ivor Novello has inherited the mantle of Owen Nares'. The whole point of gossip is to hand it on. It has been my secret until now.

During the week we read the *Daily Mail*. We did not see a Sunday paper for years. My father's mother had set a pattern of behaviour, hiding the weekly paper under cushions on the sabbath. However, a semi-religious magazine, the *Quiver*, staggering in its dullness, was allowed. I remember only one rare, enlightened sentence – a mother comforting her tearful, persecuted son, 'Don't cry, my dear. The baby Jesus had an olive skin too.'

This routine changed when Uncle Ted arrived. He drove to Somerton to collect the *Sunday Dispatch* and spent the day peering at it through his owl-eyes. By the time he went back to Bristol my father was a convert and the *Dispatch* stayed with us on Sundays. There was a quick shuffle of papers one morning when I came upon my father sneaking a look at the scandalous serialisation of *Forever Amber*.

Sundays also featured church. Kingweston shared a parson with neighbouring Barton St David. The parishes alternated matins and evensong. As the years went by my father, though not changing his attitude to religion, certainly changed his mind about God's representatives here on earth. As he grew older and they became younger his respect for them diminished and their authority faded. Services were occasionally enlivened, especially at harvest festivals, by exchange visits with neighbouring preachers. A rural dean from Wells once woke us up with a joke and another explained the Bible's error in having Jonah swallowed by a whale. 'Modern science tells us', this enlightened man explained, 'that Jonah was not swallowed by a whale.' He waited for the heresy to sink in. 'It was a shark.'

If my father had another religious prejudice apart from younger clergymen, it was Methodist parsons. 'Chapel passons', he preferred to call them. His suspicions were easily voiced. A 'chapel passon' was a man who would enquire with infinite concern about your wife or children while seeking in the welter of goodwill to buy your cow for a few pounds less.

I assume that every child growing up sees his family circumstances as the norm. It is impossible for me to imagine one brother more or less, certainly not a sister, in any variation on the unit I knew. We were a self-contained quartet. My father, breadwinner and domestic autocrat. My mother, supportive, dutiful and affectionate. I could never have envisaged a crack in their relationship. In childhood my brother was dark, better looking (he still is), more extrovert and more popular. I was shyer and inclined to tag along in his shadow. Alfred was always going to be a farmer. I never for a moment considered such a future. However, we got along well together, sharing interests in sport, cinema-going and the wireless, and the occasional conspiracy to mock our father behind his back when some bit of twentieth-century modernisation irritated or confused him.

Driving out of a multi-storey car park in Bristol after a pantomime (*Jack and the Beanstalk* with Nita Croft and 'Monsewer' Eddie Gray) unnerved him. As a result he was defeated by the unfamiliar one-way system which he entered incorrectly. It provided a perfect opportunity for two youngsters to stifle superior giggles in the back of the car, while my mother loyally tried to calm him.

Another joint activity as we grew into our later teens was Mrs Somerville's dancing class in Yeovil, which we attended along with Derek Maunder from Home Farm who was almost my brother's age. Mrs Somerville, short and amply padded, was assisted by Valerie, young and attractive. Needless to say Alfred and Derek monopolised Valerie and I was left to push Mrs Somerville across the parquet floor.

Alfred and I were happy in each other's company but our separate moments saw my brother busy on the farm and me behind a book. Sixty or so years on we meet infrequently but find it easy to pick up the old familiarity. The security provided by our parents must have played a part in this.

My mother was a woman of self-effacing modesty, her character shaped by her authoritarian father. Her devotion was simple, complete and sincere. She carried her Christianity lovingly into her daily life and showed extraordinary forbearance with my often impatient father and her two radically different sons. She had been brought up in gentler surroundings than the large, cold farmhouse where she spent most of her married life, but she worked as hard as only farmers' wives work without complaint for over thirty years. Before her marriage she had for a time been a secretary to Sir Arthur Hobhouse at Hadspen. She had gone to Switzerland briefly after the First World War to accompany one of her brothers, convalescing in vain after his return from the front. Thin, wasted and latterly wracked by arthritis, she was the most unselfish person I have known. To my father's occasional impatient or frustrated outbursts she would murmur, 'Oh, Tom!' Any incident in life, on the radio or on the television which was outside her experience prompted the comment, 'Most uncommon!'

Just before I went off to boarding school she thrust a pamphlet into my hands, saying quickly, 'I'm sure you know more about this from biology at school; but I think you ought to read it.' Years later she asked me, 'What was Oscar Wilde's crime?' Searching for the right words I compared it to the comparatively recent 1950s homosexual scandal with Edward Montagu. 'Ah, yes,' she said, 'I thought it must be, but we weren't allowed to discuss it when I was a girl.'

My brother had been established at Sexey's Trade School, Bruton, for three years when I joined him there as a weekly boarder, aged eleven. We came home at weekends, he willingly, I with some reluctance. I had too good a time at school and my hands stayed cleaner than on the farm. Sexey's was founded in the last years of the nineteenth century, named after Sir Hugh Sexey, a Master of the Horse for Queen Elizabeth I. He had also endowed almshouses at Bruton. Down the road from us loomed the upmarket shadow of King's, Bruton, the local public school. In the other direction, Sunny Hill School for Girls, where my mother had been taught. At Sexey's fee-payers and 'scholarship boys' were mixed, as were day boys and boarders, spiced by Londoners sent away from the Blitz. They seemed amazingly worldly.

As war filled up the 'Cliff' boarding house with the evacuees, my brother and I were farmed out to a spare bedroom in the house of an old master, Mr Crowther. A thin, ineffectual, caricature 'Chips', he was monstrously henpecked by his mountainous, silk-swathed, bedridden wife. She frequently berated her husband and her sad, overawed daughter; but no bleat was as potent as her aversion to the BBC newsreaders' phrase 'Mopping-up operations', applied to human beings, even though they were the enemy, in wartime. Such a sensitivity sat oddly on her lips but every time the offending words were spoken on the news Mrs Crowther would shift her enormous shiny bulk in her bed and splutter and growl, 'Mopping-up operations! What words to use about human beings! Mopping-up indeed!' My brother and I would hurry upstairs to get away from her malign growls.

The headmaster was Mr W. E. Page. He was only the second head the school had had, succeeding a local legend, W. A. K. ('Whacker') Knight. Mr Page was short and he bounced. The only time he beat me was for playing pitch and toss for very small sums of money behind the bike sheds. He took a little spring and bounced up and down, swishing his stick. He then bounced across his study and launched himself at me. Six sets of bounces and stings and it was all over.

He bounced into prep one night and startled us all with a threatening statement: 'It has come to my notice that some boys have been playing with other boys penises . . . This has got to stop!' It was not as funny as Peter Bull's memory of his headmaster's sex lecture which began, 'You may have noticed between your legs . . .' but it was good enough to be going on with.

On my arrival at Sexey's I followed my brother slavishly everywhere, earning the nickname 'Trailer'. As I gained confidence it switched to 'Eggs' or 'Eggy' – based on my initials, E. G. S. Food at Cliff House was awful. My particular aversion was the rice pudding, my worst moment a midday meal when it was so inedible that nearly everyone left theirs. Expecting trouble from Miss Mudge, a mean, pink, marshmallow of a matron, I ploughed through mine like a good little boy. Plates were passed up. Waste was perceived. Plates were sent back down the table and a full one finished up in front of me. Made to finish it, I felt a keen sense of injustice.

On one occasion we coveted the tomatoes which filled the school greenhouse. Word of our moans reached the ears of Mr Page. He addressed the dining room. He improvised angry variations on his single theme. 'They are my tomatoes. They are not *your* tomatoes. You may think that they are *your* tomatoes but they are not *your* tomatoes. They are *my* tomatoes . . .!' Yes, we had no tomatoes. Another fit of phrase-making was inspired by his discovery of a group of Sexey's boys slouching through Bruton, 'Like a lot of mill girls, kicking salmon tins down the high street!' At last Miss Mudge retired and was replaced by a splendidly correct Miss Bridges and a sympathetic young housemaster, Mr Faulkner; and the food improved.

Old Mr Thomas coughed yellow gas damage from the First World War into a jam jar during arithmetic. Bill Barnes was a 'card', bald-headed and rumoured among the boys to be addicted to beer. D. J. Williams had a Welsh freedom with words and a great ability to provoke affection for literature. He later wrote to me sadly to say he was shocked by *TW3*. Poor Miss Boome came to teach French during the war. She was, we learned, Miss K. A. M. Boome, born in Trichinopoly, daughter of General Boome. She was gentle and genteel. Baiting Miss Boome reached its peak one morning in Five (B). The desks were raised in tiers. Miss Boome stood in front of the class holding a large French dictionary. One of her persecutors, Klaus Blensdorf, who was not only an evacuee but also a refugee, was in the front row. We watched fascinated as he crawled across the floor in an attempt to peer up her skirt. Miss Boome, concentrating on her dictionary, appeared to be unaware until he reached his destination and was raising his sights. Then she withdrew her hands from the heavy book and let it fall mightily on Blensdorf's head. One up to Miss Boome.

From school we made occasional theatre outings to Bristol and Stratford for Shakespeare at the Old Vic and the Memorial Theatre. William Devlin had been a celebrated Lear in 1934 at the Westminster Theatre, when he was twenty-five. I am surprised to find that he was still only in his late thirties when I saw him at Bristol. It gave me a yardstick when I saw the great Wolfit in the role a few years later. Robert Eddison's Hamlet offered other joys. A full row of schoolboys watched as fascinated as a Wimbledon crowd while in the moments of high emotion gobbets of spit flew from side to side across the stage. The *Bristol Evening Post* called it 'a princely Hamlet'. To cap the feast of saliva one of Catherine Lacey's breasts popped out of her Gertrude costume, riveting all our eyes for a moment in a single stare. Then, as though we had not had enough Shakespearean thrills, Hamlet came to his 'motive and the cue for passion' speech. For some time a much-thumbed novel called *Cue for Passion* had passed from grubby hand to grubby hand at school – giving us unofficial sex education on the page at which it invariably fell open. However, we had never heard the words in context before and as Eddison spoke the line a loud guffaw came from our solid row of schoolboys in the stalls. Over dinner some time in the late seventies I asked Robert if he had ever tried to recapture the laugh but sadly he had no recollection of our enthusiasm. (We got a similar laugh when Sunny Hill Girls staged *The Merchant of Venice*. A well-upholstered prefect playing Antonio had the fatal line, 'My griefs and losses have so baked me that I can hardly spare a pound of flesh.') The memorable evening at *Hamlet* was rounded off with my seduction by a senior boy in the back of the car in which a master was driving us back to school. The next summer we went to Stratford and I was able to oblige a hitherto unavailable day boy in the middle of Godfrey Tearle's 'tomorrow and tomorrow' speech in *Macbeth*. It was the production in which Diana Wynyard, playing the Lady, had on the first night fallen off a rostrum in the sleepwalking scene. Breaking an arm, she managed to stay asleep for the rest of it. There were no accidents at our matinée but her arm was still in a sling. Jill Bennett, who was Godfrey Tearle's very young lover at the time, played the boy Fleance. When they got back to London the relationship prompted one of Coral Browne's most stinging observations: 'I could never understand what Godfrey Tearle saw in Jill Bennett until I saw her eating corn-on-the-cob at the Caprice.'

There was no dramatic tradition at Sexey's at the time – though I see from a recent copy of the school magazine that nowadays they even have a go at Sondheim. A sixth-former gave an excellent notice to their *Sweeney Todd* but found no room to mention the composer. The nearest we got to a play was an annual end-of-term concert at the boarding house. I was especially proud of a platinum-blond wig made somehow out of binder twine from the farm. I thought it the last word in realism until we sent away to London for wigs for a production of – was it Patrick Hamilton's *Rope* or *Ambrose Applejohn's Adventure*?

Alfred had left Sexey's to start on the farm at sixteen but, having finished school certificate, I moved up to the sixth form to specialise in chemistry, physics and biology. Bad idea. It was a wasted term. These subjects mystified me. The only one to which I could do justice was the botany part of biology. I was still collecting flowers and, given half a chance, arranging them. Give me a font or a pulpit at Christmas, Easter or harvest festival and I was off on a Constance Spry trip. Much later an aunt asked Caryl Brahms (my late collaborator) where she thought I acquired this enthusiasm. 'From his mother?' Caryl tried. 'Certainly not,' said the aunt. 'What about his father?' Caryl offered. Cousin Phyllis pounced: 'Have you ever seen Uncle Tom arranging flowers?' Caryl Brahms played a critically important part in my life, but I shall deal with it later as the story of our collaboration unfolds.

Getting off the science treadmill was not easy. There had never been an arts sixth form in the school's history. Mr Page, a physics man himself, was obdurate. However, I had allies on the staff who were frustrated by having no one to teach their special subjects above school certificate level. A quick conspiracy with Messrs Brockhouse, Morgan and Williams (D. J.) led to a successful coup. I switched to English and history as main subjects and Latin and botany as subsidiaries. As I was the entire arts sixth it meant one-on-one teaching, though others followed suit after I left.

It did the trick in terms of state and county scholarships. The Latin was a near thing. I had to take it because at the back of my mind I knew I might have to read law at Oxford; but it remained almost as unapproachable for me as chemistry and physics. The only side-effect was a precocious attempt to write a verse drama inspired by Sallust's *Jugurtha*. It was no more successful than my bright idea of making a musical out of Shaw's *Pygmalion*. I wrote an opening chorus set in Covent Garden, 'Come out of the rain', and a spirited point number, 'Emancipation, is a big sensation, it will sweep the nation . . .' Lerner and Loewe were to mine this seam more profitably in the 1950s. My 'One of the Undeserving Poor' for Doolittle was not a patch on either their 'With a Little Bit of Luck' or 'Get Me to the Church on Time'.

In 1949 I tried for scholarships and exhibitions at Oxford and Cambridge. At Oxford I was hoping for Exeter College, which has a strong West Country connection. I recall nothing of the exam papers or the interviews, only the shows which I grabbed the chance of seeing. At Oxford, at the Playhouse, was the Victorian melodrama, *The Drunkard*, starring John Moffat. At the New Theatre there was a pre-London tour of a French-windows piece called *A Woman's Place*, starring Leslie Banks and Elizabeth Allan. I thought it marvellously smooth and sophisticated and was disappointed when it failed ignominiously in London.

At Cambridge I tried Emmanuel College, to which I did not want to go. However, it seemed wise to hedge my bets. The Arts Theatre offered only an amateur production of *Trial by Jury* paired with *The Pirates of Penzance*. For entertainment on my second night I was reduced to a sparsely attended Labour Party meeting addressed by Frank Beswick, MP. This, and the cold, damp winds which came chillingly off the Fens, confirmed my preference for Oxford. My faith was rewarded.

Towards the end of my school career I played cricket and football for the first teams, eventually as captain – but with little distinction. The nadir of my career on the football field as centre half (or 'pivot' as we knowingly called it in those days) was when an opposing centre forward, whom I was supposed to be marking, scored eight out of the nine goals they ran up against us. It was small consolation when he emerged a few years later as the England striker John Atyeo. On 'Athletics Day' in my last year I won the school mile in the slowest time ever recorded by a winner at Sexey's.

I left the school in 1949 with considerable curiosity to see what the Army was like. National service for me was a year in Catterick and Aldershot with the Signals and then a year in Austria. For a country boy it was a crash course in the outside world. Apart from that jaunt to Upminster the week after the Coronation my only acquaintance with the capital was a day trip to Bertram Mills' Circus with the local Young Conservatives.

The Army helped a lot towards de-countryfication. I am not aware of having changed my accent although there must have been some modification as I grew up. The only word with which I am aware of tampering is 'garage'. In Somerset it was 'garidge'. I learned to say 'garage' as I emerged. Much later when I went to America I changed again to gar-*aage*', if I wanted to get a laugh out of Americans who would otherwise stop and ponder the unfamiliar word instead of hearing the joke.

My first Army lesson was simple and basic. I learned it at my medical in Exeter – another venture outside my patch. The lesson was: 'Don't go to the loo before one of these encounters.' I spent a very embarrassed morning trying to contribute to a specimen bottle.

I was drafted into the Royal Corps of Signals and told to report to Catterick. This complicated manoeuvre caused a great deal of planning in the Sherrin household. We were not used to travelling vast distances. This would be my furthest trip from home. My parents had friends in Leeds so it was arranged that I should stay the night there to break my journey and travel on fresh and rested the next day.

On arrival at the barracks more lessons were quickly learned. School names were being swapped among the minor public schoolboys from Worksop, Blundell's or Stonyhurst. For the first time I became aware that Sexey's was susceptible to double entendre, an idea which had never occurred to me. I also came to realise that certain schoolboy practices were carried on outside school. Smartly, on lights out, the cockney recruit in the next bed whispered in a very matter-of-fact manner, 'Race ya, Ginge!' Before I could puzzle out this terse challenge there was a rhythmic creaking of springs and then a contented blend of gasps and sighs. 'Beat ya!' he said, before I had even solved the conundrum.

Next lesson. It seems incredible to believe that in all my sheltered Somerset life it had never occurred to me that Jews existed outside the *Quiver*, *The Merchant of Venice*, the Bible or the horrors of Nazi Germany. Now, when I commented on the distinctive appearance of another soldier it was loftily dismissed by one of the public schoolboys: 'Jewish, old man.' Apart from my father's firmly held, idiosyncratic conviction that Jews had a wickedly clever method of cooking old boiler hens so that they became as tender as young chicken, Jewishness had never touched my life. We had seen blacks in Kingweston – the occasional tramp passed through before the war and then the GIs – but Jews, never!

After four weeks or so of basic training a number of us were selected as potential officers and removed to Gallowgate Camp above Richmond Hill. A training base for Royal Signals subalterns, it was also a course in combating the cold. The walls of the barrack-room huts were abnormally thin. The contractor had apparently laid the bricks vertically instead of horizontally, producing a surplus which he flogged. It was small consolation to know that he did time inside a warm, thick-walled prison.

Continuing on course to become an officer meant passing a War Office Selection Board – WOSB. We were sent to Eaton Hall on the other side of the Pennines, watched while we used our knives and forks, monitored in public-speaking exercises, set various classroom papers and, most daunting of all, put in charge of a small group as we attempted to cross various obstacles on an assault course. The group I had temporary command of was required to propel an object over an obstacle to safety on the opposite side of a stream. I could see no way of getting the object across. Fortunately the examining officer turned his back on us for a second and I cheated, lobbing it underneath. By the time he looked round it was mission accomplished. I like to think that my enterprise transcended dishonesty. I was confirmed in this view in 2004 when I read a *Telegraph* obituary of the Army officer who devised this apparently notorious test. My solution was not his.

However, it entitled me to six weeks of much more rigorous infantry training at Mons Barracks, Aldershot, presided over by RSM Britten in the last few years of his reign of terror. I only tangled once and modestly with Britten (though I did employ him in the sixties to put the fear of God into our young actors in *The Virgin Soldiers* before we flew them out to Singapore for filming). On some sort of royal parade I saw him break off from the main inspection party and take a relentless straight line in my direction. As he drew nearer there was no doubt that I was his target. He came to rest in front of me and loomed above. 'Get your left boot one half-centimetre back, sir!' was all he said before rejoining the others.

At Catterick I had found that an unexpected reply usually

threw a young inspecting officer off guard. At least it worked on two occasions. 'This brass on the front of your belt is very dirty, Sherrin.'

'It's not as bad as the ones on the back, sir.'

'Why isn't this button clean?'

'I didn't think you'd look under there, sir.'

I would never have risked that technique on Britten or on CSM Bennet, who was more closely responsible for our discipline at Mons. Certainly not on the sadistic sergeant from the West Kents who ruled our platoon and who, rumour reached us after we returned to Catterick, went mad while supervising the next intake. CSM Bennet had particular pet aversions – especially public schoolboys, Roman Catholics and people who bit their fingernails. When he found one of our number who qualified on all three grounds he had a field day.

The drinking lesson was the next to be learned. It was an age of gin and orange, about a decade before gin and tonic superseded it, and long before vodka. Back in Catterick for the rest of the officer training course, life was more comfortable, gin and orange was more plentiful and I was back in 'amateur dramatics', along with Humphrey Burton, who was to go on to a distinguished career as an arts broadcaster.

Catterick ended with a passing-out parade to which my mother and father came by train. Well, they came as far as Sheffield by train. Here they were required to change. That meant crossing Sheffield to a second station. My father had had enough of trains by then. It was his first journey on the railway since his honeymoon in Torquay and he was fed up with it. Impatient, he made a deal with the taxi driver who was driving them across town to take them the rest of the way across Yorkshire to Richmond where they were to stay. Yorkshire is a large county. Guests once arrived at Chatsworth hours late for dinner with the Devonshires. They had driven all the way from Scotland. 'Sorry,' they said, 'we forgot Yorkshire.'

They stayed in a hotel in Richmond for two nights – the first they had spent away from home together since 1927. My brother was left in charge of the farm for three days for the first time.

I had the luckiest posting from Catterick to Austria setting up a string of 'firsts'. My first trip abroad: by train to Harwich, from Harwich to the Hook. First time at sea. On arrival at the Hook we were kept waiting a couple of days for a connection. First exploration of foreign parts. Then the long journey to Villach. First sleeping compartment – shared with a boozy regular captain. I woke in the morning to picture-postcard views of snow-clad hills – an exotic journey for me.

I was posted to Klagenfurt in Carinthia, the promised land where the Israelites of the Eighth Army landed after battling up through Italy. Few of the originals survived; but there were a couple in the Signals officers' mess in Beethovenstrasse, number 42, a large house a short walk from the barracks.

My work was not onerous – just incomprehensible. I was Motor Transport officer. A non-driver, I soon learnt to fake vehicle inspections by crawling earnestly under lorries and concentrating on dirt and dust. The main part of the job was operating a minicab service for myself and the other officers. The good news was that I could always call on a car and driver when I needed them. The bad news was that I frequently cocked up the orders for cars from senior officers. The experience has given me a sneaking sympathy for the despatchers of radio taxi firms.

I had two civilian drivers who were Carinthia's champion skiers – one for speed, the other for jumping. They knew the best slopes around Klagenfurt and we would go off on unofficial skiing trips at weekends. After one or two disastrous attempts on the lower slopes they would leave me happy with my tea-*mit*-rum by a blazing fire while they skied until nightfall. Then they would put me between them in a sandwich and, keeping a tight hold, scream down the winding paths to the parked truck at an exhilarating speed which took my breath away.

In retrospect I regret how little I made of my time in Carinthia. It served as a buffer state between school and Oxford and I know that I enjoyed Oxford more because I was two years older and, if not wiser, at least more experienced. However, the sense of missed opportunity in those twelve months does lie on my conscience. I did not take leave to see Venice. I visited Vienna only once. Not only did I not learn to ski, I did not learn to swim or skate either. I spent days lounging by or in the Werthersee, a large lake surrounded by holiday hotels. The more I tried to swim, the less I succeeded. Old colonels would watch my efforts and swear that they had taught whole platoons of men to swim a couple of lengths in full-kit-and-marching-order in the course of an afternoon. However hard they tried to work their magic on me they never succeeded and would walk away disgruntled.

I did not learn to speak German, except in restaurants and tailors' shops, where I ordered a lot of unsuitable clothes in lurid, shiny foreign materials. My theatre-going was mostly confined to the Stadttheater at Klagenfurt – though I did manage a night at the opera in Vienna and, on a visit to Graz, a very odd operetta, *Czar und Zimmerman*. At the Stadttheater an unusually plump, blond male dancer, Rene Estée, seemed to feature in all the entertainments offered – ballet, opera, operetta, even Skakespeare. The Klagenfurt *Merchant of Venice* was graced by a visiting star Shylock from Vienna and ended in a frenzy of curtain calls which went on longer and longer as he tried to achieve one on his own. The more he came back, the more he was foiled by one or other of the small-part actors – usually Rene Estée, who had been playing one of the Salads. Somehow the star never got his solo call.

The routine of mess dinners, films at the AKC cinema and Saturday night dances at the Hotel Moser stole the spare time. The Moser was the centre of Army social life. Occasionally an

Army entertainment troupe would arrive. The singing comedienne Joan Turner and the pianist Bob Harvey were a big hit. Outside the door stood a sad Austrian lady who, we were told, had seen her husband enter the hotel just before the war and never emerge. She arrived each day at the same time, still expecting him to show.

The British Troops in Austria Amateur Dramatic Society took up a lot more time, and a second lieutenant's rank gave me much bigger roles than Ian Holm, who was a lance corporal. The memory makes me blush. An affair with a major's wife fizzled quickly and one with a colonel's daughter foundered when walking through the woods behind the mess I tripped over her lying in the grass with one of my despatch riders who was making her very happy. I 'lusted in my heart' for two stalwart cipher clerks and, drunk after one mess night, I jumped into Lieutenant Scott's bed and he jumped very quickly out the other side. That was the sum of romance for me for my two years of national service.

A gleeful memory is a ceremonial presentation of the Colours to a regiment by the late Princess Royal. It was performed on a parade ground surrounded by hills which produced a formidable echo with the Tannoy at full blast. The echo and HRH's open vowel sounds reached a peak of eccentricity in a sentence which started, 'My fathaaah in Indiaaaa in nineteen hundred and fouraaah!' She echoed around the mountains like an imperial yodel.

The Army became a tempting career prospect, so easy and unchallenging were its disciplines. I would have been an appalling soldier. Had my Oxford place not been assured I might have embraced that cosy career. My father was never keen on the idea of Oxford, though he did nothing to hinder my progress and, since, thanks to a means test, I got no benefit from my state and county scholarships, paid for me. What puzzled him was how it was going to help. When he heard that I intended to read history and English the only prospect which he could think of was 'schoolmastering'. All farmers have a contempt for schoolmasters and he had no intention of letting me become one. However, my mother's father was a solicitor and my father held him in some awe. The loophole through which I slipped in order to avoid a family row was to opt to read law.

So I went up to Exeter College, Oxford, and had the very best of times. Emerging from my country chrysalis, I plunged into all the freshman activities, playing football and cricket indifferently for the college – one day distant cheers just audible on the cricket pitch announced Roger Bannister's four-minute mile. I joined the Oxford University Dramatic Society (OUDS) and the Experimental Theatre Club (ETC) as well as the Union, and wrote occasionally for *Isis*. Quite soon I was cast by John Wood for an ETC production of *'Tis Pity She's a Whore* in the small but showy role of the cardinal who closes the play sonorously with the lines, 'Of one so young, so rich in nature's store, who would not say, 'tis pity she's a whore.'

After my first rehearsal I was summarily dismissed and replaced by the priest who spoke the opening lines of the play – one of the quicker promotions inside the Catholic Church. Then I failed to get Sir Toby Belch in an OUDS production of *Twelfth Night* in which Maggie Smith played Viola and John Wood, Malvolio. Patrick Dromgoole, later head of Harlech TV, got Sir Toby. Discarded by the OUDS I turned to revues for the ETC and spent most of my time at Oxford producing them. By now I was established as 'Ned'. In the Army I had been lumbered unhappily with the name of Ted, which I hated. My father always called me Ned so when I went up to Oxford I adopted it, slightly to his annoyance. He felt he had some sort of copyright on it. However, I was determined not to be Ted and happily the alternative stuck.

With Desmond O'Donovan, who went on to be a monk and thence a director at the Royal Court and then at the National Theatre, I produced a series of revues and pantomimes – *The*

Candlelight Revue, Etcetera, Loud Sing Cuckoo as well as *Dick Whittington*, and *The Babes in the Wood*, which was conflated with *The Sleeping Beauty*. This ingeniously gave us a Victorian first half written by my friend Brian Brindley, an expert in Victoriana. In the second half, when the Beauty awakes after a hundred years, it was a modern pantomime. Brian's half included a memorable couplet. Discovering a letter pinned to a tree in a forest the surprised character says,

It would have been less heterodox
If she had put the letter in the letter-o-box.

Looking back through old programmes, Nigel Lawson as a slim chorus boy with extravagantly long eyelashes was perhaps the most eccentric casting. There was one further excursion into serious drama. Kenneth Tynan, not long down but already a legend, came back to judge a one-act-play contest organised by the ETC. I dramatised a short story by Somerset Maugham in which God featured strongly. It was a very moral tale and 'dramatised' is an overstatement. I did little more than copy it out and make the lines shorter than the width of the page. It was the era of T. S. Eliot and Christopher Fry and I reckoned that this made it a verse drama. I was impressed. I can't remember who won. It may have been Colin Shaw, who went on to become director of television for the Independent Broadcasting Authority (IBA) and then something senior at the BBC. He wrote a piece called '. . . *As Flies* . . .', a tense little Central European frontier incident. Tynan said in his judgement that he always mistrusted plays with three dots in the title. My own play he dismissed out of hand with a splendid swipe at God, who was played by Desmond O'Donovan. Desmond has a rolling 'R', a highly individual lisp. 'I couldn't understand', Tynan stuttered, giving his judgement, 'how, if the Almighty could create the consonant "R", he could not pronounce it.'

Oxford is a mellow memory. Exeter was a mellow college. Distilled are recollections of the ascetic Rector Barber's official welcome: 'Exeter is the second-oldest college at Oxford – the fourth if you count lodging houses.' His sherry party for freshmen when Mrs Barber, a charming Swiss, mixed up the sherry and whisky decanters and a dozen or so undergraduates broke the ice quicker than usual. Later he took us round the pictures in the college hall. One eager freshman pushily claimed an early rector as a direct ancestor. 'Interesting,' said Rector Barber. 'Of course, all rectors were celibate in those days.' The poet Peter Levi was interested in Barber's special field – the Latin poet Propertius. Barber's expertise was in his difficult grammatical idiosyncrasies. Peter once asked him what he thought of Propertius 'as a poet'. 'Ah,' said Barber, 'you mean the slush side of poetry!'

R. M. Dawkins, Baron Corvo's 'blubber-lipped professor of Greek', still haunted the quad. Professor Atkins, who loathed women at his lectures and who, rumour suggested, had once taken off his trousers to discourage them from attending, was still a walking legend. Nevill Coghill, the English literature scholar, still had his rooms on No. 1 staircase. He gave leisurely lunches and produced an *As You Like It* in Worcester College gardens. It opened with the University Society of Archers blasting a dozen arrows to within feet of the front row and closed with Hymen's procession judged to a split second to arrive from the furthest corner of the garden. I was too late to see his *Tempest* with Ariel's famous exit skipping across the lake on supports driven down through the water. An air of unfulfilment sat heavily on Nevill's melancholic shoulders for all the success of his Chaucer translations which had not yet transformed *The Canterbury Tales* into a West End hit musical. Occasionally a gleam of enthusiasm lit up his eyes and his conversation.

Most individual of all was Dacre Balsdon, long ago a Devonian, speaking now in some favourite but extreme version of an Oxford accent which tradition told us he had painstakingly acquired. He teased, challenged, cosseted and provoked his chosen favourite undergraduates out of hobbledehoydom to some vantage point from which they might espy sophistication.

I fell into step with him one day in the front quad. I was not his pupil, academic or moral, but I was anxious to register with this college character. He asked where I had been to school. By now I was sufficiently self-conscious of the double entendre which the name Sexey's embodied to strike first and reveal it as a joke. I waited for the expected laughter. He received the information with the straightest face and I felt properly gauche and disloyal. I did not take such a reaction for granted again. Just before he died, I did a BBC anthology broadcast, *With Great Pleasure*, from Sexey's, sharing the reading with Robin Phillips. Dacre wrote from retirement outside Oxford to say how good it was to choose to do it from 'the school for which you have such an affection'.

I have lost the letter which he wrote to break, with simple care and concern, the news of a dear mutual friend's sudden early death. He was much disliked by some colleagues and misunderstood by many undergraduates, but to those whom he inspired he was the essence of their Oxford experience.

I did not shine at law. The late Derek Hall, my tutor, managed a reluctant tolerance which accepted that I was doing other things. I lived in Exeter for three years, two of them shared with a Welsh friend, Dai Williams, later to become a distinguished QC and judge. Then he was fun and a college favourite. On the first night of a college production of *A Midsummer Night's Dream* set in Exeter garden, he played Puck and reckoned his exit on the line 'I'll put a girdle round the earth in forty minutes' gave him plenty of time to stop off for a pint in the Stapledon Bar. He miscalculated and had to be fetched out after Oberon had waited some minutes for his return. The Fairy King's next line, 'Welcome wanderer', has never had more relevance. Dai's oddest foible was a fascination with fire. I once awoke to find him playfully lobbing a burning wastepaper basket at me. I just managed to punch it past him to safety out of the window. It dropped to the Turl where our neighbours below – Firth and Mucklow (names soon spooner-ised) – thought they had witnessed a falling comet. Ironically the only time any real damage was done was when I inadver-tently set light to a wastepaper basket myself and blackened an entire panelled wall.

A one-off charity concert was another showbizzy event. A Greek earthquake disaster shocked the world in August 1953. Over a thousand people died and around a hundred thousand were made homeless. A wave of sympathy prompted fund-raising schemes all over. We staged a modest show at Oxford. I remember little of the programme – apart from some sort of dis-turbance by Alexander Weymouth – now Marquess of Bath – and the 'handbag' scene from *The Importance of Being Earnest*. Daphne Levens, wife of a don at Merton, gave her Lady Bracknell, and Maggie Smith, still feeling for her own voice, did a devastating impersonation of Joan Greenwood in the then recent film as Gwendolen. We raised a substantial sum. Those of us who helped to organise it were thanked at a national commit-tee meeting in London before going on to the professionals' midnight gala at the Theatre Royal, Drury Lane, for which we had bought comparatively cheap gallery seats. At the committee meeting in a Greek shipping magnate's house in Avenue Road, I found that I had lost my ticket. Seeing my confusion, the guest of honour – Princess Katherine of Greece – Lady Katherine Brandram in this country – said she would look after it. I had hopes of another ticket. Not at all. 'Stick with me,' she said and I did, out of the door, into the car, out of the car, into the theatre, up the staircase and finally, happily, into the back of the Royal Box.

It was my first visit to the great theatre. I thought the royal party were remarkably blasé about the entertainment. There was a special prologue written by Christopher Hassal, sonorously spoken by Olivier. Alec Clunes emoted. A Brazilian group danced up a storm and Christopher Hewett did Sandy Wilson's revue sketch about Sir Christopher Wren, 'Hush, hush, whisper who dares/Christopher Wren is designing some stairs.' Starved of West End entertainment – my sole taste had been Paul Scofield in *Ring around the Moon* on my way to being demobbed – I was enraptured. About halfway through the show my benefactress wafted discreetly out into the night, followed at intervals by the rest of her party. I would not be moved. At last the curtain fell. Calls were taken to the applause of those Graecophiles in the audience who had remained. Suddenly the band struck up a strange tune which stopped in their tracks patrons making for the exits. They were standing to attention. I worked out that the band was playing the Greek national anthem. Loyally I threw out my chest. Round came a spotlight in which I basked; sole surviving representative of the Greek royal family, much to the puzzled annoyance of my friends in the gallery who had guarded their tickets better. I hung on for an encore with our own national anthem. There has been a slight sense of anticlimax on all subsequent visits to Drury Lane.

I made occasional forays into semi-professional entertainment from Oxford. I auditioned for BBC Drama, West. I sold a couple of dialect short stories to the West Region – one was called *Not as Green as I'm Cabbage Looking*; happily it does not survive. I made an inglorious trip to Birmingham to report on a Villa versus Pompey match in Aston. The BBC allowed expenses for a taxi to the studio but, thinking I knew better, I decided I could do it on public transport with time to spare. Emerging with the crowd, I got hopelessly lost. I tried begging a lift from cars crawling away from the ground. 'I'm from the BBC,' I said hopefully. I finally gained access to one car. It took the driver about twenty yards to find out that I was not Wilfred Pickles, Richard Dimbleby or one of his other heroes and I was pitchforked back into the street. Finally I jumped a bus which turned out to be the right one. I made the studio just in time to give my report on the match. I added a couple of bits of colour. Both were inaccurate. I was not asked again.

One Sunday I was summoned to Bristol to do a radio play about the invention of the steam engine. I was cast as 'an eighteenth-century voice' and 'the voice of inspiration'. It was the beginning and end of my career as a radio actor.

Immediately after Oxford I submitted a musical to Owen Reed, the head of drama at Bristol. It was based on a novel by Walter Raymond, Somerset's Thomas Hardy, called *Gentleman Upcott's Daughter*. The music was by Leopold Antelme, who had composed some revue music at Oxford. The cast was led by Jane Wenham and Denis Quilley, supported by all the West Country actors whom I had heard broadcasting for years from the studios in Whiteladies Road, Bristol. Those were the days of enormous BBC regional orchestras – the Bristol band was conducted by Frank Cantell. The sound mixer was Paul Bonner, who later became second in command when Channel 4 opened. I was very proud of *Gentleman Upcott's Daughter* and especially of a riotously rural number called 'Grass':

> Yas! Yas!
> You must 'ave the weather for Grass! Yas!

It was heady wine at that age to have a loving production, a perfect cast and an enormous orchestra. Nothing could come of it and nothing did.

My emotional life at Oxford had consisted of occasional bouts of satisfied lust and two long states of miserable unrequited love. The low point was the Queen's Coronation day in 1953 when we awoke to learn that Hillary and Tensing had climbed Everest and that it was raining. The current, unresponsive object of my affections ('I do understand. My major in the Army in Kenya had a crush on me; but I still find the idea disgusting.') had gone off to London. I went to the Bull, a little pub off Merton Street, and drank earnestly. On my way back to college I was about to cross the high street when my progress was halted by the remains of what had promised to be Oxford's grand cele-bratory Coronation fancy-dress parade. All that remained to brave the rain was a single float of Oxford's railway workers, bedraggled in their bizarre costumes. For some reason they had chosen to appear as matadors and mantilla-sporting gypsies. As the rain dripped off them it seemed to sum up my Coronation. Perhaps I would have been happier back in Kingweston. My brother, by now well established on the farm, told me that the village hired a television for the occasion. It was a first for Kingweston. It was installed in one of my father's barns. Food and drink were laid on and everyone turned out. Squire Dickinson made a memorable appearance to view the event through binoculars, perched on a shooting stick, taking the occa-sional sandwich from his picnic box.

The much-travelled ground of Oxford hardly needs another road map. When I had covered it I left with two calling cards. One was an unremarkable second. I was convinced that I only passed my viva by invoking a case called *The Queen* v. *Dodds* – the Victorian 'fuck-a-duck' case which made the examiners pass on hurriedly in some embarrassment. The second was another revue called *Oxford Accents* which the BBC televised. I kept that card in my pocket while signing up for legal cramming at Gibson and Weldon in Chancery Lane.

CHAPTER 2

Yesterday, When the World Was Young . . .

Even had I not fainted before a judge during a mock trial at Gray's Inn in 1954 I would not have stayed with the law. As I floundered before Mr Justice Skelhorn a heavenly choir began to sing in my ears, bright purple colours danced in my eyes, the room revolved gently and gracefully and then faster as I fell to the floor.

I was finishing my time at Oxford, scraping my second by cramming in the last term to make up for two and a half years of enjoyment. I had no idea what I wanted to do; but I knew that by signing up with Gibson and Weldon I would get six months' grace before making up my mind. I was already 'eating dinners' at Gray's, leaving Oxford at teatime and returning late-night on British Railways' 'Flying Fornicator'.

The moot that poleaxed me was a debate in which four junior members of the Inn argued an abstruse legal point before the learned judge. I was two nights underslept, moping my way through another disastrous, unrequited love affair. My colleague and I divided the arguments between us. I hoped to get by with a minimum of preparation. What I did not allow for was a cock-up. My leader covered all the points we had allocated to me. I was left to argue those which I assumed he had prepared and I certainly had not. Mr Justice Skelhorn became more and more tetchy and demanding, precipitating my ignominious collapse.

I came round in a few minutes and milked recovery with a glass of water. I finished the case only because I was now helpfully prompted by the suddenly sympathetic judge. But I realised that I could hardly rely on frequent fainting fits to sustain a practice at the Bar.

In a long career of happy accidents perhaps the most useful was to have been born in 1931 and to complete national service, Oxford and Bar exams precisely in time for the opening of commercial television. *Oxford Accents* came about because in 1953 the BBC outside broadcasts department had decided to visit Oxford for a week. They would cover a debate at the Union; they would eavesdrop on the pearls of wit and wisdom dropped by senior members of the university after dinner in Nevill Coghill's rooms in Exeter; and they would cover various sporting events. One of these was to be an undergraduate boxing match.

In those days of television's infancy it was against BBC policy to broadcast a fight if there was a professional bout on the same night. As our luck had it a modest professional contest tucked away in a public baths somewhere in the East End was announced just in time to force the BBC to change its plans. Desperate for an alternative thirty-minute live programme Anthony Craxton, producer, and Brian Johnston, commentator, decided on a revue. By then I'd done three for the Experimental Theatre Club. It was a simple business of choosing our 'greatest hits' and prising Maggie Smith out of her job as an ASM (Assistant Stage Manager) at the Playhouse for the night. Most of the material was the work of Jeremy Bullmore, who had gone down the year before and was struggling to start a writing career.

The next day the television critics used us as a stick with

which to beat professional entertainers. We were 'fresh', 'literate', 'witty' and 'high-spirited'. We were 'bright and a breath of fresh air'. All the usual adjectives were taken down and dusted off. I was invited to go to Television Centre to meet Ronnie Waldman, the head of light entertainment. He received me solemnly, regretted that he had not seen the programme (no recording) and advised me to join a good repertory company and learn the job from the bottom.

More promising was an invitation to meet George Dixon, a director at J. Walter Thompson, the advertising agency. I added Bullmore's name to the invitation. He was nursing a legitimate grievance. His name had been left off the TV credits. Separately we visited head office at 40 Berkeley Square and were subjected to creative writing tests and the fashionable psychological battles with ink blots. Jeremy sailed through both and was hired on the spot. Eventually he went on to head the firm. I was politely found wanting and let go.

My first 'digs' in London were smack in the middle of St James's. Duke Street, in fact. They belonged to a friend of Jeremy Bullmore who was abroad, and were presided over by a 'treasure' – Mrs Winch. Mrs Winch was a kindly, stately lady who was not used to impoverished young gentlemen camping out on the premises she dominated. She was always eager to go to market and buy vegetables. Market was Fortnum and Mason. 'Fortnum's only two doors away,' she would say, and return with everything elaborately wrapped and hideously expensive. 'Winch', it turned out, was a 'freelance butler to royalty'. He had been employed by the same class of person on a regular basis but found that he was making more money on his nights off. He had gone independent and done well. Every summer Winch took his Mrs Winch on a little European holiday. That year they had gone down the Rhine, 'All them grapes', and returned 'via Paris'.

I asked, 'How did you like Paris, Mrs Winch?'

She was wonderfully dismissive. 'Very small to London,' she said.

Eventually I settled in Chelsea in a large flat on the Embankment owned by Michel Raper, a writer, and Kenneth Fortescue, an actor. They had room for three lodgers. During the eight years that I lived there Peter Nichols (then an actor and teacher, not yet a playwright), Roderick Cook, Jeremy Sandford and Julian Pettifer were among my fellow tenants. We called it the Chelsea Palace.

Peter had served in Army entertainments in the Far East with Kenneth Williams, Stanley Baxter and John Schlesinger. A good mimic and a fine raconteur, he fumed in impotent rage when Williams came to tea and insisted on taking over his half-told stories, embroidering and developing them to some extravagantly bawdy punchline of his own. Kenneth was playing the Dauphin to Siobhan McKenna's Saint Joan at the Arts Theatre at the time. He delighted in impersonating an elderly actor-laddie, Frank Royde, who was cast as the Archbishop. Royde had been directed to spend most of the play downstage, with his back to the audience looking upstage towards Saint Joan. Asked about his make-up he boomed back at the director, John Fernald, 'Don't know! Never had to make up me arse before!'

Jeremy Sandford was just starting on a career as a writer. *Cathy Come Home* was several years away. He spent many hours of the day in bed, fully clothed, peering at empty sheets of paper. One day, as water poured through the ceiling of the landlord's sitting room below, it took precious minutes to get Jeremy to unlock the bedroom door, realise that his hand basin was running over and turn off the tap.

Hardly less eccentric was his encounter with a burglar. Strange people were always coming and going at Chelsea Embankment. Tactfully, no questions were ever asked. Jeremy came home with his girlfriend Nell (*Up the Junction*) Dunn one day to confront a visitor who was just leaving carrying a pile of clothes and a typewriter. They greeted the departing 'guest' politely. When the theft was discovered the police interviewed Jeremy – the only man who had seen the culprit. Could he give them a description? He certainly could. Notebooks poised, they waited while Jeremy weighed his words carefully. At last he felt able to give details. 'He looked . . .' he said in an inspired flash, '. . . he looked like a rather bad journalist.' No more could they elicit.

The King's Road was another country in 1954. The urge to swing had not hit it. Bakers, family butchers, greengrocers, florists and drapers still confirmed the village atmosphere. Boutiques were for the next decade although espresso bars were appearing – notably Roy's, heavy with *trompe l'oeils*, near the pheasantry. On my first excursion along the pleasant, shabby street the real Chelsea Palace was still active (not as it is now, a 'reject' shop), and Monty Norman 'The Singing Barber' (later to be the controversial composer of the Bond theme) topped the bill.

By the time I finished cramming and was due to sit for my Bar finals, I had adopted Caletta's restaurant in the King's Road as a perfect place to plan my attack on the examiners. Caletta's walls were brown and discoloured, partly through age and partly due to a vague sepia mural. We speculated that it might have been painted in the twenties or thirties by a non-paying diner-artist. The *table d'hôte* at luncheon was a legendary three shillings, all included. The tablecloths were white and soup-stained. The soup was soup-stained. It was also anonymous, thick and gravelly. Basic things were done to lamb, beef and chicken. Thick spaghetti came with a brown, meaty sauce. And yet the spindly chairs and creaking tables had their faithful aficionados – Noel Coward's favourite designer, Gladys Calthrop, occasionally Sybil Thorndike and Lewis Casson, Julian Slade and Angela Thirkell.

I used it a great deal. When exams loomed it was the perfect place to prop a book up against a jug of water or a half bottle of wine and mug up on torts. The sparsely attended room was presided over by a benign, shaky old gentleman – an Italian version of the bumbling waiter in *You Never Can Tell*. The peaceful atmosphere stemmed from the waiter and from Madame Caletta who commanded the cash desk in black and a young Mr Caletta who divided his time between the restaurant and the tobacconist-cum-sweet shop next door. Caletta's has long gone. First it was sold and re-established as a Chinese restaurant called Marco Polo. The old waiter survived until the opening party, greeting his faithful customers with frail warmth; but the variety of new and mysterious Chinese dishes brought fear and confusion to his eyes. I never found the heart to go back and see how he was doing. Now the Marco Polo has long gone too.

I celebrated the end of Bar exams by going to the Haymarket to see *The Matchmaker*. Ruth Gordon and Sam Levene and Eileen Herlie starred in a magical production by Tyrone Guthrie. The play would later provide the book for *Hello Dolly*. Arthur Hill and Alec McCowen played the two apprentices. Prunella Scales was a pert maid. The evening ended with a bang. On the way home our bus unaccountably crashed into the front of the Ritz hotel. No injuries; but a lot of jokes about caviar and chips.

After an anxious wait in Somerset the news that I had scraped through brought me hurrying back to London in late September 1955 to eat my last dinner at Gray's and formally to be called to the Bar. The morning after I was walking along the Strand when I bumped into Stephen Wade, who had been the BBC floor manager on the Oxford revue.

'What are you doing?' he said.

'I'm a barrister,' I replied grandly.

'Well,' he said, 'we're starting commercial television next week. Why don't you come and join us?'

We had lunch and he took me back to Television House at the end of the Kingsway where Associated Television (ATV) had set up shop. He introduced me very flatteringly to his boss, Keith Rogers, who was head of outside broadcasts.

'What are you doing?' he asked.

It had worked once so I tried it again.

'I'm a barrister.'

'I'm afraid we can only offer you a producer's job,' he said apologetically.

I had arrived with visions of starting as a tea-boy and inching my way up by talent, hard work and determination. However, seeing a possibility that none of those qualities might be required I kept quiet and asked what salary I could expect. He looked even more apologetic.

'I'm afraid I can only offer nine hundred pounds a year.'

I knew most of my contemporaries were being offered £450 for jobs advertised by the university appointments board and even I could work out that £900 was twice £450. I said I thought I could manage on that for a year. It was a Thursday. I reported to ATV the next Monday. Three days later ATV went on the air for the first time with a variety show from the Wood Green Empire.

It was as easy as that. The problem now is that when school-children ask how you can get into television I can't very well advise them to walk down the Strand and hope they meet a man.

It did not take ATV long to discover that my legal training had prepared me for precious little in a television studio. However, I was in, paid and established as a producer. There was an air of happy improvisation in the early days. We camped above Associated Rediffusion in Television House. Apart from a stiffening backbone of professionals who had abandoned the BBC, most staff members had drifted into their jobs from some outpost of Moss Empires and the variety circuit. We were aware of the showman Val Parnell, of the impresario Prince Littler and dimly of Little Lew Grade, the agent, though no one thought of tipping him as the ultimate survivor in the ATV power struggle. We laughed condescendingly when we heard his response to a deal for the coverage of athletics meetings which Keith Rogers had proudly negotiated with 'the three As'.

'What's the three As?'

'The Amateur Athletics Association, Mr Grade.'

'I don't want any amateurs – get me professionals!'

Most conspicuous, pacing the corridors was the stout, pudgy, pale-grey figure of Harry Alan Towers, a veteran of commercial radio, who was the first to go, while Norman Collins, who did so much to lobby for commercial television, soon faded into the woodwork of the boardroom.

For the company it was a period of turmoil and substantial loss. In the studios it was a time of cheerful co-operation. With the advent of full-time breakfast television most people have forgotten that ATV briefly pioneered it in the late 1950s – not with any great success. I was part of it.

From October to Christmas 1955 I reported dutifully to Viking Studios in St Mary Abbots Place, Kensington, on Friday evenings and prepared for the entertainment we presented from nine to ten the next morning. Two charming actors, Daphne Anderson and David Stoll, did chatty interviews in the cramped studio. Jerry Desmond, the veteran straight man to Sid Field, broadcast a live commercial for that week's London Palladium show. There was a weekly domestic sketch by the revue writer Leslie Julian Jones which did not extend two experienced actors, Tom Chatto and Hannah Watt. My particular task was to find out by various subterfuges what our celebrity guests would like as a gift. It was presented on air as a glorious surprise, in lieu of a fee.

Gracie Fields, who topped the bill of Val Parnell's first *Sunday Night at the London Palladium*, was rumoured to covet a Parker pen. Wrong. Her husband, Boris Alperovici, took one look at it as it was presented. 'We got one of those already,' he said firmly. Donald Wolfit wanted a combined alarm clock and teapot; Dorothy Tutin, a small, white lambswool rug from Harrods for her houseboat on Cheyne Walk.

On Sunday afternoons I used to hang around the London Palladium watching Parnell complain about Tommy Steele's guitar, or the choreographer, the late George Carden, bawling out his dancers. 'But Mr Carden,' said one, after a severe dressing down, 'I'm not queer!' Carden advanced on him from the stalls. 'Never mind,' he shouted, 'no one will know from the front.'

Tommy Trinder was the first host of the show and *Beat the Clock*, its game-show centrepiece. The epitome of cockney repartee, Tommy never found the same commanding fluency on television which he achieved in the halls and in cabaret with his long-forgotten catchphrase, 'You lucky people!' and his table-hopping routine, handing out cards inscribed, 'Trinder's the name.' On one occasion at the Café de Paris before the war he approached a drunken Orson Welles, saying, 'Trinder's the name.'

'Why don't you change it?' slurred Welles.

'Is that an insult, Mr Welles, or a proposal of marriage?' was the reply.

One night Trinder was confronted on *Beat the Clock* by a particularly obnoxious contestant. The woman was infuriating but, with an ageing comedian's instinctive reluctance to alienate his audience, whose sympathies he knew would be divided down the middle, Trinder persevered politely. The more she got wrong the more points he showered on her. Finally he let her through to the final round. She was in for the jackpot. Again she failed. Indecision creased his face. Again he favoured her and wheeled on the prize. It was a hairdryer. Ungrateful to the last, she considered it balefully. As the music struck up the audience did not hear her comment, 'I've got one already.' Nor did they hear Tommy's riposte as he finally snapped: 'Never mind, madam. One day you may 'ave a two-headed baby!'

After the Saturday morning show I floor-managed a children's afternoon programme. An attendant humiliation was squeezing a small rubber toy to provide the squeaking voice of an 'invisible' character, 'Charlie'. Charlie was the naughty charge of the lovable presenter (another vaudevillian survivor of the cannibalisation of the old variety circuits) – Uncle Fred. With some relief I inadvertently killed off Charlie when I was seen in shot as I moved his props about on the studio floor at precisely the wrong moment, breaking the spell of his invisibility

One of our occasional studios was the old New Cross Empire. It was, of course, another Moss Empires variety relic. Here on occasion the fog came up from the Thames so thick that it cast a ghostly haze across the studio – a sad anticipation of the death of music hall. It is now a garage forecourt.

On Christmas Day 1955 ATV decided on a live broadcast from the children's ward at the hospital on Paddington Green. There were two snags. We arrived to find that most of the patients had been sent home for Christmas – so we had to dress twenty-odd beds with four or five children; and one of the children's entertainers was rumoured, unfairly, to take an unhealthy interest in little boys. We congratulated ourselves that, by keeping the kids on the move, we managed both to give the appearance of a ward full of festive tots and to help them elude any possible unwelcome advances.

At the time there was a rigid rule that any programme with religious content must be separated by several minutes from the commercials which paid for it. Thanks to a couple of extra prayers improvised by the enthusiastic local parson who had been conscripted for the occasion, we looked like overrunning into the forbidden time-trap. My last memory of the show is hearing, over my headphones, the director, Anna Lett, pleading with central control and screaming, 'You *can't* fade a blessing!'

Inevitably the breakfast programme was scrapped. There was no evidence that anyone had ever watched it and our little group became the nucleus of the production staff when ATV started transmission in the Midlands in the spring of 1956. The London franchise had been for the weekends. In Birmingham we programmed Monday through Friday. The next regional commercial television, Granada in Manchester, came a little later.

An old theatre in the suburb of Aston was adapted as the Birmingham studio with an outside broadcast van drawn up by the stage door. A line of prefab huts alongside the building provided the office space. We were commanded by an old BBC hand, Philip Dorté. The three producers were Noele Gordon, Reg Watson, an Australian, and me. The office walls were so thin that when Noele Gordon chose to phone London to bawl out Val Parnell, who had been her lover, her theatrically trained voice could be heard loud and clear throughout the building.

The opening night of the new station set a pattern for the network with a cast of lord mayors, bishops and local bigwigs spouting civic pride in time-worn platitudes. This being ATV there was also a variety show. I had the undemanding role of cueing the lord mayor at the town hall to declare the station open. However, I got a call early on in the day telling me that I had been switched to studio-manage the variety bill – an altogether more complex job.

I had never worked on such a show before. The director was Bill Ward who had a fearsome reputation for harrying his staff. He kept shouting 'segue' through my headphones. I had no idea what a segue was and did not like to ask. I had looked everywhere for 'it' or 'them' before I discovered that it was a musical term addressed not to me but to the musical director.

The star guest was the American film actor Tyrone Power who was touring Britain in a production of *The Devil's Disciple*. The hosts were Bob Monkhouse and Dennis Goodwin. Monkhouse sensed my insecurity early on and was tirelessly supportive. What I didn't know until I read his autobiography some forty years later was that he had called on Power in his hotel suite early in the day to discuss the banter they were to exchange. The film star greeted him from his bathroom and when Bob entered stood up in his bath, revealed a large erection, and asked Monkhouse what he intended to do about it. Bob made his excuses and left.

No sign of this embarrassment hung over their exchanges during the bizarre little variety show. Barbara Lyon sang, the Buddy Bradley Dancers danced and the veteran Richard Hearne, as Mr Pastry, performed his timeless Lancers sketch supported by the rest of the company.

We all ended up in Prince Littler's suite at the Queen's hotel to celebrate. Littler still seemed very much in charge but the veteran showman and chairman of ATV was soon to be outmanoeuvred by Lew Grade. As others listened to a local bishop delivering the epilogue I watched fascinated as Littler's hand crept deeper and deeper into the cleavage of one of the ladies on his staff, the better to caress her breasts. 'May the Lord bless you and keep you . . .' the bishop was saying. This is showbiz, I was thinking.

After the grand opening Reg Watson, Noele Gordon and I were left to promote the illusion of regional programming. Noele had not spent twenty years on stage starring in the West End in *Lisbon Story* and understudying the Ethel Merman role in *Call Me Madam* to dwindle into a television executive. She first appeared on the screen in Birmingham hosting an advertising magazine, *Fancy That*. This pure kitsch art form, represented most vividly by a London show, *Jim's Inn*, combined light chat and fiction with a soft sell. Eventually it fell foul of advertising regulations and disappeared. Reg Watson produced *Fancy That* and went on to devise *Crossroads* with the writers Peter Ling and Hazel Adair. Later, back at home in Australia, he started *Neighbours*, and *Prisoner Cell Block H*, a soap set in a women's prison. Right now he came up with another vehicle for Noele, *Lunch Box*, a sort of *Family Favourites* dressed up as a greetings card.

I was left to dogsbody the other nooks and crannies of the schedule to give the Midlands viewer the impression that he was watching a station bursting with regional character. My standard-bearer was a tabloid journalist, Douglas Warth. I cannot remember how we met; but I knew of Douglas from a notorious piece of *Sunday Pictorial* scandal-writing, 'Evil Men'. In it he had exposed homosexual communities in London and around the country. It was the era of Wolfenden, the Montague/Pitt Rivers/Wildeblood trial and the scaremongering of Sir David Maxwell Fyfe, the home secretary. That Douglas should have joined the witch-hunt was puzzling. His instincts were progressive and liberal; but he was a pen for hire. He was quite open about what was for him a cynical exercise and well aware of my own instincts. He was, however, fascinated by the 'queer' scene and happy to report how, long ago, he had persuaded actor and director Peter Glenville to let him watch through a crack in the wall as he buggered another man.

Douglas's undercover exploitations threw up a bizarre coincidence. He employed a buyable gay lad to take him to clubs and pubs used by the community. No picture of him appeared with his byline so his anonymity was preserved. Visiting one 'vice den' after the series had been running a couple of weeks his informant produced a rent-boy friend whose first remark revealed how easily rumour and gossip can escalate. Douglas had a slightly deformed arm.

''Ave you been reading that Miss Warth?' his new witness said in shocked tones. 'Bitter old thing! You know why she's doing it? She's only got one arm. I should know. I've 'ad 'er.' So quickly can a grain of truth support a lie.

Douglas was a beguiling mixture of idealist and hustler, a sensitive vulgarian, a campaigner whose commitment came and went, brash and bashful, cunning and gullible. He was short, stocky and swarthy, with a stubbly shaving-brush beard.

He convinced me, and we persuaded Philip Dorté, a languid survivor and refugee from the BBC news department, that it was time television tried an equivalent of tabloid shock techniques. We called it *Paper Talk*.

Douglas's range of interests was wide. He loved debate and especially devil's counselling. He could combine theatrical tub-thumping with Jesuitical argument in varying degrees, depending on how much, if anything, he knew about the subject he was discussing.

The first programme woke the Midlands up with a start. We had devised an opening routine which revealed Douglas as a caricature tabloid journalist – tousle-haired, unbuttoned shirt, tie awry. The camera pulled back to reveal a half-empty whisky bottle and a full glass, a cigarette half-smoked, an ashtray over-flowing, and an old typewriter on which he was pounding between swigs and slurred sentences. A monstrous, talking, drinking, smoking, swearing, fighting image was created and the phones rang. The impression of 'reporter as drunkard' was compounded by Douglas's voice, which was hoarse and strained. He had not been drinking heavily before the show but he had been attacked by a psychosomatic assault on the vocal cords which can silence performers before a particularly nerve-racking first night. It left no doubt in the minds of viewers who did not want to harbour doubts. It had a far bigger impact on the Midlands than the opening variety bill.

For me it began an exciting roller-coaster ride of programmes and my introduction to the lesson – fully assimilated later on *That Was The Week That Was* – that it is infinitely better to have your programme violently attacked on the front pages of news-papers than carped at in the columns of television criticism.

Douglas engaged in wild attempts to provoke MPs and their wives; Lady Docker and her husband, Sir Bernard; racist coun-cillors; stately home owners; comics; and beauty queens.

We failed to nail Sir Oswald Mosley who was due to speak in Birmingham. Philip Dorté ducked a decision and referred me to Val Parnell. I painted an enthusiastic picture of the probable bloodletting.

'No, Ned,' said Mr Parnell, 'Mosley's not a nice man.'

'But Douglas would give him a rough time, Mr Parnell.'

'No, Ned, we can't touch it. It's politics.'

'But what about your Free-Speech programme on ATV on Sundays with discussion by a panel chosen from people like Michael Foot, A. J. P. Taylor, Woodrow Wyatt, W. J. Brown and Randolph Churchill?'

'That's not politics, Ned. That's impartial politicians talking.'

Soon after Douglas was accused of anti-Semitism – how the charge arose on a programme about boxing and brain damage, I'm not sure. This time Douglas had to defend himself to Lew Grade.

'Mr Grade,' he pleaded, 'I'm Jewish myself.'

'How much?' said Lew.

'A quarter.'

'It's not enough.'

Douglas showed a childlike joy when Norman St John Stevas said 'masturbation' on *Paper Talk* in 1957 ('Is this a television first?'). And he had a famous encounter with Bishop Watson of Birmingham. Asked afterwards how he had enjoyed the encounter, the bishop said, 'I felt as though I was being mentally raped, then I realised I was being paid for it, so I said to myself, "Makes you a prostitute, Bishop, get on with the job."'

Teddy boys were a new phenomenon at the time. Douglas interviewed a group. We dined them before the show as we did with our more senior guests. The next day we were walking past a pinball alley. Inside a row reached punch-up level. One of two opponents was one of our interviewees. He spotted Douglas, rushed out, grabbed him and pulled the other boy across to face him, 'Go on,' he shouted, almost in tears, 'you tell 'im, we did 'ave table wine, din't we?'

First in farce was a programme to reveal to the Midlands the 'serious face' of nudism. After a recce on a damp day in a soggy nudist camp near Coventry we recruited a group willing to appear naked and designed a studio set so that they could be discreetly photographed carefully posed behind deckchairs or box hedges.

Rehearsals started badly when the mother-hen nudist heard that press photographers were in the building hoping to catch indiscreet snaps of her chicks. She strode on to the set clad only in her kimono and dropped it unattractively to her feet under my nose, threatening that all her brood would do likewise live, on camera, if she caught sight of another press peeping Tom. Clearly on her side, my very young floor manager, Terry Yarwood, had already decided that anyone over thirty was a dirty old man not to be allowed on the studio floor. Most of the older electricians and stagehands clustered at the back of the control van where rehearsal cameras allowed more revealing close-ups.

There were incidental joys in the programme. Douglas's eye wandering down as he introduced a young woman warmly: 'I wish you could be sitting where I am.' A young male Midlands nude asked his job: 'I'm a tool-maker, i'n'I?' Best was a respectable married couple whose two shot would be koshered by a *Daily Telegraph* held up before them. Then they would lower it as I cut to close-ups. Nervous on air, they started to lower it before the agreed moment. I am still not sure if my barked command was in time or not. The next morning half the Midlands thought they had seen all. The other half said they had been denied.

After I left Birmingham Douglas failed to find anyone else who enjoyed to share the excitement of *Paper Talk* with him. I tried but failed to engineer a place for him in the more decorous atmosphere of the BBC. Mrs Wyndham Goldie, of whom more later, could not abide him. For a time he became a television critic and a producer with the Central Office of Information. It did not satisfy him. In the end, a disappointed man, he took his own life. He was a brave original, more sensitive under the pugnacious exterior than he would admit.

By the time ATV's Midlands station was in full swing it proved a perfect busy apprenticeship for an earnest television trainee. Looking at the interminable rolls of credits which follow current affairs programmes these days, I am shocked at the output which Beryl, my poor overworked secretary, and I used to foist on the Midlands audience.

At the busiest period on Mondays I was responsible for producing and directing three programmes. A half-hour live outside broadcast called *Seeing Sport* hosted by Billy Wright ran from 3.30 p.m. to 4.00 p.m. At six there was five minutes of local news – commercial television's first regional bulletin. At 10.00 p.m. there was another fifteen-minute live programme, *The Midlands Storyteller*, in which old gentlemen reminisced about past glories, mysteries and mishaps.

On Tuesday the regular news was followed by the controversial twenty minutes of *Paper Talk*. On Wednesday afternoons Noele presided on camera over *Tea with Noele Gordon*, thirty minutes of celebrity interviews and household hints. R. St John Roper, the late spangle-king of London Palladium costumes, demonstrated over six weeks how to make your own shirt – a skill he had to learn specially for the show. Dorothy Ward, the famous principal boy – now in her seventies and determined to be 'with it' – sang, 'I never felt more like singing the blues!' clutching and waving a blue chiffon handkerchief. A couple of hours later, another news bulletin.

On Thursdays the news came first at six, followed at 8.30 p.m. by *Midlands Affairs* – a local *Any Questions* forum. Two MPs, George Brown and Gerald Nabarro, were the regular stars supported by a revolving roster of local politicians, mayors and councillors.

Friday was the easy day – only the news, unless Reg Watson was exhausted by four days of *Lunch Box*. Noele Gordon's vehicle was a request variety show featuring Noele, other singers and the local Jerry Allen Trio. If Reg flagged I was called in on

Fridays to wet my toes in the world of variety. On one tempestuous day a particularly rude anti-fan letter got past the secretary to Noele by mistake. She was not best pleased to be accused of making a 'disgusting old fool' of herself while singing a duet with a much younger baritone. She stormed on set and insisted on reading it aloud – which, of course, produced as many letters in support of the poison-pen artist as it did from the correspondents who took Noele's side.

Seeing Sport gave me the distinction of being the first person to televise Mick Jagger. We did half an hour from his father's basketball class and I was unaware of greatness in waiting – no close-ups.

In *The Midlands Storyteller* we discovered a natural broadcaster, a distinguished, elderly criminal pathologist, Professor Webster. He had shared celebrity with his contemporary, Sir Bernard Spilsbury, a rival whom he disliked until the advent of Dr Francis Camps, whom he despised. Webster's headline career had started with the notorious Buck Ruxton and 'the Nodder' cases – both famous 1920s trials in which he appeared for the prosecution. These are still much discussed in popular crime anthologies. His last front-page involvement was in the James Camb/Gaye Gibson case in which a ship's steward was accused of pushing a chorus girl through the liner's porthole.

Webster had been an undergraduate at St Andrews at the same time as the future stage star Lionel Mollison. Both were enthusiastic amateurs actors, but only Mollison turned professional – leaving Webster as a frustrated performer. He made his debut on *Paper Talk* but it was immediately apparent that he did not need an interviewer. He was the most compulsive talker to camera that I have seen. His power was enhanced by one slightly wayward glass eye. He revelled in the fifteen-minute length of his spot. If a story required thirty minutes to tell, he would spread it over two weeks – leaving the first with a splendid cliffhanger. He liked the studio manager to give a five-minute sign, a two-minute sign, one-minute, thirty-second – and stop. He always signed off on the dot, always with a flourish, and sometimes with a twist that would have sent O. Henry to bed happy.

One day when lunching we were disturbed by the proprietor of the restaurant who ushered in a policeman. The constable bent low and whispered something to Webster who smiled briefly and excused himself. He returned with a broad grin on his face. A crowd had gathered around his car and another policeman was standing guard over it. Inside a blood-covered skull lay on the back seat – its covering blanket dislodged. The crowd were convinced that they had stumbled on a murder. On another occasion he arrived at the studio chuckling. He had come on from a post-mortem examination and the widow, told that he was doing it, seemed much comforted and said with some pride, ''E's going to 'ave to hurry to get to the ITV in time i'n' 'ee?'

No other *Midlands Storyteller* achieved the same popularity, though Phil Drabble had an enjoyable run with Black Country stories and Leslie Sands with mysteries. My big disaster was inviting a much-respected old Birmingham journalist, Harry Bush, whose conversation was as elegant as his prose. However, alarm bells should have rung when he arrived at the studio with a neatly typed script which he said he had learnt. On air he was hardly able to get past his opening sentence, 'I want to tell you about the day I went into the lion's den . . . I shall never forget it . . .' He did. Very soon I found myself sitting at his feet, out of shot, prompting him line by line for the rest of the agonising fifteen minutes.

One of the perks of *Midlands News* was that I could beg free tickets for first nights at the Shakespeare Memorial Theatre at Stratford and then give a ten-second review on ATV the next night: 'Last night *Hamlet* opened. It ended unhappily.' It was my first taste of TV celebrity. I went to a crowded Birmingham cinema, climbing over two Teddy boys on my way to my seat.

'Look who that is.'

'Who is 'ee?'

'It's Ned Sherrin. 'Ee's on television. 'Ee's famous – like Lassie!'

The Mickey Mouse character of our news bulletins was another humbling experience. News was provided in pristine journalese paragraphs by the Birmingham *Evening Despatch*. They also supplied the occasional still photograph. A local firm, whose speciality was weddings, filmed silently the opening of a supermarket, the unveiling of a statue, the laying of a foundation stone, a village fête, a pancake race, the oldest, the youngest, the fattest, the highest, the prettiest, the biggest, the smallest, the flower show, the beauty show, the fatstock show – as long as they had a couple of days' notice. We never got to know about real news in time to film it.

The ragbag of items was held together by the newsreader, Patricia Cox, a drama student who looked a little like the Queen and was gentle, dignified and reassuring. Using a woman to read the news was considered daring, but when Pat had her first holiday we thought we would dare more. Birmingham was one of the first cities to identify an aggravated 'colour problem'. After a search we found a charming black girl who looked ravishing, spoke sweetly and seemed perfect. We were within hours of unveiling her before we found that she could not read. In retrospect I suppose it was an unsuspected case of dyslexia, a condition not easily recognised in the fifties.

It was a perfect if crowded apprenticeship. Serving it, I shared an uncongenial flat in a suburb of Birmingham on weekdays with my colleagues Reg Watson and Terry Yarwood. There was the Birmingham Rep to visit, there to monitor the emerging young actor Albert Finney in *Henry V*, and to have an introduction to Schnitzler's *Anatol* and Garrick and Coleman's *The Clandestine Marriage*. There was the congenial Greek Cypriot restaurant where I had entertained the Teddy boys and Professor

Webster. And there were Friday trains on which I hightailed it
back to London and No. 6 Chelsea Embankment. My weekends
were spent working with Caryl Brahms, the distinguished ballet
critic and novelist, as we began a writing collaboration. This was
mixed with visits to the theatre and cinema, but we would often
meet finally on Monday mornings at a café near Euston Station
to polish the pages we had laboured over during the previous
two days.

After nearly two years in Birmingham – and the routine of
coming home to Chelsea for weekends and leaving from Euston
every Monday morning – I wanted to work in London. Reg
Watson was allowed the occasional trip to the capital to produce
that ultimate achievement, 'a modest spectacular'. I asked for an
interview with Bill Ward, who was in day-to-day charge of ATV
programmes. I put my case. There was a long pause from the
other side of the large desk, and then, 'No, Ned, we see you as
a Birmingham person . . .'

With the experience of directing some three hours and thirty
minutes of varied live television a week under my belt, it seemed
a good time to knock again on the door of the BBC.

CHAPTER 3

Tonight, Tonight Won't Be Just Any Night . . .

One evening during February 1957 Dr Jonathan Miller performed a monologue on the new, trailblazing BBC *Tonight* programme. The doctor was photographed by a single camera, mounted on a 'dolly', a moving platform that could be pulled smoothly back or pushed smoothly forward the better to contain his generous gestures in the picture. As bits of Dr Miller billowed out of shot the cameraman crooked his finger to indicate to his 'dolly-pusher' that they needed to retreat fully to encompass the flailing arms. Taking his cue from what was to him a beckoning finger, the doctor obediently stepped forward, recreating the problem the cameraman had solved. With each advance the camera backed away. Subject and camera hunted one another in and out of lit areas across the studio floor until, inevitably, the camera dolly hit the back wall and the doctor finished his monologue armless and in semi-darkness.

Again my timing was fortunate. *Tonight* had premiered on 18 February 1957 – my twenty-sixth birthday. Soon after Caryl Brahms, with whom I had begun collaborating when I came down from Oxford, gave me an introduction to Cecil McGivern, who was then in charge of BBC television programmes. He handed me down to Grace Wyndham Goldie (talks and current affairs), a critical influence in the development of BBC television.

She sent me further down to Donald Baverstock and Alasdair Milne, who had just started *Tonight*. I had been at Oxford with Alasdair. He went on to become one of the best director generals of the BBC, never adequately appreciated. On the night of the Miller debacle he was the unfortunate director of cameras. He and Baverstock made a formidable editorial team. Handling cameras was not Alasdair's best skill. I arrived to meet them trailing my two years of television control-room experience, hoping to answer their prayers for some order in the studio. I am grateful to Sir Jonathan for highlighting the opportunity for me.

The revolutionary *Tonight* programme came about in a curious way. It is difficult now to believe that in the 1950s the BBC conspired with parents in the absurd fiction that television closed down in the early evening, so that the kids could be packed off to bed. When they were assumed to be safely asleep transmission started again. Soon after the advent of commercial television the ITV companies realised that this period, fancifully known as 'the toddlers' truce', presented a perfect opportunity to advertise products designed to rot a toddler's teeth. It was a market place with rich pickings. Where ITV led the BBC had to follow.

After attempts to divide the hour from six to seven between outside broadcasts, drama, current affairs and light entertainment all the BBC's eggs were finally put in the one basket of *Tonight*. The original regular hosts, led by Cliff Michelmore, were Derek Hart and Geoffrey Johnson Smith. Kenneth Allsop joined later. The reporters chosen were characterful, idiosyncratic men, not picked for conventional good looks, but with a background in journalism – often on *Picture Post*. People like Fyfe Robertson, Trevor Philpott, Chris Brasher and Macdonald Hastings. In Alan Whicker's case, it was the agency, Exchange Telegraph. The film department, brooded over by Tony Essex,

was a training ground for future features directors like Jack
Gold (who once had a phone call from a Hollywood producer
asking, 'Jack, have you heard of a guy called Peter Ilyich
Tchaikovsky?'), Michael Tuchner and Kevin Billington. Bruised
by Tony Essex's disciplines, the apprentice John Schlesinger soon
found a more congenial home in the *Monitor* team. Antony Jay,
Gordon Watkins and Cynthia Judah were early associate producers. It was a dedicated and ambitious group and the amount
of mutually respectful but unyielding infighting among them
was remarkable.

Mrs Wyndham Goldie hovered over her department with
hands-on concern. She had been the *Listener*'s first television
critic in the thirties and, in the fifties and sixties, she brought a
ruthless and relentless intellect to current affairs programming.
In her book *Facing the Nation* she spelt out her attitude to
Tonight:

> One morning I walked into the sordid little office at Lime
> Grove which was shared by Donald Baverstock and Alasdair
> Milne. I was on my way to the airport for a fortnight's holi-
> day. The Editor and the Deputy Editor of *Tonight* were lying
> across their desks with their heads in their arms. Startled, I
> asked what was the matter. They did not raise their heads but
> simply said, 'You must take the programme off. We can't go
> on'. With a mixture of concern and alarm, I asked whether
> they could possibly manage for another fortnight. When I
> came back we'd sort it all out. Wearily they agreed. After an
> anxious holiday I rushed to see them to discover how things
> were. They couldn't even remember what I was talking about.
> 'Come to the cutting room,' they cried, 'and see some marvel-
> lous film that's just come in' . . . *Tonight*, to those who worked
> on it, became a way of life. They were *Tonight* people. They
> strutted around Lime Grove, respecting the audience but
> despising other broadcasters . . . They particularly resented

the resources which were put at the disposal of *Panorama* and of documentary producers, with a bitter pleasure they worked out tables showing the cost per thousand viewers of these productions compared with *Tonight*. But they did not want to leave *Tonight*.

However, *Tonight* would occasionally mount a spoiling item if they heard that *Panorama* was featuring a particular big story later in the evening.

Donald Baverstock's great strength was a mind prodigal of ideas. In a world in which few television people lay claim to a single original notion he would produce a hundred in as many minutes. Of the hundred, on a good day, one might be valuable, two mundane and the rest rubbish, but Donald had surrounded himself with colleagues who were prepared to shoot down the rubbish at early-morning meetings or at fiercely argued screening sessions of near fine cuts of film stories.

And that is my abiding memory of *Tonight*.

The relentless post-mortems. How rarely one heard the nervous reassuring phrases which are obligatory now in a more frightened broadcasting age –

'Good show, yes?'

'I think that went rather well, don't you?'

'Not a bad show, eh?'

'Were you happy?'

You might hear that sort of thing after a single interview or film item on *Tonight*, but never about a whole show. The arrogance never precluded self-examination.

Alasdair Milne's contribution was no less important. If Baverstock sparked a flurry of ideas, Milne had a better mind for analysing the results. For me, *Tonight* was an extension of my ATV apprenticeship in Birmingham, albeit in a more demanding, sophisticated and metropolitan arena. Once again I was in the studio five days a week, planning and directing some forty-five

minutes of television a day. The differences lay in my colleagues – in the first place I now had some – in their standards
and in the national audience to which we played.

Tonight believed that too much of late-fifties television patronised the audience. They were determined to be on its side. 'If we
failed to communicate that was our fault, not the audience's
lack of understanding,' Alasdair Milne wrote. *Tonight* started to
change the face of television in Britain. There are detailed
accounts of its genesis and its character in Mrs Wyndham
Goldie's book, *Facing the Nation*, in Alasdair Milne's *D.G.:
Memoirs of a British Broadcaster*, and in Asa Briggs' monu-
mental official *History of Broadcasting in the United Kingdom:
Competition 1955–1974*. All testify to its lively, challenging attitude. Having no old battles to fight, I shall confine myself to the
fun backstage.

On the very first night Ed Morrow reassured his interviewer,
Derek Hart, that the programme had a great future. In those
days it was broadcast from the studio in St Mary Abbots Place
where I had cut my teeth on ATV's breakfast show. Production
staff and paperwork were bussed over from Lime Grove each
evening. As well as Morrow on that first night there was a live
FA Cup draw, and Eleanor Roosevelt, who complained about
'That young man [Alasdair Milne] in short sleeves blowing cigarette smoke in my face.' There was also a topical calypso sung
by Cy Grant and written by Bernard Levin, a film report on a
statue which was upsetting the people of Richmond, the Dame
of Sark, the great fado singer Amalia Rodriguez on film, and
Jonathan Miller making his first appearance standing still and
properly lit.

Tonight loved animals. While we were still in Kensington Derek
Hart had to interview a tiger. It later escaped into the High Street
where it appeared far more frightened than the passers-by. An
item on *Lawrence of Arabia* was jazzed up with a live camel
borrowed from Chipperfield's Circus. As the camel walked down

the line of blow-ups of Arab chiefs it became fascinated by the pineapple-shaped mic boom which swung over its head towards the interviewer, Magnus Magnusson. Its large tongue came out to investigate. That was soon followed by a crunching noise over the sound system. Anthony Nutting spoke about Lawrence into a surviving microphone and revealed off-camera, after the pro-gramme, that he had been overruled (as technical adviser) by David Lean and Sam Spiegel about a famous incident in the film – the shooting at the desert well by Omar Sharif. 'No Bedouin', he said, 'would ever harm even his worst enemy at a desert well.' Spiegel overruled him and had to pay the son of the real Arab fifty thousand pounds for defamation of his dad.

A cockerel and a pig that had just made successful appear-ances on the show were held for collection in the pine-panelled, deep-carpeted hospitality room borrowed from deadly rivals *Panorama*. All went well until a motorbike backfired outside the window. The cockerel flew at the pig. The pig panicked and opened its bowels. The room was out of action for days and *Panorama* did not easily forgive. There was a kangaroo which behaved beautifully until a sudden studio blackout frightened it into kicking out violently, and a golden eagle was booked from a man in Ealing. In the late afternoon a PA rang to check that it was ready. 'Fine,' said the handler, 'we're about to catch the underground.' The PA was just in time to tell him a van was on its way. As I remember, interviewees were paid some five or six pounds for their trouble. There was a classic encounter when Peter Sellers plugged *Brouhaha*, a play by George Tabori, in which he was opening at the Aldwych. Sellers, playing an oil sheikh, arrived for the interview in flowing robes. On the air he improvised prodigally and hilariously. The allotted five or six minutes spread to more than ten. Everyone was delighted. Sellers left happy. Next morning I heard from his manager – hooting with laughter. The BBC booking lady, whose job it was to negotiate the contract, had telephoned him early. 'We were so pleased with Mr Sellers last night,' she cooed. 'He was so funny – we let him go on for rather longer than we had agreed.' The agent detected a note of caution through the charm. The booker made her offer: 'We would like to suggest increasing his fee from six guineas to seven.'

Kenneth Allsop, a precise, elegant and concerned journalist, had an artificial leg. I became aware of a curious ritual on the odd occasions when a guest, similarly disabled, came to the studio. As one made towards the other across the floor of the hospitality room, the stiffness of the legs became apparent and they would home in on one another. A formal Pinteresque exchange followed.

'Left?'

'Yes . . . You too?'

'No . . . Right. War?'

'Yes . . . Yours?'

'Yes . . . Wood or tin?'

'Tin . . . Yours?'

'Tin . . . Above or below?'

'Above . . . Yours?'

'Yes . . .'

Kenneth was a civilised interviewer, so there was general surprise when Sir Barnes Wallis was invited on to the programme and snorted down the telephone, 'I don't see why at the age of seventy-seven, on a cold November night, I should come all the way to Shepherd's Bush to be insulted by Kenneth Allsop.' The antipathy was never explained and later Kenneth and a film crew went down to talk to Barnes Wallis at Weybridge. There were smiles all round.

At one point Kenneth spent some time in America investigating the Chicago police. Speeding on the freeway with his host and his host's small son in the back, he became aware of a traffic cop screaming up behind on his motorcycle. The car was flagged down and the host whispered that he would demonstrate the nature of police venality in Illinois. He took out his licence and laid a twenty-dollar bill in a visible but not too obvious position. The cop approached the window, looked at the offering and said in an ugly voice, 'Get out of the car.' Allsop thought the plan had gone wrong. 'Come round the back,' snarled the cop. Allsop and the child were left anxiously in the car. When the host came back he was grim-faced, an expression which did not relax until he had put a few hundred yards between his car and the patrolman. Then he began to laugh. The cop had quickly pocketed the twenty-dollar bill and snapped, 'What ya tryin' to do? Corrupt the kid?'

Allsop was a great magnet for girls, which sometimes required drastic evasive action. Once he asked to be told immediately if one turned up at BBC reception. He got the message and when the innocent Cliff Michelmore turned to him for a final comment the director's cut showed an empty chair. Kenneth had legged it down the fire escape.

A favourite *Tonight* interview ploy was to set a subject up in a suitably theatrical setting. (Not unlike our ATV nudists, come to think of it.) When Lord Thomson (of Fleet) made a bid to take over a rival group of newspapers and magazines the camera tracked and panned long, lovingly, interminably across yards of the journals and magazines in question. Lord Thomson replied to my thank-you letter: 'I was glad of the opportunity. I would enjoy to do more of this work.'

Dorothy Lamour was surrounded by an appalling tropical beach setting, which she hated. We were not best pleased when the projected film of a sleepy lagoon in the background ran out long before the interview was over. Harold Lloyd was quizzed on a rafter high above Studio 5 at Lime Grove. Brigitte Bardot was chatted up before my arrival; but I enjoyed photographing Mylene Demongeot, curled up in white fur. I curled up when Geoffrey Johnson Smith, sitting next to Jayne Mansfield on an old-fashioned love seat, said, 'Tell me, Miss Monroe . . .'

When Nubar Gulbenkian bought a London taxi, decorated with filigree gold basket-work, he bowled happily down to Shepherd's Bush in it and up in the lift to the studio. He was interviewed through the cab window by Derek Hart; there he coined his famous explanation of why he bought it. 'I'm told it can turn on a sixpence. Whatever that may be.' I also like his definition of the perfect dinner table: 'Me, and a good head waiter.' But he didn't say that on *Tonight*.

An interview with Mike Todd, the showman who was Elizabeth Taylor's third husband, was one of our better pieces of staging. Todd was opening his mammoth film *Around the World in Eighty Days* in grand style. Before his gaudy Battersea Park Funfair launch party he came to Lime Grove dragging Miss Taylor in his wake. While Todd came up to the studio, she kicked her heels and narrowed her violet eyes impatiently in the hospitality room, plainly disenchanted at hanging around as an extra (out of shot) in her husband's starring vehicle.

Derek Hart was the interviewer and we used the slender resources of the studio to recreate the atmosphere of a tycoon's office. Todd, a short man in Cuban heels, was to sit behind a huge mogul-sized desk surrounded by telephones, his throne-like chair raised on blocks. Derek, not tall either, was perched unimpressively on a stool, at his feet. Looking down on Hart and puffing on a large cigar, Todd dismissed Derek's early questions nonchalantly. The pay-off was a bonus.

'Have you ever done anything you've been ashamed of, Mr Todd?'

'Come on, Derek, we've all done things we've been ashamed of.'

'Yes, Mr Todd, but you do things on a bigger scale than most people.'

Odd settings were sometimes forced upon us, particularly during an electricians' strike. On the first day we transmitted an entire show from the fire escape outside the studio, with the sound often drowned out by passing trains on the Metropolitan Line. The next night we moved to the roof of the Television Centre. Marcel Marceau produced one of his snappiest demonstrations of the art of mime when a gust of wind parted his toupee from his head, giving the viewer a glimpse of clear blue sky between skull and rug before he could slap it down. Another night Cliff Michelmore was trapped in a lift and introduced the programme through the bars of the door. He was extricated while a short film was running.

I confess to playing a terrible trick on the songwriter Lionel Bart, who was in his heyday. He was opening a new show and was to be interviewed by Derek Hart. For a new film he had written a song for Tommy Steele called 'It's All Happening'. It was virtually his latest hit and I said in the green room how much I admired it. Perhaps the best song he had written, I insinuated falsely. Lionel lapped it up and on the air Hart asked him about the difficulties of lyric-writing.

'Easy,' said Lionel.

'Where do you do it?'

'Bath . . . top of a bus . . . wherever I get an idea. Some of my best songs I've written in half an hour.'

'What do you consider your best song, Mr Bart?'

'Could be "It's All Happening",' said Lionel, plainly inspired by the praise that had been so recently lavished upon it. 'Yes, definitely.'

'How does the lyric go, Mr Bart?'

'It's all happening,'

'It's all happening,'

'It's all happening to me!'

'It's all happening,'

'It's all happening,'

'It's all happe . . .'

The voice trailed off as he realised he had been reciting what he had said was his best lyric.

The occasional interview was pre-recorded during the afternoon. One we taped with Joan Sutherland had its farcical side. After the first question Richard Bonynge, her conductor husband, leapt forward displeased with the way the encounter was going. The problem was straightened out and the interview started again. Unfortunately the tape-editing process went awry and when the insert was slotted into the live programme viewers were treated to Dame Joan's first answer complete with Bonynge's spirited interruption, arms waving, eyes flashing, vocabulary vivid, before the item limped on to its conventional conclusion.

The film director Stanley Kramer was live and present for his faux pas. Again Derek Hart was the interviewer. Kramer answered his first question with, 'Well, blah . . . blah . . . blah.' Hart tried again. Kramer replied again, 'Blah . . . blah . . . blah.' The interview was brought to a sudden end. Kramer had thought it was a voice test or a rehearsal. It was live. He was mortified.

The joy of directing a regular live show was the element of danger and the improvisation it inspired. An escaped piglet loose in the studio had to be followed by an available camera and cut to between interviews and film items. After interviews with Edith Sitwell had become a cliché, I shot a whole conversation focused on her eloquent, claw-like hands encrusted with enormous rings (I also carried her in my arms from car to studio and then back out again).

There were moments of agonised waiting to see if film which had been shot, edited and rushed to the projection room would be there in time for the last words of Michelmore or Hart or whoever was introducing it. The closest shave was a memorable despatch from Saigon. The reporter, Trevor Philpott, and cameraman, Slim Hewitt, sent home dramatic footage which showed them surprised in crossfire in the middle of filming their report. It was a Friday night and by Monday the story would be interesting rather than exciting. Cliff had a longish introduction. I decided to let him start it even though there was no sign on the preview monitor that the film had arrived and been loaded. A misty number, the cue, should have been visible. My act of faith had a happy outcome. I shouted 'Run telecine!' (equivalent of 'Roll film!') at the last possible moment and somehow it ran – a hail of gunfire exploding on the screen around Trevor Philpott as a steady Michelmore finished his last syllable.

At his best on *Tonight*, Cliff was a rock. There was always a telephone on his desk in the studio. Often when chaos about the next item reigned in the gallery he used to chat away to no one at all until he could hear that a conclusion had been reached. These became known as Cliff's 'Pinter' conversations – on account of the pauses.

A favourite device which *Tonight* did not invent but of which it grew very fond was the 'vox-pop' – grabbing passers-by on a busy street to canvass their views on an issue of the day or on some more self-conscious question dreamed up by a desperate production team short of material at the early-morning conference. A favourite site was the King's Road, Chelsea – just beginning to be colourful, even in black and white. At the top of Royal Avenue was a particularly wide stretch of pavement in front of the shop of Thomas T. Crapper, the famous sanitary pioneer. Typically one day a housewife, asked her opinion of the Common Market, said that she found it made shopping easier. She thought she had been asked about the new, neighbouring supermarket.

Crapper's has gone and the forecourt no longer seems fashionable for itinerant 'news' 'n' 'views' gatherers, but during the sixties the whole of the King's Road was to become their paradise. I once tried to get into Alexander's, the friendly basement restaurant on the corner of Markham Square which Mary Quant – whose first shop was above it – opened with her husband Alexander Plunket Greene. The narrow steps down to the restaurant were cluttered with uniformed Nazis, some carrying camera equipment, some not. Trying to get to the food, I asked what was going on. The Italian waiter looked surprised that anyone would even ask. 'Is swinging King's Road movie,' he shrugged.

Decades later the downmarket vox-pop migrated to the North End Road market – transformed into a shrine by Esther Rantzen's arrest for microphone importuning. The upmarket favourite remained the north-east corner of Harrods. In the mid-seventies I had occasions to ask questions on Esther's North End patch. Her special star, the aged Annie, a little old lady who sucked, nibbled or spat out everything Esther gave her to taste, spotted a man with a microphone in seconds.

'Are you from Esther?' she asked.

'No,' I said. Discovering Ms Rantzen, a radio studio manager in 1964, and giving her a job on one of the late-night satire shows had been distinction enough.

'I thought not. She told me she wasn't coming back until January.'

'Is it true?' I teased, 'You must know her as well as anyone. Is it true she's going to have her teeth shortened?'

A look of horror crossed Annie's face.

'No,' she said, 'no, Esther won't have her teeth done. She's known for her teeth!'

I had little to do with *Tonight*'s film stories – with very few exceptions. Memorably there was one joyous day just before Christmas, persuading a series of highly unphotogenic music publishers to croak-sing their coy, quaint, cute or sentimental special Christmas songs to Trevor Philpott.

My most useful contribution to filming was a late one. I arranged for Julian Pettifer, whom I had seen doing good work for Southern Television, to join as a reporter. The original intention was for him to be studio-based but, although his journalistic flair and general brightness were undoubted, he seemed ill at ease in the antiseptic surroundings of the studio. To make it worse, the majority of the reporting team were a homely looking bunch. He was about to be 'let go' when a reporter was needed for some unglamorous film chore and Julian was sent off to fill in. Immediately he was seen in front of a slag heap his golden good looks fell into unobtrusive context. Audiences started listening to him instead of wondering what he was doing there.

My main editorial contribution to the content of *Tonight* was on the showbiz side, easily the most thankless part of the programme. If a toothless grandmother in the Hebrides or a gurgling child in Bude said something amusing it was a bonus. The moment we cut to a professional entertainer everyone, audience and production team, became a critic.

There were various ways of injecting performed items into the show. At the beginning Cynthia Judah made two inspired bookings. Robin Hall and Jimmy MacGregor, the Scottish folk-singing act, alternated with Cy Grant, whose calypsos and folk songs were equally popular. Later I introduced Noel Harrison when we needed a replacement. He had been singing in clubs around Italy, came home for the programme and went on to make such records as 'Windmills of My Mind' and to launch a long career around America appearing in his father's role in *My Fair Lady*.

Then there were the 'girl singers'. *Tonight*'s original concept as an all-round magazine programme always included an 'entertainment spot'; a hangover from an earlier era. At first the girls were booked on a night-by-night basis after sketchy auditions. They were accompanied by the Ted Taylor trio – piano, bass and drums. Ted was an endearing figure who had once had a vaudeville act. He buttonholed me one day to recall a triumph of which he was particularly proud. 'I had this wonderful piece of business,' he said. 'I used to cut my toenails with a pair of shears – of course, it was a false foot!' He rocked with laughter at the memory. Some two or three hours later I found myself giving Bob Hope a lift back to the West End from Lime Grove. Something had gone wrong with the limousine which should have collected him. He was charming, but the similarity at all levels of the great family of comedians was striking. He was full of his latest television sketch, performed with Robert Wagner and Natalie Wood. The obsession with the detailed mechanics of the gag was just as single-minded as Ted's. So was the opening line: 'I had this wonderful piece of business . . .'

After I joined the programme we rationalised the girl singers, booking them for a week at a time. Donald liked clean, scrubbed sopranos like Diane Todd and Marion Grimaldi. Carole Carr, Maxine Daniels, Sheila Buxton and Tonia Bern were others who did their weeks. On one chaotic day we were hardly expecting to get in a musical contribution at all. We were virtually pre-empted by a live outside broadcast from Copenhagen. It was a royal visit to Denmark, compered by Richard Dimbleby. No studio interviews were planned, no interviewers, apart from Cliff, were called and there was one small piece of standby film in case of an emergency. And emergency there was. Timing in Copenhagen went wildly wrong and after a piece of scene-setting from Dimbleby we had to permute the resident folk singers (thank God folk singers always have an unlimited repertoire) with Maxine Daniels. It was a Friday night and she had used up all her rehearsed songs so she had to busk. The improvisation was only interrupted by occasional admissions from Denmark that nothing was happening yet. We barely managed to last the course without repeating ourselves when doors opened and the royal party entered just in time for Cliff's sign-off.

The next time I saw the Queen of Denmark was years later in the eighties when she came to dinner with her son-in-law and daughter, the King and Queen of Greece, with friends, the Neil Bensons, in Hampstead. Another guest, George (Speaker) Thomas, told the Queen, now dowager, that they had met before. She thought not. He protested that he had given her a conducted tour of the House of Commons. She established that he had not.

'Oh, dear,' said George, 'wrong queen.'

European royalty do not always have an easy ride in Britain. The King of Norway, turning up to broadcast to his beleaguered country during the war, was kept waiting at the reception desk in Broadcasting House. When the receptionist got off the phone and returned to deal with him she apologised, 'Sorry, which king did you say you were?'

'Norway!' he thundered, not best pleased.

Tonight introductions had a shamelessness which was all their own. The presenter would look brazenly into the lens and say, 'On this day a hundred and fifteen and a half years ago . . .' No further justification was required for a well-researched, well-illustrated subject which fascinated one of the production team. My own excuse was usually the death of any songwriter, however obscure. I scanned the obituary columns and the moment I saw that someone had gone to the great Tin Pan Alley in the sky I would chase up any well-known songs they had written, scratch around for a few less well known and see how quickly Peter Greenwell could cobble snatches together in a medley. Millicent Martin and David Kernan would arrive to coo the songs at one another – Miss Martin with iron-clad aplomb, Kernan with many misgivings, but always winning through in the end. Parodies, however contrived, were another favourite form. There was a four-minute saga called 'Rembrandts are a Girl's Best Friend' prompted by the slender thread of a news story which hinted that smart girls were now investing in old masters.

It was possible to get away with songs and parodies on *Tonight* – much harder to get away with topical sketches. Not only were they played to studio silence, they also had to compete with unconscious humour which often bubbled up in interviews. We persevered with several attempts to dramatise Michael Frayn's very funny columns in the *Guardian* but the comedy evaporated. Worse, we attempted a genuine television strip cartoon ignoring the basic problem – that readers of a newspaper have the option of following a strip if it amuses them or ignoring it if it does not. *Tonight* viewers had no escape from 'Evelyn' while she held the screen for some sixty seconds. She came with impeccable credentials. Bernard Levin wrote her. Tony Hoare devised paper scenery and paper costumes for the two principals. Prunella Scales was the schoolgirl, Evelyn, and Ronnie Barker her irascible uncle to whom she posed unanswerable questions. 'Evelyn' lasted some few weeks and brought down much wrath on her head and ours.

At the end Bernard Levin gave me a copy of John Evelyn's diaries, from which I have had far more pleasure than foisting Evelyn herself on an unwilling public.

Although it made no impression at the time, I had better luck with a ten-minute dramatisation of a scene from Anthony Burgess's just-published *A Clockwork Orange* to illustrate an interview with the author. James Bolam 'created' the Malcolm McDowell role. Burgess said he had never expected to see his book on the screen.

Occasionally we featured the emerging local pop singers and rock 'n' rollers. A vivid picture of the plump Belgian statesman Paul-Henri Spaak waiting to be interviewed stays in the mind – he sat incongruously next to a ten-year-old pop-singing prodigy, Little Laurie London, who was clutching his guitar and waiting to sing 'He's Got the Whole World in His Hands', with which he had just had a hit on both sides of the Atlantic.

On one memorable morning I auditioned two would-be rockers, Wee Willie Harris and Tommy Steele's brother, Colin Hicks. *Tonight* was firmly of the opinion that if you couldn't lure the real thing on to the programme, get a near relation. We'd already interviewed Tommy's mother; here was a chance to hear his sibling sing. Colin's performance was very like a second carbon copy of his brother's but it paled against the eccentricities of Wee Willie, whose shocking red hair would pass unnoticed these days. Wee Willie offered three songs. His approach to the first was fairly conservative. He stood at the piano and accompanied himself. For the next he played guitar. The third was obviously the climax of the act. With the first chorus his coat came off, with the second a waistcoat and with the third his shirt. He was skimpy, pasty and, apart from the violent hair, unprepossessing. As he started the fourth song, he began to fiddle with his belt and trousers. The gesture fizzled out. 'Thank you very much, Mr Harris,' I said, 'I thought for a moment you were going to take off your trousers.'

'Nah!' he dismissed the idea, looking more abject than ever. 'I just fiddle with me flies – makes the girls go mad!'

In another encounter with the 'new music' I shocked Larry Parnes by asking Billy Fury if he could shake his hips a bit more provocatively for another *Tonight* perennial – 'Is Rock 'n' Roll Finished?'

'They usually ask us to tone it down,' he said.

I had my first sight of Ivor Cutler playing songs in the dingy offices of Box and Cox, music publishers in seedy premises at the end of Denmark Street. 'Boxy' was a cockney–Runyonesque–Charing Cross character. 'I publish Hermione Baddeley's brother's songs, y'know – and 'ee was Bishop of Australia [*sic*].' I arrived by appointment with Caryl Brahms one evening after transmission. The office appeared to be empty apart from Ivor, a fey, gnomish figure idly tinkling on a harmonium. Further into the room I spotted Boxy behind the door, peeing in the sink. Seeing Caryl he buttoned up sharpish. He explained that he had thought of me because no one else in Denmark Street could make head nor tail of a talent so original, so 'way out'. Caryl and I found the repertoire of surreal, Edward Lear-like, offbeat, blackish, folksy songs intriguing. The only disconcerting thing was Boxy's tendency to break up in giggles every time his artist started on a new number. I booked Ivor for a week on *Tonight* and although he was not the overnight sensation we had hoped it did give his career an early push.

A ragbag of memories of incidents forty-odd years ago stays in the mind. For a time *Tonight* was preceded by a dire light entertainment show. Cliff Michelmore got so fed up that one night he introduced the programme saying, 'Good evening, if any of you are still watching.' On a rare occasion *Tonight* took a live feed off an outside broadcast from a mine disaster in Germany. The gallows introduction suggested was not broadcast – 'In the mine disaster today the number of Good Germans has risen to seventy-nine.'

Malcolm Muggeridge made frequent appearances. He used to come up from his home in Robertsbridge in a hired car driven by a retired local police constable. They either arrived an hour early or with minutes to spare. Muggeridge would apologise: 'He can't always find London.' Malcolm came on the programme on the day he was asked to resign from Pratt's Club for criticising the monarchy. He told the camera that an Englishman loved his club because it evoked 'that rosy afterglow of homosexuality'.

Some interviewees were unexpectedly nervous. Gerald Gardiner, QC, then lord chancellor, explained his anxiety saying that he had spent his life cross-examining other people, not answering questions. Indira Gandhi had no such problems. Interviewed by Derek Hart about the Kashmir problem she decided she had had enough and suddenly said, 'What would you do?' No answer. Subcontinentals have a technique for disconcerting interviewers: on *Highlight*, a programme which predated *Tonight*, Krishna Menon replied to Cliff Michelmore several times, 'That question is not cast in the mould of my thinking.'

Ed Sullivan on the other hand was unused to challenging questions and left in a huff. Claudia Cardinale, fascinated by Kenneth Allsop's neatly barbered hair, enquired 'Is eet a weeg?' Some were casual. David Montague, a banker, asked in 1963 if there were signs of a depression in London, replied, 'If you mean that one could fire a gun across the Savoy Grill without hitting either a diner or an Italian waiter the answer is no.' Ex-King

Simeon of Bulgaria confessed that as he was booted out of his country at the age of seven he had very little to remember about it. Now he is back as its prime minister. The old American actress Bessie Love was booked to talk about Scott Fitzgerald. When she arrived at Lime Grove she said, 'You *do* mean Scott Fitzgerald, the polo player?' No item. Another veteran Hollywood actress, June Havoc, refused to discuss her age or her contemporaries and swept out leaving an empty chair.

The hospitality rooms were behind the main reception at Lime Grove, christened 'the Polish Corridor' by James Mason when it was a film studio, dominated by 'mittel' Europeans. An amazing variety of people met up there. An unusual pairing was Lord David Cecil and Fatty Arbuckle's widow – Lord David was there to talk about his biography of Max Beerbohm, Mrs Arbuckle was telling Hollywood secrets. As luck had it they were about the same age and had many friends in common. There was some embarrassment when Mrs Arbuckle was handed a gin and tonic and an assistant enquired, 'Ice, Mrs Arbuckle?' There had been some argument whether the showgirl who lost her life at Fatty Arbuckle's hands in a San Francisco orgy had been penetrated by a large piece of ice or a Coca-Cola bottle. Mrs Arbuckle was unfazed.

James Cameron came to discuss the Profumo scandal and the reaction of Fleet Street. In hospitality after the broadcast the producer for the night, Gordon Watkins, protested that surely no old Harrovian would lie in the House of Commons. Cameron laughed so much he choked over his drink.

David Jacobs, a showbiz solicitor who had organised Liberace's libel action against the *Daily Mirror*, was often used by *Tonight*. On the first occasion a visit to 'make-up' was suggested. His assistant said it wasn't necessary. 'Mr Jacobs is already made up.' During his court appearance he had famously worn more make-up than his client, Liberace. Eventually he was found hanging in the garage of his house in Hove, apparently the victim of an erotic manoeuvre which malfunctioned. *Tonight* turned to David Napley.

When King Hussein of Jordan visited Lime Grove he was taken to a more rarefied hospitality room with the director general, Hugh Carleton Greene, Mrs Wyndham Goldie and Alasdair Milne. Carleton Greene offered him a drink which as a strict Muslim made him pause. Then he caught the eye of his entourage (who couldn't drink if he didn't). 'Ah,' he said, 'perhaps a little Muscadet for my throat,' so that the others could hit the hard stuff.

The Irish actor Patrick Magee came in to do some readings from Beckett. Afterwards hospitality became hostility as someone said 'Ulster'. Magee lifted him up and would not put him down until he said, 'The six counties.'

People often got lost in the rabbit warren off 'the Polish Corridor'. Cardinal Heenan in full purple robes for a *Panorama* interview went for a pee and, emerging, was helpfully shown to a drama studio where a play about Cardinal Richelieu was in production. At the time of Suez Anthony Eden was making for the same lavatory but mistakenly went through the door of a neighbouring broom cupboard and couldn't find the light switch. The door closed on him and he had to be rescued after much banging.

Grace Wyndham Goldie made frequent sorties to hospitality not always sure to whom she was talking. Meeting Louis Armstrong after a programme she asked why he hadn't played his trumpet. He said he couldn't for contractual reasons and continued to talk about the subject which obsessed him on air. It was bowel control. A few months later a not very sober Mrs Goldie was introduced to Duke Ellington. 'I see you haven't brought your trumpet yet again,' she said roguishly. Very puzzled, he smiled and said politely, 'No, ma'am.'

The most controversial *Tonight* incident pointed up dramatically the different approach of Baverstock's team and the old guard, frequently marched to the top of the hill by the then director general, Sir Ian Jacob, and then marched down again. During the investigation of a particularly nasty murder of a small child, suspicion fell on the child's uncle, aged about twenty. After some days of police investigation the suspect was released and snapped up by a Sunday newspaper. It was a Friday and during the morning the paper offered him to *Tonight* before whisking him off to continue his literary collaboration with a couple of journalists.

Baverstock and Milne agonised about the propriety of such an interview. With no highly placed BBC official available to consult on the weekend they went ahead. Geoffrey Johnson Smith was assigned to the interview which dwelt on the subject's restatement of his innocence, the strain of several days' inquisition and an appeal to an acquaintance who could give him an alibi. He was a sad little figure with a lisp. On the critical night he had been 'up West with a mate' whom he had just met. He didn't know his name but he had spent the whole night with him. 'He was wearing a blue shirt, tight blue jeans and black shoes – and I wish I knew who he was.' The interview over, the youth was given back to his minders and, after a spirited scene where one car blocked the exit from the cul-de-sac in which the studio stood so that rival journalists could not follow, he was spirited away to a country hideaway.

Little more was heard of the suspect, who was cleared in the end, but some protests got through to the BBC. Sir Ian Jacob apologised to viewers on Donald Baverstock's behalf. Baverstock hovered on the brink of angry resignation and most of his staff felt like going with him. Not long after – 1959 – Sir Ian Jacob retired. As Mrs Wyndham Goldie reports, he 'tended to treat television producers as subalterns who were there to carry out orders issued by their seniors at Broadcasting House'.

His successor, Hugh Carleton Greene, brought a more sophisticated, sage and adventurous attitude to the director general's suite at Broadcasting House, as well as a readiness to encourage experiment – without which the adventures of the sixties might have been put on hold.

During my years on *Tonight* Caryl Brahms and I were to cement our collaboration. Most weekday evenings we came together to write in her flat in Regent's Park or to attend the various theatres where she might be writing criticism of a play, an opera or a ballet. The weekend gave us Friday nights to map out work for Saturday and Sunday. It was an intensive programme. There was little opportunity to socialise outside the two disciplines.

I did occasionally get a chance to get home to Somerset. Once I was enlisted to move some sheep from one field to another. During the few moments we were on a main road a car drew up behind. A man got out and walked alongside me. He had a clipboard and a lot of questions. Did I, he wanted to know, watch much television?

'All the toime,' I said in as broad an accent as I could risk.

'What is your favourite programme?'

'Oi think oi'd 'ave to say that *Tonight*.'

He wrote it down. 'D'you like Cliff Michelmore?'

'Yas.'

'Alan Whicker?'

'Yas.'

'Fyfe Robertson?'

'Yas.'

He went on happily filling in affirmatives. Finally he said, 'What quality do you think makes *Tonight* such a good programme?'

I pondered the question. 'Oi suppose, on the whole it's the outstandingly foine quality of the direction,' I said.

He was about to write it down when a terrible thought struck him and the pen hesitated. 'You aren't Tom Sherrin's son, are you?'

I confessed. He was very forgiving about the time I had wasted.

CHAPTER 4

The World is a Stage/The Stage is the World of Entertainment

'Light entertainment? Who the hell does heavy entertainment?' was the stock comment by American television executives visiting the BBC during the fifties and early sixties. In 1959, with a sure instinct for making the wrong decision, I thought I should move on from *Tonight* and apply for a producer's job in 'LE'. I was a disaster. However, in retrospect, I dare say this bruising couple of years did go some way to completing my television education.

Most of the department's programmes at the end of the fifties were mindless, escapist or anodyne. Commercial television competition had goosed up the BBC's news and drama departments but commercial variety shows were even less ambitious than those of the BBC. The range covered naive, rudimentary sitcoms, vaudeville bills, quiz games and sing-a-longs.

Although it was no longer current the notorious BBC guide to acceptable humour – the *Green Book* – cast a long shadow over the Television Centre. I shared a caravan in the grounds with a splendid survivor, Kenneth Milne-Buckley, whose proudly worn original twenties Oxford bags he reckoned came back into fashion every decade or so.

In the words of the *Green Book*: 'There can be no compromise with doubtful material. It must be cut . . . music hall, stage and, to a lesser degree, screen, standards are not suitable for broadcasting.' Helpfully the guide went on to give examples: 'Well-known vulgar jokes (*e.g.* the Brass Monkey cleaned up) are not normally admissible since the humour in such cases is almost invariably evident only if the vulgar version is known.'

There was an 'absolute ban' on 'lavatories; effeminacy in men; immorality of any kind; suggestive references to honeymoon couples; chambermaids, fig leaves, prostitution, ladies' underwear (*e.g.* winter draws on), animal habits (*e.g.* rabbits), lodgers, commercial travellers'. 'Extreme care' was urged in dealing with 'references to or jokes about: pre-natal influences (*e.g.* his mother was frightened by a donkey); marital infidelity . . . The vulgar use of such words as "basket" must also be avoided.'

The guide could not make up its mind about biblical jokes. 'Jokes built around Bible stories, *e.g.* Adam and Eve, Cain and Abel, David and Goliath, must be avoided or any sort of parody of them. References to a few biblical characters, *e.g.* Noah, are sometimes permissible.' Why poor old Noah? And what about Ham, Shem and Japhet? 'Since there is seldom anything to be gained . . . and since they can engender such resentment they are best avoided'. Comics were advised to keep off religion altogether, including 'jokes about A.D. or B.C. (*e.g.* Before Crosby)', as well as 'spiritualism, christenings, weddings and funerals, . . . parodies of Christmas carols and offensive references to Jews (or any other religious sect).

'All such words as God, Good God, My God, Blast, Hell, Damn, Bloody, Gorblimey, Ruddy, etc., etc., are to be deleted from scripts and innocuous expressions substituted.' On commercial TV Peter Sellers was reprimanded for using the word 'berk' – too many viewers knew that the rhyming slang derived from Berkeley Hunt.

Impersonations were another minefield. John Bird, who was

to pioneer Wilson and Heath as comic characters – and Mike Yarwood, Alistair McGowan, Rory Bremner, John Culshaw, Jan Ravens and Ronni Ancona who followed – would have had a thin time. 'Artist's repertoires', the book said, 'are usually restricted to (a) leading public and political figures; (b) fellow artists.' As to (a), 'the Corporation's policy is against broadcasting impersonations of elder statesmen, *e.g.* Winston Churchill.' As to (b), 'there is no objection but certain artists have notified the Corporation that no unauthorised impersonations may be broadcast; Gracie Fields, Vera Lynn, Ethel Revnell (with or without Gracie West), Renée Houston, Jeanne de Casalis (Mrs Feather), Nat Mills and Bobby, Harry Hemsley.'

It must have made life difficult for the great female impressionist, Beryl Orde, and Peter Cavanagh, 'The voice of them all.'

The *Green Book* had its own idea of political correctness: 'Avoid derogatory references to professions, trades and "classes", *e.g.* solicitors, commercial travellers, miners, "the working class", coloured races.' Avoid any jokes or references that might be taken to encourage strikes or industrial disputes, the black market, spivs and drones. Avoid any references to 'the MacGillicuddy of the Reeks' or jokes about his name. Do not refer to the Chinese as 'Chinamen', 'Chinks', 'Yellow Bellies', etc . . . Do not refer to blacks as 'Niggers' ('Nigger Minstrels' is allowed).

There were 'special considerations for overseas broadcasts, where humour is limited by different social, political and religious taboos from our own'. The guide warned that 'Chinese laundry' jokes may be offensive. 'The term Boer War should not be used – South African War is correct. Jokes about "harems" are offensive in some parts of the world.' And my favourite? 'Jokes like "enough to make a Maltese Cross" are of doubtful value.'

An enlivening presence was Eric Maschwitz, who had run wireless light entertainment before the war and was now imported to head its television equivalent some twenty years on.

Maschwitz had a more sophisticated, broader-based attitude than his junior colleagues although he was able to do little to change things during his brief tenure. He was also one of the most accomplished English lyricists. 'A Nightingale Sang in Berkeley Square', 'Room 504' and 'These Foolish Things' were among his songs; *Love From Judy*, *Carissima*, *Balalaika* and *Goodnight Vienna* were some of his shows.

He was an engaging raconteur. *Goodnight Vienna*, which started life as a radio musical and edged its way to the stage via a film version with Jack Buchanan and Anna Neagle, provided one of his favourite stories. Driving back from the coast one night he passed the Lewisham Hippodrome. To his delight he saw that *Goodnight Vienna* was playing. He stopped the car and bounded up the steps to ask the commissionaire how *Goodnight Vienna* was doing in Lewisham. The commissionaire was unenthusiastic: 'About as well as you'd expect *Goodnight Lewisham* to do in Vienna.' Eric could do little to lighten the mood of his deputy. Tom Sloan, a Scot, was not one to embarrass a programme with ideas if he could see a way of keeping them out. Later, one of his brainwaves was to scoop the Eurovision Song Contest by offering a kilted Kenneth McKellar. He ran true to the form of many of his producers. The traditional LE figurehead gloried in a successful series in which his comedy star carried the burden of the show, but he was quick to distance himself from a flop.

My first task was to prepare a variety show around Henry Hall, a legendary, veteran bandleader from the early days of wireless, a man of great sweetness and good manners. His signature tune was 'Here's to the Next Time', his distinctive introduction, 'This is Henry Hall – and tonight is my guest night.'

I was to be his Waterloo.

With optimism and arrogance in equal measure, I decided that Henry needed a new look. The guest-night formula was outmoded and my solution was to surround him with youth. Accordingly I collected a team of young and largely untried singers, provided them with obscure and unfamiliar songs and expected the old gentleman, who had in his heyday presented most international comedy and music stars, to introduce them with every sign of enthusiasm. This he managed to do with impeccable courtesy before a listless audience at the Television Theatre for the delight of a home audience which crossed over to ITV in droves.

As my incompetence became obvious after the first pro-gramme youth was banished and senior variety names rode to the rescue. Terry Scott, before his resurrection with *Terry and June* in a dire, small schoolboy sketch, an unfunny Dutch come-dian, Wim Sonneveld, and a second-ranking, ageing French singer, Irene Hilda, did nothing to stem the flow of deserters to the commercial channel.

There was a humiliating final cock-up on my last programme. We had returned to a certain amount of embarrassing banter between Henry and his guests. One set-up with the veteran musi-cal comedy star Evelyn Laye depended on the two of them being 'vanished' by camera trickery. To achieve this they had to stay firmly on their marks. At the critical moment on the live trans-mission, no doubt mistrusting the skill of their young director, the two veterans helpfully stepped aside, effectively destroying the illusion.

My fate had by then been decided and I was replaced by a more experienced director who improved the shows but failed to erase the full stop with which I had punctuated Henry's career. He remained kind and friendly until his death, never reproach-ing me, but I have no doubt that I finished him off.

I was moved on to an altogether less challenging chore. *Ask Me Another* was already a successful general knowledge quiz hosted by Franklin Engelman. The questions were set by John P. Wynn, who had a corner in those quizzes along with his wife

Joan Clark, a radio producer. He was also the deviser of *Brain of Britain*. He liked to celebrate his successes with what his heavy, mittel European accent declared to be a glass of 'chumpine'. Earlier he had contributed the *Meet Dr Morell* mini-mysteries on *Monday Night at Eight*. He told a story of a visit by a policeman to his house in Hampstead one Sunday morning during the heyday of *Meet Dr Morell*.

'Are you Mr Wynn?'

Putting aside his glass of chumpine, John P. admitted that indeed he was, wondering what crime he might have committed. None.

'It's like this, sir. Every Monday night my wife and I listen to your programme *Meet Dr Morell* – with all the clues and everything. At the end of the mystery when they ask what the solution is I can never work it out and my wife gives me a terrible time – "Call yourself a policeman" and all that. Now, if you could tell me the clues and the solution this week, sir, so I could come out with the right answer, that would shut her up for always. Just this week, sir.'

John gave him the clues and the identity of the culprit in that week's riddle and never heard from him again. He guarded the standards of *Ask Me Another* jealously. The infallible stars Reginald Webster, Olive Stephens, Professor Thomas Bodkin and especially Ted Moult are sadly forgotten but we were nearly touched by one scandal. There had been a sensational success on a commercial TV quiz show by a woman who became a national heroine. She asked to be on *Ask Me Another*. We booked her for three weeks. On the first two programmes she barely got a correct answer. Before the third recording I got an anguished phone call from a man in her close circle saying that she was in despair. I weakened and gave her sight of her questions and answers. She sailed through the first half but then Engelman, brightly alert, switched the questions so that she was once more adrift. She got nothing else right. At least she left with some small tatter of her reputation restored. As far as I know she never tried a general knowledge quiz again. I hope not.

I did some very odd things at the sink end of light entertainment. Pleasant and undemanding was a series with the pianist Semprini tinkling while the George Mitchell Singers fluted. The bottom was a bizarre monstrosity, a summer replacement quiz imported from America called *Laugh Line*. I was shown an American pilot which the BBC had bought. It was compered by Dick Van Dyke and starred Mike Nichols, Elaine May and Dorothy Loudon as panellists. Contestants were presented with cartoons which came to life, courtesy of posing actors. The panellists could order them around at will to change the picture and create alternative 'laugh lines'. Finally satisfied, the panellist spoke the new punchline as the actors mimed the predicament.

Our chairman was an actor/light comedian, Digby Wolfe, who later went to America to work as a writer on *The Laugh In*. The panellists ran the gamut of English television personalities. My favourites were Beryl Reid and Kenneth Williams. The pleasant by-product was the chance to give a lot of talented, amusing, out-of-work actors a chance to pick up some pocket money posing in the tableaux.

As we were only a summer replacement, the show, which emerged as an asinine mistake, escaped almost unnoticed by the critics. However, the upper echelon of light entertainment was so delighted at having started a new, moronic, comedy quiz without bringing the wrath of the nation down on its head that it decided to bring it back. Winter, as the *Green Book* had it, 'draws on', and after Christmas they rescheduled it. Indeed, they elevated it proudly to prime time. The wrath which it had been spared was now unleashed on it with a vengeance. It landed on the head of poor old Albert Stevenson, the amiable veteran who was now in charge. I was lucky enough to have been sacked and was back on *Tonight* by then.

The one definite plus in joining the light entertainment

department was that I had more time to work with Caryl. We divided our time between the 'Chelsea Palace' where I was still living and her flat in Regent's Park. She would drive to Chelsea or I would go from the Television Centre to NW1. In that far-away year of 1961 I could get a taxi home to SW3 for ten shillings and sixpence. Often I chose to walk my way home after a session. The distance seems impossible to imagine now but in those days nocturnal ramblings often resulted in chance meetings. The days of plentiful gay bars, then clubs, then discos, then lonely hearts columns and now Internet chatrooms as convenient meeting places were years in the future.

We worked on radio plays, a stage adaptation of the Caryl Brahms and S. J. Simon novel *No Bed for Bacon* and one commission which came directly from television light entertainment. It was the only job with the department which I enjoyed without reservation. It was *Parasol*, a musical which Caryl and I wrote with a splendid composer. With his background in theatre musicals Eric Maschwitz couldn't see why they shouldn't work on television. He had already mounted one of his own, *Carissima*, a 1948 West End show, for the BBC. He had imported Ginger Rogers to star and flooded a studio with water to realise the Venetian setting. It was a brave gesture as even the *Stage* had said of the original West End production, 'One knows what is going to happen next at approximately fifteen minutes before it happens.' *The Times* found that 'the words that have been given to the singers are as banal as the story is clumsy' and the *Star* complained, 'Some day an entirely new plot for operetta will be discovered. Meanwhile we must make do with the one they use in *Carissima*.' Nevertheless it encouraged us to make a pitch to Eric.

We had enjoyed reading Schnitzler's *Anatol* dialogues – a series of one-act sketches for a man-about-Vienna, Anatol, his friend Max and various girlfriends. I had seen them played in Birmingham at the Rep. The scenes were sharp and funny – not

unlike the author's *La Ronde*. The atmosphere invited music
and Viennese snow scenes, restaurants, churches and boudoirs
provided an attractive, traditional spectacle. Any mention of
Vienna was immediately reassuring for Maschwitz with his
Goodnight background. He wanted a star composer and a star
actor to play Anatol.

We were lucky from the first with our composer. *Parasol* – to
which the musical had changed its name on account of a linking
device of parasols which Anatol collected from his lovers, rather
like notches on a bedpost – is the only musical composed by Sir
Malcolm Arnold. Caryl knew Malcolm well and he leapt at the
idea. It was a happy collaboration, yielding a tuneful score
which I still enjoy. Waltzes dominate it and one, 'Only a parasol/
left here for Anatol', has a great, simple beauty and, as it is
often repeated, could have benefited from more varied words by
the lyricists.

Working sessions were highlighted by lavish lunches with
Malcolm at Wheelers in Old Compton Street and after-lunch
visits to Muriel Belcher's *Colony Room*. Casting Anatol was
more difficult. For a long time we thought we had persuaded
Paul Scofield to play the part and planned on that understanding
until a few weeks before rehearsals started when he gently but
firmly told us that he was not going to do it. A frantic search followed. Keith Michel, Louis Jourdan, John Neville, Peter
Wyngarde, Jean-Pierre Aumont were all wooed but not won. I
made a flying visit to Paris – first time in the air – in a vain
attempt to persuade another handsome French film actor and
recording starlet, Jean-Claude Pascal, to accept. He didn't. We
auditioned William Franklyn, who roared with laughter when
we told him he couldn't sing.

We were due to start rehearsals on a Monday. On the
Thursday before that we had all the girls but no Anatol. I was
sitting in the Kenya coffee bar in the King's Road, despairing of
rustling up anyone at such short notice when a Canadian

woman started to talk to me. We soon got around to theatre, television and my little problem. She explained that I was in luck, Canada's finest actor was between engagements and happened at that very moment to be in England. I was suspicious of 'Canada's finest actor', as the last Canadian actor to whom I had spoken was the good-looking and able but very serious Leo Ciceri, who told me that he was going to throw up his promising English career to go home to play the title role in *Everyman* at the Vancouver Festival. I expressed some surprise. 'Ah,' he said solemnly, 'I can't let Canada down.'

Our last chance for Anatol took himself much less seriously. William Hutt is still one of Canada's leading actors. He has played the range of classical roles often, at Stratford, Ontario, with *Lear*, *A Long Day's Journey into Night* and Lady Bracknell among them. In the eighties I saw him and John Neville as the two old ladies in Robin Phillips's production of *Arsenic and Old Lace* in London, Ontario, the only time that I have laughed at that play. However, in the early sixties he was a solid, well-set-up character actor who was examining the possibilities of working regularly in England. Spurred on by his enthusiastic fan, I arranged to meet him the next day and by the weekend he was cast.

Modern television productions are miracles of complexity, pre-recordings, taping in small sequences over days. *Parasol* in 1959 was a seventy-five-minute musical, transmitted live, with a cast and chorus of over thirty and an orchestra of fifty conducted by Marcus Dods in a different studio. There was a large church set, inside and out, a snow-covered street with a shopping arcade; there were bedrooms and sitting rooms, a huge restaurant set with an enormous dance floor for Alfred Rodrigues' dancers to waltz around, as well as a lot of filmed links with whirling, animated parasols. 'Only a parasol/left here for Anatol/Only a parasol/left of our love . . .'

William Hutt battled splendidly, a fine actor but not

essentially a matinée idol. Peter Sallis supported him wittily as Max, and the girls – Moira Redmond, Pip Hinton, Irene Hamilton and Hy Hazell – were impeccable.

As I cued the start of the programme I had an odd sense of unreality. The enormity of the undertaking hit me. I had never directed a professional cast in a play, let alone a big new musical. Hours spent in studio control rooms all had to do with current affairs, immediacy or vaudeville splash. Suddenly the idea of getting away with a musical high comedy was daunting. When I went down to congratulate Bill Hutt at the end I found tears forming in my eyes and a lump in my throat. They were from tiredness and relief but he, poor man, nursed for years the notion that I was tearfully disappointed by his excellent performance.

The next day's reviews were positive but, fortunately, it was too late to save my career as a light entertainment producer. The axe had fallen. Eric Maschwitz departed the BBC. His place was taken by the heavy hand of Tom Sloan. But there were encouraging signs in the department. Frank Muir and Denis Norden were brought in as comedy advisers. More forward-looking ideas were coming from Bill Cotton, Duncan Wood, Galton and Simpson, and Dennis Main Wilson.

I hightailed it back to the warren of dingy terraced rooms at Lime Grove with great relief.

CHAPTER 5

That Was The Week That Was/ It's Over Let It Go . . .

Being sacked from light entertainment was the best break for me.

Forty years on in November 2002 Greg Dyke hosted a BBC party for the anniversary of the first *That Was The Week That Was* programme. I had sent a careful note to remind him of the birthday. I was aware that the claims of other venerable fifties and sixties programmes for a celebration had been ignored. 'I did the thirtieth at home myself,' I wrote, 'let me know or I'll have to get the caterers in again.' Greg quickly acknowledged the significance of the show and the party was planned.

Whatever else it was, *TW3*, as it soon became known, was a broadcasting landmark. If I had not been dismissed in Tom Sloan's office it would not have happened – at least not as it did and with that title. 'Going back' is rarely an attractive prospect, but a return to *Tonight* was different. Unlike my departure two years earlier, it could not have been better timed.

Baverstock and Milne, who had filled the 6–7 p.m. slot so successfully, were looking for fresh fields to conquer. Critically they noticed that nothing much happened on television after 10.30 p.m. on Saturday nights – incredibly hard to believe these days. Surely it was a spot with a special character? We started to talk about it. I wangled a trip to the States to look at late-night shows there – particularly *The Jack Parr Show* which was ahead of the pack. Parr produced one of the craftiest first questions I have heard. He was greeting Michael Dunn, a clever dwarf actor. 'Tell me, Mickey,' he said, after Dunn had hopped up on a stool to sit beside him, 'how do you put people at ease?'

Over the *Tonight* years I managed to justify two or three trips to America. On one I was supposed to return with a comprehensive report on the new-wave American humour. It was just beginning to surface in England. There were admired recordings of Nichols and May, Mort Sahl, Shelley Berman, Bob Newhart, Jonathan Winters, and the Smothers Brothers. I saw Mike Nichols and Elaine May in their after-dinner Broadway revue and Mort Sahl at the Basin Street East but I never got within a mile of fixing an interview with any of them. A team of two helpful but hopeless young Americans offered 'film services' and in the end we did corral Jonathan Winters, the Smothers Brothers and the veteran king of one-liners, Henny Youngman, into a dismal Sheraton hotel suite where I asked earnest questions and they tried to work out why they were there. Who was this doing the asking? Were they getting paid? No. We shot miles of unviewable film which never appeared; but once home I became an unstoppable authority on the new American humour.

Ironically Mort Sahl's unfavourable reception when light entertainment imported him to do a show at the Shepherd's Bush Empire was one of the reasons Hugh Greene gave a green light to the current affairs offer of *That Was The Week That Was*. Denis Norden has explained that it wasn't really LE's fault. They flew Sahl over in time to acclimatise him, took him around, offered him writers and filled the theatre with heavyweight fans of his LP. On the night, to their dismay, he produced no new material and fell back on his album, repeating the gags which the enthusiasts had played hundreds of times. The inclination for spontaneous laughter had long gone.

TW3 grew directly out of *Tonight*. The *Tonight* brief was to be 'on the side of the audience'. *That Was The Week That Was* took the relationship a step further – from a conversation into a conspiracy. We were looking for a 'them' and 'us' relationship. 'Us' constituted the programme-makers (the performers as far as the viewers were concerned) and the sympathetic part of the audience. 'Them' were the public figures or establishment forces whom we investigated, challenged, mocked or pilloried, and those viewers who tut-tutted in shock.

In the early stages of pondering the programme I knew that the high points on *Tonight* had usually been factual, unscripted and spontaneous. The scripted and performed inserts which I usually provided were rarely show-stoppers and suffered by comparison. In thinking about the new venture I rejected the American chat-show formula. It relies on a dominant host and a circus of extroverts. Schooled on *Tonight*, I had no other option. I was looking for a show which was considered, structured, edited and controlled.

Television programmes are more often shaped in performance than on the drawing board but the guests at Greg Dyke's celebration, shown a copy of my memo outlining the show, seemed surprised to find that what finally appeared on the screen was – with a few tweaks after the first pilot – more or less what I put into my proposition. Some of it is reproduced on p. 101 – notice the 'copy-to' initials to a generous selection of BBC personnel.

The critical decision was to book a band and invite an audience. Once a theatrical ambience was established it dictated the content. The show became a revue, not a magazine. I wanted a cast of new faces. Throughout my period on *Tonight* I had done the round of West End cabarets, Murray's (later made notorious by Christine Keeler), Churchill's, L'Hirondelle, the Blue Angel, the Embassy, and Quaglinos. By 1961 the Establishment was flourishing and became another major influence on the pro-gramme. If *Tonight* was one factual, documented, researched parent of *TW3*, it was an injection from *Private Eye*, *Beyond the Fringe* and the Establishment which fertilised the new show. They called the baby 'satire'.

All this was happening in the context of a changing world. In 1956 John Osborne's *Look Back in Anger* opened at the Royal Court Theatre. Suddenly there was room for an alternative voice in the theatre, on television and in print. The phrase 'Angry Young Men' was coined by the Court's publicist, George Fearon. Soon it blanketed plays by Wesker, Bond, Storey, Willis Hall and Keith Waterhouse; and books like Amis's *Lucky Jim* and John Braine's *Room at the Top*.

Television plays acquired their own label, 'kitchen-sink drama', pioneered on ABC Television's *Armchair Theatre* by a Canadian, Sydney Newman, with writers like Alun Owen and directors of the order of Philip Saville, Ted Kotcheff, John Moxey, Dennis Vance and Wilfred Eades. Newman had also been influenced by Osborne's play. As Peter Black wrote in *The Mirror in the Corner*, Newman 'had seen the new drama and it worked'.

In 1960 John Bassett, who later became a valuable production assistant on *TW3*, paired two Cambridge graduates, Peter Cook and Jonathan Miller, with two from Oxford, Alan Bennett and Dudley Moore, earning himself the nickname 'The Father of Satire'. At a café off the Euston Road he invited them to make *Beyond the Fringe* for the Edinburgh Festival. Legend has it that Julie Christie, unknown at the time, was considered as a 'run-ning gag' – an idea which never got off the drawing board.

While *Beyond the Fringe* was having its initial Edinburgh suc-cess and edging its way to London, Richard Ingrams and John Duncan (later another essential member of the *TW3* team) were running a touring theatrical company. One play which they pre-sented was Spike Milligan's *The Bed Sitting Room*. William Rushton was in the cast. Ingrams, with Rushton and Christopher

FROM: Ned Sherrin

SUBJECT: "SATURDAY NIGHT"   7th February 1962

TO: Editor, 'Tonight'   copy to: C.P.Tel., A.C.P.Tel., A.C.G.A.T.Tel.
                                      A.H.T.TEl., Asst. Editor 'Tonight'

For some time we have discussed the possibility of a late night programme
with a satirical approach:

Such a programme would have to find a new style, new personalities, and a new
format but there is every chance that it would also find a new audience if it
could start at 10.30 on Saturday nights and run for 45 minutes. If it works
it might come forward to 10 and be open ended; but the later, limited time
seems better as a start.

STYLE

The programme would be aware, pointed, irreverent, fundamentally serious,
intelligently witty, outspoken in the proper sense of the word, and would
provide an opportunity for saying things worth saying and not usually said on
television.

It would contain a number of complimentary ingredients: Rehearsed and possibly
recorded, satirical injections; ad lib political satire, personality interviews;
invective; no-holds barred discussion; music; but its aim would be to amuse
and arouse the audience.

For this sort of show at this particular time it is essential that there should
be the right studio atmosphere and to achieve this there would be a small band
as well as a small studio audience. It is not necessary to try to recreate
a phoney nightclub atmosphere but much of the humour will need immediate
audience response.

However, this is not a magazine programme as we know magazine programmes at
the moment. The approach would not be as conversational as 'Tonight'. It is
not desirable that the people appearing should all be informal and relaxed.
The programme must necessarily be an irritant to some and if we are going to
make people scratch, the object of the programme would be to give them something
worth scratching.

Booker, had another iron in the fire, the magazine *Private Eye*, a direct descendant of the *Salopian*, a school magazine which Ingrams and Rushton had hijacked at Shrewsbury, and of *Parson's Pleasure* and *Mesopotamia*, Oxford undergraduate magazines which Ingrams, Paul Foot, John Wells and William Rushton (visiting from London) produced.

I watched as *Beyond the Fringe* made its bumpy journey towards the West End. There were shocked walk-outs in Brighton – always a good sign. Peter Lewis had used the word 'satire' in his Edinburgh review. When the show opened at the Fortune Theatre Ken Tynan and Bernard Levin followed suit. Tynan wrote, 'English satire advances into the Sixties.' The word was to be bandied about for the next decade as indiscriminately as had been 'Teddy boy', 'Beatnik' and 'Angry Young Man'. 'Satirists' became a convenient label of abuse in some mouths. The old West End targets – 'Binkie', 'Noel', 'Cecil' – were replaced by politicians, royals, bishops and other public figures. Bright choruses and sentimental songs were banished. Dudley Moore's fiendish parodies of serious composers provided musical relief.

The four stars were reluctant to be seen as missionaries. Jonathan Miller has said, 'I honestly don't think we tried to *do* anything in *Beyond the Fringe*.' Peter Cook agreed: 'We don't expect to be specifically didactic.' From outside John Wells said, 'They were fooling about on the stage in exactly the same way they fooled about off it.' Alan Bennett concurred: 'It has always seemed that what was subsequently labelled "satire" was this kind of private humour going public.' The nearest he got to a 'sense of purpose' was a sketch of which he quirkily remembers, 'I have a dreadful feeling that I may have thought I was doing some good.'

By now Christopher Booker's writing and Willy Rushton's cartoons for *Private Eye* were being noticed. Soon after the triumph of *Beyond the Fringe* in October 1961 Cook opened the Establishment Club in Greek Street with John Bird, John

Fortune, Jeremy Geidt and later Eleanor Bron as the resident performers.

The Establishment had been a dream of Peter Cook's since he visited the Porcupine in Berlin as an undergraduate – 'I thought, why isn't there the equivalent of this in London? For a long time my major fear was that somebody would do the obvious and start it before me.' As soon as the club was announced cash rolled in to speed the redecoration of the old Club Tropicana at 18 Greek Street ('All-Girl Strip Revue – Dancing to 3-D Sound'). Founder members included Graham Greene, J. B. Priestley, Yehudi Menuhin, Lionel Bart, the octogenarian playwright Ben Travers, the future lord chancellor Gerald Gardiner, QC, and the academic Isaiah Berlin.

The opening-night targets made attendance essential for someone planning *TW3*. They included Macmillan, Lord Home (foreign secretary), R. A. Butler (home secretary), John Bird as Jomo Kenyatta – 'Ah . . . shall soon be rushin' on to de assumin' of even more gigantic powers as de Queen.' The boundaries of blasphemy were tested with a sketch about the Crucifixion with John Fortune as Christ and John Bird and Jeremy Geidt on lower crosses complaining, 'Why are you getting all the vinegar and sponges an' that . . . an' that bint down there washin' your feet?'

The nucleus resident cast always played to capacity when I visited in the early months. Occasionally the regulars got a night or a week off. Frankie Howerd was to make a famous comeback there before I booked him for *TW3*. 'The most controversial visitor was Lenny Bruce. I saw him a couple of times in witty form, performing with great charm. I never caught the uncharming, unfunny side of his act which some people deplored. One night I saw him harassed by a particularly annoying drunk. He battled sweetly but after about twenty minutes of heckling a note of irritation crept into his patter. Finally the heckler stood up in front of him, swayed and just managed to slur, 'Why don't you tell us an English joke?' After a pitying pause Bruce said, as gently as possible, 'But you *are* an English joke.'

I spent one deserted evening at the Establishment when the unknown Barry Humphries made his British debut as Edna Everage. Not yet honoured with her title, the great dame had none of her later effrontery and plumage. She came over as a well-observed, slightly pathetic matron in a homespun sack-dress – the gladioli were not yet in evidence. However, John Betjeman at once declared his allegiance.

By the time I started to recruit a cast for the pilot of *TW3* – still unnamed – we had the support of the director general, Hugh Carleton Greene – who was expecting a political cabaret of the sort he had enjoyed in Berlin where he was a correspondent reporting on the early years of the Nazi regime following on the collapse of the Weimar Republic. Kenneth Adam, controller of programmes, was also on our side, though he was anticipating something more like Herbert Farjeon's *Gate Revues* in the late twenties and thirties.

Lance Percival was an early recruit. I had seen him in cabaret at Quaglinos and the Blue Angel and in a revue, *One over the Eight*. It starred Kenneth Williams and Sheila Hancock and featured several sketches by Peter Cook. In cabaret Lance improvised topical calypsos which were soon to be a feature of the television show. He was a ready mimic. Roy Kinnear I spotted in Joan Littlewood's company at the Theatre Royal, Stratford East and in a revue at the Shaftesbury, *England Our England*, written largely by Keith Waterhouse and Willis Hall, who would provide material for all the late-night 'satire' shows. I went to Ilford to find Willy Rushton. An unlikely cabaret devised by Stephen Vinaver for the even more unlikely 'Room at the Top' (the 'Top' of a soulless store) featured Willy along with John Wells, Richard Ingrams and Barbara Windsor. Millicent Martin was an automatic choice after the instant performances she had run up for me on *Tonight*.

The main search was for a link man. I wanted John Bird. We had lunch at Bertorelli's on Shepherd's Bush Green. He was guarded about committing himself to the show, perhaps because he had already been involved in some sort of talks with the BBC – nothing to do with my plans. The Establishment team was not yet committed to following *Beyond the Fringe* to New York. John was an invaluable sounding board for me as I talked through ideas. In summing up after a long lunch I said I was trying to make a programme for a particular time on a particular day of a week which was nearly over. We wanted to put the memories of the week behind us, shrug and look forward to the next.

John echoed and adapted the Shell advertising slogan 'That Was Shell That Was', murmuring, 'a sort of That Was The Week That Was'. It leapt at me as the perfect title. When Caryl Brahms and I came to write the lyric for Ron Grainer's signature tune the second line supplied itself: 'That was the week that was/It's over let it go . . .!' The only moment of doubt about the title occurred when Stuart Hood, the new controller of programmes under Kenneth Adam, now director of television, admitted at a press conference that there would be a new late-night revue but insisted that whatever it was called it would not have a clumsy title like *That Was The Week That Was*.

At around the same time I saw a review in Peter Hepple's 'Nightbeat' column in the *Stage* newspaper. He reported that a young Cambridge comic, David Frost, was appearing in cabaret conducting an improvised press conference as Harold Macmillan. It was the centrepiece of his act at the Blue Angel. After Peter Cook's *Fringe* triumph, a Macmillan mimic was essential.

I set off for the club, which had become a regular place for talent-spotting. I once heard a very drunk 'debs' delight' dismiss a waiter there, drawling, 'Oh piss off and put it on Daddy's bill.' The waiter stood his ground, pointing a few tables away. 'Daddy's over there.' Sobriety set in.

My account of the evening is much disputed by Sir David. However, as I remember it, I arrived at the club at cabaret time. It was in a basement off Berkeley Square run by Max Setty, whose brother Stanley had notoriously come to an untimely end some years earlier. His body cropped up as several dismembered pieces scattered from an aeroplane over the Essex marshes.

Hovering in the lobby with the surviving Setty was a formidable old agent and booker, Beatrice Braham, who was always busy on the cabaret circuit. Some distance away sat a tousled young man looking despondent. Welcomed by Mr Setty I asked at what time David Frost was due to appear. Mr Setty said that the act had not been going too well so he was unlikely to put him on that night. I said that in that case I would be off. Mr Setty tempted me with the news that Hutch was topping the bill. I'd often enjoyed Hutch but he wasn't the fresh young Macmillan impersonator I was looking for. Mrs Braham, a motherly old soul intervened. 'Give the boy a chance, Max,' she said, and Mr Setty relented.

In David's autobiography *David Frost: Part One – From Congregations to Audiences* (we eagerly await *Part Two*) he writes, 'My version is that I had certainly never been told that I was getting the night off – it would have been a first – and that Max Setty was far too budget-conscious a businessman to pay somebody and then not use him. But Ned and I have agreed to disagree about this story for thirty-one years [now forty-odd] and no doubt we will continue to for the next thirty-one.'

Whichever version you believe the story has a happy ending. David did perform that night. His Macmillan lacked the easy charm of Peter Cook's earlier interpretation but he was adept at provoking questions from his audience and at the improviser's knack of segueing from an unpromising question to a prepared premise and banging home an apparently spontaneous punchline. 'Ask me a question, any subject,' one exchange began. 'What about the Queen?' someone shouted. 'The Queen is not a subject,' was Frost's prompt reply. In his book he quoted my memo to Donald Baverstock. 'Ex Footlights (Cambridge) looks promising. Have seen him conducting press conference as cabaret turn at a nightclub where he was limited by the stupidity of the customers.'

We met for lunch at Bertorelli's the next day, 9 January 1962. The late Willi Frischauer, Frost's first biographer, reports that he was wearing a turquoise, plastic raincoat bought from a corner store 'to protect him from icy rain'. Mind you, on page three of the same book the biographer writes, 'David rises, stretches his wiry, athletic body . . .' which makes one doubt the accuracy of the whole book. However, David confirms the turquoise cloak. I lunched him with Tony Jay of the *Tonight* team to get a second opinion. We decided that he would be a valuable recruit.

A few weeks before we were due to record the first pilot programme, John Bird decided not to appear. Plans to take the Establishment team to America were firming up. Promoting David to front man was the obvious step. From the moment that I switched him to the central position he was tirelessly inventive and energetic in helping to shape the programme. Above all he was closely in touch with recent graduates and undergraduates at Oxford and Cambridge and was already looking for set pieces for himself by young writers like John Cleese, Ian Lang and Ian Davidson.

David was one of the first graduates to know no other job than television. He went straight from Cambridge to Associated Rediffusion as a trainee. There he was attached to a topical magazine, *This Week*. He gave himself a quick acquaintanceship with the technical set-up of a studio. I missed his interview with a young Jane Fonda and his first dance competition show, *Let's Twist*; but I enjoyed a truly awful sequel, *Let's Twist on the Riviera*. Here he was working with Elkan Allan, later a television journalist but then a key figure in Rediffusion's light entertainment hierarchy. He had a scrappy, dun-coloured beard and once famously told a busy office that he was off to a fancy-dress party. 'What shall I go as?' he asked, unwisely. A mousy secretary risked, 'Why don't you spray yourself with talcum and go as an armpit?' When we needed a witty alternative to one of Muriel Belcher's would-be-funny put-downs in *Jeffery Bernard is Unwell* it still worked well.

Elkan Allan and Rediffusion heard rumours of a BBC late-night revue and planned one of their own. With his Footlights background they were beginning to think of Frost as their house funny man. This put him in a spot. Although unaware that I was after him, Rediffusion started to offer him a better contract, while *TW3* was still a highly speculative venture. Frost managed to temporise.

My first intention had been that the programme would be open-ended. I'd been impressed by some of David Susskind's early shows in America – although they were entirely conversational. Two items promised to be unpredictable in length. I planned a confrontation between Bernard Levin and a group of opponents, and an unchaired discussion between three celebrated conversationalists due to last for thirty minutes. The rest of the programme was to consist of topical songs and sketches, rounded off by Lance Percival's improvised calypsos commenting on the events during the programme.

The set and the camera plan fell quickly into place – seats for the audience, no attempt to disguise the bare studio walls, space for a small band, a projection screen and cameras moving in and out in full view. With topical material coming in at the last moment cameras were bound to get into shot by mistake so I decided to show them intentionally from the beginning. I had always found the opening credits for *Armchair Theatre*, which were run over shots of a busy studio, attractive and dramatic.

Our first pilot for *TW3* on Sunday, 15 July 1962 lasted two hours and forty minutes. Millicent Martin sang the opening song

and was on a plane taking off for a Spanish holiday before we finished. The main topical sketch dealt with the first satellite
transmission from America and the giant dish on Goonhilly
Down through which it was received. Frost had a good time with
the giant dish, and stronger items to do with the neo-fascist Colin
Jordan, the *Daily Express* and abortion. He shared the host role
with Brian Redhead, who was working on *Tonight* at the time.
The chemistry didn't work and as the emphasis moved relentlessly towards scripted performance Redhead opted out.

Bernard Levin's appearance was an immediate hit. He confronted a group of Conservative women – including their
chairwoman, Peggy Shepherd. They wore their splendid hats
and rose to Bernard's bait. He prompted marvellous impromptus
out of one. Several times she shouted, 'Mr Macmillan has always
satisfied me', and later, as the discussion moved on to law and
order, 'Mr Levin, how would you like it if your daughter was out
walking up a dark lane late at night and nothing done about it?'

The discussion section was a disaster. Ken Tynan had told me
that his pick of the most magical conversationalists in London
was Seth Holt, the film director, Harold Lang, the actor, and
George Melly (who also sang on the pilot show). In other circumstances Ken was probably right. We looked for an amusing
thirty minutes. I decided that a serious subject would provide a
less self-conscious opportunity for wit than something frivolous.
In a moment of laughable solemnity I settled for 'human unhappiness'. God knows what I was thinking. The moment the
discussion started a powerful gloom settled over the studio and
the conversationalists. It lasted throughout the episode.

The reaction inside the BBC was curious. People sneaked into
preview theatres where *TW3* was being screened. It was talked
of as some sort of blue movie. I sat through one blazingly hot
summer afternoon at the Television Centre watching the telerecording with Baverstock, Milne and Grace Wyndham Goldie.
We enjoyed the opening songs and sketches, turned down the

sound on 'human unhappiness' and finished the afternoon depressingly uncertain about the show's prospects.

We were right to be depressed. In *Facing the Nation* Grace wrote that she found it, 'Long . . . amateurish in its endeavours to seem casual, and politically tendentious and dangerous.' Fortunately the Tory ladies had disliked it even more. So shocked were they that Central Office complained to the BBC. Kenneth Adam had to see it. He watched it with another executive, Joanna Spicer, more sophisticated than Grace. She also had the bonus of a sense of humour. We had chopped out 'human unhappiness' and she jangled her beads happily and laughed unselfconsciously. As a result we got the green light for a second pilot on 29 September. Sadly no record exists of the first. John Bassett smuggled the 16mm film out to show it at his old school, Bedales. It never came back.

The second pilot delivered more or less what was wanted. Roy Kinnear and David Kernan joined the team. Bernard Levin harangued a group of lawyers. More topical material came in. I earmarked several items that we might repeat in the series. There was a demolition job on Norrie Paramor, a long-serving A&R man at Columbia Records whose habit was to put his own innocuous songs on the B-side of big-selling hits; an old Footlights send up of the fatuities of the advertising magazine *Jim's Inn*; and a musical item by Steven Vinaver in the manner of Annie Ross's jazz pyrotechnics which Milly sang confidently.

With the date of the second pilot only eight weeks before the first transmission date, there was a tacit assumption that we were going to get the formula right with a little fine-tuning. David Frost took a risk and cut his links with Rediffusion before his BBC future was finally assured. The ITV company mounted its own Thursday-night spoiler 'satire' show, *What the Public Wants*, in October. The public didn't and it soon perished.

All the performers took a chance. It was expected to be late-night, ghetto television likely to attract a fringe metropolitan audience. As Millicent Martin said later, 'If I'd known I was going to be part of an era I'd have taken more notice.' She was torn between *TW3* and an offer for pantomime in Bromley. She was worried that the BBC might pay her no more than she got for her occasional appearances on *Tonight*. Kenneth Cope, who had just had a good run on *Coronation Street*, came in about now on John Bassett's recommendation.

During the lead-up to *TW3* I continued to direct the cameras on *Tonight*. There was a brief distraction by the Cuban Missile Crisis. In September 1962 Russia was installing nuclear missiles in Cuba. Congress granted Kennedy the power to call up 150,000 reservists if they were required. This manoeuvre meant that he would not have to declare a national emergency before calling them to arms. Khrushchev's threat was that any American attack on Castro's Cuba would be met by a nuclear response from Russia. They were head to head for a week. The world held its breath. On the eve of the denouement the editor of *Panorama*, Paul Fox, decided to mount a *Panorama* special. He waylaid me at Lime Grove studios. He had no director to point the cameras at what promised to be an international disaster.

It was the only time I worked with the redoubtable Richard Dimbleby. There were inserts on satellite from America – the Goonhilly giant dish was earning its keep – film and tape interventions, an outside broadcast from the Trocadero, where the foreign secretary, Alec Douglas-Home, had to insert a major policy statement into his after-dinner speech. Harold Wilson, his shadow, crouched in a chair in the studio. Fox had a fearsome reputation for shouting at his directors. I was similarly supposed to impose silence on my control room. We reached an amiable compromise. He shut up.

Dimbleby was a revelation. There was no time to write introductions for these various elaborations on the narrative. He said he would cue each bit of film, which in those days needed a few seconds to gather speed, by tapping his nose. We kept in touch by studio telephone as the various connections to film or tape or satellite presented themselves or failed to materialise. The nation was weighing the chances of war. In the studios, at close quarters, my concerns paled before Dimbleby's technique. In the event Khrushchev promised that Russian missiles based in Cuba would be dismantled and shipped back to the Soviet Union. Kennedy agreed not to invade Cuba and to lift his blockade. Next morning I was back on *TW3* duty.

At 10.50 p.m. on Saturday, 24 November 1962 before a studio audience primed with mulled claret served by girls in black fishnet stockings and the cast, inspired by just enough but not too much BBC hospitality, *TW3* took to the air.

Frost had been joined by Christopher Booker, then editor of *Private Eye*, and together they wrote an opening topical sketch which they continued to do throughout the series – usually put together on Friday morning. Keith Waterhouse and Willis Hall supplied a brilliant party political broadcast for Roy Kinnear as a squaddie taking advantage of a new provision allowing soldiers to stand as candidates for Parliament. In its suggestion of the Army party's prospective cabinet it was about as politically incorrect as it was possible to be: 'Our shadow secretary for Commonwealth affairs is Provost-Sergeant MacMichael J., 'oo 'as done extensive tours of the Commonwealth and is in fact married to a wog bint . . . so, get your knees brown, Lord Home . . . Our shadow colonial secretary, Signalman Cooney, is 'imself an Anglo Banglo . . . and can chat up the blackies as if they was man to man . . . Common Market . . . Fusilier Geordie Woolerton . . . Our Common Market policy? . . . You cannot trust the Krautheads. Also if the price of a bottle of lager at Helga's Bar, Windelstrasse, is indicative of Common Market trading you can stuff it.'

It was with some trepidation that we repeated the Norrie Paramor sketch from the second pilot; but the BBC's senior lawyer, Mr Walford, who had been extraordinarily helpful from the start – 'If we're going to do it, let's do it properly' – gave the green light. It was a tradition that the BBC's solicitor Lawrence Roche followed up nobly.

As Bernard Levin's victims, a group of PR men were led to the slaughter. On the Friday we had looked for a way to illustrate an item about identikit pictures. There was a murder in the news. Frost introduced me to Timothy Birdsall, one of his contemporaries at Cambridge and now a contributing cartoonist to *Private Eye* and the *Spectator*. Tim's speed, good looks and infinite charm as he drew and explained his identikit caricatures were a revelation. It was obvious that he must talk to Frost and cartoon at the same time – which he did throughout the first series. Millicent Martin sang the first of her 'jazzers' – 'Take a Little Time', Stephen Vinaver's words set to a Wardell Gray jazz instrumental – and Willy Rushton and Kenneth Cope had a conversation sketch about the Bomb. We repeated the *Jim's Inn* advertising magazine item from the second pilot. Frost revived a Peter Cook Cambridge monologue about sports reporters: 'On the red shale track, it was a black, black day of gloom, despair and despondency for the British lads and lassies who ran their hearts into the ground in the sizzling cauldron that is Rome . . .'

Only one warning note was struck. I came upon David Kernan almost too tearful to go on just before the show. Donald Baverstock had been explaining the political significance of one of his songs to him – as he might have done to a *Tonight* interviewer. The singer found it thoroughly confusing and Baverstock had to be banned from talking to the acting cast.

After the show we piled into taxis and headed for the Casserole in the King's Road – which was very much my local, a splendidly camp restaurant. It became our regular Saturday-night destination and went through a heady period when regular visitors included the emerging Beatles and the Stones. You nodded and got on with your meal. Beef and mango casserole at seven shillings and sixpence (old money) was a popular favourite. It remains more vividly in the memory than the mop-heads and their rivals.

Frost's debut was extraordinary. His curious, classless accent, sloppy charcoal suit and overambitious haircut concealed a man who had come into his kingdom at a bound. John Duncan, whom I hired to direct actors in sketches on the studio floor, quickly saw that sketch-acting was not David's forte but once he was limited to linking dialogue and to monologues he was secure. George Melly credits him with changing the whole image of the television presenter. 'He stood out as the first compere who, instead of helping to keep the children from becoming over-excited, seemed determined to make them behave even worse.' Christopher Booker, who knew both 'before' and 'after' Frost, wrote, 'Suddenly, at the age of just twenty-three he had entered a magic new world – expensive restaurants, taxis, newspaper interviews – where every day was like a royal progress through a wash of compliments ("loved the show", "super", "bless you") . . . the transformation in him was remarkable.'

We met the morning after the first show in the Kenya coffee bar in the King's Road for a post-mortem. We were not expecting reviews until, perhaps, the Monday morning. We shared a feeling of anticlimax. Everything had gone as well or better than we expected. Five viewers had telephoned to complain; but there were eighty-three calls of congratulations. Miraculously, trawling the Sunday papers, David turned to the back page of the *Sunday Telegraph* and came upon a review by Pat Williams. Her single column ran the length of the page. We might have written it ourselves.

'Without reservations *That Was The Week That Was*, the BBC's first late-night satirical show, is brilliant. It based itself securely on the week's events, repeating and expanding its idiocies, invectives and near libels. It did so with intelligence and dislike . . . This is the first late-night show I have seen on television which uses the licence of the late hour and the smaller audience to be adventurous both visually and in its material.' The audience was not to be small for long. Donald Baverstock was soon predicting eight million. It proved a ludicrous understatement. I liked Ms Williams's last sentence particularly: 'For the first time it seems reasonable that one should need a licence for a television set – it can be as lethal as a gun.'

On Monday the *Daily Mail* and the *Daily Sketch* followed the *Telegraph*'s lead. Dennis Potter, who was soon to write for the programme, joined in in the *Daily Herald*: 'Satire – or how to laugh when something is gripping your throat – is getting a foothold in the most unlikely places nowadays. Even Auntie BBC . . . is having a go . . . more than enough blows thudded home for the purple bruises to be counted'.

Hugh Carleton Greene, the director general, sent immediate congratulations and some time later wrote, 'I was delighted. The programme sprang fully armed into life – almost every item seemed to be on the ball, and I thought, really we have achieved something.'

Reginald Bevins, the postmaster general, did not share the enthusiasm and reassured the prime minister that he would take steps to stop the show. Macmillan, wiser and more sophisti-cated, replied: 'I hope you will not, repeat not, take any action about *That Was The Week That Was* without consulting me. It is a good thing to be laughed over – it is better than to be ignored.'

There was one sad figure that Monday morning. Roy Kinnear after his triumphs in '*Jim's Inn*' and as '3246098 L/Cpl Wallace, A., Royal Signals' had heard nothing and sat through the Sunday wondering how it had gone. On the Monday morning he plucked up courage and rang his agent, Freddie Joachim. Roy was treated as though recently bereaved: 'Don't worry, Roy – it was horrible, and they have a contract. But I have talked to people in very high places in Broadcasting House and I am assured it cannot last three weeks.' Like the rest of us, Roy had thought he might be on to a success so, depressed, he went out on to Hampstead Heath for a little air. There he bumped into

Tom Bell, who clasped him warmly by the hand, treated him like a hero and banished any thoughts of suicide.

It took a couple of weeks before we began flying by the seat of our pants. A certain amount of material had been prepared earlier or hung over from the second pilot. The last surviving examples were broadcast on episode two:

Lance enters in a policeman's uniform.
ROY:　Good evening.
LANCE:　Evening, sir. [*He beats up Roy*] Just a routine inquiry, sir.

Now we introduced an extra topicality – we revealed the headlines from the next day's Sunday newspapers. It is incredible today to realise that the proprietors believed that seeing their stuff read out on television the night before would kill people's desire to buy the paper in the morning. Clement Freud volunteered to hang around the vans at the back of the Fleet Street presses and beg, borrow or steal the copies from the delivery men.

Assembling the programme very soon fell into a routine. After 'winding down' at the Casserole I often fled to Brighton with Caryl Brahms to write. We went to ground at the Royal Crescent hotel until my cover was blown by an earnest little reporter, Anne Nightingale, later a popular radio DJ, who bribed the tipsy night porter with a ten-bob note to tell her who was staying there.

On Tuesday the routine of collecting material began again. It was important not to make decisions early on Tuesday. The weekend and Monday papers have a habit of cleaning up the tail end of the previous week. It is too early to feel the pulse of the week ahead. Some stories do begin to emerge on Tuesdays. It was a good day to start making lists and phone calls.

Some regular writers were contracted to supply a sketch or a song a week. Some trusted contributors rang in when they had an idea with a fair certainty that it would be commissioned;

others took a chance; or, if the idea was particularly attractive, *I* took a chance. Many writers new to television submitted ideas. A number of journalists recognised the possibility of combining research and a little dramatisation in the mock-documentary style we applied to some exposé items.

Keith Waterhouse and Willis Hall were already established both as playwrights and journalists. *Daily Mail* colleagues Peter Lewis and Peter Dobereiner (who went on to be the golf correspondent of the *Observer*) soon became regulars. Quentin Crewe and Julian Holland formed an alliance. David Nathan spent a week following the programme for his paper and then brought in Dennis Potter as a collaborating sketch writer. Jack Rosenthal came in occasionally through the *Coronation Street* connection with Kenneth Cope. David Nobbs telephoned with an idea and was recruited by Frost, a Cambridge contemporary. He introduced his journalist colleague, Peter Tinniswood. Our musical director Dave Lee had already had a hit with Herbert Kretzmer, then dramatic critic for the *Daily Express*, with 'Goodness Gracious Me' for Peter Sellers and Sophia Loren. Kretzmer took a little persuading but together they usually managed a song a week – some of the sharpest critical items.

Keith Waterhouse has described the last-minute efforts to keep the programme up to date:

> Willis and I tended to write our *TW3* sketch at the last minute on Friday morning, when the BBC would send round a taxi to whisk it over to Lime Grove for the cast to learn and rehearse for the following evening. Sometimes, if inspiration faltered, we would hear the cab meter remorselessly ticking away in the street below even as we wrestled with the final lines. The fashion at the time for sketches without blackout punchlines was put down to the influence of *Beyond the Fringe*. I am inclined to think it was often more to do with the impatient presence of the cab at the door.

Every week everyone in the cast hoped the 'Waterhall' sketch would come their way. David Nobbs had similar experiences. 'Peter and I once wrote a complete sketch on a Saturday morning, sent it by taxi and saw it performed that night.' Gerald Kaufman, who was working as a researcher on the *Daily Mirror* at the time, discovered the programme one weekend while staying with his parents in Leeds. 'I watched the topical sketches with interest and, what is more, a certain degree of annoyance. I was certain I could do better.'

He called me at the BBC and was surprised to be put straight through. He quickly sold me an item about 'Crossbencher', the *Sunday Express* political column. Hugh Cudlipp, his editor, had pointed out to him that it contained a risible number of inaccurate predictions. No taxi this time. The script arrived by post the next day impeccably presented. Gerald had clearly absorbed the split-screen techniques I employed. On one side Crossbencher (Willy Rushton) would quote neat examples of the columnist's buttonholing style: '1 July. Cluster around now, all you hopeful Tory backbenchers . . . what of the big government reshuffle which everyone has been expecting this month. And what is my news? There won't be one.' Kenneth Cope – on the other half of the screen – as the voice of fact: '13 July. Macmillan carries out biggest-ever government reshuffle.'

Gerald's script finished up, 'Don't miss tomorrow's *Sunday Express* for the latest glimpse into Crossbencher's amazing crystal balls.' There was a tragic postscript to the sketch. When the Sunday papers arrived Christopher Booker, who had a few minutes to read them and brief Frost, turned immediately to the column. Hugh Gaitskell, leader of the opposition, had been ill. Crossbencher had inside news: 'Despite his mysterious minor illness, Hugh Gaitskell is on the way to recovery. In no time at all he will be fit and back at work again.' David put down the paper and looked at the camera and said, 'Sorry, Hugh!' Sadly this proved horribly accurate. Three weeks later Gaitskell was dead.

Gerald caused a stir in the House of Commons with another lethal piece about 'thirteen silent MPs' who had not spoken in Parliament for lengths of time up to ten or fifteen years. Again the research was impeccable and damning. 'Salute Sir Norman Hulbert, Tory MP for Stockport North . . . Sir Norman is chairman of Associated Motor Cycles. Last month he hit out at "Ton-up boys" because of the "noise they make". No one could hit out at Sir Norman for this reason: the only noise he has made since the election has been to ask a question about naval survival rafts . . .' Sir Norman tried to protest in the Commons and get the matter referred to the Committee of Privileges, but he was laughed out of the chamber.

Much later in the series I wanted to do an item on Sir Reginald Manningham-Buller (or Bullying-Manner in Bernard Levin's famous phrase in his 'Taper' column in the *Spectator* – as perceptive as his other damning nickname, Sir Shortly-Floorcross for Sir Hartley Shawcross). Manningham-Buller, who went on, as Lord Dilhorne, to be lord chancellor, was not a lawyer I admired. Some time before Norman St John Stevas was appearing on *Tonight* just after his appointment and was persuaded by Baverstock that saying, 'At last we've got a Woolsack on the Woolsack' was not a good career move.

The first Dilhorne script I commissioned was caustic, amusing and wild: at about the same time I got a warning from Hugh Greene that it was politically inadvisable to treat him as a target. Disappointed, I filed the script and waited until another, more admirable judge, Lord Devlin, came into prominence. On a week when everyone who knew of the BBC's unease about nailing Dilhorne was going away for the weekend I did a sneaky thing and got Gerald Kaufman to reshape the earlier material as a tribute to Devlin, letting him shine the brighter in the light of comparison with Dilhorne. Mrs Wyndham Goldie, who was not privy to the Dilhorne ban, was chaperoning the programme that weekend. I deceitfully showed her the 'Devlin' script without giving her the background. She found it strong but acceptable and we broadcast it. All hell broke loose and I got a rare, furious call from Hugh Carleton Greene. Dilhorne's brother had been raging down the phone at him, trumpeting inaccuracies. Had I relied on the first script I would have been worried. Gerald's record was too reassuring. Finally the accusations came down to three errors of fact – which Kaufman was easily able to rebut – especially one of a political link by marriage which the lord chancellor and his brother appeared to have forgotten.

Apart from contributions by journalists it was exciting to coax scripts from celebrated writers in other fields. My routine began early in the morning and I was usually in the office before seven. I would share a pot of tea with the cleaners, read scripts and write notes for two largely uninterrupted hours. I was exercise-conscious for a mad moment and used to nip up to a fashionable gym in Notting Hill Gate which was also patronised by Laurence Olivier and Robert Stephens. The practice soon palled. The production staff arrived around 9.30 a.m., and from 10.00 a.m. I had time to wheedle contributions by telephone or over lunch. In London that usually meant the Grill Room at the Café Royal – conveniently splitting the difference between Shepherd's Bush and Fleet Street. Other lunches were pot luck in the oak-panelled rooms at Lime Grove. Roy Hattersley reminds me ruefully that we met at this time but he was not chosen. Tony Benn was not keen to be involved. Cyril Connolly produced an immensely scholarly sketch about Shakespeare in a cramped long hand which would have played half the length of a programme. Rejecting it was an uneasy business.

One day David Frost and I were to lunch Nigel Dennis, from whom we hoped to cajole a script. He was very late. Finally I found him stumbling around the corridors of Lime Grove, lost and distracted. He had been waylaid by Huw Wheldon, who took him for Ernest Milton, a distinguished old actor who was due to appear in a *Monitor* programme about Hamlet. Huw had been his usual effusive self: 'Orson's coming! O'Toole's on his way!' Nigel Dennis's confusion grew until the real Ernest Milton arrived and Wheldon turned on Dennis accusingly: 'Then who are you?' Nigel slipped away guiltily, feeling vaguely that he'd been accused of gatecrashing lunch, masquerading as an eighty-year-old Hamlet. I never persuaded him to write for us and have always blamed Wheldon.

Caryl Brahms provided occasional topical poems which were an excuse to invite guests like Michael Redgrave, Edith Evans and Max Adrian and vary the texture of the shows. For Redgrave there was a lament over the closure of railway branch lines.

And oh the silence when the stations die
In Tewkesbury, Ripple, Brill, Fairford and
Ardingly

And a protest when Madame Tussaud's melted down the waxworks of some prominent figures who had gone out of fashion – they included Selwyn Lloyd, the boxer Terry Spinks, Vivien Leigh and Marilyn Monroe:

Ashes to ashes,
Wax to flame
Selwyn and Terry Spinks the same.
Spare, friend, a sigh for Vivien there,
But for sweet Marilyn a prayer.

Dame Edith bewailed a plan to redevelop the ballerina Pavlova's old home:

Where on a lawn that's gone
Pavlova in a green world, watched a swan.

We recorded the verses in advance. Edith flirted relentlessly with the cameraman. Peter O'Toole, Paul Scofield, Ian Holm and Coral Browne all made guest appearances in one or another of the late-night shows. Coral, apparently the most assured and easily the most elegant of actresses, rarely did television, certainly not live. She wrote her first line on her immaculately manicured nails and entered with her hand held up and her fingers stretched out. Her hand was shaking so much she was quite unable to read the blur.

Dame Sybil Thorndike was twice a guest. Caryl and I had worked with her on a radio play with music, *The Sunday Market*. The score was by John Dankworth. The *Daily Express* provided a photograph memorably captioned, 'Thorndike sings Dankworth'. During the early weeks of *TW3* she was playing St Teresa of Avila in the West End. The play did not have a long run but during the course of it she fell while leaping for a bus in the King's Road, triggering the arthritis which plagued her last years. She made rueful little jokes about the saint's levitational skills and her own failure to land safely.

The week after her play closed I collected a sketch from Keith Waterhouse and Willis Hall. On this occasion they parodied an agony aunt column. Current Tory ministers put problems to Super Aunt in the enquiring, naive style of 'Puzzled Surbiton'. Without much hope I rang Dame Sybil's agent and sent the script round in a taxi. I was surprised and delighted when she said 'Yes'. When she arrived at Lime Grove she was surprised in her turn to find that we were broadcasting live the next day. She had never worked in front of a live studio audience before and she had never seen a teleprompter. She confessed that she had no idea about the programme or the furore it was creating. She had read the sketch when it arrived and was about to tell her agent to say, 'No . . . Too frivolous, too risqué,' when her husband, Sir Lewis Casson, asked what it was. When she told him it was for 'something called *That Was The Week That Was*', he was adamant that she should do it. 'You must,' he told her. 'The programme's practically communist.'

She got to know the teleprompter next day but I think she thought it was cheating. However, she relished the studio guffaws from the crew and wanted to know if she was overdoing it. 'I always do in comedy, you know. You must cut me down.' The contention was that Annabel, the agony aunt, dictated replies into a dictaphone after each minister had stated his problem. When we came to the sketch on transmission Willy Rushton, as Harold Macmillan, was the first applicant – even then Europe and the intransigence of France, and particularly de Gaulle, was a prime subject. 'Dear Annabel,' he said, 'I am a prime minister and for the last sixteen months I have been having an affair with a French boy called Charles, even though I knew he had other friends . . .' I cut to Sybil at the end of the letter over audience laughter. The moment is still vivid in my mind. I saw that her right hand clutching the dictaphone was shaking slightly, betraying the nervousness which had overtaken her. There was a brief pause. Then she raised her left hand, whacked it down on her right wrist and launched into her reply with both under control. She went on to get all her laughs and enjoyed herself a lot.

Often *TW3* was attractive to writers who were used to filling a whole evening in the theatre with a large theme. If they realised that an idea which had pleased them would not stand up to a two-hour play or even to one act they could recast it as a sketch. Eight or ten minutes on *TW3* gave them a convenient shop window, a huge audience and the satisfaction of instant reaction. John Mortimer, Frank Marcus, John Antrobus, Kenneth Tynan, John Braine and Peter Shaffer were among those who contributed occasional pieces.

Shaffer's first sketch was a classic rumination on the immense scandal surrounding the Vassall case. William Vassall was a gay civil servant who had allowed himself to be entrapped in a sexual encounter in Russia. He was subsequently used by the

Soviets. Much play was made in court of his homosexuality. Wild and sinister implications were read into the routine salutations and sign-offs of his correspondence with a junior minister, the late Thomas Galbraith. Lance Percival, as a senior civil servant, hauled David Kernan, his junior, over the coals, pouncing on innocently ambiguous phrases in an official letter like 'my dear'; 'pursuant' ('it has an erotic penumbra'); 'favour' (the *Oxford Dictionary* defines it as 'to look kindly upon'); 'thinking of you in anticipation' ('positively whinnies with suggestiveness'); 'yours faithfully' ('even "yours" is dangerous – it suggests a willingness to surrender!'); 'your obedient servant' ('an *ipso facto* confession of sexual deviation. And that, as we all know, is an *ipso facto* confession of treason').

I wooed Noel Coward for a contribution and got a very quick 'no'. I had a long correspondence with Terence Rattigan but in the end he decided that sketch-writing was not for him. John Osborne never wrote for us but when *TW3*'s successor was at its most beleaguered he wrote a supportive thunderbolt to the *Sunday Times*.

David Frost and Christopher Booker wrote a lot together – getting together on Fridays or as late as Saturday mornings so that the sketches at the top of the show could be as topical as possible. Again, David's first biographer, Willi Frischauer, had a romantic view of their sessions: 'the thoughts were philosophical, sublime, esoteric . . . David was the one who barked most fiercely and showed his teeth – literally with the greatest ferocity'.

One of Booker's great strengths was as a parodist. His *Private Eye* piece, 'The Decline and Fall of the Emperor Macmillianus' was wonderfully sustained. I commissioned a piece from him in the style of Disraeli when Alec Douglas-Home rather than Rab Butler was pitchforked into No. 10 by the machinations of Harold Macmillan. As a lifelong Disraelian Conservative it was the nearest I got to mounting a personal pulpit on *TW3*. It always puzzled people that my politics were conservative – my responsibility to the programme was to approach each item on its merits. This was probably the only time I allowed a prejudice to sway me.

No such savage attack on a politician had been broadcast on BBC television and it caused a storm – nearly six hundred phone calls and over three hundred letters – all in protest. David himself supplied the splendid pay-off, 'And so the choice for the electorate: on one hand Lord Home and on the other hand Mister Harold Wilson. Dull Alec versus smart Alec.' Years later Lord Home confessed in a television interview that it was the only thing that hurt him in many years in politics. *TW3* was, he said, 'an attack on the establishment – it wasn't satire'.

In fact it was one of the few pieces that really measured up to that demanding label. Frost and Booker produced another sketch which qualified. Again the form was parody; the vehicle, Eamonn Andrews' lugubrious style on *This Is Your Life*. Andrews was not, of course, the target – that was the home secretary, Henry Brooke. Willy Rushton played Brooke. George Nelson Rockwell and Georges Bidault, who had cocked a snook at him and the 'victims' of his administration, Carmel Bryan, Robert Soblen and Chief Enharo, were wheeled on to greet him. Frost/Andrews' pay-off was 'This is your life, Henry Brooke – and was theirs!' – to which Rushton/Brooke muttered, 'It just shows if you're home secretary you can get away with murder!'

When people asked what practical effect *TW3* ever had on politics this is the only example to which I can point with some certainty. Henry Brooke's subsequent election defeat in Hampstead was materially affected by it. Edward Heath was of that opinion, inveighing against it for ten or fifteen minutes at a rumbustious *Punch* lunch. At the fortieth anniversary party of the programme Tam Dalziel went further. He told me categorically that *TW3* was a critical factor in Wilson's victory.

David and I were lunching one day at the Café Royal. It was after a series of scandals – Profumo, Vassall, etc. Across the

Grill Room we spotted Ted Heath, then Tory chief whip, in conversation with a decidedly dodgy-looking character, coiffed hair, a suggestion of make-up, eyebrows plucked. We enjoyed devising a scenario which made him a senior civil servant, ripe for exposure, ready for scandal. Obviously Heath was counselling him to behave and get the boy out of his house. On his way past our table the chief whip stopped to introduce us. 'I don't think you know the Czechoslovakian ambassador,' he said.

For me a special attraction of *TW3* – a great bonus – was that producing it combined three of my main interests. To be licensed as a news junkie to address the news in a vaudeville style and at the same time indulge my taste in music represented layers of icing on a cake already stuffed with plums.

I commissioned a lot of light music for the show – an activity often neglected by the BBC. John Bassett's contacts with jazz musicians produced some of these composers. John Dankworth, John Scott and Duncan Heath wrote many of the jazz improvisations to which words were set in the manner of Annie Ross's 'Twisted'. Forty years later when she appeared on *Loose Ends* a new generation of producers wondered what Annie had to do with Barbra Streisand's number! The defining lyrics were by Steven Vinaver. When he tired of the task Caryl Brahms took over. Ron Grainer, who wrote the signature tune for *TW3*, *Not So Much a Programme* and *BBC-3*, Carl Davis, Peter Greenwell, Dave Lee and Sandy Wilson also wrote for the programme.

Millicent Martin's jazz solo was a regular highlight. She usually got it as late as Thursday, and always performed in a little black dress. She only nearly fluffed once when I superimposed the fingers of the virtuoso bongo player Barry Morgan on her breasts. 'Beat out that rhythm on the drum' was the nearest she came to losing her cool.

Herbert Kretzmer had a special talent for turning a topical news story into impeccably rhymed, hard-hitting lyrics. An announcement that one London baby in eight born in 1961 had been illegitimate inspired a moving lullaby sung with beautiful simplicity by Millicent Martin, rocking a cradle:

> There's no reason any longer
> Why you ought to feel so blue.
> The world is full of bastards
> Just like you . . .

The most chilling musical parody, 'Song of Nostalgia for an American State', performed as an innocent, exuberant Black and White Minstrel number, was provoked by a racial outrage in the Deep South:

> I wanna go back to Mississippi
> Where the scent of blossoms
> Kiss the evenin' breeze,
> Where the Mississippi mud
> Kinda mingles with the blood
> Of the Niggers
> Who are hangin'
> From the branches of the trees . . .

It was irritating forty years on when it was rebroadcast in the anniversary show to find a smart-ass correspondent to the *Radio Times* dismissing it on account of Billie Holiday's magnificent 'Strange Fruit'. In 1963 it was necessary to say it again.

Milly had a deeply ingrained mistrust of new material. 'Why can't I have a song as good as last week?' was a regular moan – never louder than when I gave her a topical Kretzmer lyric which started, 'I've been testing contraceptives all day long . . .' However, with the suggestion that Lance Percival might like to sing it instead she buckled down and by the next weekend it too had become a benchmark.

Milly and Roy Kinnear were a potent pairing in sketches from an early show when they shared the Steven Vinaver 'Fly Buttons' sketch. In it social embarrassment spirals as 'she' tries to tell 'him' something discreetly.

HE: You don't have to whisper.
SHE: I don't want no one to hear.
      [*And after much protesting*]
HE: Just say it out loud.
SHE: [*Loud*] Your fly is open.

It's impossible to convey the explosive effect of those words today. Baverstock had refused to risk the sketch until the third programme – although it played to great laughs on the second pilot. It typified the sort of funny titillation which some viewers looked for in the show while being sharply observed.

Keith Waterhouse and Willis Hall summed it up and sent it up with Roy and Milly in an epilogue to the last programme of the first series. After the credits they were discovered watching an empty television set.

SHE: Well, it was something different.
HE: Well, it was satire, wasn't it? What we call satire.
SHE: All jokes and skits and that.
HE: Yes! Mucky jokes. Obscenity – it's all the go nowadays.
      By law, you see. You're allowed to do it. You can say 'bum',
      you can say 'po', you can say anything.

So we became the 'bum and po' show. Another battle cry – pounced on by Bernard Levin who extrapolated it from the words of various hostile critics – was 'Filth, Sedition and Blasphemy!' On the blasphemy front – or at least on religious topics – there were two early warning signs. A line from an old favourite Cambridge sketch of David's, 'The Bible Condensed', in *Reader's Digest* style – 'The Resurrection: You can't keep a good man down' – had the press scurrying to Beccles to grab a quote from his father, the Reverend Paradine Frost. 'I am thinking of David as an actor who just speaks the lines put in his mouth' was the Methodist minister's loyal verdict.

He was soon to be bombarded by Fleet Street's finest. Unsurprisingly they reported what suited them. When the *Daily Mail* ran a headline, 'Frost was wrong says his Clergyman father', the *Sketch* registered approval: 'Caused me no embarrassment.' Elsewhere the Reverend Frost offered that, 'if it wakes people up and makes them alive to the church and religion', it was on the side of the angels. Meanwhile the *Daily Telegraph* harvested a quite different verdict: 'I had a busy day and was rather tired. I dozed off during it.'

The trigger for the second row was the 'Consumer's Guide to Religion', written by two actors, Charles Lewsen and Robert Gillespie. It was a simple idea which Charles Lewsen says I suggested to him. It rigorously applied the language and standards of consumer guides to the great world religions. I tried to diffuse an outcry with little success by having Willy Rushton speak an introduction suggesting that if religions sought to make an ever more worldly appeal to their flocks they must not be surprised if they found themselves judged by the standards of the world.

The sketch made for a tense atmosphere in the hospitality suite where we gathered before the show, fed and watered by the wonderful Mrs Reynolds, who dispensed BBC hospitality, a calming, motherly figure and on occasion a useful spy ('You want to watch that Tom Sloan. When I was serving the DG this week he was trying to do you down').

I had discussed the sketch with Alasdair Milne. He was aware of the dangers but agreed that we should broadcast it. On the Saturday night Kenneth Adam decided to visit the studio. It was becoming fashionable to be seen in the audience. Alasdair showed him the script. He told him he had already made the decision to play it. Adam would have preferred to cut it. Alasdair's firm stance made that impossible. The Milne/Baverstock protective umbrella was always invaluable.

The 'Consumer's Guide' is a long sketch but it still holds up in the age of the soundbite, the one-liner and the endless cycle of comic quickies. I read it recently at one of those City churches possessed of two pulpits where the incumbent enjoys to debate with a visitor. It held the congregation for its ten-minute length. For those housewives keen to know, the best buy was:

'The Church of England . . . It's a jolly friendly faith – if you are one there is no onus on you to make anyone else join – in fact no one need ever know. And it's pretty fair on the whole, too. With some of these products we've mentioned . . . you start guilty from the off. But the Church of England is English. On the whole you start pretty well innocent, and they've got to prove you guilty.'

It was a tour de force for Frost, who delivered the long monologue to camera in front of blow-ups of photos of typical representatives of each religion. The BBC logged 249 complaints and 167 appreciations. All this pre-email. A parson from Sussex phoned Frost to ask the score. He was preaching a sermon in favour of *TW3* and wanted to get his facts right. The *Daily Express* thundered, 'Do you believe a man's religion should be mocked?' (It was about now that they produced a vast spread with photographs of Frost and me under the headline, 'These Guilty Men Must Go!') Surprisingly Peter Simple in the *Daily Telegraph* took the same line as my introduction: 'As I understood it, the intention was not to mock at religion, but to mock at the idea that religion is a product.'

Millicent Martin was quoted as saying, 'It's just a send-up of those consumer guides.' A Catholic priest wrote to me, 'I'm sure you will have a lot of trouble and a lot of protests about this. Don't take any notice. It was very good and the sort of people who complain will all be converts.' On the other hand an

Anglican preacher on the Isle of Man told his flock: 'If we were 100 per cent Christian we would storm the BBC building and make it drop this horrible programme.' There are few more potent instruments of publicity than a bishop banging on against you from his pulpit, a politician railing at you in Parliament or a newspaper screaming abuse in its headlines. By now we had a full house.

The see of the bishop we most upset was Swansea and Brecon. He backed up his protest with a letter to Hugh Greene saying that the sketch was in 'deplorably bad taste, and gratuitously offensive to many viewers'.

Sex, politics, religion and royalty. These were the major taboos of the *Green Book*. Our attitude to the royal family was not to mock the Queen but the reverential, forelock-tugging way they were reported. The most famous sketch, and one of our biggest rows, was prompted by Princess Margaret. Frost and I were at a party given by Quentin Crewe. It is very pleasant to be flavour of the month and we were. Our social lives were on a roll. David's networking skills were already in full flower. Caryl had always provided an entrée to arts circles for me. She was particularly miffed (understandably) when David Astor and his *Observer* hacks entertained the team to lunch. She heard one straight-faced young woman ask me if she could touch the hem of my garment. David was now lionised by most sections of society. He swanned through them to the manner born. At Q's party the princess enthused about the programme and asked why we didn't do something about the way 'we' are reported. Frost remembered a Footlights sketch by Ian Lang. Ian, now Lord Lang of Monkton, had auditioned unsuccessfully for the replacement cast of *Beyond the Fringe* and appeared as a stand-up in Clement Freud's club at the Royal Court before surrendering to politics. The monologue had Frost as a Dimbleby figure reporting in hushed tones a royal occasion from the Pool of London when disaster strikes:

The Royal Barge is, as it were, sinking. The sleek royal blue hull of the barge is sliding gracefully, almost regally, beneath the waters of the Pool of London . . . perhaps the lip-readers amongst you will know what Prince Philip, Duke of Edinburgh, has just said to the Captain of the Barge . . . And now the Duke of Gloucester and Mr Angus Ogilvy have rushed forward to the end of the quay – to get a better view. And Lord Snowdon has just taken a colour photograph . . . Now the Queen, smiling radiantly, is swimming for her life. Her Majesty is wearing a silk ensemble in canary yellow . . . and now the Royal Marine Band strikes up, 'God Save the Queen'!

A moment which lingers in the memory of most over-fifties is the assault on Bernard Levin. It has overshadowed one of the funniest sketches which appeared in the same programme – 20 April 1963. It was the week the London Hilton opened, and Peter Lewis and Peter Dobereiner gave the ethos of Hilton hotel management a biblical welcome, declaimed by our new American recruit, Al Mancini: 'And there was a great gushing of ic-ed water and a great puking of pip-ed music and a great charging of fifty guineas a night without breakfast . . . And a library where you may read the Hilton Milton and 850 Hilton manservants and maidservants smiling Hilton smiles, which they smile not saying "Cheese" but "Hilton Stilton" . . .'

Bernard inspired his own diversion. That week in his paper he reviewed a performance of Brecht and Weil songs by the cabaret singer Agnes Bernelle at the Duchess Theatre. Ms Bernelle was married to Desmond Leslie. Bernard did not pull his punches. 'She does not talk well, walk well or stand well, overlays everything with a horrid archness that makes one squirm, and when she reaches for a high note does so with a kind of throaty vibrato that made me think of a line by Mr H. F. Ellis to the effect, if memory serves, "that the great white ox of Patagonia makes its peculiar hunting cry by banging its nostrils together".'

Mr Leslie was furious – it was suggested later that he felt guilt for the fiasco of his wife's performance because he was in charge of the sound balance and had royally screwed it up. However, he knew John Bassett and begged a ticket for the Saturday show without telling him why he wanted it. As Bernard prepared to launch into his dialogue (with a nice irony he was to confront a group of pacifists), Leslie came down through the audience and confronted him. 'Excuse me, Mr Levin, but would you stand up for a moment?' Bernard, surprised and puzzled, turned to face him. 'Before you go on, Mr Levin, your review of *Savagery and Delights* was not a review, it was . . .' Bernard had managed, 'Yes, yes, but . . .' when Leslie started to throw punches at him. Before he could land one Peter Chafer, the floor manager, closely followed by Frost, pulled him off. Chafer bustled Leslie away. Bernard dusted himself down, resumed his seat and said, to applause, to the CND group, 'Can we concentrate on non-violence, you and I?'

The *Daily Express* was convinced that the incident was fixed. They were constantly on the lookout for reasons to attack. As Herbert Kretzmer was their drama critic and was writing songs for us with Dave Lee, our musical director, they assumed that Dave might have the inside story. A reporter rang him at home on the Sunday. Dave led him on. 'I can certainly tell you what Ned Sherrin said when Levin got punched. I had headphones on. I heard every word.'

'What did he say?'

'Have you got a pen?'

'Yes, of course!'

'And paper?'

'Yes. Yes. What did he say?'

'He said, "Who the fuck's that?"'

No story appeared but there was an epilogue. A few years before Desmond Leslie died he and Bernard bumped into one another, quite by chance, in the Gresham hotel, Dublin. They had an amiable tea together and never mentioned the incident provoked by the performance of Leslie's ex-wife.

Towards the end of the first season of *TW3* early rumours of Christine Keeler's simultaneous liaisons with the Tory war minister, John Profumo, and a Russian naval attaché/spy, Ivanov, began to surface. *TW3* is remembered by many as being obsessed by the scandal but our references were few and fleeting. I hinted that we knew what was going on by inventing a spurious peg – the centenary of the original performance of a Victorian song:

> See 'im in the 'Ahse of Commons
> Making laws to put dahn croime,
> While the object of 'is passion
> Walks the streets to 'ide 'er shoime

and inserted it into Millicent Martin's opening number. She was also given a David Nathan and Dennis Potter sketch delivered in negligee and dark glasses:

> I was on first-name terms with top
> politicians and we often had discussions
> which went on far into the night . . .

When Ms Keeler disappeared to Spain to avoid giving evidence in a court case not directly involving Profumo we used the cast as court ushers placed around the studio yelling, 'Call Christine Keeler . . .' who, needless to say, did not appear. During the last programme before the summer break Frost offered some predictions of news items which might surface in the coming weeks. 'May 23rd Christine Keeler appointed Conservative Party's Chief PRO . . . June 13th Christine Keeler becomes Conservative Party Chief Whip . . .'

The climax of the drama was played out during the interval

between the two series. I heard of Profumo's eventual confession to the House of Commons in New York over the radio in a taxi travelling along Fifth Avenue. In those days New York taxi drivers spoke English and were always keen to give you an opinion. My man had not quite got the cast right. 'I don't see why this Macmillan guy shouldn't sleep around,' he said. 'At his age it's to his credit!'

Our last contribution to the incident was an item on the first programme after the break. It was a beautifully animated collage of headlines and photographs put together by the late Geoffrey Martin to the Rodgers and Hart song 'I Could Write a Book'. It greeted the publication of the Denning Report into the scandal. The frenzy to buy a copy was of Harry Potter proportions.

My visit to America was clouded by the news of Timothy Birdsall's death. I was told over the telephone and had to break it to John Bird and Eleanor Bron, who were close Cambridge friends. They were having a great success at the New York 'Establishment'. Timothy had been ill for some time but his wife, Jocelyn, had kept from him the news that the illness was a form of leukaemia – much harder to treat at that time. Joss made the decision that Tim would not want to know that he would not live to see their very young sons, Adam and Toby, grow up. She came to ask me if the BBC would offer a contract for the next season at a much inflated fee so that Tim's mind would be relieved of financial worries over the last few weeks. Touchingly, she guaranteed that he would not live to fulfil it. The bureaucratic image of the BBC cracked and a way was found to do what she asked. Sadly Tim did not live to test it.

One highlight of the first series had been Frankie Howerd's sensational comeback. After a lean period he made a success of his run at the Establishment but it was the vast audience who saw him on *TW3* who turned the tide. He reworked his view of the Budget which was the principal plank of his Greek Street show, but I was struck by the care and concern with which he embellished it. For a week we hired a rehearsal room for him which had a telephone in it. Each day he conscientiously paced the floor and battered the new stuff into his head. He only stopped to telephone his scriptwriting friends for updates and refinements. Galton and Simpson, Johnny Speight, Muir and Norden, Sid Colin, Eric Sykes, Barry Cryer and more were relentlessly put on the spot.

When he got to the studio he ran through it routinely for me behind a scenery flat. When he performed it on the show he flowered. Part of his uneasiness on previous shows, especially on commercial television, had come from the discipline of time. Often on *Sunday Night at the Palladium* when his 'oohs!' and 'ahs!' expanded to the delight of the theatre audience the viewer at home would see the credits rolling over his uncompleted act. It was intriguing to see him relaxing after a few minutes on *TW3*. He went on and on, encouraged that no studio manager waved his arms to stop him. Two memorable images which he conjured up stay in the mind. Frank's trick was to reduce national politics to kitchen comedy – over-the-garden-wall gossip. Robin Day was condemned for his 'cruel glasses', and Harold Macmillan was absolved of guilt: 'I blame her, Dot . . .' He overran by many minutes, the time added by his trademark grunts and groans and more especially by laughter. At the end the applause was deafening and prolonged.

David led the clapping with enthusiasm. The ovation went on a lot longer than any of us had expected. Finally David looked down at his notes to remind himself of the next and last item – the Sunday papers. The glance down happened exactly as I cut to his enthusiastic cheerleading. All the audience saw was a bowed head and a frown of concentration. An alarming number of viewers and some critics thought, quite wrongly, that they had witnessed one of the 'young amateurs' jealous of the success of a 'real professional'. However, nothing could spoil Frank's triumph. He came on, euphoric, to the Casserole and confirmed his return to public favour with huge spreads in the national papers. His next success was *A Funny Thing Happened on the Way to the Forum* in the West End and then its television echo, *Up Pompeii*. He didn't need another comeback until the eighties.

By now the 'satire' label was firmly fixed on the show. There was a court case where a mother, giving evidence on behalf of her son, pleaded, 'Oh, he got in with some of them satirists, your Honour.' And a letter arrived at the office from a muddled man who asked, 'Which school should I send my son to so he can be a satirist when he grows up?' At the Montreux Festival where we showed a compilation out of competition there was a lot of puzzlement about a very verbal show. The exception was a mime devised for an Oxford revue by Ian Davidson in which Frost conducted an orchestra of gun noises killing all signs of life. A Swiss television producer remonstrated with us: 'You should not make fun of war. We Swiss have lived through two world wars!'

We had been careful not to use the word 'satire' ourselves. I had a sixth sense that it would rebound and that we would not live up to a proper definition except in the sense that the original Latin, *satura*, means 'Hotch potch'. Unlike the great satirists we had a mass audience. On most Saturday nights we 'played to' more people than Bion, Juvenal, Lucian, Petronius, Pope, Dryden and Voltaire put together. George S. Kaufman said, 'satire is what closes on Saturday nights'; we often strayed into Sunday morning. Harold Macmillan was nearer to it in our case when he came down to the Television Centre one day and murmured to Hugh Greene, 'I hear you have some sort of Saturnalia here on Saturday nights.' Keith Waterhouse and Willis Hall provided another classic sketch for Roy Kinnear which skewered the feeble attempts of more conservative comics to catch on to the new fashion. They called it 'The Safe Comedian'. A baggy-trousered, check-suited figure, Roy bounced on.

Oh, he's vicious, is David Frost. I'm not saying he's got a cutting tongue but he's the only man I know who doesn't have to
slice his bread before he eats it. [*Smarmily*] No, but seriously,
David, you're doing a grand job and it's a great pleasure and
privilege to be working on your show tonight. Work, eh? Half
a million unemployed. My brother's unemployed. Still, he's
lazy. Well, I won't say he's lazy, but he's the only person I know
with elbow patches on his pyjamas! Still, we don't want to get
maudlin about it, do we? Geddit? Maudlin', Mr Maudling.
No, but seriously, boys and girls, *he's doing a grand job*.

David picked up the phrase and used it a few times to underline a political joke. It became a 'catchphrase'. I was rather
puritanical about catchphrases, which seem too easy, and phased
it out – but it stuck anyway. Reginald Maudling was the second
leading politician to visit the show. The first was George Brown,
who arrived as Cliff Michelmore's guest. He was duly caught on
camera laughing and applauding. The next week Maudling
arrived with the director general – no doubt looking for some 'we
can take a joke too' balance. Unfortunately I had a message from
on high to say he was on no account to be photographed so I
carefully kept the cameras off him. He was very disappointed.

TW3 ended for a variety of reasons. One was the initial success of the programme. In a few weeks the audience rose to ten
or twelve million, probably more. Unprecedented at that hour.
The phenomena of *TW3* parties and pubs empty on Saturday
nights ballooned. The romance was too hot not to cool down.

There was some unease among the governing body led by the
vice-chairman, Sir James Duff. During the summer break political suspicions grew stronger. To attack a popular show is a
tricky track to take. However, Stuart Hood, who had earlier
said, 'It won't have a clumsy name like *That Was The Week
That Was*', made a speech in Blackpool – saying words to the
effect, 'Yes, the programme will certainly return in the autumn,

but the element of "smut" will be omitted.' We had not been much concerned with smut but once a BBC spokesman had lit the blue touchpaper political opponents realised that they could stand well away and watch. Reaction gained momentum.

Our first four shows after the summer break were dull. There is a self-consciousness about a second series. Diaghilev, returning to London for a second ballet season, said to his designers, 'Paint the colours twice as bright. That's how they will remember them.' Our efforts to be bright produced stilted and self-conscious programmes. People said the show had lost its magic. The anti-brigade, led inside the BBC by Duff, had more ammunition at their disposal. It is much easier to knock a show which looks in trouble.

The second season began on Saturday 28 September. On 13 November the BBC made a formal announcement that, 'The present run of *That Was The Week That Was* will end on 28th December and not continue, as had originally been intended until the spring.' The explanation given was that 1964 would be an election year and rather than 'dilute the content and so alter the nature of the programme' it should stop. 'Election year? Tell that to the Marines,' one viewer wrote. In those days, whenever I had a programme taken off it always seemed to be Barry Norman, then a showbiz reporter on the *Daily Mail*, who was first up the stairs of the flat into which I had moved in Dover Street to ask if I knew and had I any comment to make.

Mrs Wyndham Goldie gives a moving account of the strain *TW3* placed on senior BBC executives. Describing one occasion when she was nominally in charge, she wrote: 'I felt I was being asked to ride a tiger.' In this uncomfortable period she was also on the horns of a dilemma: 'The problem came later: when the general consensus had to be translated on Saturday into a script for the next edition of the programme . . . overtly there were never any difficulties. Ned Sherrin, if told that a particular item must not be included, did not argue. He was too cool a character.'

He was also concerned with getting the programme on the air. Grace mentions a sketch in October 1963 which she found 'humanly offensive'. She does not identify the sketch and I do not remember the incident. Apparently I said, 'Oh, don't you like it? Then of course we'll take it out.' A programme's running order was never sacrosanct until we were on the air. It may well have been in my mind to drop it in any case.

Theatre revues are difficult to put together because the actors jealously guard their sketch opportunities. We had a more family atmosphere on *TW3* and less jockeying for exposure because if your role was diminished one week there was every chance that you would be overloaded seven days later. It was a running joke that if Peter Chafer on the floor said to one of the cast, 'pick up the phone,' it meant that I was about to say that a sketch had been cut. I only remember one tearful response when I told David Kernan that I was cutting a very funny William Rushton song for an Italian gigolo:

Fornicatione
is Italian for love
Copulatzione
Sent from heaven up above.

Baverstock had found it too suggestive in its account of the American matrons who were the gigolo's clients:

Frustratzione
Flutters in their withered loins,
I bring senzatzione
For a fountainful of coins.

Sadly, out it went, to Kernan's cries of 'foul'. Mrs Goldie quotes Donald on the item she had described as 'humanly offensive': 'I told him what was in the sketch. He said, "Oh my God!" There was a pause, then he added slowly, "It's important to understand that if a group of people are expected to go to the limits of what is permissible, they must have it within them to go beyond those limits."'

Mrs Goldie's final verdict is that '*TW3* died not so much from excessive censorship as from confusion of purpose.' It died as a result of its extraordinary success. I had set out to produce a service programme not a sensation. It was as though I had designed an aeroplane and come up with a rocket. When the rocket had run its course it fizzled out. This was one fault we would have to rectify when we started to plan its successor, *Not So Much a Programme More a Way of Life*. At that moment, however, a successor seemed an unlikely prospect and, anyway, we still had to do six more programmes.

On 22 November 1963 I was going through the revolving doors that lead to the ballroom at the Dorchester to pick up a BAFTA for *TW3*. I was told of the assault on President Kennedy as I entered the hotel. Soon the assassination was confirmed. I picked up the gong from Dame Sybil having spent the meal wondering what to do with the programme next day. Fifty or sixty minutes of topical comedy were being typed up at Lime Grove to be fed to the autocue in the morning. In the development of *That Was The Week That Was* all the new ideas which made the programme memorable had come from the writers. My first task was to reach as many of them as possible, see what they could offer and then make up my mind at the last possible moment. Frost, who had to get hold of Christopher Booker, and I kept popping in and out of the ballroom using small change for the telephone.

At the Television Centre I found Kenneth Adam, Rex Moorfoot, the head of presentation, Mrs Wyndham Goldie and for some reason Bill Cotton, the assistant head of light entertainment, huddled in front of screens where commentators were trying to gild the gruesome pictures with appropriate words and failing miserably. It was difficult to see how we could add any-thing to the mass of verbiage the next day. The atmosphere in that central control room was stunned and maudlin; words were slurred. Public grief was drowned in private glasses and Grace, who was going through her own 'unhappy hour', was murmur-ing, 'News has failed us again.'

I tried to assess what the mood of the audience would be in twenty-four hours' time. Would they be able to take any more? Would they want a change? Would they want to be reminded? Would they want to forget? Would they want to escape or would they want to wallow? It was a critical test for us to sum up the mood we felt in the nation at the end of that dramatic week. I talked to Donald Baverstock and Alasdair Milne and changed my mind at least three times during dinner and three times more at the Television Centre.

I continued to phone the writers. I tracked down Gore Vidal in Rome to try to get him to write a special piece. He was pack-ing his bags to fly to Washington. I went to Quaglinos where David was doing his cabaret act in the Allegro Room. I seem to remember that he cut the Hilton hotel monologue which he had incorporated into his act. I went to bed in the small hours and got up at six.

Had too much fuss been made of the whole business the night before? In the distorting goldfish bowl of television, events often loom larger. The cast of *TW3* were called for rehearsal as usual at 11 a.m. John Bassett and John Duncan started to rehearse the prepared script on the studio floor. I went down to Christopher Booker's house in Chelsea where he was working on a piece which might preface the programme we had originally planned to broadcast. Back at the Television Centre more and more mourning news films were coming in from America. At last it became obvious that it was no good doing anything but a Kennedy special programme. We could forget combining it with the other sketches which had been rehearsed from eleven to one o'clock. Alasdair Milne and Donald Baverstock agreed. Donald urged us to raise the standard of the writing to an elegiac formality – not a quality much sought in television, but wise advice. He felt that no one had found the eloquence the occasion demanded and urged us to feel for it.

At one o'clock I sent the cast home. There was nothing yet written for them to rehearse except the song Herbert Kretzmer had half finished for Millicent Martin: a pastiche Western ballad commemorating the assassination in Dallas, 'In the Summer of His Years'. She was able to start learning the tune of the first eight bars. A redoubtable old cockney actress, Rita Webb, had been booked for the original programme. She was reluctant to be let go. 'I'm always the cockney voice of the bleedin' Blitz,' she protested. 'I should be speaking for bleedin' cockney London, like I always bleedin' do.'

By now I was expecting two pieces by Bernard Levin: his own hopeful contribution on Lyndon Johnson's potential and a second item, a reflection on power, for which we hoped to harness his ability to let his prose soar as Donald had suggested. I checked that Robert Lang, a fine speaker who had often been a member of the team in the second season and was appearing in the first production at the National Theatre (*Hamlet*), could get away to deliver the piece if Bernard could come up with it. David Frost and Christopher Booker were polishing David's linking dialogue and writing introductory paragraphs for the whole team. Early in the afternoon I remembered that we had planned no mention of the widowed Jacqueline Kennedy, so I phoned Caryl Brahms, who was at a recording of one of our radio plays at Broadcasting House, to ask her to write this. So it came about that Dame Sybil was back with us at 10 p.m. less than twenty-four hours since she had presented the BAFTA. Her only question when I telephoned her was 'It won't be funny, will it?' Reassured, she came in and gave a magisterial reading of 'Why, Jacqui?'

We had one run through. It was a curious, quiet occasion. Donald Baverstock then made a decision which had far-reaching consequences. He saw that this programme which could be effective at home might be even more moving in America. We always recorded *TW3* – unusual in those days – because of potential libel. Donald decided to record it so that it could be transmitted on both the British and American systems. This required a special, rarely used machine. That way it could be flown immediately to America and shown on American television within twenty-four hours. In the event they repeated it many times during the following days. The long-playing record won a Grammy and eventually we were all, writers and performers, flown over to restage the whole thing in the old Madison Square Gardens for a massive Jewish charity show.

On 23 November 1963 we skipped the usual cheerful audience warm-up and Frost simply told those who had come out to the Television Centre that there would be no party, we were doing a twenty-minute valedictory show and those who wished to stay were welcome to do so.

We went on air.

Frost led off with the introductory comments which he and Christopher Booker had written in a simple statement: 'The reason why the shock was so great was because it was the most unexpected piece of news one could possibly imagine . . . If anyone else had died – Sir Winston Churchill, de Gaulle, Khrushchev – it would have been something we could understand and even perhaps accept.' Roy Kinnear said, 'When Kennedy was elected three years ago, it was as if we'd been given some gigantic, miraculous present . . . And now that present has been taken away from us when we thought we still had five more years before we need start worrying again.'

David Kernan's paragraph saw Kennedy as a father figure for young people. Al Mancini talked of the Kennedy family's unhappy history, and Kenneth Cope of the breadth of the appalled world reaction. Willy Rushton commented on the film-star image and Lance Percival saw Kennedy 'simply and superlatively as a man of his age, who understood his age'. David Frost summed up, remembering that we had lost Tim Birdsall during the year: 'Yesterday one man died. Today, in America, sixty lost their lives in a fire. And yet, somehow, it is the one that matters. Even in death, it seems, we are not all equal. Death is not the great leveller. Death reveals the eminent.'

The last sentence came from Baverstock's pen. 'In the Summer of His Years' followed, a small tear unmistakably sliding down Millicent Martin's cheek. Robert Lang read Bernard's reflections on power. Sybil spoke Caryl's poem, Bernard's essay on Lyndon Johnson set out to refute the many hearts-on-sleeves commentators who had sought to emphasise Kennedy's greatness by belittling his successor. He praised Johnson's record in civil rights: 'Though a Southerner . . . it was he who steered through Congress the only successful civil rights legislation of recent years.' He concluded, 'We, citizens of the alliance he now leads, have "the duty to wish him well with all our hearts".'

A poet hymned an earlier, narrower moment of crisis in the life of the United States: how much more bitterly relevant are those words today,

Sail on, oh ship of state
Sail on, oh Union strong and great,
Humanity, with all its fears,
With all the hope of future years
Is hanging breathless on thy fate.

In the last minute of the twenty-two the programme lasted Frost concluded, 'The tragedy of John Kennedy's death is not that the liberal movements of history that he led will cease. It is that their momentum may be lost. That is the aftermath of

Dallas, 22 November. It is a time for private thoughts. Good-night.'

There were about thirty protests on the phone log. Some were from people who felt that we should not have been allowed to broadcast at all; some who felt that it was our job to be amusing and that we should have continued to be amusing; some who felt, God knows why, that we were trying to be funny at the expense of the late president.

In the longer term the balance lay in our favour. Some continued to maintain that it was sentimental – Malcolm Muggeridge reflected, 'They are probably now all thoroughly ashamed of it.' Grace Wyndham Goldie snidely recorded, 'Strangely enough *TW3* went out in a blaze of glory.' She was referring to the Kennedy programme; but, given a second wind, the last four or five were some of our best shows.

It is difficult to assess how valuable our comments were, conceived and delivered in the haste and emotion of the moment. I tried to be consistent with my brief for the whole series. We were not trying, any more than on other nights, to provide a lasting document. The week which had just gone by had been obliterated by one event. All we could do was try to gauge the feeling of that evening and distil it in a way which we felt appropriate. The impact in America meant that on 4 December Senator Hubert Humphrey read the script into the Congressional Record with the words:

> 'Art', said the philosopher Santayana, 'is the trick of arresting the immediate.' This programme did indeed arrest the immediate. In all its ugly hardness but also in its searing tragedy, and in its depth of meaning in history, hope and duty, we have apparently been studied deeply – far more than from Friday to Saturday night – the time it took to write and produce the programme.
>
> It is humbling to know what our friends think and hope. I

wish to thank the British Broadcasting Corporation and through them the individuals who wrote and produced the programme. I ask unanimous consent to have the BBC copyright transcript printed in the Congressional Record.

Many Americans became aware of the existence of the BBC for the first time and it served to sell an American version of *TW3*, which they proceeded to botch with wholehearted American thoroughness, enthusiasm and showbiz know-how. It took American television more than a decade to realise what a potent period late-night Saturday is. They judged its value eventually with *Saturday Night Live*, which still totters on.

The last *That Was The Week That Was* was broadcast on 28 December 1963. It was an emotional occasion for participants and audience. Almost entirely retrospective, it was a trip through some of the best-remembered times. Viewed again some years later, it is so full of plums that some of them don't seem as juicy when juxtaposed as they did when they were highlights in a routine show. I miss the ballast of minor stories and nostalgic detail which crops up in the weekly programmes. Donald Baverstock led cries of 'More!' after the opening song, and the mood of nostalgic euphoria continued throughout the hour and a half.

Reaction in Kingweston was muted. Since I moved into television my father had his favourite programmes and his bêtes noires. He and my mother had long since given up concerning themselves with what my next move would be. *Ask Me Another* and *Tonight* passed muster. Everything else was suspect, especially *TW3*. On the whole he kept quiet about it. He only attempted one intervention. The BBC had broadcast one of its periodical indictments of Freemasonry. My father was a Mason. He rang me before going milking one morning to ask me not to touch the subject on Saturday. As we had no intention of doing so it was easy to comply.

Very early and very late calls when one is in bed always seem to mean extraordinary news. I was once woken in the early hours by Lionel Bart's then agent, calling from America. He said, without much conviction, how thrilled he and Lionel were that I was to direct Lionel's new Broadway show *La Strada*, based on the Fellini movie.

It came as news to me. Then I remembered that the latest Broadway hit *The Great White Hope* was directed by my near namesake, Ed Sherin. Broadway producers always go for the latest hot name. I suggested that 'Mr Ed' not 'Mr Ned' was the likely choice. The relief was tangible as he expressed disappointment. Poor Lionel's score was ripped apart on tour and the Broadway run was a one-night fiasco.

Australia produced its answer to *TW3*. It was called *The Mavis Bramston Show*. I never found out why, but sitting in bed with *The Times* early one morning I came across a sad little paragraph saying that the producer of *The Mavis Bramston Show* had been found dead in bed. He had committed suicide surrounded by scripts.

I knew how he felt.

CHAPTER 6

Pick Yourself Up, Dust Yourself Down and Start All Over Again

The election was over, the alibi exploded; but the blaze of glory from the Kennedy programme lingered, reinforced by the success of the last editions of *TW3*. All combined to fuel a 'bring back satire' cry. We were anxious to avoid the hysteria which the weekly show had inspired. The first idea was to broadcast a 'service' show five nights a week. However, plans were already forming for David Frost to commute between London and New York, which would make this impossible.

We settled on a three-night schedule – broadcasting on Fridays, Saturdays and Sundays. We knew we would not be able to provide enough sketches for three nights so we broadened the scope of the show. Conveniently David had fallen in love with the job of 'talk-show host' in America and was anxious to indulge this new romance.

We did six pilots – contributing to Denis Norden's quip, 'And that is David Frost who's had more pilots than the average BOAC air hostess' – and I began to assemble an impressive roster of performers. New to the screen and quickly popular were Harvey Orkin, an American film agent, and Patrick Campbell, the humorous writer and elegant stutterer. They joined Denis Norden as conversational sidekicks for Frost. Campbell took the spare chair on Fridays, Norden on Saturdays and Orkin on Sundays. I made a foolish attempt to lighten David's load by giving him Willy Rushton and the essayist and poet P. J. Kavanagh to share it. David didn't want his load lightened, and Willy and Patrick had little enthusiasm for the job. Willy wrote, 'Neither of us wanted to be in the programme. So we got elbowed to one side a bit; and in the end we were being paid £80 a show for nothing – it was the best job I ever had, except that it was driving me absolutely up the spout.' It was about this time that Willy came upon David's folder marked 'Airport quips' – a file of ready-made gags which the international traveller could fire off on arrival anywhere in the world.

The other members of the *TW3* cast were all branching out by now. I did not try to hang on to them. John Bird, Eleanor Bron and John Fortune were back from New York and were keen to join, along with Doug Fisher. I saw Roy Hudd in a Clarkson Rose music-hall show at Richmond. His broad vaudeville style complemented the 'university comedians' and he provided a range of show-business impersonations to balance the George Brown, Edward Heath, Harold Wilson and Jomo Kenyatta of John Bird, the Conservative ladies of Eleanor Bron and the occasional de Gaulle or Selwyn Lloyd of John Wells.

I also booked the versatile, virtuoso actor Leonard Rossiter. Unfortunately Leonard's debut was complicated by an overrun on the film he was making in Paris – *Hotel Paradiso*. He flew in on Fridays and out again the following Monday. He never felt part of the team. In the early weeks Bron, Bird, Fortune and John Wells provided much of their own material while I was trying to explore Leonard's range and make the contributing writers aware of it.

I had discovered on *TW3* that it was not until a fresh actor was *seen* to be doing something funny that scriptwriters started to write for him. After a successful Rushton, Kinnear or Percival sketch, a batch of scripts would arrive designed for Willy, Roy or Lance. Indifferent writers simply named the actor and assumed his mannerisms would make the sketch funny. Better writers realised the actor's skills and extended his range. However, Leonard soon became impatient at the lack of material. He asked to be released. Ironically this was the moment that the first tailor-made vehicle arrived for him. Dick Vosburgh wrote a Groucho Marx routine – a five-minute hint at the sure-footed, sustained pastiche he was to deliver some fifteen years later for *A Night in the Ukraine*. Leonard performed it with lightness and subtlety and a batch of scripts poured in for him, sadly too late. He had committed himself to a theatre role.

I had more success with Michael Crawford, whom I had seen in Neil Simon's *Come Blow Your Horn* with Bob Monkhouse, David Kossoff and Libby Morris and as Feste in Colin Graham's production of *Twelfth Night* in Inner Temple Hall. Peter Lewis and Peter Dobereiner created a character not unlike J. D. Salinger's Holden Caulfield in *The Catcher in the Rye*. They channelled the views of the teenage generation through this youngster, whom they named 'Byron'. He talked directly to camera for three or four minutes. Michael was virtually unknown. His first film, *The Knack*, had not yet been released and he was funny.

By this time I had moved out of Chelsea and was living in Dover Street in a four-floor walk-up – my first flat, at the age of thirty-three. I had woken up there one morning and persuaded my friend Gavin Robinson, in whose bed I had spent the night, that he needed somewhere more grand. He was about to change his career from model to model agent. It was tiny but convenient. It had previously been a Piccadilly lady's pad. Occasionally elderly colonial administrators puffed their way up the stairs and knocked hopefully on the door looking for the delights of long ago. They left sadly disappointed.

I moved in on the night of another television ball at the

Dorchester. Apart from collecting a second award, I won an electrically illuminated plastic water fountain in the raffle. After the ball I got home to find my predecessor had left no other bulbs in the flat. The weird water fountain was the only illumination until the next morning. By the time Michael came for an interview the lights were in working order. In fact Michael interviewed me. Relentlessly. That he was a very young, virtually unknown actor being offered a solo spot in the successor to one of the most talked-about shows in the history of television did not inhibit him. He grilled me rigorously about the attitude and background of the character, his point of view and the place he would occupy in the programme. Conveniently I had scheduled him for Sunday night which would not conflict with any theatre engagements.

In becoming a star Michael has acquired a demanding reputation. Apart from my initial third degree, we had few problems. It undoubtedly helped that he had the camera to himself and could deliver a good topical script with skill, charm and aplomb in medium close-up, unsupported or, perhaps in his mind, unhindered by other actors.

The only hiccup occurred one weekend when I thought the Lewis and Dobereiner sketch was not up to scratch; I warned Michael that I might have to drop him. He would, of course, be paid. Meanwhile the writers would try to produce a better script. They failed. Michael fretted and fumed. His immense new following of fans would be mortified. He would be shamed. Finally, tantrum spent, I sent him home. However, since then he has been overgenerous in insisting that the experience taught him a valuable lesson. Never go on unless the material is absolutely right.

Three nights required three singers to replace Millicent Martin, who by now was appearing in the West End and in everything Lew Grade put on television. Barbara Evans sang on Fridays, Josephine Blake and later Annie Ross did Saturdays. On

My mother and father.
(Author's collection)

With my brother
Alfred. I tagged
along in his shadow.
(Author's collection)

My home from the age of three – Lower Farm, Kingweston. *(C. Pursey)*

Some of the Army's finest recruits, fighting the cold at Gallowgate Camp. I am on the extreme right. *(Author's collection)*

Klagenfurt Signals Squadron, 1951. I made a wretched Motor Transport Officer, more a Minicab Controller. *(Author's collection)*

At Exeter College, Oxford. Now firmly established as 'Ned'. *(Author's collection)*

Maggie Smith (left) and Pamela Harrington (right) define glamour in one of my Oxford revues. *(Getty Images)*

Floor-managing ATV's 'Breakfast Television' in the early days at Viking Studios.

Paper Talk (ATV Birmingham), 1957. Frankie Vaughn (seated left) and Douglas Warth (seated centre) prepare to discuss the 'Teddy boy' phenomenon. ('Table wine' had been taken.) *(Willoughby Gullachsen)*

In the heart of it on *TW3*'s studio floor. *(Radio Times)*

Some of *TW3*'s pioneers, January 1963. From left: David Frost, Al Mancini, Millicent Martin, me, Roy Kinnear, Kenneth Cope, David Kernan, Lance Percival and Willy Rushton. *(Getty Images)*

Filming *The Virgin Soldiers* on Singapore's infamous Bugis Street in 1967. 'Trixie' became captivated by Hywel Bennett. In front, John Dexter (dark-haired) tries not to be aware of her.

With lighting director Ken Higgins (right) and my vastly experienced co-producer Leslie Gilliat (left).

At work with Terry Glinwood, co-founder with me of Virgin Films, on the second of the *Up* films, *Up the Chastity Belt* (1971).

Eartha Kitt purred mischievously on *Up the Chastity Belt*, causing some embarrassment for her co-star, Frankie Howerd. I stand in.

Sundays Cleo Laine obliged. Occasionally they were backed by dancers led initially by the Japanese-Canadian David Toguri. Very soon Alan Bennett nicknamed them 'the Viet Cong Dancers'. When David left to twirl Anna Neagle around the stage of the Adelphi Theatre in *Charlie Girl* a handsome French-Swiss, Rene Sartoris, took over and the troupe soon became 'the Pompidou Dancers'.

Deciding on the semi-regular conversationalists was the most intriguing part of assembling the show. Undimmed by half an hour of human unhappiness on the *TW3* pilot, I consulted Kenneth Tynan again. This time he suggested Patrick Campbell (Lord Glenavy), the patrician Irish journalist and humourist. We had lunch at the Café Royal Grill, and Paddy and Ken, two celebrated stutterers, competed in hesitation. Paddy had an irresistible set piece – how he had only appeared on one television programme in his life and how it had been an unmitigated disaster. In the early days of ITV he was tried out at ATV's New Cross Empire studio. It was all very glamorous. A limousine purred him to the place; champagne was produced and poured and placed before him. Beautiful women were on hand to minister to his needs. Never had he felt more cosseted. He hardly realised that the programme had begun. Famous people talked earnestly and confidently. Early on someone turned to him and put a question, 'Does your editor think of your ideas or do you?' Patrick was stunned by the idiocy of the question. No words came. From that moment he was ignored. He remained silent throughout the ninety minutes which the Sunday afternoon programme lasted.

He was anxious to know if this encouraged me to engage him. He went on to particularise the consonants, which inevitably led to disaster. 'S' was his Waterloo, illustrated by a story of trying to spit out a telephone number compounded of sixes and sevens. If there was one subject on which Patrick Campbell could talk with hilarious authority it was his disability.

We arranged that Frost's first question to him on air would get him off to the flying s . . . s . . . s . . . start he needed. Later he developed a rich vein of anecdotage around his wartime exploits in the Irish Navy.

Harvey Orkin's elevation was almost accidental. Harvey was a film agent. His clients included Peter Sellers and Paul Newman. I stumbled on him through an introduction from Burt Shevelove, a witty Anglophile and co-author of the book of *A Funny Thing Happened on the Way to the Forum*. I had tried to involve Burt but public performance was not his line. He recommended Harvey. The segment in the show I wanted him for was a mock trial. I was self-consciously looking for ways to avoid the basic chat-show simplicity of a host and one or two guests by creating a dramatic situation. It worked perfectly on the pilot but disastrously on the first weekend. I asked Gerald Kaufman, another debutante, to assume the persona of a historical monster and defend his record against a cross-examiner. As a closet film buff, Gerald chose to be Louis B. Mayer. Burt's introduction to a Hollywood insider with a taste for performance gave me the perfect questioner. Harvey crossed swords so wittily with Gerald, a brilliant devil's advocate, that it looked as if we had hit upon a winning formula. With a different subject on the first weekend the idea sank hopelessly; but at least we had found a sharp, new, potential talker in Gerald and a star in Harvey.

There was one unfortunate side-effect of the announcement that *Not So Much a Programme More a Way of Life* was to take the air three nights a week. An unknown woman in the Midlands – Wednesbury, I think – announced that she was giving up her job in order to monitor what promised to be a 'festival of filth'. The *Daily Mail* rang me for a comment. I speculated on what could be the job she was giving up to check on a show that was airing on Fridays, Saturdays and Sundays at around eleven o'clock at night. The *Mail* printed my speculation with the obvious implication that she must have been plying a dodgy sexual trade. Mary Whitehouse sued. Not me, fortunately, but the *Daily Mail*. They paid her five thousand pounds, which became the seed money to form the National Viewers and Listeners Association. Thus in creating a monster did I do most harm to television in my entire career.

Mrs Whitehouse was always quick with a writ. Dennis Potter's mother got the better of her when Mrs W. asserted on Radio 4's *Midweek* in the eighties that one of Dennis's TV plays showed his mother in flagrante. The character was a fiction. Mrs Potter collected fifteen thousand pounds. A few years later A. N. Wilson libelled Mrs Whitehouse on a technicality on my Radio 4 show *Loose Ends*. The redoubtable Mary stood out for fifteen thousand and got it.

The first transmission was on Friday, 13 November 1964. Much as we had refined the formula during the six pilots we had not refined it enough. Fans of *That Was The Week That Was* found too little that was familiar. Enemies found too much which revived old grievances. We strengthened the resolve of our opponents and divided our friends. Friday night produced a mass of attacking phone calls including one from the young drama producer Tony Garnett, who had been rowing with Baverstock about cutbacks in drama production. He congratulated Donald on having 'fallen flat on his face'. It was a far cry from the euphoria of *TW3* and we still had Saturday and Sunday to go.

One undoubted success was Patrick Campbell, whose stutter and wit kept viewers somewhere between the edge of the chair and the aisles. Eleanor Bron was also an instant hit. She introduced her Conservative Party supporter, Lady Pamela Stitty: 'It's never easy to choose a leader. You see, leaders are not made in a day. Of course Alec was. He's rather the exception. That's why we're trying to find another method of choosing . . .' John Bird's Jomo Kenyatta, developed from his Establishment monologues, now sounded like Idi Amin. He announced peaceful plans to take over Britain. 'No doubt there will be the occasional blood bath. But, I always say, you can't make an omelette without layin' eggs. I myself will temporarily assume the office of Queen until a reliable native replacement can be found.' This went down well with everyone except the Kenya High Commission. John Bird was able to give Mr Kenyatta's reply the next night. 'Good Evenin'. Well, as I always say, in the words of an old proverb, he who is without stones let him throw himself into the glass house . . .'

A fairly typical press reaction was Peter Black in the *Daily Mail*: 'The formula is not as good as the old inspired casualness of *TW3* (why does TV stick to this superstition of never repeating good ideas?) but will work well enough if it can find . . . more speakers like Kaufman and Patrick Campbell.' As the weekends followed the balance between talk and sketches settled. In addition to Paddy, Harvey, Denis Norden and Bernard Levin, other visitors included Jonathan Miller, Norman St John Stevas, Brigid Brophy, Malcolm Muggeridge, Ian Macleod, A. J. Ayer, Nicholas Tomalin, Peter Sellers, George Melly, Peter Hall, Claude Cockburn, James Mossman, Robert Shaw, Henry Fairlie, Dee Wells and many others.

John Bird's Harold Wilson monologues began to draw blood. John was asked to provide the cabaret at a Press Club evening. The prime minister was guest of honour. The pre-dinner Wilson was affable and encouraging but, Bird remembered, 'I said things that the pressmen knew Wilson knew and was thinking but wasn't saying out loud . . . afterwards he didn't speak to me at all'. John was encouraged by the prime minister's reaction which was typical of the new government's attitude. Satire was something ordained by God with which to beat the Tories. It was entirely inappropriate to use it against a Labour administration. 'Bad show, chaps,' as the Western Brothers might have chorused twenty years before. New Labour reacted in much the same way thirty-odd years later.

Eleanor Bron continued to pillory Alec Douglas-Home – 'I think people have been jolly unkind about Alec . . . I do rather wish that people could get a chance to see him in committee, because he is absolutely staggering there – he's forceful and dynamic – you wouldn't recognise him'. She and John Fortune found a new rich vein of 'relationship dialogues' in the manner of Mike Nichols and Elaine May. On one of the Sunday pilots Eleanor had improvised two sketches with Mike Nichols, who was visiting England. Now she and John developed some of the ideas they had played with at the Establishment and were a few years later to turn into a stylish BBC 2 series, *Where Was Spring?* Wiped now, of course.

Roy Hudd's finest hour was a manic performance as Ken Dodd. Dodd's season at the Palladium had made him a society favourite. Harold Wilson and John Osborne were his most famous and eloquent fans. Dick Vosburgh wrote a brilliant ten-minute sketch on the premise of Ken Dodd as Jimmy Porter berating his wife across the ironing board.

By now we were well removed from a pious original intention to let the chat-show content of the programme spring exclusively out of the issues raised in a preceding sketch. However, the biggest public row did start with a sketch by David Webster. The subject was birth control. I had commissioned it during the run of *TW3*. The moment passed before I could use it but I kept it on file. In mid-February 1965 there were two headlined reports of Catholic priests who vowed they would leave the Church if it did not change its attitude to birth control. In Webster's sketch a reactionary priest, played by Brian Murphy, calls on an Irish mother (Patricia Routledge) in a Liverpool slum. Miss Routledge's casting was an added irony. She had turned down a John Mortimer sketch the week before on grounds of taste. Beryl Reid then had a great success with it. However, to show no ill feeling I offered Patricia the role of the mother. She accepted it without a query, only to find a gigantic storm of controversy bursting around her.

Father O'Connor enquires after the health of the fifteen or sixteen of Mrs O'Hara's children. Mrs O'Hara offers him a drop of whiskey. After asking about another two of her kids the priest says, 'Won't yous have one yourself?' Mrs O'Hara replies that she can't afford it. 'Now,' says the priest, 'talking on that subject . . .' And she forks out two pounds for the church. The priest then remarks that he sees, 'no signs of a future blessing on the way'. 'No, Father,' says Mrs O'Hara. The priest is immediately suspicious. 'Have you sinned, Mrs O'Hara? Have you been using those dirty, black Protestant pills?' She denies this and explains that her husband needs his expensive fill of Guinness before he can perform and, 'it's hard to make a decent living in Liverpool unless you play an electric ukelele. He's too old now to join a group.' The priest gives her back ten shillings: 'Spend it wisely, won't you?' he says. 'God bless you, Father. I'll buy some little shoes for Michael.' This does not find favour. 'You will not, Mrs O'Hara. You will give it to himself for his porter. A working man needs it.' Mrs O'Hara agrees and the priest finishes his drink: 'Well, now, I'll be off.' He mentions three more children: 'Oh, and give my regards to Declan and Terence and Eileen.' Then in a final aside to camera, 'We'll catch the Chinese up yet . . .'

Norman St John Stevas eloquently and vigorously argued the Catholic case. Dee Wells opposed him. The sympathy of the studio audience was with her, especially in her condemnation of the Catholic Church for refusing to allow the United Nations to distribute contraceptives in the Third World. So intense was the argument that another guest, the American humourist Al Capp, sat for twelve minutes in unaccustomed silence.

Simon Mahon, Labour Member for Bootle, tabled a motion of condemnation in the House: 'The BBC . . . have outraged the conscience of the people of Merseyside . . . by transmitting a disgusting and grossly offensive sketch in their production of *Not So Much a Programme More a Way of Life* . . . deplores this flagrant and nauseating attack on the dignity of family life . . . and demands an apology.' Early in the office on Tuesday I fielded an anonymous challenge to a duel from a caller from Liverpool. Hugh Greene made a half apology, arguing that the matter was one of public interest and that St John Stevas had properly presented the Catholic case. More MPs joined in the condemnation. In the Lords Lord Longford denounced 'a revolting programme', *The Times* thundered against us. The *Mail* pleaded for a sense of humour: 'Let us discuss the current question and not should David Frost and Ned Sherrin be whipped through the streets? . . . Britain is largely run by puritanical pressure groups of one sort or another. I don't accept their claim that nobody must make fun of them. They should be good-humouredly and steadily made fun of. I object to the apologies offered them.'

Punch concentrated on the viewing figures. 'There are now more than six million viewers each night it's on – twice as many viewers as the BBC has ever had before for a Friday series at that hour and three times as many on Sunday evenings. The Saturday evening figure is the biggest since *TW3*.' Not bad for a series which, in retrospect, tends to be written off as an anticlimax. Not quite 'limping', as Humphrey Carpenter implies in *That Was Satire That Was*.

By now David was well into his weekly commuter trip to the States. Flying out on Mondays to broadcast from New York on Tuesdays and returning to us on Thursday. Although the American version of *TW3* is still remembered fondly over there as a breakthrough, it was a limp, lacklustre affair. It was produced by a charming, senior 'man of the theatre', agent, film producer, Leland Heyward, at that time married to Pamela, originally Digby, previously Churchill, subsequently Harriman. A dignified legend, Leland was probably the only producer who could have put *TW3* on in America in that nervous era. He acted as a Trojan Horse to transport the wild young men

through the gates of the NBC establishment. However, once let
loose inside its walls they found that their swords had been
blunted en route.

With an irony that had been forgotten by the time *Saturday
Night Live* was a late-night triumph for NBC a decade later in
the seventies, the network ruled that in 1964 nearing midnight
was no time for comedy. *TW3* was scheduled for 8.30 p.m. on
Tuesdays. They still clung to the opening words, blithely singing,
'That was the week that was – it's over let it go . . .' before it had
really started.

I watched the first programme. Admirable writers and performers had been assembled, including Eliot Reid, Tom Lehrer,
Henry Morgan, Robert Morse, Tom Meehan, Tony Geiss and
Buck Henry. With the usual instinct of Americans who invest in
success, Leland wanted to preserve everything he had bought.
That included our studio. His set designer recreated the grotty
old BBC bare-walls setting complete with pipes, wires, hooks
and air vents. However, as this was colour television he bathed
everything in delicate pastel shades, giving the overall effect of a
deliciously edible birthday cake. Without the 'grotty' background the 'gritty' intent of the material was diluted. In another
slavish, misunderstood attempt to mimic the British show the
script was buttoned up days before transmission. Our carelessly
intrusive cameras were directed impromptu out of topical necessity. In America the moves in and out of shot were carefully
choreographed since last-minute news was not to be catered for.
Leland made sure that the content was defused, and Nancy
Holmes, a lone new face, cast in Millicent Martin's role, lacked
both her striking singing voice and her comic punch. She provided yet another antiseptic ingredient.

David had to fight harder for his spots in America. On the
first camera rehearsal I watched him fight determinedly to preserve his second featured moment. He had earned an easier
passage. However, he won in the end and the programme

became generally identified with him. It limped into a second season but eventually, to quote David's autobiography, it 'had just not prevailed in the ratings over the combined strength of *Peyton Place* and *Petticoat Junction*'.

David used his opportunity brilliantly to gain entry into the American television system. His shuttling to and fro across the Atlantic was an awesome spectacle. 'Sorry, Mr Frost, caviar again' was the BOAC air staff's standing joke. I once travelled back with him. We approached Kennedy Airport long after the normal check-in time. His car telephone ensured that the plane was held. We were ushered obsequiously through an emergency luggage vent. Getting him on board at the last possible moment seemed to be a matter of pride for the young crew. Once in his seat he lolled into grey somnolence and then deep sleep until we touched down at Heathrow. By then, I suppose, the effects of a sleeping pill, slipped down on leaving the office in Manhattan, had worn off.

The double life made it hard for him to keep a perspective on the impact of American news on an English audience. It provoked our only serious studio disagreement. John Bird wrote a particularly sharp sketch dealing with the ironies of a white, liberal television producer patronising a cultivated black newsreader, played by Kenny Lynch. Over the weekend the news of Malcolm X's assassination came through. David reacted to it with the awareness of how much it would mean in America. Having played a key part in the *TW3* Kennedy programme, he wanted us to stage a similar memorial show. I did not judge that Malcolm X's death had caused shockwaves in Britain comparable with those aroused by the Kennedy tragedy. We played the sketch.

It was clear that our careers were ready to go in different directions. Happily we have stayed friends. David's American experience confirmed for him that in American television the face in front of the camera controls the show. The role of the producer is to service the star, who frequently owns the controlling company. This was not a role that any BBC producer who had been trained for the responsibility of current affairs programmes would have found appropriate at the time.

In the end the divorce was a shotgun affair. The BBC wielded the weapon after the last weekend of *Not So Much a Programme*. It was the end of March. On the Friday night show Eleanor Bron discussed Sir Alec Douglas-Home's leadership again in her Lady Pamela Stitty character. In the ensuing discussion (chaired by David) between Ian Macleod, Patrick Campbell and Bernard Levin, Bernard dropped the word 'cretin' into his assessment of Douglas-Home. It became a famous red herring. Campbell first picked up the word and belaboured Levin with it. Macleod engaged him on the more serious side of his argument. Patrick Campbell persisted in putting Levin in the wrong; Frost drew from him first a modification then a withdrawal and finally an apology. He controlled the incident impeccably but the scent of scandal lingered.

There was a lull on Saturday 27 March. The final programme of the series and the one that broke this particular camel's back was on the 28th. The error of judgement was entirely mine. For some time we had been preparing an elaborate animated film – a mock-operatic treatment of the Duke of Windsor's abdication crisis written by the critic B. A. Young. Mild to a fault, its stance, if anything, was sympathetic to the duke. Just as it was completed the duke was admitted to hospital for an eye operation. I shelved it until he was better. However, I worried that it had cost about five thousand pounds of licence-payers' money. That was an enormous sum for a seven- or eight-minute segment forty years ago. It preyed on my mind. Eventually the duke went home. I breathed a sigh of relief. We had just time to put out the highly polished piece on film on that last Sunday night of the series.

Early on the Sunday morning the duke's sister, the Princess Royal, died. Neither Frost nor Alasdair Milne had any idea of the closeness of the family relationship – brother and sister. I knew perfectly well but I decided to take this last chance to justify the expenditure and included the sketch in the running order. The timing was interpreted as a deliberate and tasteless lampoon on the royal family in their moment of grief. Compounded by the 'cretin incident', it provoked a decision, sudden and irrevocable, that *Not So Much a Programme* would not return in the autumn. Barry Norman's footsteps were back on the walk-up in Dover Street.

One consolation was a fine piece of invective by John Osborne which he published in the *Sunday Times* on 11 April 1965 under the title 'Middle Class Poison'.

As we all know, most of the stones have been hurled up at Mr David Frost and Mr Ned Sherrin, two faces which seem to loom in the dreams of many, and can even be seen by some leering out of every window at the Television Centre. In spite of a great deal of simulated boredom expressed about these two figures they have set more typewriters rattling in Fleet Street than anyone else who has ever broken and entered our homes from the little box of faded promises . . . But why have these two particular young men aroused even old, Lib–Lab lions like Cassandra from their lairs? First, because they are both what is still considered, even in these treacherous days, young. Secondly they work in a perversion of creative democracy called a medium in which every viewing Jack likes to think he is as good as his masters. Almost everyone, from dealers in stolen goods to property-developers to schoolgirls and newspapermen, wants to get up there and show that they can do just as well if not better.

Third, almost no one *listens* or watches. For instance, no one seems to have grasped that Bernard Levin withdrew both the 'cretin' and 'imbecile' (used in reference to Sir Alec Douglas-Home) on the programme. Some twenty weeks of the programme passed by before anyone saw the prurient possibilities of attacking it and went for the birth-control sketch. It is not surprising that no one understood the point of the Duke of Windsor's sketch, which was not an attack on royalty but on the British public's insistence that their totems play out an idea of marriage that is as unreal as a comic opera . . . The English Bourgeois – or bourgeoisie – is violent because his intuition is faulty and his loyalties collusive. His objectives narrowed down to a nagging, painful sore of human under-nourishment, he is understandably inaccessible to the relaxation of wit, irony, tones of voice or the delicacy of affection or even love that often huddles beneath the most outrageous lampoon.

It was in this year that my father died. As his strength began to fail he and my mother had moved up the road to a house on which he had had his sights for some years. It was a pleasant, detached house in the village of Alford – Parson Woodforde's parish centuries before. Set apart from the daily business on which he had worked so hard and presided over so autocratically for so long, his energy diminished and he hugged his fireside. My brother was running the farm – at last on his own.

In 1965 I was driven down to Somerset to spend a night, knowing that he would not live long. He had shrunk into himself. He was very small and frail. Cutting myself off from the farm left us little conversation which we could share unselfconsciously. We spent a few unreal hours and I had to leave on the Sunday evening. All his life he had been an undemonstrative man, with one exception. He assumed, expected, looked for, a goodnight, or goodbye, kiss from his sons. My brother and I had gone through all the stages of doing it happily when small, beginning to be self-conscious about it as we grew older, hating it, rebelling against it and finally coming round to it. As I got up to go that last weekend to say goodbye

I knew it would be the last. A car drew up outside. By an odd coincidence the driver was the friend of my father who had knocked us over twenty-six years earlier, before the war, when we were on our way to book seats for the pantomime. The party came in, aware, gently, consciously genial. Suddenly the occasion became public and I did not like to go across to kiss him. I saw his sadness, but I left. I did it a week later when he was dead.

My mother lived a dozen years more, lovingly looked after by my brother and his housekeeper. Towards the end she became very vague and would gaze intently at the television screen if I was on and say, 'I know that man!'

One Boxing Day we settled down together in front of the set after lunch and watched the opening sequences of the American musical *The Unsinkable Molly Brown*. It starts with a long, energetic dance routine choreographed by Peter Gennaro for Debbie Reynolds. Miss Reynolds, playing a tom-boy, runs, jumps and romps for what must be at least ten minutes with a group of equally frenzied chorus boys. The scene is a farmyard and they cover haystacks, fences and barns. The routine builds to an all-out climax designed to draw a round of applause in the cinema. As Miss Reynolds finished her stint with arms spread wide the scene faded. My mother leant forward with a look of faint disapproval on her face.

'Oh dear,' she said, 'I do hope those aren't local children.'

Two series having been taken off the BBC was contemplating a third. I was at some pains to get it right. In the later weeks of *Not So Much a Programme* a palace revolution had ousted Donald Baverstock. Alasdair Milne soon followed him voluntarily into exile. Nobody was very keen to handle a potential hot potato but Michael Peacock took some responsibility and Huw Wheldon moved into Baverstock's role as controller of programmes.

The coup was announced on a Friday. On Monday morning I was required to present myself in Wheldon's office to discuss the final weeks of the series. The change was instant and dramatic. All Donald's effects had been removed, none of Huw's yet installed. Floor, walls, desk were bare. I took in the room at a glance and said bitchily, 'Ah, Huw, put the stamp of your personality on the office already.' He laughed and we went on to discuss the situation. I told Frost proudly about the remark immediately afterwards – ignoring the fact that whatever Wheldon lacked it was not personality. The incident rebounded immediately. It duly appeared on the *Daily Mirror* gossip page the next day. As there had only been the two of us in the office and as the leak was unlikely to have come from Huw, I immediately suspected Frost. However, it was never mentioned.

The chairman of the governors, Lord Normanbrook, the director general, Sir Hugh Greene, the director of television, Kenneth Adam, and Wheldon were all involved in the last 'satirical' throw. Indeed, I had to fly back from a holiday in Cannes to meet Huw and Normanbrook at the Television Centre. There was one point on which all my masters were agreed: Frost must go. The insistence that the major royal error on the last weekend had been mine alone cut no ice. Officials in broadcasting always identify the success of a programme with the face on the screen – their wives want to meet it, they themselves want to hobnob with it. Their children want its autograph. Unfortunately in this case custom was working the other way. They polarised their fear of the late-night monster around a determination to behead it by sacking David. It was unfair, but I was intrigued by the challenge of being without him. I had done three winters with David. Now facing a third series without his support was both daunting and alluring. It was to be called *BBC-3* to suggest a certain independence from the BBC monoliths, BBC 1 and BBC 2.

I broke the news to David over breakfast at the Ritz on Monday 17 May. We agreed that I would let him say that he had opted out. I kept to that until the truth became general knowledge and he had secured his future. David reacted with magnificent resilience. If Kitty Muggeridge suggested that he had 'risen without trace', Bernard Levin was already beginning to polish up his vignette of Frost as Britain's 'Man of the Sixties'. Now, David took on the two men who had been his greatest enemies and wooed them with a skilful offensive. Having done some groundwork with the LE producer Bill Cotton, he invited the head of the department at the BBC, Tom Sloan (who always resented *TW3*) to a glamorous dinner at the Top of the 6's in New York. In the course of the evening he sold him a revue series, *The Frost Report*. He was to star in it. He also introduced Ronnie Barker and Ronnie Corbett as a comedy team as well as John Cleese and Julie Felix. Simultaneously he returned to the doors of Associated Rediffusion which he had been told never again to darken and developed the *Frost Programme*, three nights a week, which gave full scope to his talk-show ambitions.

Meanwhile, back at the BBC, Huw Wheldon enthused about a mystical Corporation instinct for defusing awkward situations. David, he said, had never acquired it. We needed someone with a sixth sense of what was right and proper for the BBC, someone who would instinctively intervene at the right moment in any discussion to rob it of outrage and offence, magisterially guiding argument on impeccably acceptable lines. We searched and emerged with Robert Robinson, an admirable broadcaster who gave loyal service, especially when he was called upon to introduce and lend his apparent approval to sketches which he disliked or thought unfair or unfunny. He had been handling the interview side of *BBC-3* as well as Wheldon had hoped when after about three weeks he was ambushed by Ken Tynan and the word 'fuck'.

I was aware of a long 'feud' between Tynan and Mary McCarthy which had been fought over the years in the letters columns of various literary magazines. Since Mary was to be in London, I liked the idea of presenting them in public combat. Experience of famous feuds sounded a note of caution. Tynan and McCarthy had never met. Celebrated enemies are frequently charmed by meeting their opponents, especially when they are as bright as were Tynan and McCarthy. I lunched them with Robert at the Café Royal. We set about finding a premise for the debate. Sure enough, they agreed about almost everything. They could hardly remember the cause of the original disagreement. They both felt that writing to the papers is a prime source of misunderstanding and a subject in itself. We nearly settled on a critical analysis of Truman Capote's documentary novel *In Cold Blood*. Had we done so, 'that word' would never have been uttered. In the end the only area on which they could agree to disagree was censorship. Tynan was against it unreservedly. McCarthy could visualise a case for censorship in some circumstances.

Ken said nothing about his intentions in the hospitality room before the broadcast. He had decided that he could not properly argue his case against censorship and at the same time censor himself. On the other hand, he felt that to tell Robert or me beforehand that he was going to use the word 'fuck' would embarrass us into forbidding him from saying it. So he said nothing. In the discussion he introduced the word in as quiet and low-key a manner as possible, saying, 'I doubt if there are any rational people to whom the word "fuck" would be particularly diabolical, revolting or totally forbidden.' I hardly heard it. I was saying, 'Cut to two,' or something like that at the time. Neither Robert nor Mary looked surprised or lingered on the moment. The reason Mary was unsurprised was made clear in Kathleen Tynan's biography of her husband. In it she reveals that she and McCarthy's husband welcomed their partners back to the Tynan flat in Mount Street after the programme with cries of 'You said it!'

The furore seems the more incredible in retrospect. At the switchboard all hell was let loose. Asked to comment immediately after the programme, I could only manage, 'Well, it's a better word than "super",' which was much in vogue at the time. My favourite postscript came from a woman who taught a class of inner-city infants in London. So many Monday morning front-page headlines featured 'That word!' that her charges pestered her all through their lessons to find out what it was. She hedged until the lunch break when her patience ran out. 'What did 'ee say, miss? That man on telly on Saturday?' She braced herself. 'He said "fuck".' There was a groan of disappointment. One little boy voiced the feelings of his classmates. 'Is that all? We thought 'ee said "cunt".'

It was saddening to see the disproportionate space and emphasis given to 'Tynan's word' in Ken's obituaries. Apart from his critical brilliance, I valued his enthusiasm and his keenness to find or recommend new talents and give them a platform.

In the programme the incident had one obvious benefit. The viewing audience found us. *BBC-3* was certainly the wrong title. It had failed to indicate our independence from the mainstream of BBC 1 and BBC 2. Early viewing figures were disappointing. If quizzed, people were inclined to say, 'BBC 3? I can't even get BBC 2.' The Tynan incident solved that. I had nearly called the programme *It's All Been Done Before* in an attempt to pre-empt criticism. I wish I had. Instead I saved the phrase for Lynda Baron's opening song: 'It's all been done before/But so has spring and summer'.

Robert Robinson had no chance of rescuing the Tynan moment and in general he handled the discussions skilfully, though I missed sometimes the sense of danger, of balancing on a knife-edge which Frost often brought. On one occasion Peregrine Worsthorne (soon to flourish the f-word himself on ITV) had advanced a theory that there is indisputably a ruling class. It was a proposition which Gore Vidal was anxious to demolish. On the air Gore was dazzling. Eventually he cornered Perry into a position from which there was no escape. Sadistically I was enjoying sending the cameras slowly in for the kill – that moment when the talking-head has no more to say, the mouth is open and defeat shines clearly from the victim's eyes. Infuriatingly Robert filled the dramatic silence with a supplementary question and Perry, the panting fish, was off the hook. He reminded me of it ruefully at the Barbican years later: 'What an escape!'

In many ways *BBC-3* (Saturday nights only) contained the best sketch material of all three shows in the series. John Bird, sometimes working with Alan Watkins, sometimes alone, perfected his Wilson, his George Brown and Ted Heath impersonations. We had moved on towards visual as well as vocal effects with the skills of the brilliant make-up artist Sandra Shepherd.

People commented on 'lack of bite'. This was often because 'attacking' sketches had become the norm rather than the six-day wonder they had seemed on the breakthrough *TW3*. John Bird's Wilson is a good example:

> Now, I imagine you'll think it a bit peculiar for me to appear on such a gay, lighthearted programme as this. But, you know, I don't have to go on being prime minister for a living – I could always go back to being a socialist . . . I'll be frank with you, I'll admit in the privacy of the television studio, that all is not well with the government. Some of my colleagues have not performed as well as I expected them to. Even worse, some of them have. But there are better prospects to come. This morning, for example, George Brown told me he had seen the Queen. Well, there it is – some people see snakes, some people see elephants, George sees the Queen.

John Bird has quoted Marcia Falkender in suggesting that he and Watkins were sufficiently successful at thinking Bird into Wilson's mind to provoke some paranoia at No. 10. Not too hard in retrospect.

Alan Bennett joined on a whimsical contract. He would meet John Bird and John Fortune towards the end of the week and see if the spirit moved him. If it did not, he went home and the other two, perhaps with Doug Fisher, improvised without him. It was during *BBC-3* that Alan first tried out his Virginia Woolf monologue which later found a place in his play *Forty Years On*: 'Of all the honours that fell upon Virginia's head, none I think pleased her more than the *Evening Standard* award for the tallest woman writer of 1933, an award she took by a short neck from Elizabeth Bowen, and rightly, I think, because she was in a very real sense the tallest writer I've ever known. Which is not of course to say that her stories were tall – they were not. They were short.'

Towards the end of the run I was approached by Columbia Pictures to develop a film project on a two-year contract. The alternative was yet another round of Saturday-night trouser-dropping from which my BBC typecasting made it hard to escape. It was a chance to do something new in a medium which I imperfectly understood. I said 'yes.' I was not sure I was right.

The last moments of *BBC-3* were emotional. I knew that I was ending my loose arrangement with the BBC and going off to do other things. The four seasons of the late-night shows had been special. Music quickly evokes nostalgia and the potency was strong on that occasion. Peter Greenwell arranged Ron Grainer's three themes in counterpoint. They were sung by Lynda Baron, the resident singer on *BBC-3*, by Cleo Laine, representing *Not So Much a Programme*, and finally – the link back to the first pilot, the musical corncrake sound with which it all began – Millicent Martin, hitting in with 'That was the week that was/It's over let it go . . .'

CHAPTER 7

Hurray for Hollywood . . .
It's So Terrific It's Not Even Good

Sexing up porridge is an unlikely subject for a film, but it was
the motor for the plot of a movie treatment which two dramatic
critics, Herbert Kretzmer and Milton Shulman, sold to Columbia
Pictures in 1965. Their hero was an impressionable advertising
man faced with a sluggish porridge account. They explored the
emotional strain that selling it with sex would have on his hitherto happy home life. They called it *Goldilocks*. The deal was
engineered by John Van Eyssen, a South African ex-actor who
had been Shulman's agent before joining Columbia with one of
those whimsical movie executive titles like 'Vice President with
Responsibility for Creative Endeavour (Europe)'. He was easily
embarrassed by any reference to a faltering, by now faltered,
career as an actor – usually playing blond, uniformed Nazi officers. He answered to the head of the European office, Max
Setton. Setton had an endearing habit of saying, 'Before I can give
you any decision on that I must make a hemisphere to hemisphere telephone conversation.' He meant, 'I have to call New
York.' He also had a penchant for lunching at the Jardin des
Gourmets in Soho, advising visiting Americans, 'It is very good for
lunch, but do not come in the evening. Then it is a notorious

haunt for homosexuals.' Which probably hoisted the evening trade in visiting Americans.

The *Goldilocks* material could be loosely described as 'satirical' so Herbert and Milton suggested that I be invited to produce it. Columbia offered a generous two-year contract, negotiated by John Heyman, father of the producer of the current Harry Potter series of films, at that time my agent. My choice was simple. I could stay at the BBC and embark on yet another round of the Saturday-night sensation or I could decamp to explore a different medium which I imperfectly understood.

Just how imperfectly it took me some time to realise. As a country child I had not been raised on Saturday-morning kids' cinema clubs or regular twice-weekly visits to the local fleapit. Occasionally my brother and I had cycled the ten miles to Yeovil for a film 'event' at the Odeon – like *Desert Victory* or *The Overlanders*. My father had also taken us on a rare outing when a film based on A. G. Street's novel *Farmer's Glory* was advertised – William Hartnell was the agricultural juvenile. It was a disappointment. Too much romance not enough cows. I had cycled to Glastonbury to see Barry K. Barnes in a *Scarlet Pimpernel* story and to Street for *The Birth of the Blues*. At school I had persuaded the headmaster to let us off prep one night because *Great Expectations* was being shown in Bruton and it was 'educational'. Somehow I managed to catch all the Gainsborough romances – *The Wicked Lady*, *The Man in Grey*, *Blanche Fury*, *Jassy*, *Fanny by Gaslight* – and the pick of the Ealing comedies. In the Army a visit to the AKC had been one of the few easy entertainments available. At Oxford I must have seen more, but one double bill is all that stays in my mind. *Wages of Fear* was teamed with Harold Lloyd in . . . was it *High Dizzy* or *Safety Last*? When I started to work with Caryl Brahms in the fifties I fell in with her regular attendance at the Academy or the Curzon but without zeal.

It was an odd time to choose to break into films. The industry was embarked on its slide into penury. Money was scarce – though not as scarce as it was to be ten years later. In my innocence I determined to make as many films as I could as quickly as possible. I hoped to achieve a crash apprenticeship in cinema in much the same way that I had learned to produce television programmes in my early days at ATV, and then move on to more prestigious projects. Initially it seemed an exciting, glamorous step up to be a film producer.

When I had joined the BBC people were still paid in guineas rather than pounds. If they were not, they had been until very recently. Producers were not allowed to negotiate fees. We had been protected by a community of genteel but tight bookers and negotiators. Communication inside the Corporation was usually by reams of memoranda.

No one wrote memos in the movies. The exception was John Trevelyan, the secretary of the Board of Film Censors, whose manner was much more BBC. Complementary to his role of cleaning up the cinema he had an obsessive penchant for telling dirty jokes. Having no memos to send, I trailed around from office to sound stage to editing suite trying to learn to be a film producer by osmosis.

Although Kretzmer and Shulman had worked out their storyline in considerable detail, it was not yet a screenplay. A team of writers was needed to achieve the mixture of parody, fantasy and satire which they envisaged on the screen. I made some practical moves to develop the treatment. I talked to writers. I wooed directors. I listened to the wisdom, or at least the anecdotage, of experienced producers whom I met at cocktail parties, screenings or premieres. Anthony Mann, Sam Spiegel, Carl Foreman, David Deutsch, Irving Allen, Mike Frankovich were all around.

I learned how to schedule and budget my film once I had a screenplay from Marty Feldman and Barry Took. (All this was before Marty Feldman's great celebrity, although he and Barry were already successful radio and television writers (*Round the*

Horne, Bootsie and Snudge). Marty was beginning to emerge as a television performer on *At Last the 1948 Show*.) However, even with writers, scripts, schedule, budget and, in theory, Columbia's backing, there was still an unreal air about the project.

Nothing more excited the front offices of film companies in the 1960s than an orgy of speculative casting. If they didn't know that George Segal was determined to make a film in England, they were sure that Albert Finney was keen to have a go at comedy. A part written for Alec Guinness could easily be rejigged for Richard Chamberlain with a minimum of rewriting. If an actor did show an interest in a role, the front office couldn't wait to report that, although he may have been box-office gold last week, this week he was box-office poison and you couldn't finance a trailer on him, let alone a movie and certainly not at the price the agent was asking. Confusingly, the agent had not heard that his client was box-office poison.

The months slipped by and after two years I had still not assembled what Columbia considered a 'package'. I was told that they were not going to pick up their option on my contract. It seemed a very reasonable decision. I began to think of going back into television. One advantage of these unproductive years had been that I was able to dip my toe into theatrical waters, directing Danny La Rue in *Come Spy with Me*, and to give more time to writing with Caryl. She was always sceptical of my ability to make a movie – even after I had produced nine.

In 1965 Danny La Rue was at the peak of his cabaret success. From dominating the revues at Winston's, the Mayfair night club, he had set up his own club off Hanover Square and was very much the toast of the town. Single-handed he removed the stigma attached to 'drag' and turned it into an accepted family entertainment. When he went out in pantomime he became favourite coach-party fodder. When he performed on his own premises he was lionised by the Nureyevs, Fonteyns, Cowards and Dietrichs.

I was never quite sure why I was drafted in to direct *Come Spy with Me*. I suppose it was the reputation which still clung to *TW3*. The musical was a James Bondian romp by Danny's regular sketch-writer at his club, Bryan Blackburn. It was not about to win prizes but it was an efficient vehicle for the star, who could dress up as a lady in the service of his country, foil diabolical plots and emerge as a man in the finale with a reassuring, deep-voiced cry of 'Wotcher, mates' proving his virility beyond any reasonable doubt.

Nearly forty years on in the development of the musical it is hard to imagine such a glorified cabaret being staged today. How's this for a period piece? 'The villains, Dr Sigmund Fink, his devilish Momma and his vile accomplices, Tamara Flesch and "Greensleeves", are after a fantastic pre-Viagra fertility drug invented by a Professor von Schlumpf – deceased. In pursuit are a crooning heart-throb, Agent VO3, and Agent Danny Rhodes, who is required to disguise himself in drag for the assignment because Fink knows him. However, before he died, von Schlumpf, in a final, fatal spasm, planted the magical drug on Mavis Apple who was operating the lift in which he was done to death.' 'The chase', as one account puts it, 'is on'. Fink chases the drug, Danny chases Fink, Agent VO3 mistakenly chases Mavis until all our heroes are captured, escape, are recaptured and then 'Mavis swallows the beastly drug'.

This inspired farrago enabled Danny to appear in, among other guises, those of an Irish nurse, a diplomat's wife and an Oriental entertainer performing a striptease cabaret in the 'Rice Room', the villains' headquarters. Richard Wattis was the head of MI6 giving exactly the performance as a precise civil servant which one would expect but arriving at it by painstaking, searching rehearsal. Barbara Windsor, a regular at the La Rue club, was Mavis and the popular singer Gary Miller played Agent VO3. We opened in Oxford and toured to Brighton and Golder's Green, the theatres filled by Danny's growing stardom.

Golder's Green remains in my mind because of a huge laugh on the first night caused by the similarity of the words 'Pssst!' and 'Pissed' in an exchange between Danny and Dickie Wattis. It stopped the show for at least a couple of minutes. I was standing at the back of the stalls with the leading lighting designer, Richard Pilbrow. As the house fell in at the simple joke he turned to me sardonically and whispered, 'That's what you came into the theatre for, isn't it?'

Sadly at the end of the week Gary Miller had a slight heart attack and the West End opening was postponed while we rehearsed a temporary replacement. After some argument this was the understudy, Craig Hunter. The crisis period lasted over a Whitsun weekend. We had a run through on the Friday, let a few friends in on the Saturday and, on Danny's instinct, performed the show for a packed, excited invited house on Whit Sunday. To this his fashionable following – the Nureyevs, the Fonteyns, the Cowards and the Dietrichs – all flocked. For the one time in the thousands of lives of Danny's audiences, they sat on their hands for him. Barbara was cheered to the rafters; for Danny they gave nothing. This made for an overtly tense Whit Monday but by Whit Tuesday – our opening night – the equilibrium was restored. The *Observer* was fascinated by the star: 'Never having seen his nightclub act, I wouldn't have believed the extent to which he disinfects the drag joke with humour, finesse and affection . . . For a start, he makes no real pretence of being a woman . . . like Dietrich, like Dors and Mae West he draws a laughing cartoon of the woman every man partly dreams of – absurdly seductive, preposterously available, yet under it all somehow one of the fellows.'

It ran for a year and a half – well over four hundred performances – and came off eventually when the producer realised that in the small Whitehall Theatre he wasn't making a weekly profit, even with full houses. This was 1965: 'Stalls and Circle 15/-, 12/6, 10/6, 8/6, Balcony 5/-. All bookable. Programme one shilling.'

One surprising result of directing *Come Spy with Me* was an invitation from the National Theatre. Incredibly, Ken Tynan had spotted a 'Brechtian' style in the production (God knows how). As Laurence Olivier's dramaturge he asked me to direct a new docu-drama about the Cuban Missile Crisis. It involved one meeting with Olivier, and long poring over the detailed synopsis the writer had drawn up. This was to be a sort of Latin American *Oh What a Lovely Crisis!* Irving Davies, the choreographer with whom I had done *Come Spy*, and I spent a deal of time trying to enliven it with Carmen Miranda routines. It didn't happen. My directing career ground to a halt. And my life as a film producer seemed to be drawing peacefully to its close.

Just in time Carl Foreman threw me a lifeline. Carl was a senior screenwriter and a producer with *The Men*, *High Noon* and *The Bridge on the River Kwai* among his credits. He had a near-impregnable position as an independent working through Columbia. In 1966 he had encouraged them to acquire Leslie Thomas's best-selling novel, *The Virgin Soldiers*. The book generously mixed slapstick, melodrama, wry humour and touchingly accurate observation as raw national service recruits tried to lose their virginity before they lost their lives in Malaya during the emergency back in the 1950s. The book held an artful balance between autobiographical reminiscence and optimistic sexual fantasy. Carl sat on the property for some time but his mind was on weightier matters – especially a mammoth Western starring Gregory Peck, another of his literate action-epics. Columbia was growing impatient to see a return on their investment; Leslie Thomas and his tiny but flamboyant agent, Desmond Elliot, were equally keen to see the novel on the big screen; Carl was embarrassed. I was only too available. I was, perhaps, twenty years nearer the age of the main characters and – hell! – this was the sixties. Youth was in. So Carl enlisted me to give the project a nudge.

To watch him handle Columbia politics was a revelation. After stumbling in the wilderness for two years I was magically translated from a contract producer on his way out to an independent with an exciting subject handed on a plate on improved terms. Better still, I was awarded a co-producer who knew what he was doing. Leslie Gilliat had produced innumerable English movies, many with his brother Sidney and his partner Frank Launder. With great tact and patience Leslie shouldered the detailed practical business of planning the film, leaving me to look after the 'artistic' tip of the iceberg.

Carl had already selected a director. John Dexter, a complex, difficult man, had a superb theatrical record at the Royal Court and the National Theatre. Dexter's long-time companion was Riggs O'Hara, an American-Italian actor whom John met when Riggs came to London with the *West Side Story* company in 1958. Riggs had a small part in *The Victors*, a Second World War epic which Carl wrote and directed. During shooting he formed a firm friendship with Carl's second wife, Eve. This led to John's introduction to the circle.

In *The Honourable Beast*, a 'posthumous autobiography' edited by Riggs, Dexter states his credo: 'Fury for perfection makes me difficult to work with. The pressure that people feel is merely the aftermath of the blast off. They have no right to stand too close unless they are insured against fire.' Not all his victims would agree that this is the last word. I knew John slightly. Caryl Brahms had given him a good notice for an early Sunday-evening production at the Royal Court. We were disposed to get on well with one another. I admired his theatre work: *Roots*, *Black Comedy*, *The Royal Hunt of the Sun* and *Chips with Everything*, which also dealt brilliantly with young national servicemen. Arguing with the author, Arnold Wesker, Dexter famously said, 'If you interfere again, Arnold, I'll direct this play the way you wrote it.' In the case of *The Royal Hunt* he claimed to have wanted to direct Peter Shaffer's play simply because of one stage direction: 'They cross the Andes'. Not a man to shirk a challenge? We would see.

In the beginning was the word. Leslie Thomas had written a script as part of his deal. It did not do justice to his novel. First we approached John McGrath, a playwright who had a sound, gritty, stage and television reputation. John loved the premise and settled down to produce a first treatment some hundred pages long. Unfortunately it sprang far more from his interest in war and his left-wing politics than from the events in Leslie Thomas's book. A lot of it excited Dexter and me. It dismayed Foreman and Thomas. McGrath was reluctant to go back to the original book so we moved on to another fine theatre and television playwright, John Hopkins. He solved most of the problems of adaptation with great speed. Low comedy was not his speciality, but there was enough of that and to spare in the original novel. He clarified the storyline and extracted the tender tale of young people struggling towards some knowledge of their sexual potential. At the same time he preserved the infectious sense of fun with which Thomas remembered so many essentially autobiographical incidents.

Now that we had enough to go on we could start thinking about casting, testing and location-hunting. When the time came for more rewrites Hopkins was not available and we needed some jokes, so Ian La Frenais, who with Dick Clement had written *The Likely Lads* and would one day deliver *Auf Wiedersehen, Pet*, came in and supplied them. (One, about 'A case of syphilis', 'It'll make a change from Lucozade', was to surface again in the last movie I produced.)

Dexter, Leslie Gilliat and I set off to do a recce in Singapore and Malaysia, where part of the film was to be shot. We first based ourselves in Raffles hotel, unrecognisable today but then everything that reading Somerset Maugham and Noel Coward had led me to expect: imperial furniture, wickerwork and leather, punkahs whirling and purring, gin-slings, and in the

evening a grassed courtyard with tables laid for dinner illuminated by pink-shaded, moth-beckoning lamps, insects buzzing
over mulligatawny soup, lamb chops and trifle.

Riggs O'Hara includes a letter from Dexter at this time in *The
Honourable Beast*. He described our trips up country again to
Malacca and Serembam. We found a filthy swamp which he
was happy 'to drop you in'. He reported that we had not yet got
anything like a barracks that would do. He was pleased with our
attack on Ian La Frenais's rewrite, 'except for half a dozen
jokes'. We did do a lot of cutting, chopping around and repasting,
working every evening until dinnertime, 'when I pick up my
chopsticks and go out to cover my new John Michael suit with
sweet and sour sauce!'

He goes on to speculate on the possibility of persuading Sean
Connery to play a leading role as Sergeant Driscoll in the film. I
have no memory of this but Dexter writes, 'Sean is our insurance
policy . . . as he owes Columbia a film at a cheaper rate, and
Max wants me to go with the new script which is being typed
out here and is *much* stronger for Driscoll, then Ned and I are to
chat him into it . . . If the film is to be made we have to have one
more star to balance the cost of bringing the unit out here . . .
having seen Singapore we *must* come out here. Sean is in
London but is on his way to Philadelphia and if he expresses
even a vague interest, we'll see him there . . .'

Connery's interest must have been less than vague. We didn't
go to Philadelphia to see him; I did fly from Singapore, via
Copenhagen, and over the Pole to Los Angeles to try to talk
terms with Tommy Steele's Hollywood agent for the same part.
That trip proved abortive and we cast Nigel Davenport as
Driscoll. The other stars were Hywel Bennett and Lynn
Redgrave. There was one other Columbia attempt to upcast a
cameo. Max Setton heard that James Mason was doing nothing
very much in Switzerland, and might agree to play a sympathetic colonel. I was despatched to Vevey, where we had a

pleasant lunch. I returned to cast the excellent Michael Gwynn in the part.

Back in London we began what seemed an interminable parade of young actors who tripped up the steps to my new house in Bywater Street in Chelsea. On leaving the BBC I had sold my story to the *Sunday Mirror* (*The Man from Auntie*) to provide the deposit and I worked from it as an office. We needed at least a dozen new faces who would carry conviction as the motley crew of raw recruits whom Leslie Thomas remembered. Dexter was looking for a definitive Army 'shower'. Many of the actors we saw were, of necessity, new to the game. In order to perk them into some sort of animation, to engage their minds and make them forget their nervousness and their best behaviour, he devised a series of staccato questions – 'Can you shoot?', 'Can you drive?', 'Do you ride?', 'Do you swim?', 'What games do you play?', and then, when it was least expected, 'Are you a virgin?' Often this relaxed the interviewees into a joky, confidential mood and they opened up easily. There was one disastrous comeuppence. A young man from Leigh-on-Sea sent in a photograph of himself in his mother's back garden dressed as a Home Counties Tarzan. He took a day off work and came up to audition. He got the routine quick questions climaxing in 'Are you a virgin?' At this he burst into tears. 'Yes, that's the whole problem of my life.' He had to be led sobbing from the house.

Another intriguing interviewee was the young David Bowie, who had no problem with the 'virgin question'. At that time he was an aspiring singer and mime working with Lindsay Kemp. It was difficult to assess his acting potential so we asked him to stay on for lunch at Alvaro's, the Chelsea restaurant round the corner which was so '*in*' that it was ex-directory. Bowie weaved a fascinating story about his apparently glass eye. He insisted that he had lost it in a fight with another man over a girl. After the eye came out the two men forgot the girl and started a relationship. Dexter and I could not decide whether the story was true or run up on the spot to increase our curiosity. We gave him a screen test along with half a dozen hopefuls but decided against giving him a feature part. In 1967 his strange quality was too elusive to capture on the screen. However, we did give him a crowd part in a NAAFI dance sequence. He had his hair cropped to a severe military length and did five days' filming. I have never been able to identify him in the finished cut although Bowie fans are always writing to ask which is their hero. We also, encouraged by Columbia, had lunch with Mick Jagger and his agent. There was talk about an important cameo. Mick didn't think it was the 'right career move'. John and I felt some relief. We were able to cast a proper actor – James Cosmo.

Finally we flew off to the Far East towards the end of the summer of 1968, with a motley crew of actors and technicians filling a chartered plane. In the sixties the various unions required that everyone fly first class. Champagne and caviar were anticipated within seconds of take-off. Sadly the charterer forgot to put the champagne on board. There was a good deal of wiring ahead so that the chorus of discontent could be silenced. We took on supplies at our first stop – Tehran, and suitably refreshed, we flew in to Kuala Lumpur. The jungle sequences up country in Malaysia were to be filmed first. We arrived in late evening, trucked in convoy to a beach hotel which overlooked the Indian Ocean and settled in, ready to start shooting the next morning.

The jungle was hot, damp and sweaty. There was a scatter of warm rain as we filmed the first shots. Our magnificently unprepared platoon of raw recruits was fording a stream. Little Wayne Sleep on leave from the Royal Ballet was too short to be seen above the muddy water. Stones had to be thrown in to make a platform before his head broke the surface. For lunch the Asian caterers, reckoning that the actors would be missing home cooking, thoughtfully offered fish and chips. Hywel Bennett, our leading Virgin, was dismayed. Hywel had and has a tendency towards podginess. He was on a strict diet and did not intend to break it for fish and chips. Unfortunately I didn't take his complaint as seriously as he did. Without thinking I said, 'Just up the driveway there, through the jungle there's this Belgian couple who run a little bistro. You get very good onion soup and they do amusing things with veal.' Before I knew what was happening Hywel had called his driver and set off up the jungle track, heading for the Belgian bistro. It took him half an hour to find that it did not exist. When he got back there were no fish and chips left either. He was unamused but at least he hadn't got any plumper.

That night we ordered some appalling champagne and drank a good deal sitting on a verandah looking at the Indian Ocean in the moonlight. Nigel Davenport suggested a nightcap. Drambuie all round. I forgot that it is whisky-based and my constitution can't take whisky and champagne together. I awoke at two o'clock with a splitting headache and was violently ill until six. To hang on to my newly acquired producer's authority I had to pretend that I had been struck down with a violent form of Asian flu. There was a lot of it about and my shame was concealed.

I soon had to use the Asian flu gambit again but in another cause. John Van Eyssen collected jade. He wanted an excuse to come to Singapore at Columbia's expense and pick some up. He did what all film executives do if they feel like a rich trip to another location. He invented a crisis. Just as we were leaving he started to raise objections to some of the language in the script – which had been on his desk for months. In particular he spotted the word 'lesbian'. In a tense scene an RSM (Nigel Patrick) accuses his daughter (Lynn Redgrave) of frigidity and lesbianism. John's ruse was to warn us that a clean-up scare was going on in Hollywood and certain words would prevent a subsequent lucrative sale of the film to American television. 'Lesbian' was high on the list. When we arrived in Malaysia cables started flying saying, 'p 103 delete "lesbian".' Leslie Gilliat and I fought a rearguard action.

I telexed back an enthusiastic welcome to John. I confirmed that I had reserved the Dragon Emperor suite (or some such name) at the Goodwood hotel for him. Fortunately I remembered that he was a king-size hypochondriac. I added a cautionary postscript advising him to have all possible vaccinations against Asian flu as the whole peninsula was in the grip of a virulent epidemic. We were lucky in our filming. The message reached him in Los Angeles where he was in conference with the Columbia top brass. It was passed ritually from the head of the company down the table via various vice-presidents until it got to our man at the bottom. John decided that perhaps he didn't need to go to Singapore after all.

However, the awful spectre of lesbianism had not completely disappeared. Columbia bombarded Dexter and me with telexes and telegrams. For John, already insecure in a new medium, it was doubly disconcerting. He had accepted the film under the wing of Carl Foreman. Now here he was on location in Singapore with two quite different producers. Leslie Gilliat had great experience and efficiency – but he and John found it difficult to communicate. Turning to me, on my first film, it was clear to Dexter that I knew no more than he did. There was another factor. Many victims have written about John's need to have a whipping boy (or girl) among his casts of actors. He also had a destructive instinct to fight managements. In receipt of another irritating telex one morning he exploded. I was never, in any circumstances, to show him another message from 'that old fool Max Setton'.

When we had completed the jungle sequences in Malaysia (which included blowing up Kate Winslet's uncle, Robert Bridges), we moved down to Singapore for the parade-ground locations. We filmed those sequences on a beautiful tarmac square surrounded by leafy, imperial barracks, imposing palms and beautiful tropical flowers. In the officers' mess hung a very different picture. It was a panoramic view of the same scene secretly taken during the war. The Japanese filled the entire tarmac space with British servicemen who were kept there for days in the baking sun, suffering and dying.

We were fortunate to get the parade ground. Dick Lester had recently made a movie called *How I Won the War*. He obtained Army co-operation without revealing to the War Office that it lampooned the military. When it was screened stern questions were asked about why the Army had collaborated in sending itself up.

During the years since *TW3* Gerald Kaufman had gone on to be an influential member of Harold Wilson's 'kitchen cabinet'. Gerald wangled permission for us to use the essential location – but only just in time. The moment Michael Carver, the GOC in the Far East, got word of our film plans he withdrew all further support. We had the parade ground in writing but not the soldiers we hoped to fill it with as extras. He forbade any participation. Eventually we made do with men from the Singaporean Army, relegated to the back rows because they were not only very short but the wrong shade. The foreground was stocked with schoolboys, sons of serving soldiers over whom Carver's writ did not run. They were happy to take the pocket money denied their fathers.

Off the set Singapore offered a rich harvest of anticipated delights. The Far East yielded all the expected funny Chinese names and pronunciations, which I was naively unable to take in my stride. There was 'Lai Kee Fun'; there was 'Mr Wee, a sanitary engineer'; there was a camp and flustered counter clerk for whom the job of rerouting a Russian flight to Moscow from Singapore via Delhi proved so daunting that he flung all his travel documents at his superior, screaming, 'It's all Gleek to me!'; I was getting used to 'flied lice' by now; there was a little, old Chinaman of great sweetness whom we cast for the role of F. Yew, a Chinese tailor. We found him in an old people's home run by nuns. His name was Hallelujah – he was seventy. He had lived in Singapore for forty years and his favourite film star was Norma Shearer.

An eclectic range of entertainment was available: 'The Great Royal Circus of India'; 'The Greatest Show of Culture and Geste' from China; countless touring Chinese operas running five hours and performed by the roadside. At a local fleapit, *2001, A Space Odyssey* – 19th Big Day! Season Ending Soon! *At Last the 1948 Show* and *The Forsyte Saga* were on television with 'Ilene' the toast of Singapore. *Show of Swords* was a Shaw Brothers production in Shawscope, in Malay with English and Chinese subtitles (a screenful). It starred Wang Yu and Li Chin. The premiere of *The Tragedy of a King Poet*, at which both Yam Kim Fei and Pak Suet Sin, two actresses who took the leading male and female roles, were mobbed. *Up the Junction* was doing a few days with the subtitle, *Don't Get Caught Was What She Wasn't Taught*. Across in Indonesia an attempt to revive gladiatorial contests in the presence of the foreign minister failed. The Javanese gladiator, Bandot Lahargo, was confronted by an unusually sophisticated lion who sensibly declined to put up a fight.

Singapore was well stocked with traditional seaport facilities. Cabaret restaurants like the Car Park, featuring 'Five Korean Lovelies' and conversations with not very chatty hostesses at twelve dollars an hour, represented it at its most respectable. Down the road drag queens patrolled Bugis Street after midnight like giant Kewpie dolls, painted and fantastical, saving up for their sex-change operations in Tokyo. When Trixie and Edna and Lulu had to cross the causeway into Malaysia and show their passports, official photographs required short haircuts and a brief reversion to Jim or Fred or Omar.

One lotus-eyed Edna or Trixie captivated Hywel to such an

extent that he did not identify her as a Fred or a Jim until it was almost too late. She became his devoted admirer, visiting him formally on the set, to John Dexter's considerable irritation and embarrassment. When we left she invested in the Singaporean custom of airmailing orchids, which were waiting for him when he returned to England. A few days later she telephoned from a girl's home in Windsor. Cathy McGowan, Hywel's girlfriend, put her foot down. Trixie was last heard of working in a drag club in Birmingham. One or two of the crew sampled the attractions of Bugis Street. On leaving Leslie and I offered a free medical check, especially against venereal disease. The only crew-member casualty to require treatment was the one who had poured scorn on the Bugis Street girls and plumped for legitimate ladies.

Discreet pleasure parlours offered terms of three Singapore dollars a drink and three dollars more for treatment in the sawdust-floored back rooms. One was known as the Winky-Wanky Bar with the alluring slogan, 'One on the Rocks and One off the Wrist'. Round the corner men with gold teeth offered blue movies, exhibitions, girls or boys or boys and girls. The traditional 'girl meets donkey' film evoked the time-honoured film technicians' thumbs down: 'Not a very good print.'

The political climate was set by Prime Minister Lee Kuan Yew's strong arm. As I left he was starting the last phase of his 'Keep Singapore Clean' campaign, giving Singaporeans one final 'voluntary' month before 'enforcing discipline on those who do not yield to social suasion'. It was not easy to imagine 'social suasion' having a lightning effect on the muddle of Singapore – a tumbledown kampong under each towering new block, the smell of rubbish surging from open drains, and the pong of pigs alternating with clouds of frangipani scent in more open country. Yet when I returned to Singapore a couple of times in the nineties it was transformed. Much sea was reclaimed, few of the

old open spaces remained and a gleamingly efficient underground moved its magnified population across the island.

I met two local censors during our brief stay. A Malaysian
who had just viewed John Wayne's hawkish *The Green Berets*
announced, 'I pass it clean.' And there was a female censor who
had a highly original test: 'If a film gives me a funny feeling I
know it is dirty; but if I feel nothing I know it is culture.'

Evenings in Singapore (if we were not night-shooting) were
enlivened by a very sociable cast and crew – Lynn Redgrave and
her mother, Rachel Kempson, Hywel, Nigel Davenport and Jack
Shepherd, who played two warring NCOs, and the other
Virgins, Don Hawkins, Geoffrey Hughes, Wayne Sleep, Gregory
Phillips, Riggs O'Hara and Jolyon Jackley, were invariably up
for a night on the town. We dined well in a number of happily
discovered Chinese restaurants. There was 'Faty's', where Faty
cooked exquisitely on the open pavement and was rumoured to
have a Rolls-Royce at the back and a son at Eton. There were
meals at the Hong Kong Bowl, one in the middle of a Chinese
wedding, incredibly noisy as the guests put away baked crab
claws, turtle, suckling pig, 'flesh flied milk' and all those vegetables that taste so much nicer in the East. And there was
entertainment at the Hollywood-style home of the film mogul
Run Me Shaw. Run Me, based in Singapore, and Run Run, his
older brother, based in Hong Kong, straddled the entertainment
world in the Far East. An evening with Run Me meant drinks, a
nine-course dinner including the inevitable suckling pig and then
a struggle to keep awake in the lavish screening room, viewing
the latest imported film.

Legend has it that the two brothers had lowly beginnings.
Run Run got his name from his first job as a messenger. One day
when he was sick his little brother turned up and said, 'Run Me!'
Legend is, perhaps, too cute and convenient to be true.

We finished our schedule in Singapore and returned to shoot
a jungle ambush near Saffron Walden. Leslie Gilliat arranged to

transport a massive old steam engine from Wales, install it in a disused British Rail siding and convert it to look like an authentic period piece. The small copse which lined the track was tricked out with bamboos and palm trees to make a fairly convincing jungle setting. However, by now October was giving way to November and spots of telltale yellow were appearing in the trees. We were filming a night ambush. In the cold English night air we had to be careful that breath which steamed out of shivering soldiers' mouths did not give the game away.

Leslie and I wanted to get out of East Anglia before all the leaves turned brown. However, before we left Singapore there had been minor frictions with John Dexter. He tensed up before shooting any particularly big set piece, finding reasons to delay dealing with it and seriously threatening the schedule. The ambush was the biggest, most complicated sequence and it produced maximum procrastination. We began to fall behind. It also threw up a favourite scene of farce. We were about to film the master shot – smoke, explosions, gun-toting terrorists, fleeing soldiers – when Lindsay Anderson visited the set. Lindsay, a long time Royal Court colleague of John's steeped in film, was staying at Grayshotts, the nearby health farm. John was nervously impressed by the visit and turned away to talk animatedly to his visitor. The conversation went on so long that the first assistant director, Claude Watson, finally called 'Action!'. All hell broke loose until he yelled 'Cut!' John turned away from Lindsay and said 'Good.' Lindsay sidled over to me and said innocently, 'Does John always direct with his back to the action?'

We recreated the interiors of the Changi barrack rooms in a disused old Army camp near Crowthorne and Bracknell in Berkshire. It was now that John became particularly recalcitrant and the Columbia front office in Wells Street became seriously concerned at the overrun. They found it hard to accept that John, so good with the actors, was dragging his feet. Finally

Leslie and I were summoned to a crisis meeting. We found Max Setton and John Van Eyssen there with Carl Foreman. Max did the talking. 'Carl has explained to me', he said, 'that John is an artist and you don't really understand him. All that is needed is for me to send an encouraging letter to him saying how pleased we are with the rushes and then he will speed up.'

I said that it was a good plan but it wouldn't work. 'Why not?' Max wanted to know. I explained, 'Because I was given strict instructions early on in the shooting never to bother him with another letter from "that old fool Max Setton".' It was risky, but it worked. John, Leslie and I were summoned to Carl's house that evening. John made the mistake of appealing to Carl's socialist principles, insisting that the crew were being over-worked. Carl was on the notorious left-wing Hollywood blacklist during the McCarthy era: as a film producer he at last had an idea of the problems Leslie and I had been facing. He read the riot act and we finished on schedule. My easier relationship with John was slowly restored over the years.

Hywel Bennett went on to star in several movies and to mature into a formidable character actor. Lynn Redgrave's career bloomed in America. Nigel Davenport seemed always to be in work, as his son, Jack. Jack Shepherd developed as a writer and director, and as a television detective starring in *Wycliffe*. Geoffrey Hughes became a mainstay of *Coronation Street*. Don Hawkins pursued a career as a film producer. Dexter continued as a formidable stage director and had a dazzling period at the Metropolitan Opera in New York. He did make other films but not on the same scale as *The Virgin Soldiers*. He died in 1990 after a series of heart attacks.

The subsequent history of *The Virgin Soldiers*, once shooting was over, completed the first stages of my apprenticeship as a film producer. There was the long editing process, cutting, rejigging and finding the right music. Ray Davies of The Kinks wrote a memorable, haunting march theme and Peter Greenwell arranged the rest of the score. The movie was a great success in Britain, getting good notices and taking more money at home than any other film that year except the then-current Bond offering. However, Columbia was in no haste to show it in America. For a long time they considered it too inflammatory to offer laughs alongside death in the jungle at a time when the Vietnam War was still being fought. Suddenly, albeit a year later, I began to sense a change in attitude. They were hearing good things about Twentieth Century Fox's *M*A*S*H* – wartime laughs in Korea. At the same time American public opinion was beginning to swing against the war. It was comic to watch the speed and thoroughness with which a large company can do an about turn.

I flew to New York for a sneak preview only to find that the print had been impounded in customs at Kennedy Airport on the suspicion, based on the title, that it was pornographic. At least it enabled me to get to the second night of *O Calcutta!* in the time suddenly made available. Kenneth Tynan had earlier asked me to direct it. Second choice, I think, after Harold Pinter turned it down. I had had to say no because it would have conflicted with my commitment to *The Virgin Soldiers*. Nor could it have passed the lord chamberlain's office at the time – hence its transatlantic opening.

The crowning irony in this sorry postscript was the engagement of a pair of elderly protest writers to write a lyric to Ray Davies's march, expressing the universal antipathy to war of 'young people the world over'. The enthusiasm with which the company suggested that this 'moving treatment' would be 'plugged' on peace marches in Washington was not shared by the youthful protesters. Eventually we opened in New York in 1970 almost unnoticed. *M*A*S*H* had long stolen a march on us. Ten other films were premiered that week, and among the ten *Patton* said most of what the United States wanted to hear about war and said it in American accents.

The Virgin Soldiers sank without trace. In Britain it has continued to have a television life. There was a grubby sequel, *Onward Virgin Soldiers*, with none of the original principal players. Our film still works well when it is often aired on TV in the wee small hours of the morning.

CHAPTER 8

What'll I Do?

The Virgin Soldiers was financed by Columbia, sponsored by Carl Foreman, directed by John Dexter and administered by Leslie Gilliat. It left me basking in their success; but without a 'property', a play, a novel, an original idea to follow it up.

There was one faint hope. Since I had commissioned Barry Took and Marty Feldman to write *Goldilocks* nearly three years earlier, Marty had become a television star. The Boulting brothers, Roy and John, had recently had a huge success with a movie version of the sitcom *Till Death Us Do Part*. British Lion made a fortune out of it. Columbia, particularly the Californian and New York offices, no longer had any interest in *Goldilocks*. However, they were not averse to getting their money back. I went to see the Boulting twins, always an odd couple to deal with. As you entered John's office Roy seemed to materialise beside him like ectoplasm without a door having opened. They were tight negotiators, but they were encouraging.

Marty, always highly strung, was nervous but intrigued. Considering the other actors we had discussed for the role – Alan Bates, George Segal, Tom Courtenay, Albert Finney – it was hardly typecasting.

For a generation unfamiliar with Marty Feldman, who died in 1982, he was a gnome-like figure of manic energy, his face dominated by a pair of enormous thyroid eyes. Although a strict vegetarian, on one drunken occasion he decided to eat a little fish. Consulting the menu, he thought whitebait sounded harmless. When the plate arrived all he could see was a shoal of small creatures, apparently close relatives, all staring up at him reproachfully with their huge eyes. He was very sick and never tried fish again.

Barry and Marty did another draft for the Boultings, accommodating, indeed exploiting, Marty's bizarre appearance in a series of fantasy sequences and extravagant parodies. For various reasons we changed the title to *Every Home Should Have One*. Without Leslie Gilliat to guide me I poached Terry Glinwood as associate producer from my friend and agent, John Heyman. Terry's experience was long and varied. He started as an accountant and worked in several capacities on various films. Judging by his rosy reminiscences of Stanley Kubrick's *Lolita* he spent most of his time on that film playing table tennis with the director. He worked with Polanski on *Repulsion* and moved on to Michael Klinger, a buccaneering English independent producer, for whom he kept a tight rein on the purse strings of films like *Penthouse*, a small-budget shocker which did well for Klinger in the early sixties.

For John Heyman he started by making *Privilege*, an apocalyptic vision directed by Peter Watkins. Heyman, a multifaceted entrepreneur, combined managing Burton and Taylor, Trevor Howard and Hughie Green with raging ulcers and one deaf ear. He used this devastatingly in negotiation to hear only what he wanted to hear. He went on to produce Tennessee Williams's *Boom* with Burton, Taylor and Noel Coward and L. P. Hartley's *The Go-Between*, scripted by Harold Pinter, with Julie Christie, Alan Bates and Michael Redgrave – both directed by Joseph Losey. Terry was practical, optimistic and imaginative. I depended on him on *Every Home* as much as I had on Leslie on *The Virgin Soldiers*. More as time went on and we set up more films.

To direct *Every Home Should Have One* we chose Jim Clark, a distinguished film editor who had worked on many of John Schlesinger's movies. Some years earlier for the first episode of *BBC-3* he filmed a funny sketch for me. It sent up naturist films. Beryl Reid played a leading nudist. I had first invited Schlesinger, who was doing nothing in the wake of *Darling*, to direct it. I thought he might enjoy to let his hair down. We were all set to go when John had an attack of nervous jitters. He was heavily tipped for an Oscar for *Darling*. Suddenly to direct a comic ten-minute television nudie short looked as though it might prejudice his chances. He pulled out a few days before we were due to shoot. By now I had committed quite a lot of BBC money. John suggested Jim Clark, who wanted to break into direction. It was good advice. Jim did it with style and humour, with some particularly funny moments when clapperboards appeared to collide with the private parts of naked actors.

Jim quickly established a rapport with Marty. His thoroughness and his experience as an editor for the big screen impressed the comedian. We were due to film at the British Lion Studios at Shepperton with a certain amount of work on location in the countryside around. The rest of the cast was a roster of fine British character actors, including Patience Collier, Alan Bennett and Jack Watson; and a number of young English comedians. Judy Cornwell played Marty's wife. Frances de la Tour and Penelope Keith had small parts: Frances as a Mary Whitehouse figure; Penelope a massive, leather-clad, motorcycling, German, lesbian au pair.

We had a discouraging search for another au pair – the beautiful Scandinavian sort whom every home should have. We scoured Britain without success. Then Terry and I tried Sweden. We enjoyed the light nights and long drinks but found no one whom we could afford on our modest budget. Returning in despair we were visited the very next day by the remarkably lovely Julie Ege. She was just delivered of a baby. This was the reason we had not been shown her earlier. It was the start of a short but lively career in movies. She had appeared as a back-ground Bond girl in *On Her Majesty's Secret Service* and, having played for us in *Every Home*, would feature in *Up Pompeii* and *Rentadick*, as well as a few more films, including one of those fur-bikini, all-grunting, prehistoric epics. An enchanting girl, her frail command of English meant that she was never quite sure what a film was about until she saw the final cut. When she returned to Norway she played some serious roles in the theatre in her own language, raised two daughters and became a senior nurse.

The other leading actor was the American comedian Shelley Berman. He played a conniving colleague who led Marty's innocent-at-large into trouble and excess. I had always admired Berman's work but I was not prepared for his insecurity. An able character actor, it did not bolster his confidence to arrive in Britain and find that his co-star, a comic of whom he had never heard, was a household name and, even more, a household face, receiving columns of coverage in the press. Marty's bizarre appearance cried out to be photographed. The publicity depart-ment had an impossible task interesting journalists in writing stories about Shelley or taking his picture.

His morale wasn't helped when one of our extras set another up to play a trick on him. They were part of the crowd in a trendy Chelsea restaurant. The girl asked for Shelley's auto-graph. So far, so excellent. Unfortunately she had been briefed to say, 'Thank you . . . and I loved your "Driving Instructor" record.' Everybody but the girl knew that Shelley's classic rou-tines are telephone conversations – the 'Driving Instructor' belongs to his rival Bob Newhart. The sulk lasted for days.

A second offence was innocent but it produced another

explosion. Towards the end of shooting Miss Godfrey, my house-keeper, who sports a fine line in stylish hats, came down to visit the set and lunch with Jim and Marty, whom she knew well as visitors to my house. Halfway through a happy meal I spotted Shelley across the room getting more and more agitated. Finally he came over and hissed in my ear, 'This is the final insult.' I was nonplussed. 'What d'you mean?' His whisper swelled to a whine: 'You have this important lady journalist down here and you haven't asked her to meet me.' Miss Godfrey's hats were in the best Hollywood tradition of gossip-columnists like Hedda Hopper and Louella Parsons. It took some time to persuade Shelley that she did not wield a gossip-writer's pen.

Miss Godfrey (who, as I write in March 2005, has just passed a hundred) came into my life at a very convenient time. Having moved from Dover Street to Bywater Street, a pretty cul-de-sac in Chelsea, in 1966, I needed to be looked after. My baptism of fire was a woman I will call Mrs O'Rourke. She started by explaining that she did not have to do the job. 'My husband is a builder in a very big way of business . . . I don't need the money. I shall spend half of it on my personal appearance. The other half I shall give to the Catholic Church. If my husband knew I was coming here to work he'd be up the road in ten minutes and beating you around the face.'

Her Achilles heel was celebrity worship. 'If Mr David Frost should come to call I would be honoured to kiss the front door-mat the moment he has stepped off it.' She lasted a few weeks. The manner of her going was disconcerting. She failed to arrive one Monday morning so I telephoned to see if she was all right – risking Mr O'Rourke's wrath should he be still at home. Mrs O'Rourke spoke only one sentence: 'You know very well why I didn't come this morning', and slammed down the receiver. It was a bewildering puzzle, aggravated by a letter which arrived two days later. 'M Sherrin,' she wrote, 'You have a unique abil-ity to make people around you unhappy.'

The words lingered reproachfully in my mind for some weeks. But when I finally advertised for her successor I picked up the phone one morning and heard her unmistakable voice. 'Hello, Mr Sherrin . . .'

'Who is it?' I said, knowing full well and trying to think fast.

'It is a person of no importance,' she announced.

'Oh no it's not, it's Mrs O'Rourke.'

'Mr Sherrin, I want you to know that I've had two whiskies before making this call . . . and I want to come back.' Mercifully the unique Miss Jean Godfrey had come into my life the day before, and presided over it for some of its happiest years. She was about sixty-three. She had led a varied life, dabbling in antiques at one time but applying herself to any challenge which came along. Miss Godfrey was born and based in Battersea, 'up the Latchmere'. She was a fine cook and used to leave a full complement of dishes for me to warm up over a weekend. She had previously kept house for Selwyn Lloyd and his daughter when he was chancellor of the exchequer – a job which ended when Harold Macmillan sacked him on 13 July 1962, in 'The Night of the Long Knives', prompting Jeremy Thorpe's famous line, 'Greater love hath no man than he lay down his friends for his life.' Miss Godfrey retained great affection for the deposed minister and rejoiced when he became Speaker in 1971.

She had had to leave school early but she cherished an extraordinary range of interests. She was a great one for evening classes – especially languages – and an intrepid traveller abroad. She painted enthusiastically in oils and water, and was a devoted theatregoer – her ideal trip being a matinée followed by tea 'at Fortnum'. If she hadn't spent the housekeeping allowance at the end of the week she would invest it proudly in something I didn't need. I have several more cigarette boxes than are strictly necessary for a non-smoker to prove it. When I moved across the King's Road to a bigger house in Wellington Square she recruited her younger brother Jack and an old Battersea schoolfriend, Grace, to augment her staff. They made a happy household.

Most remarkable was Miss Godfrey's tolerance of the variety of young Americans who often occupied my spare room – though she was shocked one morning when she arrived to find Rachel Roberts creeping downstairs after a night with her lover, Darren Ramirez. Darren was in residence at the time. Jean coped patiently with two of the three young members of the Broadway cast of *Hair* whom I put up (and she put up with). Jonathan Kramer and Paul Jabarra were the easy ones. Jonathan lavished attention on her. Paul entertained but shocked her when he handcuffed himself to the railings of 10 Downing Street in 1972, protesting that he had not been given a work permit to star in *Jacob's Journey*, a companion piece to the Rice/Lloyd Webber show *Joseph and the Amazing Technicolor Dreamcoat* when it moved to the Albery Theatre. The play did not succeed but Paul returned to America to have a successful career as a songwriter – notably with The Weather Girls and 'It's Raining Men'. His disastrous Broadway musical, *My Name Is Rachel Lilly Rosenbloom and Don't You Ever Forget It*, was never going to be as good as when he performed the entire show solo to anyone who would hear it in Wellington Square. It closed before its first night on the Great White Way. Miss Godfrey listened patiently to large excerpts in the kitchen while preparing lunch. Paul has gone now to Aids; Jonathan to a lonely suicide in Seattle; Jack and Grace to age. Miss Godfrey survives, blind now but cared for in a friendly home in south London. Her one Waterloo – or perhaps it was his – was the third member of the original *Hair* cast. Hiram Keller, blond, extravagantly good-looking, had little to do in the show except stand around looking extravagantly good-looking. It got him a starring role in Fellini's *Satyricon*. After the film he swanned about to no particular purpose beyond decoration. His crime in Miss Godfrey's eyes was that he wanted to buy and bring into the house a dog. Miss Godfrey told him that if the dog came, she went. A small whippet appeared. I returned from filming to find a note from Miss Godfrey explaining that she could not stay. It was no contest. Hiram found accommodation elsewhere. He is the one survivor of the trio – training horses now in the American South. I saw Miss Godfrey on her hundredth. The card from the Queen had not arrived, owing to some bureaucratic bungle; but one of her devoted friends was on the case.

Like *The Virgin Soldiers*, *Every Home Should Have One* was one of the ten top-grossing British films of the year. Like *The Virgin Soldiers* it had no success in America. It was not released there until the early eighties. The distributors gave it the seedy new title *Think Dirty*, an oblique reference to the copywriter's attempts to think sex into the porridge. Fortunately it closed quickly.

During shooting Terry Glinwood had become indispensable. In 1970 we formed a company together called Virgin Films – pre-Branson, of course. Continuing my strategy of making as many films as possible and getting experience as quickly as I could, we contracted to make seven in the next few years. For Anglo-EMI we produced three spin-offs from Frankie Howerd's *Up Pompeii* series on television. For Rank we made *Rentadick* from an original screenplay by Graham Chapman and John Cleese. For Hemdale we did *Girl Stroke Boy*, a comedy based on a West End play called *The Girl Friend* and, for Columbia, a sequel to *Till Death Us Do Part* and a screen version of Peter Nichols's National Theatre success, *The National Health*.

Up Pompeii introduced me to a new distributor, Nat Cohen. Long the head of Anglo-Amalgamated, Nat was a short, spick and span, old-school mogul – a British version of the ex-fur-trader tsars of Hollywood. A dapper little man with a cropped, military moustache, he loved making a deal, having a pretty girl on his arm, owning a Grand National winner – Kilmore

(1962) – and showing off his flat in St James's. It had been redecorated by Jon Bannenberg with a lot of brass and leather. 'I think he's brought the masculine touch,' Nat said, proudly puffing on a cigar.

Nat, born in 1905, was the son of an immigrant butcher in Whitechapel who put some of the money he made from meat into local cinemas. As a small chain developed the son began to manage it, putting on local talent shows before the main feature. In the thirties at the Mile End Empire he engaged the dance act 'Bernard Delfont and Tokyo'.

Nat's distribution programme was two-pronged. On the bread-and-butter side there were leaden B-features using the names of Edgar Lustgarten and Edgar Wallace, and *The Tommy Steele Story*. There were early *Carry Ons*, and TV spin-offs like the *Up* series, *On the Buses* and *Steptoe and Son*. At the other pole he worked with Joseph Losey, and backed the Jo Janni, John Schlesinger hits *Billy Liar*, *A Kind of Loving*, *Darling* and *Far from the Madding Crowd*, and Ken Loach's *Poor Cow* and *Family Life*. Forty years on his old dancing discovery, Bernard Delfont, made him head of production for EMI at Elstree in 1971 – *Murder on the Orient Express* followed. Eventually EMI Films was bought out by the bizarre Cannon empire of Menachim Golan and Yoram Globus.

We belonged firmly in Nat's 'a giggle, a girl and a few innuendoes' compartment of British film-making. Once again we walked luckily into the *Up Pompeii* deal. Frankie Howerd's long-time agent, Beryl Vertue, had already sold the idea to Nat. He had spotted the potency of cheap TV spin-offs and was envious of the Boulting brothers' success with *Till Death Us Do Part*.

Frankie's unique comic quality had never been captured on the screen. Nor did we, despite the ingenuity of the director, Bob Kellett, really manage to pin it down. In the theatre he established a conspiratorial communion with the audience. Confidentially he would rubbish the show, the setting, the material, other members of the cast, even the audience. He thrived on the tightrope of live performance. Coaxing or berating his listeners, with painstaking, cunning self-rehearsal and self-absorption, he squeezed a fresh sense of occasion into each show.

On television *Up Pompeii* allowed him to continue his conspiratorial affair with the studio audience and to share it to a certain extent with the viewing public. Large close-ups of generous asides to camera drew in the home crowd and Frank was reassured by the immediate studio laughter.

In the film studio he could blow up a bubble of fun at his first rehearsal of a scene, delivering a line with rich eccentricity and setting off laughter among the admiring crew. However, when the director called 'action' and a cathedral-like silence descended Frank was robbed of his most powerful ally – laughter. He was often very funny, particularly in the first two films of the series, but still a fraction of his commanding presence on stage.

The television shows were written by the late Talbot Rothwell, who looked like a prosperous retired squadron leader. He lived outside Brighton and had written a large number of *Carry On* films. He was chary about committing himself to a series of *Up* films in case he should lose favour with the *Carry On* producers. However, with another comedy veteran, Sid Colin, he wrote the first film and it was exhilarating to turn the pages of the first draft, rich in robust music-hall routines and red-nosed double entendres, so redolent of meaty seaside postcards.

FATHER: My poor child, so lovely and so chaste.

FRANK: And so easily caught!

FRANK: Let us celebrate the Festival of the Prolific Goose. Laying all night . . .

PROCURESS: In the great court of Samarkand she once held a unique position.

FRANK: On top of the wardrobe, I should think!

Orgies, stolen parchments, gladiators, soothsayers, Nero, public baths, hippy Christians fed to lions, the entire destruction of Pompeii – all ancient Roman life was there seen through Talbot Rothwell's vaudevillian eyes.

We had another lucky break with the scenery. On an abandoned MGM lot up the road from Elstree Studios where we were to film, Terry Glinwood found most of Pompeii in a Roman set left over from Charlton Heston's attempt to film *Julius Caesar*. There were endless vistas of marble flats, Roman columns, statues and busts, including one of John Gielgud which I subsequently bagged for my back garden. We bought the lot for a song and subsequently sold it to roughly the same tune.

Michael Hordern, Barbara Murray, Bill Fraser, Bernard Bresslaw, Lance Percival, Patrick Cargill, Rita Webb and Royce Mills supported Frankie Howerd, along with crowds of extras. Since his death much has been written about Frankie's priapic tendencies. He did have a habit of asking well-built soldiers and gladiators to share a drink in his dressing room at the end of the day. As far as I could gather, after the expected pounce, he took the almost inevitable rebuff in good spirits. He worked on the principle that he might as well try. Nothing ventured, nothing gained. He escorted one actor who had turned down his advances to the dressing-room door. There he held him in conversation until he heard someone else come along the corridor. He chose that moment elaborately to pretend to zip up his fly and thank the innocent but blushing actor loudly and profusely. Kenneth Cranham (first Hippy Christian) told me that he threatened to punch Frank when he groped him in a dungeon scene. A quick climbdown was the nearest we got to violence. The only apparent consent was by an American so stoned that he lay back unaroused, thinking of America, until Frank gave up embarrassed and muttered, 'You won't tell anyone, will you?'

Up Pompeii was in 1971 a big enough hit to ensure that a sequel could be planned and put into production straight away.

By now the problem of finding and developing material was easing. We worked closely with Beryl Vertue, who ran the film side of Robert Stigwood's organisation. Talbot Rothwell returned to the *Carry On* camp but Beryl brought in two more of her clients, Alan Galton and Ray Simpson, who had written material for Frankie for years. She smoothed the way to a collaboration between them and Sid Colin. Sid delivered an initial treatment.

We abandoned Pompeii for medieval Britain – for 'slave', read 'serf'. Instead of 'Lurcio', Frankie became 'Lurkalot'. His master, 'Ludicrous Sextus', became 'Sir Coward de Custard', and his son, 'Nausius', was 'Knotweed'. The equivalent of a gladiator, 'Prodigious' would be 'Chopper', a woodsman in this epic. The double entendres were doubled. ('Oh, me chopper!') Once again, the sense of history was fanciful.

LADY DE CUSTARD: Serfs ought to be where you want them when you want them. He'll have to go.
SIR COWARD: I agree, my dear, let's swap him for one of those nice Swedish girls.

Sid Colin's plot revolved around the thesis – not supported by any historical evidence – that King Richard the Lionheart had been born with an identical twin brother – two Frankies for the price of one. The firstborn was spirited away by evil barons, abandoned in a pigsty and, by a happy chance, raised by a sow whom he regards as his mother. The younger twin, a surprise born after the barons think they have settled the succession, grows up to be King Richard. The Lionheart is not keen on the boring routine of ruling: 'Sod that for a lark. I think I'll go on a crusade.'

This time the medieval panorama included jousting, jesters, crusaders, stocks, a ducking stool and the invention of gunpowder – originally called 'Gone-powder' because, 'No sooner did you light the fuse than you were gone!' The plot involved Robin

Hood and his Gay, as opposed to Merry, Men. Their Lincoln Green was replaced by black leather cut tight across the hips. Rita Webb, the old cockney so disappointed not to appear on the Kennedy *TW3*, was a grotesque Maid Marian.

FRANK: How do you do?
MARIAN: Not very often, thank you.

The band of men just failed to corrupt young Knotweed.

LADY DE CUSTARD: Knotweed, you're not one of them?
FRANK: [*Aside*] If he's not he soon will be.

The plot turned on Lurkalot's new invention, a chastity belt, the Knickerbocker Glory, Mark Three. All ended happily and the belt gave us the title, *Up the Chastity Belt*.

There was no shortage of clever character actors to back up Frankie. Graham Crowden and Anna Quayle replaced Michael Hordern and Barbara Murray – both of whom had found 'feeding' Frankie stressful. Bill Fraser and Lance Percival returned as villains. Roy Hudd (a locksmith), Derek Griffiths (Saladin) and Hugh Paddick (Robin Hood) triggered some insecurity in the star: 'They're not supposed to be funny. I'm the comedian.' I was pleased to be able to use Dave King – a leading television comedian in the fifties. It was a tiny part but it triggered a new acting career for him. I recommended him to Tom Stoppard as the leading man in his revival of *Born Yesterday* at Greenwich opposite Lynn Redgrave. This led to his casting as Enobarbus with Vanessa Redgrave in *Antony and Cleopatra* and eventually to his role in David Hare's *Teeth 'n' Smiles* opposite Helen Mirren.

A more eccentric piece of casting was the writer, Godfrey Winn. He turned out to have a fully paid-up Equity card and played the Archbishop of All England – pink and plump and scrubbed.

For as long as anyone could remember, Frankie had worn an

appalling 'it fools nobody' wig. We had a new hairdresser on *Up the Chastity Belt* – the highly experienced, wonderfully exotic Ramon Gow. I impressed on Ramon that the fiction that the star's hair was his own could not be challenged. Ramon nodded in agreement and marched in for his first session with Frankie. 'What's this bit of old rubbish?' he said, deftly separating toupee from bald crown. They did not bond. Ramon's lady assistant applied wigs on top of Frankie's toupee for the rest of the shooting schedule and Ramon worked his magic on the rest of the cast.

Richard the Lionheart's stay in the Holy Land involved him with an exotic femme fatale. Eartha Kitt had two field days filming a seduction scene in a crusader's tent to which the plot had piloted both Frankies. She seduced them simultaneously in an ultimate twist of mistaken identity, mingled limbs and apparently impossible contortions. Fortunately no wig was disturbed. She teased him relentlessly with her low, throbbing purr and a mischievous intensity which caused her co-star a good deal of sheepish, red-faced embarrassment.

Up the Chastity Belt opened even more successfully than *Up Pompeii* and looked like beating it at the box office. However, during its first week on general release there was a nationwide power strike. Cinemas were dark or looked like being dark. Audiences stayed away and, although the film was replayed piecemeal after the strike had finished, the momentum had gone and it did little more than recoup its investment.

Filming the *Ups* was the easy side of film production. The money was there – usually just over £200,000 for a six-week schedule. There was an audience waiting for Frank. Bob Kellett knew how to handle actors and cameras. Terry Glinwood kept an eagle eye on progress and expenditure. My main role – apart from casting clever actor-friends in small parts – was to keep the visiting 'cameo' stars happy if Frank was fractious; and to keep him happy if they were funny. Both problems were usually solved by a congenial canteen lunch. I spent most of my time looking ahead and trying to set up future projects.

Our last film in the *Up* series, *Up the Front*, was a First World War saga in which the slave/serf character now became Francis, a batman. This was by far the least successful of the series, hastily concocted and released too soon after *Chastity Belt*. Robert Coote, Jonathan Cecil, Hermione Baddeley and Dora Bryan were among the cast.

Filming was enlivened by adding Zsa Zsa Gabor to the mixture as Mata Hari. We negotiated quickly for her week's work. Most of her questions concerned travel, transport, accommodation and especially costume, make-up and hair. We agreed that Zandra Rhodes, who was just emerging as a leading designer, should create a wardrobe for her. Zsa Zsa purred her delight down the phone line. She was to arrive from Los Angeles on a Friday, be fitted and fêted and fussed over during the weekend, and photographed in a tight week's schedule starting on the Monday.

Zsa Zsa has a history of trouble with customs and immigration officials – especially when trying to smuggle her pet dogs through. We prepared carefully. We couldn't afford to have her denied entry. My assistant Nicholas Page was young, indefatigable, affable and wore his hair very long. My driver was an ex-guardsman who insisted on having a uniform for special occasions. The colour he chose was a delicate powder blue. The plane was on time. Nicholas, who was also wily, somehow ingratiated himself behind the customs barrier so that he could make sure there was no trouble. He emerged with Zsa Zsa (who was travelling alone – no dog) apparently as her escort or, as some newspapers preferred, her 'hippy lover'. She volleyed her usual hail of 'Darlinks'. The hippy lover had started a good atmosphere; the powder-blue chauffeur completed it. The convoy set off for her hotel in Piccadilly.

The hotel's welcome was obsequious. They didn't know what

they had let themselves in for. She conducted an imperious examination of the accommodation on offer. Having surveyed the rooms, she rejected them. The main objection was hanging space. This was apparently quite inadequate. Whether the rejection was real or ritual, it was followed by the immediate acceptance of the next suite she was shown – which looked to me to be identical. She swung round to comfirm how undemanding she was being: 'You see, darlink, this is perfect. Why don't they offer me this the first time?'

The next evening I gave a small dinner party for her. One of the guests was Mervyn Stockwood, Bishop of Southwark, who loved life, friends and rubbing shoulders with showbiz. Some years earlier at Cathy McGowan's wedding breakfast after her marriage to Hywel Bennett I had placed him next to Roger Moore, producing the inevitable newspaper photograph captions: 'What the Bishop Said to the Saint'. This time the legend was equally predictable: 'What the Bishop Said to the Actress'. I sometimes wondered if Mervyn minded these exploitations. I was reassured later, on going through his book of press cuttings, to see that both photographs were duly pasted in.

Mild tremors started on the Saturday afternoon. This time I made the mistake of engaging a female hairdresser. A halfwit should have assessed that Zsa Zsa felt more secure with a man. Richard Mills, the make-up artist, quickly became her immediate friend and confidant. Zsa Zsa had a fixed idea that a stylist supplied by Ricci Burns – the fashionable sixties King's Road crimper – should do her hair. It did not take her long to explain to our appointee that she was unsuitable. I got a cooing call to explain that the hairdresser had left: 'Very happy, darlink! I tell her she is a sweet girl; but not for me. But you do not have to worry. I have found this marvellous man. He is divine! He understands! He works for my great friend . . . [Aside] . . . What is his name? [To me] . . . Ricci Burns!'

I was about to explain that there could be complications.

Unions guarded jealously the admission of hairdressers to studios and sets. If Mr Burns's man was not a member of the union we could not let him in. Zsa Zsa embarked on a perfectly shaped monologue which stayed vividly in my memory:

> He is so good to me, this Ricci. He has sent me this beautiful man. The girl was nice but she did not understand me. This man is wonderful . . . You are wonderful, darlink . . . He has done all the best people . . . I have complete confidence in him . . . Tell me who you have done, darlink! I am talking to my producer, he would like to know . . . [To me] He cannot remember . . . [To him] You must have done someone . . . Are you good? . . . I only have the best . . . Are you very good? . . . Me . . .! Of course I am good . . . You do not ask me this! How dare you say that! . . . What? . . . What is this? Clapped out! Go away! Get out! [Door bangs] Darlink, I do not think he will do. Do not worry. We will find someone better. *Au revoir!*

Richard Mills, having gained her confidence, found an excellent union hairdresser and no more was heard of that problem. Now the clothes became an issue. 'Zandra is the best dress maker in the world, BUT! . . . And darlink, she is so amusing, the green hair and the pink hair and the funny accent . . . BUT! . . . And I am sure the clothes would be wonderful for somebody else . . . BUT!'

It transpired that Zsa Zsa had brought with her a couple of her own 'old rags' and she thought that even these would be better than Zandra's creations. I suspect that she never had any intention of wearing anything else. The whole experience was an eye-opener for Zandra. Conspiratorially we conceded the clothes. Miss Gabor was to wear whatever she was happiest in so that she could concentrate on reading her cue cards. Zandra asked only one favour. With Zsa Zsa having given strict instructions that Miss Rhodes was not to come to the studio, she was curious to have a look at this strange creature at work. We arranged a vantage point on the set from which she watched fascinated. Eventually she returned, still shaking her head in amazement. They met again much later in America and became firm friends.

Taking Zsa Zsa to a first night was another revelation. She had revelled the previous night away at her usual stamping ground, Les Ambassadeurs. Then she worked through the day. She changed at the studio and we drove in from Elstree just in time. She was hungry and wanted a salt-beef sandwich. As we crossed north London we failed to find one. We arrived at the Globe Theatre just in time for me to buy a large box of chocolates. We got to our seats – immediately in front of the Rex Harrisons and the Carl Foremans – as the curtain rose. The play quickly put her into a deep gloom. As the first act went on her head began to sag. It was a large, pinkish-whitish head and her shoulders were swathed in a white fur. She was not inconspicuous. Sleep began to possess her. I invented a routine rather like one of Charlie Chaplin's in *Modern Times*. As the great, white head lolled I nudged her side and she straightened up. Then her hand stretched out automatically, clutched a chocolate and stuffed it in her mouth. The effect, the munching and the sugar, gave her a temporary lift with her head snapped back into an upright position. Five minutes later, down went the head; in dug the elbow, out went the hand and up went the chocolate. There were just enough chocolates to see the evening and the ritual through.

My forward planning paid off for the moment. At one period Terry Glinwood and I found ourselves producing three or four films at once. There was a time in the early seventies when we were starting one on location, finishing one at Elstree and preparing yet another at Pinewood – roughly forty minutes between each destination. Ironically this was the moment when I decided that I must have a telephone in my car. I was beginning to resent jumping out to press pennies into coin boxes en route or trying to make and take important calls during the few moments of spare time on arrival at a studio. I was spending some four or five hours in the car each day. At that time car phones were not easy to come by but I lobbied a lot and eventually a telephone was installed. From the moment I had the phone I never completed another film deal.

Rentadick, which we *did* make, came to us via David Frost. David had bought the John Cleese/Graham Chapman screenplay but had failed to get it to the screen. His flirtation with the cinema has always been an off-and-on affair. The week we discussed the subject it was very much on the blink. He had paid richly for the script. With little prospect of getting together the money to film it, he was anxious to offload it. The prospect of a screenplay by Cleese and Chapman tailored to the Python team, whom we understood were keen to be in it, was exciting. We bought it. Now we had become proud purchasers, the Pythons no longer wanted to be part of it. We had no alternative but to recruit other actors. Then, without one of our trump cards, we had to finance the movie. When you take over a script from another producer he has usually shopped it from backer to backer. We soon found that placing this package was tricky.

However, fortunately, luck stepped in again. I was asked to speak at a City luncheon. I left Elstree Studios reluctantly. We were filming. When I got to the lunch I found that I was sitting next to Graham Dowson, John Davis's right-hand man at the Rank Organisation. 'How extraordinary,' he said, 'you've never made a film for us.' 'How extraordinary,' I echoed, 'I have the perfect script.'

At the end of the lunch we made an appointment to see Frank Poole, who ran the film side of Rank. He adopted Graham's new baby with wary indulgence and we were given the go-ahead without delay. John Wells and John Fortune did a little tailoring on the script and Jim Clark collected a clever bunch of actor-comedians, including Donald Sinden, Richard Briers, James Booth, Ronald Fraser, Richard Beckinsale, John Wells, Derek Griffiths, Kenneth Cope, Spike Milligan, Michael Bentine, Tsai Chin, Julie Ege and Penelope Keith.

The film starts promisingly but somehow along the way the mixture of nonsense which Cleese and Chapman had concocted fails to rise. This disappointment can be witnessed about twice a year on late-night television. Insomniacs will notice that the denouement – an escape by aeroplane – is worked out again as the climax of *A Fish Called Wanda*. Rank lost its entire investment and Cleese and Chapman, after a chilly viewing, asked to have their names removed.

Although we were still trying to make as many films in England as possible, Terry Glinwood and I were beginning to sense that to finance British films was getting harder and harder. We made a deal with Robert Stigwood for him to buy Virgin Films. This looked like giving us some security. It also meant that we had to keep active. We bought a West End play, *The Girl Friend*, which had flopped. Caryl Brahms and I adapted it for the screen under the title *Girl Stroke Boy*. Its premise was a weekend visit home by a boy whose parents (Michael Hordern and Joan Greenwood) have begun to wonder if he will ever marry. He announces that he is bringing home a fiancée. They are overjoyed. When the pair arrive, the fiancée is black and there is room for doubt if she is a boy or a girl. On the basis of a budget of fifty thousand pounds and many deferred fees we managed to sell it to John Daly at Hemdale.

The parents and the lovers (Clive Francis and Peter Straker) gave convincing high-comedy performances under Bob Kellett's direction. It was all filmed in two weeks at a house near Elstree unhappily called Faggotts End. It seemed to delight preview audiences until the press show at which it was universally condemned. However, Daly made a television sale which recovered its costs and many years later I got a cheque for four thousand pounds for a deferment payment due to the estate of Caryl Brahms. Decades on I took a call from Paris from a French producer who wanted to stage it in the theatre. I put him in touch with the original author but I think it has yet to take Paris by storm.

For Columbia, who had now woken up to the idea of TV spin-offs, we made a sequel to the original Garnett film. It was memorable for a close-up chance to observe the detail which Warren Mitchell and Dandy Nichols put into their characterisations, for a gallery of cameos, and for two curious guest appearances by the football stars Bobby Moore and George Best. They were scripted to be heckled by Alf Garnett in a men's lavatory at West Ham FC.

The night before they were due to film I gave a small dinner party at Alvaro's – the essential sixties King's Road restaurant – the ex-directory one to which John Dexter and I had taken David Bowie. The purpose was to introduce director, writer and star to the two footballers. On his best behaviour, George didn't drink at all for most of the meal. However, he did flirt a little with Bobby's wife, Tina – to Bobby's annoyance. As a result Bobby and George embarked on an epic duel. Who could drink the most sambucas (the Italian drink, obligatory at the time, decked out with flaming coffee beans)? They finished thirteen each before the party broke up. The next morning Bobby was present for filming. George was not. We searched his favourite haunts. The general verdict was that he was holed up, hiding from us under Sinead Cusack's bed. She denied all knowledge. We filmed Bobby and then, days later, had to send a second-unit crew to Manchester to film George in a matching loo.

Finally we made *The National Health*. I had wanted to film Peter Nichols's stage play since its first night at the National Theatre in 1969. I tried to get John Van Eyssen to buy it without any luck. Four years later John asked me diffidently if I knew Peter Nichols's play *The National Health*? Tactfully I professed admiration and no back history. He asked if we would like to produce it and we were in business.

Peter Nichols's screenplay was substantially ready to go. The stumbling block had been Columbia's reluctance to entrust it to a first-time director, Michael Blakemore. Blakemore had done an excellent job with it in the theatre. His subsequent success as a film director suggests that Columbia was wrong. I had no option but to look elsewhere. We agreed on Jack Gold. Peter made some small tinkering changes and our only serious problem was to find a hospital in which to make the film. The Ministry of Health declined to help. We found a condemned barracks in Woolwich which was beautifully converted into an antiquated hospital. The cast, Jim Dale, Lynn Redgrave, Donald Sinden, Eleanor Bron, Clive Swift, Bob Hoskins, Patience Collier, John Hamill and a group of veterans, were admirable both in the moving realistic scenes and in Nichols's stylish parodies of hospital soap-opera clichés which paralleled the action. In Britain it did well and won the *Evening News* award as Best Comedy.

Although an off-broadway production had been a success, Columbia was reluctant to release it in America. It lingered on the shelves for ten years when it was finally screened on a whim in a small arthouse and highly praised by Tom Buckley in the *New York Times*. Too late. Too late.

By now Terry Glinwood and I were looking beyond the domestic market. Our last throw was a short – virtually silent – film called *The Cobblers of Umbrage*, a send-up of *The Archers* which I directed in fields around Elstree for about two pence in five days in the middle of a heavy bout of flu. My abiding memory is of standing in wet grass trying to finish a shot in pouring rain and seeing my concerned chauffeur, Roger (not the powder-blue uniform), who used to be a head waiter in a West End restaurant, making his way across the waterlogged turf bearing a bowl of hot soup, a napkin over his arm.

The Cobblers was due to be released by Nat Cohen in support of his big hit of the season – on advantageous terms for us. The big hit, *Our Miss Fred* with Danny La Rue, turned out to be the big disaster and we failed to make our killing. It has since been shown once on BBC 2.

We started to buy properties; not a cheap hobby. Jack Gold arrived one morning saying, 'I bought this book yesterday.' Obsessed with acquiring film rights, I thought that was what he'd done. How? In fact he had picked up a Penguin.

No films are made in the next few pages. They are an account of a couple of years' shopping for money for movies. Many of these projects were being juggled at the same time. All the balls hit the floor. Here is how.

Along with Beryl Vertue and Stigwood we developed a screenplay, beautifully constructed by E. A. Whitehead based on Hunter Davies's 'gritty northern' novel, *The Rise and Fall of Jake Sullivan*. We failed to shift it – or a mad medieval action romance which was to be a vehicle for the Bee Gees. It was nearly Ridley Scott's directorial feature debut. He was very hot on realism and mud; but he had to wait for *The Duellists* to wallow in both.

Tom Stoppard let us play around with the screenplay he wrote based on his novel *Lord Malquist and Mr Moon*. We talked enthusiastically about Rex Harrison and Tom Courtenay and got nowhere. I was intrigued by a novel by Eric Geen, *Tolstoy Lives in 12N B9*, a black, futuristic comedy set in '12N B9'. In Geen's world expertly planned new towns have no names – just a postal address. Tolstoy is a small boy. His father is in jail. His mother is in an asylum. His nine-year-old girlfriend is 'on a perpetual quest for a simultaneous orgasm'. His life is ruled by welfare officers, police inspectors and education experts. The progressive headmaster renames his school St Che Guevara and wants to be on TV. The swinging vicar, the Revd Kid Solomons, leads his congregation in 'All Things Bright and Beautiful' in the nude. If we thought it prophetic then, thirty years on we would probably conclude that it has been overtaken by events. It wasn't cheap. It didn't get made.

Another Stigwood idea was *Peter Pan*. He'd got Universal Pictures to put up the money for *Jesus Christ Superstar*. He wanted Tim Rice and Andrew Lloyd Webber to write the score for the Barrie play. Andrew feels that he can write anything. Tim looked forward to meeting Liza Minelli. First we needed a book. Patrick Garland had just had a success for Universal's television arm with a film of Paul Gallico's *The Snow Goose*. I suggested him.

Ned Tanen, the Universal executive responsible, flew in from Los Angeles for a meeting. He arrived in smart leisure clothes and gold chains, with a bronzed chest and an expansive manner. Patrick was brilliant. He told us the story. He told us how the story came to be written. He pointed out similarities to *Le Grand Meaulnes* and *The Great Gatsby*. After thirty minutes he paused. 'Gee Patrick,' said Mr Tanen, 'you sure do have concept!'

Fired with enthusiasm, Mrs Vertue and I set off for Paris. Liza was playing the Olympia. We went round. This was a role she had always dreamed of playing. Were we really offering it? We left feeling that we had made a talented girl very happy. Then we hit a problem with Tim and Andrew. Andrew had hundreds of tunes in his head waiting to be liberated. Tim couldn't see his iconoclastic, colloquial idiom, which worked so well on the grandiose themes of *Superstar* and *Evita*, suiting Barrie's fragile world of make-believe. Wisely he decided not to write it at all.

We tried to develop a treatment for a film version of *Joseph and the Amazing Technicolor Dreamcoat*. Again it came to nothing. We were also pursuing non-Stigwood-inspired films. We bought the rights to a book called *The Bodyguard Man*, a thriller by Philip Evans, a journalist who specialised in reporting soccer. It was set in Italy. It told an exciting but complicated story about an attempt to assassinate an Italian football idol. It seemed a good way to get out of parochial subjects. To this end we also acquired *Cage of Water*, an ingenious thriller by Alan Scott and Chris Bryant set on a luxury Mediterranean yacht with a Clouzot-style denouement. All the guests and crew are enjoying themselves in the water. The yacht is anchored miles from shore. Suddenly they realise that they have no chance of getting back on the boat and no hope of rescue. A baby, abandoned on the deck, is crying in the burning heat.

After months of negotiation we nudged both projects nearer to fruition. MGM was still producing films from England. The London office liked the script of *Cage of Water*. Terry and I came away from a couple of meetings with a brief to go to Paris and make a deal with one of a shortlist of approved directors. Terry at that time had no French and mine was schoolboy. We moved into the Hotel Lancaster and first tried Yves Boisset, who had worked on a number of English and American films. He led us a little dance, but mainly tried to concentrate the minds of the backers of another movie project dearer to his heart.

We got as far as an aperitif with Edouard Molinaro, who had just had a success with *La Cage aux Folles*. He preferred his *Cage* to our *Cage d'Eau*. After a few more rejections there was only one name left on our list. Beside it stood the initials 'NSE' – No Speak English. Jean-Gabriel Albicocco had directed one of my favourite French films, *Le Grand Meaulnes*, shown in an English version as *The Wanderer*. It is a beautiful, lyrical, primitive impression of that elusive novel. It was fêted in America where its lush, imaginative camerawork chimed with the vogue for psychedelia.

One morning we sat in the Lancaster in deep depression. Terry badgered me to call Albicocco. There was nothing to lose. He answered the phone himself and it was clear that 'No Speak English' was no exaggeration. I ploughed on. Suddenly the mention of MGM made some magic for Jean-Gabriel. He was at the Lancaster in no time, a round, dark, rumpled, friendly bear of a man with a passion for films. I managed to sketch the plot for him and we gave him a literal translation of the Scott and Bryant script.

Jean-Gabriel is dead now but I have only happy memories of him, even though we did not make the film. With his collaborator, Pierre Kast, we worked for months on the script. We talked to French actors, we examined yachts, MGM picked up our development costs – at last. They paid for a recce in Egypt where they had some currency locked away. We were within some three months of shooting when Metro suddenly decided that films had lost their charm and hotels would keep the Lion roaring in the future. Sadly Jean-Gabriel had just learnt a little English. We sat for several long days resolving script problems. Jean-Gabriel was a hit with Miss Godfrey. Her cuisine was a hit with him. After hours of agreeing and disagreeing I got into the habit of saying, 'Oh, I think it's over the yard-arm,' at about six in the evening, and handing out drinks. On the third day the going had been particularly tough. At the magic hour I became aware of Jean-Gabriel's dark eyes trained on me. A very small, hopeful voice squeezed out, 'Ees eet zee yard-arm?'

We wanted to make *The Bodyguard Man* as an Anglo-Italian co-production. So we entered the exotic world of Italian film finance. With football at its centre the best chance for the movie was in Europe not America. At that time Italian television provided a powerful boost to Italian cinema. The ubiquitous porn channels had not taken over. On our first night in Rome Terry Glinwood and I waited for our dinner guest to turn up. On the television around an elaborate relief map of the region a full-scale discussion of the drains in Calabria was in progress. An hour passed. The guest arrived. We went out to dinner. Three hours later we returned and the discussion of the drains was still going on. No wonder the cinema retained its popularity.

Our guest was Christopher Mankiewicz, son of Joseph L.

Chris had been an assistant on his father's Burton and Taylor film, *Cleopatra*. He had worked in Rome on and off ever since. When we met he was supervising productions for Alberto Grimaldi. Grimaldi had just produced *Last Tango in Paris*. Christopher was to be our guide through the tortuous byways and back alleys of Roman film-making. This time we were dealing with Warner Brothers but we had spent a lot of our own money acquiring the rights to the book, commissioning a screenplay and now finding a director who was acceptable to Warners.

Chris had an ambition to direct. He was simultaneously pushing a script by the fine American novelist James Salter called *Raincoat*, a charming, offbeat, bittersweet comedy about an amusing but very fat hero. The would-be director, himself a Falstaffian figure, passionately identified with him. Terry and I both liked the script. Our loose arrangement was that we would try to set up *Raincoat* in Britain if Christopher held our hands in Rome. He knew the vagaries of Italian film-making and had an enthusiasm for Italian food and wine which we soon realised was an integral part of it.

Warners suggested an Italian 'action' director, Sergio Corbucci. We screened some of his films in London – full of bangs and laughs. In spite of Chris's advocacy we had some trouble getting to him. When we finally did, it turned out that his wife had seen a ghastly David Bailey photograph of me in his sixties book *Goodbye Baby and Amen*. She did not want her husband to meet me, deciding that I looked evil. I agreed with Signora Corbucci.

Sergio was a vivid, buccaneering, noisy character – always addressed by his staff as 'Dottore'. All bonhomie and anecdotage, there was much namedropping, waving of arms and an infectious chuckle. There was also a tale of his disciplining a recalcitrant actor by picking up a large brick and threatening to smash his face in. He told this story accompanied by gales of laughter. From Christopher we learned that our director had some eye trouble. To disguise it on the first day of shooting he would get an assistant to disarrange a small piece of an actor's clothing. Then from hundreds of yards away he would 'notice' it and call to the assistant to correct it. This was intended to re-assure nervous actors and producers who might have started to wonder if they were working with a sightless director. This is considered a disadvantage in the movies.

Sergio embraced *The Bodyguard Man* with enthusiasm. It excited him. Football excited him. The faint hint that 'Georgio Best' might play the young footballer – lots of action, very few lines – excited him (we did not tell him that 'Georgio' had done a runner on the Garnett film).

As our meetings became more serious he began to have great doubts about the story. The characters were perfect, the plot was perfect, the action sequences were perfect. The trouble was that they were Italian. No Italian would behave like our characters. If we set the action in Spain, everybody would believe that Spaniards would behave like that – except possibly the Spaniards. This was not important. Spaniards would not matter. Also, there were many advantages. Not only would it be an Anglo-Italian co-production, it would be an Anglo-Italian–Spanish co-production. Maybe if we dealt in a couple of French actors it could be an Anglo-Franco-Italian–Spanish co-production. I do not think that working in Madrid would have hurt Sergio's income-tax dodges either.

More meetings, more food, and we got nearer to signing a contract for an option on Sergio's services. This in itself was a highly theatrical occasion. It took place in the offices of Sergio's agent, Roger Beaumont, the Roman head of CMA. Our meet-ings with Roger had always been jovial. Before, when we argued hotly about the terms of the deal, it seemed part of a Roman charade. All over the city restaurants were full of people setting up films at the tops of their voices, casting films while waving expansive arms, commissioning films over an ocean of pasta.

Now, suddenly, a religious solemnity descended on the office. As I brought out my chequebook I thought that Roger might be about to kneel. One of those restaurant romances was about to be consummated. Money was going to change hands. The reverential whispers sank into silence as pen scratched paper.

I made an explosive exit from Rome. Standing in Leonardo da Vinci Airport, I became aware of a hail of bullets spattering the walls beside me. A hijack attempt had started. Its resolution was as anticlimactic for me as the fate of *The Bodyguard Man*. We were herded on to the outside tarmac and stood for some hours singing, 'Why are we waiting?' until we were finally allowed to fly away.

There was no happy ending. I spent a lot of time in Los Angeles trying to interest stars who had some clout and were prepared to go to Italy. I failed. I nearly contracted Tony Curtis only to discover that Warners no longer wanted him. I barely extricated myself from a lawsuit and yet another expensive commitment. Long weeks at the Beverly Wilshire didn't come cheap. We went often to Madrid and looked at locations – especially at the Real stadium where we were negotiating to film the climax. Sergio worked on the script and reminisced. His stories had a ruthless Roman attitude. One day, he told us, he was sitting in the lobby of the Grand hotel with a bunch of important Italian producers and financiers and a celebrated English actor. They were joined by Raymond Stross, a self-invited American producer married to an English actress. She had some small success on the screen – none on the stage. He launched into his pitch. Even if these producers wanted her for their next picture they could not have her – no matter how much money was offered. Her English public would not let her go. The National Theatre would not let her go. Laurence Olivier would not let her go. She had just played Hedda Gabler, Juliet and Lady Macbeth for him. Olivier had told him personally that his wife was the greatest classical actress in England. At this point the senior Italian producer rose to introduce the celebrated English actor. 'I don't think you've met Sir Laurence Olivier,' he said. 'I think I'd better go,' said Stross.

Meanwhile we had been trying to set up *Raincoat* – Chris Mankiewicz's project. Chris was determined to make it with Alan Bates, from whom he had sensed some interest. The longer we worked on it the less enthusiasm Alan showed. Leading actors are reluctant to have their name attached to a script which is being peddled from studio to studio. The idea of playing a severely overweight hero was also losing some of its appeal.

All these projects (and others) led us into a curious no man's land of independent finance, and clutched straws. Persuasive Arabs materialised in hotel lobbies. Voluble Italians flew in and flourished deals which we should broker for a handsome commission. We camped out daily at the Inn on the Park, sidetracked for the moment in a greedy exercise to acquire for ourselves and our movies a share in millions of dollars which were supposed to flow from oil-rich potentates to hungry Scandinavian finance ministers.

There is no more dangerous combination than ignorance and greed. When it came to that crock of gold I could summon up both. One afternoon I found myself surrounded by expectant Italians phoning a finance minister in Stockholm and having an apparently serious conversation with him. The ragbag of 'international financiers' with whom we were dealing never inspired confidence. They invariably professed access to a trump card, usually called Prince Faisal. At one point there appeared to be some seven Prince Faisals alive and well and peddling millions in London. Confirmation of these prodigious transfers of money depended on a telex. The telex was always due to arrive on the very first day of the transaction. The small hitch that day was another regular feature of the negotiations. It stretched on for days. Dapper men with briefcases flew themselves off to Geneva or Rome or Paris and tied themselves to telephones in expensive hotels. Sensibly, no one trusted anyone else. I never heard of one of these deals going through. One Italian who had expected a fortune by telex from Crédit Lyonnais dismissed it – 'What can you expect? It's only a little provincial bank.'

I met my second genuine confidence trickster. The secret ingredient of tricksters is always that they smother you with detail. I had met one who lived in the flat above Caryl Brahms's apartment. He professed an aristocratic background and Persian family retainers known by numbers not names. His young accomplice was therefore called 'Three-five'. They were finally convicted of stealing suitcases from Euston Station in the early hours. The gratuitous detail was fatally convincing.

My second confidence trickster was a woman. We met her through a nondescript little solicitor in Kensington High Street. He had somehow been involved in the Arab–Italian charade. He said she was an 'international financier'. She would meet us at the Savoy. We should not be surprised by her appearance. She would look like a bag lady. She did. But she talked with huge enthusiasm about films. She said she knew Gwyneth Dunwoody, who, between stints as an MP, was Director of Film Production of Great Britain. This at least was true. Gwyneth confirmed it. She found the lady 'impressive'. She conducted all her business from hotels. Different hotels. She appeared to be juggling enormous financial projects. At one meeting at the Athenaeum Court we walked in as a group of directors, said to represent the threatened Mersey Docks and Harbour Board, was ushered out looking encouraged. When our time was up we gave way to the hopefuls behind a scheme for a few multistorey hotels in Rotterdam who entered optimistically. She never came near taking any money from us – she would have realised that there was little to take. She liked to create a flurry of activity. We should have smelt a rat when she used a well-worn formula – 'of course, the trouble is you only want a million pounds. It's so much easier to raise ten'. She could reel off figures as readily as

Simon Callow running through Shakespeare's sonnets. We travelled in hope for a few weeks. Gradually calls and letters were not being returned or answered. Nick Page drove down to her house near Denham and found an empty semi. He peered through the letterbox and saw a sinister pile of brown-envelopes-with-windows littering the hallway.

Finally the truth sank in. Her last inspired idea for financing one of our films was her suggestion that she could fix up an Irish–Ghanaian co-production. She had 'high-level contacts' in Ireland and Ghana. An Irish–Ghanaian co-production? We thought not. It later transpired that she had been a financial secretary to a large company. She had been imprisoned for embezzlement and was making good use of her parole when we met her. She was soon back inside.

Desperation was beginning to set in. The money, energy and emotion invested in *The Bodyguard Man* to no purpose was a huge disappointment. From the simple process of selling an idea to a studio – Cohen, Columbia, the Boultings at British Lion – we were having to juggle the irreconcilable tax dodges of potential investors from various parts of the globe and attempting to negotiate pre-sales to as many other countries as we could impress. I began to feel horribly out of my depth. My initial misgivings about film and me nagged away. I missed the immediacy of live television and the theatre. I doubted my ability to start a project big enough to have the staying power to remain valid through the many years of finding it, setting it up, financing it, casting it, filming it and presenting it to the public.

We grasped at other straws in order to keep active. Some were attractive projects which we badly wanted to do. Others were exercises in opportunism which failed to provide an opportunity. We toyed with a film comedy-thriller written for Morecambe and Wise. We had several meetings with Ernie Wise, who still wanted to be a film star. When we finally met up with the more cautious Eric Morecambe it was clear that he did not share the enthusiasm. We even contemplated a werewolf story which we reckoned could be filmed entirely in my house.

This is a cautionary tale, descending into black depths.

I regret some that got away. Alan Bennett wrote an ambitious original screenplay called *The Vicar's Wife*. It is a comedy in the Ealing manner which we offered to Peter Sellers with his agent Harvey Orkin's enthusiastic encouragement. The plot turned on the attempts of a busty young woman to exhaust to death her elderly parson husband. The script came back very smartly. It was only then that Harvey and I remembered that Sellers's recent marriage to Britt Ekland had been quickly followed by a heart attack.

Some clever lobbying by John Heyman brought Cary Grant, who hadn't made a film for years, into the frame. Rachel Roberts was to play the wife. One of Grant's conditions was that, if he was to film in England, we had to provide a role in Britain for his estranged wife, Dyan Cannon. Ms Cannon was not well known at the time. Grant's plan was to ensure that he would still have access to their young daughter. Terry Glinwood discovered that Tony Tenser, an old colleague, was planning a B-picture. We plotted to give him ten thousand pounds to engage the ex-Mrs Grant. When she was signed and she told her former husband that she was taking their daughter to England to film, he would say, 'What a coincidence! I'm going to be filming there at the same time.' At the last minute Grant's advisers persuaded him that this little local British film was not the sort of thing he should be involved in. We only just avoided a commitment to Dyan Cannon with no movie to underwrite it.

Concerned at his wife's disappointment, Rex Harrison read the script and demanded to know why it hadn't been offered to him. 'If Grant could play it, why can't I?' I had originally wanted Rachel but I had not wanted her to think I was simply using her as a way to Rex. He seemed to accept this and I spent a weekend in Portofino discussing the script with them. He was preparing to film *Staircase* with Richard Burton. Sadly, before we could proceed *Doctor Doolittle* was released and Columbia, who had been most likely to back the film, had decided that Rex was not the great draw they had considered him to be a week before.

We developed a romantic English Western, *Gentleman Abe*. A 'last of the gunslingers' cowboy rides out of Buffalo Bill's Wild West Show after Queen Victoria's Royal Command Performance at Windsor and heads for the English countryside. There he teams up with an impoverished squire's lovely daughter. Together they start a series of provincial bank raids before riding off into the sunset. Once again no one shared my expensive enthusiasm. I even asked Michael Winner to consider it. He passed.

Caryl and I adapted a Henry James novel, *The Spoils of Poynton*, which we had earlier done as a play. I sent it to Katharine Hepburn, who was conveniently in England at the time. With farcical timing an English actor's agent also called Hepburn telephoned one lunchtime to give me some unwelcome news. We had a row. Putting down the phone to return to my congealing lamb chop, I had hardly sat down when it rang again. A secretarial voice said, 'Miss Hepburn for you.' I was about to launch into another tirade when the unmistakable voice started to ask me searching questions about *The Spoils*. It didn't work out. Nor did it when I got tentative interest from Bette Davis, Glenda Jackson and Michael York. Nat Cohen wanted a 'romantic comedy vehicle' for Twiggy – we started Eleanor Bron and John Fortune on a wild goose chase for a script. It fizzled out.

A near miss was Graham Greene's novella *May We Borrow Your Husband*. The rights were owned by the old Hollywood composer Dmitri Tiomkin, holed up in Hampstead with a young wife. With his encouragement I interested Joe Losey in directing. He brought in Harold Pinter, who would write the screenplay. Dirk Bogarde, Michael York and Lynn Redgrave looked likely as the leads. Columbia was thrilled. Just as we seemed set Dmitri changed his mind and demanded a crippling downpayment for the rights. He passed on the partnership we had been discussing all along. Ironically, after his death it was filmed for television from a dull screenplay by Dirk Bogarde.

My last excursion into film finance was the least successful. It was a dying throw in our efforts to finance *Raincoat*. Optimism preceded disaster. Two old Hollywood hustler contacts of Chris Mankiewicz – one black, Bill; one white, Gene – assured us that they had everything all tied up. I was to fly to New York on a Sunday and check in to the Algonquin hotel. On Monday all that was required would be my signature on a piece of paper. The Monday meeting failed to materialise. Thursday was Thanksgiving Day in New York. On Wednesday the nation went on holiday. It would have been a weekend of gloom had it not been lightened by hospitable friends in Buck's County.

On Monday the saga started again. I was looking for the last third of the budget. The rest was secured in England but it could not be released until this final contribution was in place. I hung about for expensive days. The moment of truth came at the Plaza hotel. Gene – whose infallible deal had brought me inno-cently to New York – was still on the job. He invited me to meet a Southern millionaire. He was in coal, but he wanted to invest half a million dollars in a movie. It seemed improbable but greed and necessity won.

We are at the Plaza.

The millionaire, short, in a blue suit and an open-necked shirt, is behind the door. Gene is bobbing nervously up and down a long corridor, welcoming. In the sitting room are four men, five women and the remains of an all-day buffet. Introductions. The oldest woman is maybe Czechoslovakian, perhaps the madam. One of the others is French, one English, two are American. They look like the sum total of a last-minute, indiscriminate casting call. The English one is a model in England. No, no particular agency, but she worked with some really nice people and had a really nice time until it became really draggy and then she decided to come to New York. She arrived three months ago and really liked it because, although when she got here all her friends were out of town, she made some really nice men friends and all in all she's got to like New York a lot. Really.

I can't work out the cast yet. I'm not sure if the millionaire is the millionaire though the chances are that he is because he seems to be the worst-dressed person in the room. I know that his lawyer is here. He must be the 'distinguished-looking' grey-haired man in another open-necked shirt. He smiles a lot. More champagne arrives. I am joined by the snappiest dresser. I do not recall his name. Maybe he is the millionaire? No, he is too friendly and he lives a few blocks away. He talks about movies. He is a close partner of Gene; they've got a regular little group going. They get together a lot and have a fun time. Like tonight.

Finally, the millionaire coal-miner is declared. It is the Badly Dressed Man. His name is Joe, or Bob, or Bill. He is wheeled over. I am to tell him the story – strictly for laughs. He is not really interested in the story but if the deal is right he says he will go along. I recite and he laughs a great deal and occasionally slaps a fat thigh. The ladies laugh a little bit but only when they see he is laughing first and slapping. Halfway through my tale he gets diverted into a story about a launch he owned on a lake near the coal mines and girls and liquor and a storm . . . The investment recedes.

Sandwiches arrive. An enormous tray of club, beef and chicken – no turkey. Instead there are a lot of turkey jokes at Gene's expense because Gene has raised turkeys since he left Princeton. Gene's big thing now is celebrity turkeys and show-business turkeys. Gene, a visionary, conceptual thinker, sees a great deal of life this way because some executives also send turkeys to girlfriends. Gene can tell how important the girlfriend is by whether she gets a fourteen-pound turkey or a twenty-pound turkey.

By now the girls are beginning to look a little bored.

The coal-miner's lawyer descends on me. Are we getting down to business? No. He produces a carbon copy of a poem he suddenly felt inspired to write one dark and stormy night down south. The poem had come to him quite spontaneously, as such things do, and he called it 'Togetherness'. He has made several copies and is in the habit of giving them to friends. It starts, 'How can a man with mortal words . . .'

Business appears to be over for the night. The girls are despondent and start getting their coats. 'We thought there was going to be an orgy,' one says sadly. I suggest that there is still a fair chance and, like a reporter from the *People*, make my excuses and leave. Gene diverts me to the lobby and says that professionalism is very important and he has arranged many more meetings for the next day and that the coal-miner, who is very professional, has personally said that he may come through . . . Walking away, I could hear the girlish giggles begin. At least they were getting their orgy. The ladies prostituted themselves to some purpose; I danced to none. That much was confirmed in the morning.

I had to leave New York just before Christmas. I was contracted to appear on, of all things, *Any Questions?* It put a fitting full stop to my career as a film producer.

Unlike Terry, whose skill and experience subsequently found him a prestigious role in movie-making, I needed to find a new career quickly. Flushed by the Stigwood deal, I had moved into 19 Wellington Square in Chelsea, which I bought for £113,000. Now, approaching the mid-seventies, Stigwood shares dropped steeply, and we were making no films. The Westminster Bank and the tax man decided that something dramatic must be done. Their preferred gesture was for me to sell the house. In the housing slump of the time its value had fallen to £56,000. At least, that is what it went for. The car went too and with it the best in my collection of chauffeurs. He became landlord of a pub in

Islington and rented me his house in the New North Road on very friendly terms. Islington was as grey as it had always seemed and still does. American Express was getting stroppy about a bill for a few thousand pounds. We agreed that if I paid it I could keep my card. I paid it and they cancelled the card. The next morning a letter from American Express fell through the letterbox soliciting subscribers. I filled in the form. It asked whether I had possessed a card before. I wrote that I had. It enquired why I no longer had it. Truthfully I replied, 'Because you took it away.'

I posted the application off without much hope. I received a new card by return of post.

CHAPTER 9

It's the Little Things You Do Together

Caryl Brahms and S. J. Simon collaborated from the late thirties until his death in 1948, producing a popular series of funny ballet books, starting with *A Bullet in the Ballet*, and a highly successful set of anachronistic, historical comedies including *Don't, Mr Disraeli*, *No Nightingales* and *No Bed for Bacon*.

While I was at Oxford I had had two vague, pipe-dream ambitions. In fact they were the same. I wanted to write or direct, preferably both, two musicals, based on two novels – *Zuleika Dobson* by Max Beerbohm and *No Bed for Bacon*. Brahms and Simon were and are fiercely loved by a generation of readers but were less well known in recent years until many fans pointed out that the film *Shakespeare in Love* followed the same plot as *No Bed for Bacon*.

Zuleika was a perfect subject for Oxford. However, although Max Beerbohm was still alive and reasonably well and living in Rapallo, it never occurred to me that he would let anyone set his novel to music. I was reckoning without Cambridge. The announcement in *The Times* that *Zuleika* by a music don, Peter Tranchel, and James Ferman, much later Britain's film censor, was to hit the stage at the Arts Theatre was accompanied by a pithy sentence stating that Sir Max was overjoyed that Cambridge was giving his heroine 'theatrical life' and that he had always been disappointed that Oxford had never asked.

I watched the subsequent history of the show. It was pleasant as an undergraduate musical, dominated by Peter Woodthorpe who played Noakes. Later Donald Albery staged it for London and, while with ATV, I went from Birmingham to Wolverhampton to see a pre-London tour performance at the pretty little green and white theatre. Woodthorpe was still in it, still funny, but more subdued. Diane Cilento was acting, but barely singing, Zuleika. She left the show at Oxford among traumas. Eventually it came to the old Saville Theatre, starring Mildred Mayne, who had been promoted from inside the company. Until then she was mainly known for a bra advertisement on the underground. *Zuleika* languished and died.

However, back at Oxford Sir Max's rap on the knuckles emboldened me. 'So,' I thought, 'Caryl Brahms is still alive. I'll write to her.' As soon as I had come down and was installed in semi-permanent lodgings (semi-permanent that lasted eight years) on Chelsea Embankment, I checked the London telephone book and there she was, no ex-directory nonsense, 3 Cambridge Gate, London NW1. S. J. Simon, her great collaborator, had died some years before and since then she had finished a novel, which they started together, and written another by herself, *Away Went Polly*, which I admired. I had already started to toy with songs for *No Bed*. I wrote to her to suggest that I might perhaps send some lyrics to see if she would agree to an adaptation of the novel for the stage.

I posted it late in the afternoon, and next morning Kenneth Fortescue, with Michel Raper one of my landlords at that time, called me down to answer the telephone. I found it blearily and awoke quickly at the sound of a sharp, businesslike voice at the other end of the line. 'Caryl Brahms,' she announced. 'Is that Mr Sherrin?' I admitted it. 'Of course we have met,' she said firmly.

I doubted it. 'Oh yes,' she said, 'I'm trying to remember where. I'm sure I know your work.' I doubted this as well and said I was just down from Oxford. 'That must be where we met,' she persisted and continued until I weakly agreed that we probably had. 'There, you see, I knew it,' she triumphed. She went on to explain that she would much rather I did not send her lyrics because people were always doing that and then she lost them or failed to find brown paper and string with which to return them, provoking accusations of theft from the would-be adapters. I suggested that I should come and talk to her about the idea. She could see nothing wrong with that and suggested that I should come for a glass of sherry the next Tuesday evening. It was 1954. I was twenty-three, she was fifty-three.

As we talked we moved round to the idea of doing it together. Caryl was one of those writers who hate other hands to adapt her work for a new medium. Her humour was too delicately balanced and too personal to her and Simon. Apart from one exercise in adapting *Away Went Polly* as a stage play, with Christopher Hassall, she had not wanted to embark on another collaboration after Simon's death. However, I was very different from him and did not challenge memories of what had been a highly successful, close and idiosyncratic partnership. They both had their alternative professional interests. Caryl had her ballet criticism until she tired of dancing swans, Simon his bridge. He played as an international and his book, *Why You Lose at Bridge*, is a classic, but their joint work was the principal concern. They were both funny, and together they were formidable.

Caryl did not have the most logical mind, but her descriptions of Simon suggest a rare Russian anarchy. Together their strange imaginations took off on excursions into laughter using routes no one else had explored. They were unique, and they influenced a lot of writers who came after them.

My own collaboration with Caryl was of a very different order. If she most nearly approximated to an organiser in her

work with Simon, in our partnership she had to be the free
spirit. My instinct is more earthbound. I was inclined not to
allow her the chance to explore untravelled areas, being too
sure too soon that there was nothing there to discover.

In a late addition to her memoir, *Too Dirty for the
Windmill*, which I edited after her death, Caryl made her own
comparisons:

S. J. Simon and E. G. Sherrin: Skid and Ned . . . Skid with
nothing about which to be secret, withholding nothing. Ned,
the schizophrenic grappling to himself his secret or secrets, yet
changing as the wind changes of a March day . . . Skid working in my mind and I in his, in a creative kind of ESP . . . Ned,
withholding what he writes so that I can at most act as a kind
of corrective governess, embellishing his work . . . Often Ned
and I have furious arguments, but, as with Skid, never over
money: always in the placing or replacing of words, or occasionally on a point of creative wit . . . Skid was a clown by
birthright . . . 'That's not humour, it's wit: OUT!' . . . Ned is a
wit – at times a disturbingly arch wit . . . his close-cropped
hair somewhere between red and brown: steady, piercing eyes,
pale thin lips, not unlike an egg in a bitter mood, making a
biting and shrewd assessment of his peers . . . yet when I first
met him there was no bitterness discernible in him, only a
happy, friendly, eager ambience . . . Skid was less able but
more secure than Ned, whose insecurity takes the form of
never admitting to being in the wrong . . . He is lucky in that
he soon starts believing his own lies, and this I find half infuriating and half touching. Skid saw no necessity to lie* (*Why
bother? Shrug) . . . As I write [1982] Ned is coming up to 52,
good looking in a paunchy way and narcissistically brimming
over with confidence. However, there is, I think, a price to be
paid by the over-confident. Can it be only the thin ice covering the dark water of self-knowledge beneath? . . . Certainly

where money is concerned he is the most generous man imaginable . . . Skid was an open book for all to read: Ned is an
island under an April sky; a sphinx – I wish I had the understanding to solve his riddle and to help him in the way that he
helps me . . . speed is of the essence in his sevenfold working
fury. I like to select and, as it were, taste my words: Ned's sevenfold demons drive him on torrent-wise.

The hares that this passage starts are many and various. The
suggestion of a secretive nature is valid, but secrecy was sometimes essential to preserve a working relationship. In those
pre-Wolfenden days when homosexuality was illegal Caryl was
expansively liberal in her attitude. Her background in ballet
criticism had made her many gay friends – probably the majority of her circle was gay – and she enjoyed them and their
company freely. However, she did not consider it at all appropriate that I should have gay relationships. Indeed on the two
occasions when I embarked on attempts at sustained affairs she
did all she could to sabotage them. She need not have worried.
In both cases I was dumped. Of course, the cause was not a
rivalry for my emotions, but for my time. Caryl was a writer. I
sometimes wrote, but my main livelihood would come from
producing or directing first television, then films and sometimes
plays or musicals in the theatre. The time when we could write
together was limited to evenings and weekends. A lover, a play,
a television series or a film on location impinged on these valuable moments. Not enjoying a row, I preferred to conceal or to
leave revelation to the last moment. If I managed to involve her,
as I would with *TW3* and in getting her to devise the final
medley in *Side By Side By Sondheim*, she would eventually come
round; but shows in which she was not involved, like *Come Spy
with Me* at the Whitehall Theatre or *Only in America* at the
Roundhouse, she never attended and sniped at from the sidelines. One of her secretaries told me after her death that she had

complained about some of the 'shocking' ventures into which I had dragged her. I could only answer, 'Try keeping her out.'

I would never wish away the almost thirty years of work together. The early days were a wonderful introduction and an invaluable apprenticeship. I would not have missed the whole experience, but that is the background to the work.

It must have been infuriating for Caryl to have a writing partner less committed than she was. My main source of income was my other work. Indeed I could not have survived, nor continued to subsidise our writing partnership, without the other activities.

We started work on *No Bed for Bacon* over a ritual lunch at the Ivy about a week after our first meeting. To me, the Ivy represented West End theatre. It was my first visit. I was unaware that it was long past its heyday (and decades short of its revival). Neither of us knew that it would regain its glamour in the eighties. Caryl had used it a lot during the war and was delighted. We met on a Saturday and I began with an artichoke, another first.

As *No Bed* was to be a musical we had to find a composer. Caryl had done some work with Leslie Julian Jones, one of the composers for the Gingold revues during and after the war. He lived in West Horsley with his wife, Hazel Gee, a choreographer, and we began with him. However, rather like a Ziegfeld or a Cochran collecting tunes from a number of sources, Caryl was not happy with one composer. She was a close friend of the Australian Arthur Benjamin and admired his popular 'Jamaican Rumba'. So it was assumed that he would contribute one or two songs. Caryl kept talking airily about a drinking song which she insisted on calling a 'Brindisi'. Then there was Larry Adler, from whom we solicited a couple more. When we went to see him I carried the tape-recorder and for years he thought of me as Miss Brahms' technician. It was an odyssey of stumbling discovery. To look back on it is to shudder at our naïvety. Another potential victim was the Canadian conductor-composer Robert Farnon. Caryl wanted to purloin his popular 'Westminster Waltz' tune.

Farnon sensibly did not want to surrender it. In the end the first score was mainly Leslie's.

The novel is a warm and witty, anarchic, anachronistic examination of the court of Elizabeth I and the playhouse of Shakespeare and Burbage. The starting point is Brahms and Simon's reluctance to believe that Shakespeare could have written Cleopatra for a boy actor. Viola, a lady-in-waiting, falls for Shakespeare and the theatre, disguises herself as a boy and is taken on at the Globe. When Shakespeare finds out her secret he declares that at last he is ready to write the great woman's role now that he has found an actress worthy of playing it. It was always a problem for us to tell the story in sufficient depth and to balance it with the running gags which pepper the book and the revue numbers with which we dramatised other comic set pieces like the 'tasting of the first potato'. We played it to innumerable managers, never with much luck.

I remember the series of auditions principally because it was my first experience of a managerial excuse which I soon realised was a universal cliché for rejection: 'Of course,' they said, 'we think it's very funny, but it's too sophisticated for the public.' There were also private backers around to lead us up other garden paths. At one house we were to be dined lavishly and then, in an after-dinner glow, to play our demonstration tape. Before dinner I started to set up the tape-recorder and by pushing two plugless ends of flex into a metal fixture I fused every light in the house, putting an end to dinner, audition and that source of money. When we performed live Leslie played and sang the love songs, I chimed in with the comedy numbers and told the story, while Caryl enthused – though a manager told me years later that his clear memory of one such occasion was 'of this tall, fair young man singing away to the accompaniment of the flying hands of a wild gypsy lady at the piano'.

Auditioning a musical is a depressing business, but we were extraordinarily ill prepared. Some listeners would preserve a stony silence throughout and beat a retreat the moment it was over. Others would laugh along, tapping merry feet and smiling appreciatively. They would linger to discuss casting and theatre, unable to come out with a rejection face to face. Two days later that would arrive through the post – or they would find it easier to forget and let it fade away. Private backers often looked on these occasions as a free concert at home and asked friends, who were supposed to make the evening go with a swing – invariably they grew bored and talkative five minutes in. Ours was a hopeful, innocent approach, especially as the private backer was usually good for no more than an investment of a few hundred pounds. They never told us that until they had had their free cabaret.

It was Leslie Julian Jones who first got the play to a stage – the village hall at West Horsley. He and his wife were leading lights at the WHIPS, the local amateur dramatic society. We went to the last night, and very spirited the WHIPS were. One of them, a commuter to the City, was so impressed that he recorded the performance and, encouraged by Bernard Miles to treat the Mermaid as the City's private theatre (not unreasonably as the City had provided most of the money), he submitted the tape with an enthusiastic letter.

Bernard reacted well. He liked the idea and the frequent references to Elizabethan London. He summoned us to Puddledock and said that he was delighted by the plot: 'Bloody girl, dressed up as a boy – going to bloody Shakespeare!' The Mermaid was still an ex-warehouse just below Blackfriars Bridge. He showed us proudly over the rubble with Josephine Wilson, his wife, and Gerald Frow, his son-in-law and PR assistant. Josephine wore a permanent worried look, as though in constant anticipation of the next brick which Bernard would surely drop. She kept her distance, rather like the English lady five yards behind her husband in *Monsieur Hulot's Holiday*.

Inside the bare walls of the warehouse a theatre was taking shape among the mud and concrete, and the thrust stage was being installed. Bernard delivered a tirade against theatre in the round which was plainly a set piece. He had been to see it. He had not liked it. His neighbours in the theatre had not liked it. 'Couldn't bloody concentrate. No play's half as interesting as how far the bloke on the other side's got his hand up his girl-friend's skirt' – end of theatre in the round. Administration was being carried on in a small hut on the building site and we fin-ished up there with the Miles family, sausages, and some very sharp white wine which played hell with Caryl's digestive system on our next few visits.

These stretched into a saga. On that first meeting Bernard was expansive. What a wonderful idea! What a perfect play to open the Mermaid! A play about Shakespeare and a play about the City of London. He retold the plot of her novel to Caryl with delight – a conversational gambit which he repeated on each of our subsequent meetings. He had heard the tape and vetoed our choice of composer. This was not a battle which we minded losing. We were beginning to feel the need for a coherent score and were aware of the weaknesses in ours. Bernard suggested John Addison, whose work for the revue *Cranks* we all admired. However, first he said he wanted some changes to the script. He was glad we had written as we did because, he said, it enabled him to see clearly where we had gone wrong. He sent us off to rewrite while he went to America to appear in a remake of *Wuthering Heights*. 'A great man of the theatre,' we said to each other on the way home. 'We can learn from him . . .'

At the end of four weeks we sent in the rewrites and a couple of days later went down to hear the great man's verdict.

'I'm glad you did those rewrites,' he said. 'It's all wrong, but I can now see exactly what to do about it.'

He gave us more sausages and white wine and sent us away to do more work.

'A great man of the theatre,' we said to each other once again. 'We can learn from him.'

Two weeks later we were back again.

'I'm glad you did those rewrites. It's all wrong but now I can see exactly how to bloody do it.'

He told us the plot again and with rich enthusiasm invented a new scene. 'Nothing bloody like it has ever been seen on the stage. Just bloody think. She's rehearsing with bloody Shakespeare and he gives her this speech. Remember he thinks she's a boy and she knows she's a bloody girl. So she gets to this line, "Bare thy bloody breast", and she can't. But he doesn't know that so he keeps after her: "Bare thy bloody breast". And she doesn't so he rips her bloody shirt off and he sees both of 'em and he knows. Never been seen on the stage. Bloody marvellous!'

Accepting that he may well have been ahead of his time, we were beginning to have doubts about the direction in which our man of the theatre was leading us. However, we had one more go. Returning, we found Bernard in an exultant mood.

'Bloody marvellous!' he enthused. 'It's all wrong, but I'm glad you did it. Now I know what to do. Throw out all your dialogue. Every bloody word! Go through Shakespeare. Shakespeare has a word for everything. Find 'em all. I don't want a word of yours. All bloody Shakespeare's. I want an under-water-over-air tapestry of Shakespeare's language.' (And if anyone doubts that this flight of Milesian fancy ever dropped from his lips, I have been repeating it without embroidery regularly since the memorable day on which I first heard it.) Bernard had not yet finished. He was having a vision.

'I can see the opening night,' he said. 'We'll have the Queen and we'll have bloody Philip! Both at the Mermaid. London's theatre! She'll come down by barge, sailing down London river; and she'll get out of the bloody barge and she'll sit herself down and when the play starts every bloody word'll be Shakespeare's – not one of yours – just bloody Shakespeare's for bloody everything; and after about five minutes Philip'll get the idea and he'll dig her in the ribs and say, "That's where the bugger got it from!'"

We parted at that, gave back our, I think, £150 commissioning fee, and found that Bernard, like any sensible manager, was talking to several teams about providing the opening show for the Mermaid – Lionel Bart and Laurie Johnson were chosen, and Bernard earned his hit with *Lock up Your Daughters*.

Before we finally got *No Bed for Bacon* to a stage at the end of the 1950s Caryl and I wrote our first produced work – directed on radio and then for television by Charles Lefeaux, a senior BBC producer. We called it *The Little Beggars* because it was a loose retelling of *The Beggar's Opera* for very young kids living rough on a bomb site. Alec McCowen played the Macheath figure in both productions. David Hemmings was the child lead in the radio play but had outgrown the role by the time we got it to television. So had Michael Ingrams – later Michael Crawford – who was one of a chorus of kids.

No Bed for Bacon finally found a home at the Bristol Old Vic in 1959. A new composer had arrived on the scene. Caryl enquired of the music publishers, Boosey & Hawkes, if they knew a young writer, classically based, with a melodic gift. They suggested Malcolm Williamson, an immature Australian whose orchestral music was full of big tunes and who turned out to be keen to try a musical play.

We were also playing with a musical version of *A Midsummer Night's Dream*. I still have a reel-to-reel tape of *Make with the Mischief*, the title we gave it, having had the idea of making the fairies black following Shakespeare's hint in the line, 'We are spirits of another sort'. We made a demo with Cy Grant and Lucille Mapp as Oberon and Titania, and Rachel Roberts as a tempestuous Helena, inspired at the recording by several glasses of port – 'for the voice'.

Quite early on Malcolm showed signs of trouble. The musical gift was sabotaged by appalling behaviour, usually after drink had been taken. Once when we were working at a convenient piano in the BBC *Tonight* studio he disappeared behind the set for a piss, relieving himself on the studio floor. On a couple of occasions when we were on our way to play the score to managers he would demand a twenty-five-pound 'loan' before consenting to present his music. It came as no surprise years later to hear that, as Master of the Queen's Musick, he rarely met her commissions on time.

Much in awe of the melodic gift of Richard Rodgers, he produced some wonderfully expansive settings for ballads and bouncily effective tunes for comedy numbers. In spite of the problem of getting Malcolm to play the score to managers if he was not in the mood, John Moody, who directed the Bristol Old Vic, took it on. Having grown fat on the success of *Salad Days*, Bristol was always looking for a successor. Frank Dunlop directed. The company was full of first-class character actors – many on the brink of national recognition: Lally Bowers, Michael Bates, Peter Jeffrey, Robert Lang, John Woodvine, Donald Pickering, David King and Derek Godfrey, who played Shakespeare. Marion Grimaldi came in to play the Lady Viola.

The balance between plot and incidental diversion had still not been found and our collaboration with Williamson ended on the last week of the run. After a substantial disagreement about rewrites – we were still hoping for a transfer – we all went to the pub next door for a lunchtime drink. Malcolm surprised me by buying the first round. For himself he ordered a pint of bitter which he emptied over Caryl's head. The story has gathered variations whenever I have had it told back to me; but those are the bare facts. I still regret not having punched Williamson very hard. As an excuse I can only say that it is not every day someone pours a pint of bitter over a lady, and my reflexes were below par. The victim insisted that she would rather leave quickly than stay around to argue with the future Master of the Queen's Musick – so we went. Stephanie Cole, who was a student at the Bristol Old Vic school at the time, told me years later that witnessing this sealed her ambition to be an actress. Suddenly the theatre seemed exciting.

It was 1963 before we had another go at *No Bed for Bacon*. This time it was at the Ashcroft Theatre, Croydon. By now we had a new score composed by Dave Lee and John Scott. Again the cast was good, led by John Wood as Shakespeare, with Vivienne Martin, Angela Baddeley, Stephen Moore and William Rushton. Again incidental performances and comedy set pieces came off; but we had still not solved the conundrum of reconciling the drive of the romantic plot with the jokes that pepper the book. A pattern of disasters dogged our theatrical adventures. Here it focused its attentions on our opening night.

At the dress rehearsal the leading lady was in tears about her costume, and with good reason. Robin Phillips, now a distinguished director but then a fledgling actor not involved in the production, though a close friend, volunteered to make another overnight. He is the most prepared theatre director in the world – his versatility covers wig making and dressing, dress designing and making, the practicalities of lighting, scene construction and rudimentary choreography; box office and theatre cleaning are second nature, and his comprehensive supervision of press and public relations, though more controversial, is spirited. None of this was known to the young woman in question, who simply saw a pale young actor promising to make a suitably grand gown in twenty-four hours. If she was Cinderella, she was not going to recognise Robin as a Fairy Godmother. She burst into tears and went missing.

She was still missing the next day, and as the time for curtainup approached general nervousness spread. Not only was the girl nowhere to be found but the dress was on the other side of London with Robin and a girlfriend still stitching. Realising that time was running out, they transferred their workroom to a taxi and as they hit a traffic jam from Streatham to Croydon commuters were treated to the puzzling spectacle of a young man and a young woman bent over a mass of apricot silk, sewing pearls into it. In Croydon we had no idea where they were and no way of finding out. We hoped for the best. The leading lady returned to the fold just in time, having spent the day stalking Croydon in a successful attempt to control her emotions. She arrived rather too soon for us. Her first request was to see her new dress, which had still not turned up. Before a massive relapse could set in, the dress came through the gates of the car park and with a pin here and a tuck there brought about her complete recovery.

It was not enough to save the play. It languished in Croydon and stumbled as far as the cavernous wastes of the Golders Green Hippodrome. There was enough going for it to make a transfer to the West End a possibility, but no more.

One of the great problems of doing musicals in this country forty years ago was the prodigious effort it takes to get them produced. So often it was necessary to agree to a try-out on an undernourished repertory-company budget. Some musical shows thrive on an air of improvisation; but the very nature of most of them requires that they should have more people, more scenery, more costumes, more rehearsal, more musicians, more of everything than the average straight play, and all that adds up to more money and more risk. Nowadays it is even harder.

Caryl and I developed one sideline which helped nudge our work towards the stage. With *The Little Beggars* on radio (which became a BBC nomination for the Italia Prize) we had started a vein of ballad musicals. For a 'sort of sequel' – *Bigger Beggars* – we used English and American folk songs in a story of teenage gang warfare in south London, which we pushed as far as a student production at RADA with would-be actors like Tom Courtenay, Nicholas Pennell, David Burke and Derek Fowlds. We called it *Shut up and Sing* (echoing one of the projected titles for *West Side Story*, which was *Shut up and*

Dance). We did not succeed in setting it up in the West End, though some managers came to see it and Tom Courtenay's fighting performance in the lead focused early interest in his career. His next, and first professional, role was Konstantin in *The Seagull* at the Old Vic in the Waterloo Road.

Of our shows which started in this way, the one with the longest life is *Cindy-Ella* or *I Gotta Shoe* – the Cinderella story played out in the Storyville area of New Orleans. A mother narrating the traditional story of Cinderella to her child holds the show together, and the dialogue is an anthology of received white attitudes to black traditions. Mostly traditional Negro songs are used. They fit the moods of despair and elation that characterise Cinderella's progress to the ball and back. 'Sometimes I Feel Like a Motherless Child' spells out the loss of her own mother. 'Nobody Knows the Trouble I've Seen' heralds the arrival of stepmother and sisters. She goes to the ball to 'Swing Low Sweet Chariot', and comes rushing out at the stroke of midnight to catch the Midnight Special – 'Git on board!' The resources of radio drama enabled us in the late fifties to engage a large cast and an orchestra conducted by Peter Knight, who also composed the music for some original songs.

The large and ebullient company, which included Elisabeth Welch, Bertice Reading and Cy Grant, carried the carnival mood of the studio into the lifts at Broadcasting House. I retain a vivid picture of the producer, Charles Lefeaux, a man excellent at his job but with a rolled umbrella in his soul, being serenaded with 'Swing Low Sweet Chariot' as a lift took us up to the canteen. Bertice Reading narrated the piece during the day and then carried out a demanding nightclub routine. At the final recording the sound mixer turned up her microphone and all that emerged was silence, followed by a deeply contented snore and then a wheeze. I sympathised years later – waiting to be interviewed on a particularly dull television discussion about acting, I went to sleep during a long answer from the playwright David Mercer.

I was surprised to find the studio manager whispering into my ear that I was on next and would I wake up as I was only about two feet away from the interviewer and about to be asked a question.

Now we had an off-air recording of *Cindy-Ella* to give us something we could play to managers. To make a demonstration record is always expensive and often frustrating. Here we had in our hands a first-class cast and beautifully orchestrated songs, and we began to prepare a stage version to go with it. We took it to Michael Codron, who was to become one of the most enterprising and innovative of West End managers. At the time he was still producing musical plays. His reaction was good and prospects began to look rosy. Then Sandy Wilson finished his version of *Valmouth*, Michael produced it and we lost Bertice to the venture, in which she played Mrs Yaj.

Cindy-Ella was shelved for the theatre for the meantime, but we were still in love with the subject so we attacked it again as a novel. In 1962 W. H. Allen published the slim volume with beautiful illustrations by Tony Walton. I was waiting to go on the air with *TW3* and still directing *Tonight*. I persuaded the editors that we could make an attractive item by singing the story of a black Cinderella in five and a half minutes, and produced it by stringing together snatches of the show's key folk songs and spirituals, sung by Elisabeth Welch and Cleo Laine, using a split-screen technique to decorate the musical summary with Tony Walton's black-and-white illustrations.

By a happy chance Michael Codron was watching and became excited all over again about the show he had passed up a few years before. There was a catch. He thought it would be best performed entirely by Elisabeth Welch and Cleo Laine. The era of the two-character play was approaching. We persuaded him to accept two men as well – Cy Grant and George Browne – who had also been in the radio version. The four were to play all the parts and share the narration. We redressed the script once again.

Christmas and the start of rehearsals were perilously close, and to add to the risk Cleo was some six months pregnant and had to be dressed by Tony Walton in an apricot tent – the most pregnant Cinderella ever to meet her Prince Charming. We played matinées at the Garrick Theatre and opened in a record snowbound winter. For the revival the next year at the Arts there was no snow, but audiences were still not big enough. Since then we have done *Cindy-Ella* on record, on television, and revived it at the Criterion in 1976–7. In 2003 came a welcome reissue of the album on a new label, Must Close Saturday Records.

Other disasters come back like old friends. We tried to make a *revue macabre*, *Kiss Kiss*, out of the short stories of Roald Dahl but lost Roald when we lost the management which had been enthusing about it. Then there was a revue, *Les Pupitres* by Ramond Davos, which Caryl and I were paid to translate from the French. We did the job to the best of our ability and advised the manager who had commissioned us not to proceed. It was essentially a small-theatre, absurdist show which he was determined to tour around the larger Moss Empire provincial houses. He supplied the new title *Oom Pah Pah!* and engaged a director just down from Oxford and a perfectly respectable cast who suffered enough on tour not to be reminded of the nightmare experience. The manager thought a reasonable economy would be to leave the engagement of a musical director for this musical piece until the second week of rehearsals and a stage manager until a week later. Somehow they rehearsed and got themselves to Bristol.

It was 1964 and I was just about to start *Not So Much a Programme* on BBC 1. I arrived in Bristol late on a Monday. They had had Sunday to get the modest set in and were due to do a dress rehearsal on Monday evening. I waited until it was time for the milk train to take me back to London – nothing had happened. Next day I got back to Bristol to do a promotional interview on the local television news, and checking at the theatre found that only the opening number had been roughly run through on stage. I went to the BBC to breach the Trade Descriptions Act, lavishly assuring viewers that they were in for a feast of fun. Returning to the theatre, things were running true to early form. The audience, which no more than half-filled the enormous barn, was welcomed by the director, who stepped through the curtains to inform them that the show was not really ready and if they would prefer to go home they would get their money back. Their appetites whetted by the promise of impending disaster, not a soul moved. Or at least not until we were ten minutes into the show. Throughout the first half there was a steady trickle of absentees. At the interval I eavesdropped in the bars and would have been surprised to hear an encouraging word. I was not surprised. On our return the half an audience had shrunk to an eighth. The eighth were even more restless and kept up a movement towards the exits livelier than anything that was going on on stage.

A heavy pall of gloom hung over the two translators, especially as Caryl had a large clutch of cousins living around Bristol. They all turned up to cheer her on and we were to meet for dinner. The wake (good food and pitying looks) ended for me when I got back on the milk train, but the humiliation was not over. The press-cutting agency sent weekly reports as the show moved from town to town and bitterly reproachful criticism from local papers trickled in.

The tipping-up of theatre seats is never an appealing sound. We heard it again in our one venture into opera. Colin Graham, who had directed *Cindy-Ella* beautifully for us, asked us to translate some dialogue in a Carl Orff opera, *Die Klüge*, which he was to produce at Sadler's Wells in a double bill with Dallapiccola's *The Prisoner*. *Die Klüge* has a buoyant, tuneful score, but the dialogue scenes were as earnestly German as the revue we had translated was feyly French. There was one other stumbling block – the plot, which Caryl could not understand. It hinged on the biological fact that mules – the result of a union between horse and donkey – cannot reproduce. This was news to Caryl, and she was reluctant to believe it or to believe that anyone in the audience would know or believe it. We reached an amused compromise. Colin Graham suggested a programme note: 'NB. Mules cannot have babies'. Caryl accepted that and we set to work from a literal translation to cut and sharpen the scenes. It was not a labour of love, except in the sense that it was unpaid, but we did it, sent it off and forgot about it.

Some twelve months later Caryl got a call from a friend who said he was looking forward to seeing her at her first night at Sadler's Wells. We checked in the newspapers and there it was, a double bill: *The Prisoner* and *Die Klüge*. Getting into appropriate clothes, we shot off for our premiere. The Dallapiccola was a tremendous success. The foyer buzzed with approbation at the interval. We went back in to see what would happen to *Die Klüge*. For the first time we paid attention to the programme. There was an asterisk after the title. I looked at the bottom of the cast list. There it stood in all its inexplicable clarity: '*NB. Mules cannot have babies'. Colin is a man of his word.

The curtain rose on one of Orff's lively melodies, but as it finished every word of the appalling spoken passages rang out with that uninflected, sing-song flatness that only Welsh opera singers can produce to perfection. Whatever percussion Orff included in his score was overshadowed by the relentless seat-tipping exits of the paying public. Almost alone but for a sympathetic Arthur Benjamin, who was too polite to leave, we sat it out. We were never asked to improve another opera.

While I still worked inside the BBC there was a chance to work on other features under the loose banner of current affairs: a couple of series with Eleanor Bron and John Fortune, *Where Was Spring?*; a set of parodies of current-affairs reporting by N. F. Simpson, *World in Ferment* – very like Armando Iannucci and Chris Morris's show *The Day Today* with Steve Coogan brilliant as Alan Partridge some thirty years later; and three semi-documentary shows written by Caryl – *Steam, Sanctity and Song, The Long Garden Party* and *The Long Cocktail Party*. These were musical essays which counterpointed the events of the Victorian Age, the Edwardian Age and the 1930s with the evocative popular songs of the period, featuring among others Michael Redgrave, Joan Greenwood, James Booth, Millicent Martin, David Kernan, John Wood and Elisabeth Welch.

Together Caryl and I wrote three big shows which gave me an exciting opportunity to work with some extraordinary actors. Sir Donald Wolfit was one. Wolfit stories are legion. In theatrical memory Sir Donald is perceived as the last of a line, the epitome of overacting, a definition of 'ham', and selfish and mean to his inadequate companies. Towards the end of his life he was inclined to encourage these reports: he was well aware that he had become a character and fed the legend. Ronald Harwood's biography, one of the best theatre lives ever written, tells the famous Wolfit stories and evaluates him more accurately than most. He was the Shakespearean actor whose classical performances I would hasten to with keenest anticipation. No exceptions.

My own encounters with him were after the great days when his Lear was generally accepted as the best of the last century and when his unfashionable tours of Shakespeare, without subsidy, made him a one-man arts council. Watching his dagger scene in *Macbeth*, Caryl Brahms heard a galleryite at the old Bedford breathe excitedly, 'Cor, 'e's seein' things.' Going round to Wolfit to tell him, she found him more impressed than amused: 'Ah, Miss Brahms,' he said sagely and seriously, 'the illusion of the theatre.'

On one occasion Rosalind Iden, Lady Wolfit, was ill and not available to play Ophelia. Joan Greenwood, a young actress with Wolfit at that time, was offered promotion at short notice.

Wolfit recalled lovingly how he gave her the chance. 'Could she have a new dress for the role?' she asked. Magnanimously he let her have the run of his dressing baskets. She found the perfect dress, ransacked his supply of stage jewellery and painstakingly sewed a mass of beads and bits of glass all over the costume to her satisfaction. Happily gowned she played the role and after her success he was generous with his praise. Encouraged, she made a request. It had been a wonderful experience, one that she would treasure; might she, as a memento, keep the dress she had made? In retelling the story I could see Wolfit's awareness of his reputation for closeness fuelling the enthusiasm with which he built to his pay-off. 'No,' I said, 'no, you may not *keep* the dress . . . but you may *always* wear it when you play the role in my company.'

His 'ham' reputation makes imitators who never saw him thunder and bark when they tell Wolfit stories. In fact his voice was very flexible; its more characteristic notes were light and high and, when he was suggesting shocked surprise, as he frequently did, it approached a whine. I went round to see him once after a performance of *Ghosts*, which had moved to the West End following an initial production at the Old Vic; Sir Donald had replaced Michael Hordern as Pastor Manders. I had enjoyed Michael's performance, but the feeling of farce during the announcement of the fire went too far and I told Wolfit how much better the scene was playing. Characteristically, he agreed. 'Hordern did it at the Vic,' he said. There was a long pause and the voice became quiet and conspiratorial. 'I know Hordern . . . had him as Macduff to my Macbeth on the wireless . . .' A long intake of breath and a sad shake of the head, 'Very dangerous!'

We went on to discuss the rest of the production, especially Dame Flora Robson's Mrs Alving, which had improved a good deal since the Waterloo Road. Again Sir Donald agreed emphatically. 'I'm glad you thought that. She is better, isn't she? . . .

Much lighter . . . I had quite a battle achieving that . . . You see, what Flora didn't realise was that Ibsen didn't write for tragediennes . . . There weren't any in Scandinavia at the time. All he had were comediennes with a gift for pathos.' No one should embark on an Ibsen play without considering Wolfit's theory, and it probably explains why Joan Greenwood's savagely funny Hedda Gabler is easily the best I have seen.

On the same evening Sir Donald went on to discuss future plans. The BBC had asked him to give his Volpone on television. He viewed the suggestion with a mixture of proper pride and extreme pain. 'My old friend Stephen Harrison is doing it . . . Shan't have to worry about the cam-e-ra angles . . . But do you know? . . . Do you know what they, the BBC, have had the effrontery to ask? I am to give my Volpone to the television . . . a lifetime of study . . . Shan't be able to play it again in the theatre for ten years . . . Giving my Volpone for a paltry few hundred pounds . . .' The voice was rising: 'And they said . . . they actually said . . . [Higher!] we must have a *name* for Mosca! [It went through the ceiling.] 'A *name* for *Mosca* . . . I want me old John Wynyard. Best Mosca I ever had . . . but they want a *name*! I know what'll happen . . . Stop every two lines while the fellow says, "What does that mean?" Well, you haven't got time for that in television . . .' More head-shaking and a dying fall, 'A *name* for Mosca!'

He got his 'old John Wynyard'; and for posterity the unforgettable moments when Wolfit opens the play and bids good morning to the sun and ends it with the exhalation of breath which signifies the end of the Fox are murkily but magnificently preserved in a grey telerecording.

The occasion of my one working experience with Wolfit was a television production of the play *Benbow Was His Name*, which Caryl Brahms and I had written for him for radio under the title *Those Cowardly Captains*. He was not available for the radio production and the part was beautifully played by

Michael Hordern ('I know Hordern . . .!'). It was a naval drama set in the early years of the eighteenth century, based on an actual mutiny in the West Indies and on the literature of the sea. Our starting point had been Caryl's love of sea shanties and our wish to find a narrative which could be carried along by them, sung by the folk-singers Robin Hall and Jimmy MacGregor, with whom I had worked on *Tonight*.

The mainspring of the mutiny was the clash of personality between Admiral Benbow, a sea-dog of the old school, and Captain Kirkby, a gentleman officer, much given to foppery. Charles Shadwell's play *The Fair Quaker of Deal* concerned two such characters and we stole our establishing scenes from it. Opposite Sir Donald we cast John Wood, most elegant of a new breed of actors. John has now become one of the most sought-after stage stars, but in 1963, his career at the Old Vic having failed to prosper, he was beginning to carve out a reputation as a television star. He has a demanding temperament and a repu-tation for it. (There is a more recent story of an agent calling him in New York and telling him that a director had asked for him. 'That can't be true,' John said. 'Yes it is, I just put the phone down,' said the agent, 'he definitely wants you.' John was not to be persuaded. 'He can't. I've worked for him before.')

The parallel between the old salt and the elegant fop in the story was echoed in the contrast between the styles of the stars. We wondered how they would get along. On the first day of rehearsals Donald arrived knowing every word. 'I've got a lot on my mind,' he said touchingly. 'I don't want these young sparks to see me struggling for the words.' John Wood's approach was the opposite. He learnt his lines effortlessly during rehearsal. However, they deferred continually to one another, enjoyed and admired one another, and provided a bumpless passage. The nearest we got to a difficult moment was one day when we were going from the outside rehearsal room to the BBC for lunch. Peter Stenson – playing a small part – was getting into his car.

Donald was looking his most Wolfitian, eyebrows beetling, face flushed, the astrakhan collar on his coat spiritually, if not actually, there. The taxi I had ordered had not arrived so we rode with Peter, the nervous actor. Donald crammed himself into the small front seat. As the driver got more nervous his hand slipped from the gear lever onto Wolfit's knee. Peter's voice shot up a few octaves as he apologised. Wolfit was reassuring: 'That's all right, lad. We get used to that sort of thing in the theatre.'

Wolfit was working in the West End at the same time as we did *Benbow*, playing John Gabriel Borkman at the Duchess Theatre. The television play was scheduled to run sixty minutes and to be recorded over two days at the BBC's Riverside Studios. During those two days we were to see Sir Donald only for Saturday morning and Sunday; on Saturday afternoon he was giving two Borkmans. It was a heavy chore for a man of his age, especially as he never felt as much at home in the studios as he did in the theatre. A complicated production included film sequences cut in, simultaneous back projection and Hall and MacGregor singing their sea songs against it. Michael Byrne, then a young actor just out of RADA, stood in for Wolfit when he was absent, marked his positions and ferried him into place when he rejoined the company on the Sunday.

I do not think Donald knew much about the actual recording. Michael put him on his marks and he gave a fine performance, but the bustle of the studios, the strain of playing Borkman at the same time and the length of the role meant that he had to conserve all his energy to say the lines correctly in alien surroundings. His death scene took place on board ship at the height of a particularly dirty, smoky battle. He had one obsessive concern. He took me aside. 'Lad,' he said, 'I don't have to die with my face dirty, do I?'

Caryl and I went to stay with the Wolfits on the night the play was transmitted. They were always warm and welcoming hosts at Swift Cottage in Hampshire. He seemed very nervous. After a while we realised why: there was an unnatural concentration of admirals living in the district. Hampshire is a dormitory area for retired naval officers. Donald, playing an admiral, was worrying what sort of figure he would cut for his neighbours. It took a couple of calls from them before he felt off the hook. He had watched the transmission with a mixture of surprise and pleasure. He had not been aware of the projections and film sequences in the studio. They had all been taken from old feature-film footage – tall ships banging away at one another in the heat of battle. Donald appeared to have got it into his head that this was special film that I had run up ingeniously with a Box Brownie and tank full of models. As classic cinema sequence succeeded classic sequence, I became more embarrassed. 'Splendid shot, lad!' he kept repeating. As the sequences became more ambitious his admiration grew more fulsome. My embarrassment reached a climax with the biggest and best battle, lifted straight from *Lady Hamilton*. I decided that I had to confess, before I could be handed credit for that as well. 'That's from *Lady Hamilton*,' I whispered. His reply was immediate: 'Not as good as yours, lad.'

I was glad that the notices were good. It was impossible not to be aware that somehow at the back of his mind Donald was counting up the performances he had left to give. Some were sacrificed to cash. He played many films simply to leave as much as he could to his widow when he died. He had supported touring classical theatre single-handed for so long that he was entitled to take the sort of role that made people arch their eyebrows. Not all the films were negligible. He scored a great success as Mr Brown in *Room at the Top* – though this rebounded.

He told the story rather ruefully. He was proud of his Shakespearean readings, which he toured with Rosalind. (Somewhere in the repertoire was their two-man *Othello*: 'We've cut out Iago – do it all with lights!') On one occasion they arrived in San Francisco. 'I went down to the theatre to check the arrangements, as I always do, so that Rosalind can rest a little at the hotel. I had expressly asked for a Tudor chair – of course they gave us a Victorian one. But we are used to that. Then I went to inspect the front of house.' The great tragic actor's mask registered shock with no trace of humour. 'They had billed me as Donald Wolfit.' He paused to consider the ignorance which had obliterated five decades of distinguished service to the classics with one billboard: 'Donald Wolfit, Mr Brown, of *Room at the Top* Fame!'

When Wolfit died, Caryl and I mounted his obituary programme at the BBC. She wrote a linking commentary, spoken by Michael Elliott, who had directed his last television performance (Pastor Manders again, not at full strength; with Celia Johnson as Mrs Alving and Tom Courtenay as Oswald). I started to search for people to talk about Wolfit. It was important that it should be considered, but not solemn. Caryl called the programme *The Knight Has Been Unruly*. First I looked for other knights who would speak of their peer. I did not approach Sir Ralph Richardson, knowing that there had been some friction long ago when they had both learned their business in a touring company run by an old actor-manager called Charles Doran. (Wolfit was an encyclopedic rememberer of stage business. Once when I said I had been to see Richardson's Shylock, he hissed, 'Did he drop his dagger on the way out of the trial scene?' 'Yes,' I said. 'Ah! Ah! Doran's business!' he cried.)

The replies of Wolfit's fellow knights were magically in character. I tried Sir Laurence Olivier. But he was to read the lesson at the memorial service and thought that was enough. Sir Michael Redgrave was diplomatically ill. Sir Alec Guinness's refusal was subtly judged: 'I thought he was a wonderful film actor,' he said. 'I never really saw him much in the theatre.' Finally I went down to the Old Vic to see Sir John Gielgud between performances – without much confidence. He was disarmingly frank as usual. 'I couldn't do it,' he said. 'It would be so hypocritical. We used to think he was a joke.'

And so, of course, the West End had always thought, and I was reminded of another of Wolfit's long-held grudges going back to a forgotten Old Vic season when he played Macduff to Gielgud's Macbeth. He said that they had quarrelled on the first night, and I became vividly aware of the naked animosity that can be kindled between ambitious young actors, as Wolfit dwelt in secret tones on his revenge – 'Got him by the eye with me sword in the fight on the second night.'

Finally it was Sir Donald's most famous adversary who buried the hatchet on his behalf – Sir Tyrone Guthrie. Guthrie had directed his legendary *Tamburlaine*, then quarrelled over a revival of *King Lear* at the Old Vic. Wolfit left the company. Yet Guthrie's epilogue was just and generous, and recalled the distinction with which Wolfit spoke Shakespeare's verse and his awareness of the need to keep his voice, 'his instrument, honed and bright'; and the devotion with which he had done so.

Richard Burton remembered Wolfit in the storm scene in *Lear* on a night when the hovel collapsed on his back and he had to play the whole scene carrying a house around the stage. Sybil Thorndike still saw him as a young actor of great promise joining her and her husband in a Sunday-night try-out in Swiss Cottage; apparently most concerned about the tragic waste of this man who in her perspective was dying too soon. Members of his company – Harold Pinter, Brian Rix, Eric Porter and Ronald Fraser – told their stories. Film clips, television recordings and the sound recording of *Lear* filled out the programme. But most moving was a simple roll-call of all the Shakespearean parts that he had played in all the plays. It was an incredible roster – the best epitaph on a unique career.

Wolfit's obituary also gave me my second chance to observe Elizabeth Taylor in her role of lady-in-waiting. When Donald died Richard Burton was shooting *Where Eagles Dare* at Elstree and I went over to the studio to ask him to record a piece. He was warm and welcoming to the idea, but it was impossible to ignore the feeling of a circus surrounding him at the peak of his fame. The large suite of dressing rooms was full of odd extras, chauffeurs, hairdressers, secretaries and the Welsh acting Tafia, the feeling very much that of Prince Hal's hangers-on with the Prince doubling as Falstaff. One quiet presence saying little and sipping from a beer can in a corner was Clint Eastwood, who was making his change of career from spaghetti Westerns to international movies, and observing the hoopla with one raised eyebrow.

At Lime Grove Burton smartly cut through Miss Taylor's reluctance to wait downstairs by asking if she might sit in the control room. She had never been in one before. She spent an hour or so either fascinated or behaving with scrupulous good manners, watching the process of television – as opposed to film – from a new vantage point, and professing amazement at its complexity.

Donald's memorial service was held at St Martin-in-the-Fields. It ran much after the pattern of those occasions. I like a good theatrical service, the mixture of stars and fans, fellow workers and fellow sufferers; the determination that this is a 'celebration', a 'party' – anything but a funeral. I came in behind a little old woman, I think a member of the public, of Wolfit's public, not an actress. She was bent and she moved slowly and finally arrived at an usher. He showed her courteously to her place and gave her a form of service with some concern. As she took it to move past him she unwound to look up and thank him: she had to unwind quite a long way as he was very tall. When her eyes at last met the usher's she gave a little start. 'Oh,' she said, 'you're Paul Scofield.'

'Yes,' he said gently, 'but we're not here for that, are we?'

One irony of television is that when recording became common in the 1960s many valuable programmes were still lost to posterity because there was no space in which to store many of the tapes on which they were recorded. No trace remains of an extravagant musical I wrote with Caryl and Ron Grainer, *Take a Sapphire*, with a cast including Georgia Brown, John Wood, Max Adrian and Elisabeth Welch, and the last public appearance of the ballerina Lydia Sokolova, a name unknown to the chorus dancers until she electrified them by a stunning entrance in the rehearsal room.

It was another lavish production, with an orchestra of sixty and a cast of about the same number. Budgets were hugely different in those days but I think I had been allocated some sixteen thousand pounds to produce the entire seventy-five minutes. It cost twenty-four thousand pounds – an overspend of eight thousand. Paul Fox, who had unwittingly inherited responsibility for overseeing it, sent me a sharp memo when the full extent of the damage became known. Happily he had not worded his memo wisely. 'Would you care', he wrote, 'to explain this overspending?' My reply was simply 'No', and I heard no more.

In 1970 Caryl and I wrote a biography of Charles Dickens to commemorate the centenary of his death. It was culled almost entirely from autobiographical scenes from his novels. Gordon Jackson was the narrator, and the cast included Anthony Hopkins as Dickens, with Joan Greenwood, Vivian Pickles, Arthur Lowe, Patrick Cargill, Mona Washbourne, Dandy Nichols, Jenny Agutter, Michael Wilding, Nora Nicholson, and, in virtually their last television performances, Stanley Holloway, Dame Gladys Cooper and Dame Sybil Thorndike. Dame Gladys flew in just in time to rehearse, and spent most of the first day telephoning British Airways to argue about some articles of jewellery missing after her flight from the West Indies. She had five lines in her cameo scene with Jenny Agutter and was not going to be rattled about remembering them. By the time we got to the studio some days later for the first run through she had mastered two out of five and retained them for the dress rehearsal. At the end of that she loomed up in front of the biggest camera wearing street clothes and a headscarf. 'Boy,' she called sweetly, 'I'm going to dine at the Ritz with my agent; I'll be back in plenty of time for the show.' The next thing we heard was a call from a coin box. 'It's Gladys Cooper, I'm getting into a taxi now. Please have the money ready when I arrive. I haven't any on me.'

She got one of her two lines right when we recorded her, and patiently allowed us to record the other four in single takes as though she were humouring us. I had always admired the story of her courage when, presenting herself in a new play on Broadway, she made her entrance on the first night to find that a man in the front row had placed his hat on the stage. Walking straight down to it she booted it coolly into the fifth row and carried on with the play. It was good to find that the composure survived.

There was one farcical diplomatic disaster. Dandy Nichols's make-up as the definitive Mrs Gamp was grotesque. When we had filmed her scene and cleared the recording, I made the mistake of saying, 'They've checked the tape, Dandy. It's OK. You can take off your make-up.' She wasn't impressed. 'I've taken it off already,' she said.

Sadder circumstances attended my attempt to enlist Dame Margaret Rutherford to play Miss La Creevy, the miniaturist. She had been ill and had not acted for some time, but Stringer Davis, her husband, felt that coming out to work in a small but charming role might be therapeutic. We sent her the script for her scene some weeks ahead and Stringer heard her lines daily. Just before we went into rehearsal, I had the morbid thought that I had better check that she had been able to learn it. I took Anthony Hopkins, who was to play opposite her, out to meet her. They read the scene and then her husband encouraged her to do it without referring to the book. It was not a good idea. Time after time she forgot the lines; and each mistake added to her distress. We were as encouraging and admiring as we could be. Tony especially struck up a rapport with her; but it became agonising to watch.

Dame Margaret was a wonderful actress with a much greater range than is usually appreciated, but she was very ill and very tired and very old. The more she failed the more determined to try again she became and the more tearfully disappointed. Our difficulty was to release her without allowing her to feel that she had let us down. We left at last with heavy hearts on Stringer's optimistic prophecy that her return to acting would perhaps be best judged in a large role in the theatre. It was not to be. She died soon after. Her TV role was played by Nora Nicholson, who was in fact slightly older.

The Great Inimitable Mr Dickens was a success – in spite of a *Sunday Times* forecast that although the idea sounded good, 'the word around the BBC is that it doesn't work'. When the film was repeated I asked if we could repeat that sentence among the other raves which were added to the *Radio Times* billing – unfortunately it was not considered politic. Some years later Yorkshire Television produced a series of programmes telling the story of Dickens's life, written by Wolf Mankowitz. They announced proudly that they had found a new approach: they were going to illustrate important moments in the novelist's life by scenes from his books. I suggested to the BBC that we repeat *The Great Inimitable* the week before and the response was enthusiastic. As the time drew nearer I heard no more and rang to find out when we were scheduled for transmission. There was an embarrassed pause. They had wiped the tape. None of those fine performances – in some cases last appearances by great actors – existed. To paraphrase Shakespeare, 'These our actors . . . are melted into air, into thin air . . . and, like some insubstantial pageant *wiped* . . . leaving not a wrack behind.'

A subject for which there was no easy route to the stage was our attempt to make a stage musical out of the life of Marie Lloyd. We had by this time already dabbled in late Victorian/ early Edwardian music-hall atmosphere in a radio play called *Mr Tooley Tried*, in which we embroidered around a Crippen-like marriage between a meek little man and his overbearing singer wife. The music-hall songs ran through the play and once again we felt that we had the basis of a stage show. The music was by Anthony Bowles. A tape of the original songs which we wrote with him was generously recorded by friends who included Barry Humphries. Just as we were trying to set up a production, Wolf Mankowitz announced a musical, *Belle*, based directly on the Crippen theme, and once again we had to retreat and use our material as a novel, which we called *Rappel 1910*. However, while we researched the period music-hall material, we became fascinated by Marie Lloyd, the greatest music-hall star of her age, and her turbulent private life. We started to chase up the surviving contemporaries who remembered her.

Ada Reeve, who was ninety-one when we met her in 1965, grew up in the next street to Marie Lloyd and was some three years younger. She admitted frankly that although Marie was universally loved she herself had been rather afraid of her. The older girl was too brash and too noisy in spite of her open heart. On one occasion when Ada was playing at the Tivoli she bumped into Marie in Leicester Square. It was her first West End engagement and Miss Lloyd decided that it was an occasion for celebration. She hustled Ada into the Queen's bar on the north side of the square and called for champagne, which Ada had never tasted before. She took a sip, was disconcerted by the bubbles and did not like the taste.

'Drink up!' her hostess commanded. 'Have another!'

'Oh, no!' said the debutante.

'Go on – bloody virgin!'

'I'm not, Marie! I promise I'm not.'

Ada was always looking to better herself and felt that she had made it when she married the stage manager of a legitimate theatre company run by Sir Johnston Forbes Robertson. Recollecting him bitterly she said, 'He had all the appearance of a gentleman.' Thrilled by keeping company with her gentleman,

she married him and they went to Brighton for their honeymoon. Showing him off on the front, she was dismayed to see an
effulgent Marie Lloyd approaching. In her new-found gentility
she was sure that Marie would say something shocking in front
of her 'gentleman' husband. She tried to head him off down a
side street, but it was too late. Marie bore down on them and
looked Ada's catch up and down approvingly: 'Nice bit of cock
you got there, dear,' she said and sailed on.

Ada had another grievance, which was really against Marie's
first husband, Percy Courtenay, a racing hanger-on. She was
taken to Brighton races on this occasion and given a hot tip by
the lord who was escorting her. Courtenay offered to place the
bet and the lord handed over the money. The horse came home
at thumping odds, only for Ada to discover that her bet had not
been placed. 'Didn't think it could win, old girl; just trying to
save your money.'

As we talked to her in the upstairs dining room of a pub at
Notting Hill Gate, her strong voice rose to a pitch in moments of
excitement and swooped to a conspiratorial whisper at others.
Her stage training meant that even the conspiratorial whisper
carried throbbingly around the room, and at one point an old
cockney woman some tables away bustled across, drew herself
up beside Ada and said sharply, 'You're a wicked old thing.
Don't you say a word against our Marie, she was twice as good
as you'll ever be.' She stomped out leaving Ada no room for
reply, and for a moment the old lady's eyes looked puzzled.
Then she shook her head in disbelief and applied herself again to
her lunch, which she was attacking vigorously, carrying on with
her story between and during mouthfuls.

All the old ladies we met had the same tendency to whisper
their confidences: plainly the thirty-odd years since Marie
Lloyd's death had done nothing to diminish the aura of scandal
that surrounded her. One of the most interesting was. Clarice
Mayne, who used to feature an imitation of Marie Lloyd in her

act. Her first marriage was to James Tate, who accompanied her and wrote songs for her, including 'Oh, You Beautiful Doll'. He was billed with her on the halls as 'Clarice Mayne and That'; after his death she married Teddy Knox of the Crazy Gang. Her imitation of Marie was generally held to be the best and she was happy to slip into it. She clucked with disapproval when I told her that we had been to see Marie Kendall, whose great song was 'Just Like the Ivy'. Marie went out of her way to say what a lovely girl Clarice had been. 'I dare say she did,' snapped Clarice, 'old cat. Always trying to pass me off on some follower or other,' hinting darkly that Miss Kendall's motives in urging these introductions were not always of the purest.

Clarice also harboured a grudge against Vesta Tilley, who, unlike Marie Lloyd, had not relished her impersonations and who, as Lady de Frece (when she married into music-hall management), was in a position to make her displeasure known. 'I saw her years later in the south of France,' said Clarice with uncommon relish. 'She was very old, and I cut her dead.'

On one visit to New York I tried to track down another contemporary, 'Happy Fanny Fields', an American who had success in England before the First World War. She retired in New York and married a Dr A. J. Ronjy. I looked her up in the phone book and found that she was living on Central Park South. I had little time to spare but I did not want to alarm her with a call out of the blue. I checked with the editor of *Variety*, Abel Greene, who told me that as far as he knew she was well and that anyway if I rang the number in question I could get a switchboard operator who would be able to give me the up-to-date information. I rang and got no switchboard but a very suspicious maid. I asked if I could speak to Mrs Ronjy. 'What about?' I explained that I was researching the background to one of Mrs Ronjy's contemporaries on the stage in England. No luck. 'Ah'm sure Mrs Ronjy don't want to be bothered by a little thing like that,' she said, slamming down the phone. When I left two days later I could see her point. I opened my *New York Times* and read Mrs Ronjy's obituary.

Marie Lloyd's life runs too true to the traditional show-business story. A love life littered with unsuitable husbands, and a professional career which goes up and up as personal happiness goes down and down. In the end she was too sick to earn the huge sums she had commanded all her life, but she continued to perform and to scatter money with extravagant generosity until her death – on stage.

Once again as we thought we were near a production a rival version reared its head. This time it was Dan Farson who provided the competition. His play was staged at Joan Littlewood's Theatre Royal at Stratford in London. Joan Littlewood directed herself. It had long been her ambition to do a show about Marie Lloyd: 'Silly old Joan,' Barbara Windsor used to say, 'she's in love with cockneys'. It was not one of the productions she touched with her special magic. It languished and did not move. However, we reckoned that we had to put our version away for a few years. In the meantime we kept working at it and rewriting, helped at one stage by Peter Wood, who co-operated closely and imaginatively with us and with Ron Grainer on script and music. He cut a swath through the clutter of detail which we loved because of its accuracy but which we began to see was killing the play's theatrical life. At another stage we persuaded Alan Bennett to write a couple of important comedy scenes.

The years of research, writing, rewriting, cutting and re-examining paid off when the Greenwich Theatre opened in 1969. Ewan Hooper, whose brainchild it was, was looking for a musical which could fill the new theatre with familiar songs on a London subject. We talked to him about Marie Lloyd and he was enthusiastic – the only problem was a shortfall of a few thousand pounds on the sum required to budget it adequately. It was time to do the rounds of the London managers again. This time at least we had a theatre which was staking some of the money, so for a limited investment a punter had a chance to see if his gamble would pay off and could then complete the flutter, should he wish, by financing a West End transfer.

In fact we found Robert Stigwood, who was busily expanding his empire into theatre and films. We lost Millicent Martin, whom we had hoped would play Marie, to an engagement at the Talk of the Town. Barbara Windsor came in instead, with Denis Quilley and Maurice Gibb of the Bee Gees as two of her husbands. The Bee Gees were separated at the time by bitter differences and casting Maurice as Bernard Dillon, Marie's disastrous young husband, was as much an act of therapy on Stigwood's part to keep him happy as it was a piece of commercial casting. A few eyebrows went up among the cast on the first day of rehearsal when Maurice's road manager solicitously helped him into his rehearsal sneakers and took away his street shoes; but pop stars do get used to the attentions of their road managers, and the word when Maurice's marriage to Lulu broke up was that he was given custody of the 'roadie'. His performance, though keen, was lacklustre. Barbara has recorded that I told her that she should 'give him one', as it might liven him up a bit on stage. Apparently she did but it didn't. (After the run Maurice was reunited in harmony with his brothers, and the Bee Gees continued to prosper as a trio until he died in Florida in 2004.)

Robin Phillips directed *Sing a Rude Song* in a set by Roger Butlin with Tim Goodchild's costumes. It had plainly benefited from the long history of rewriting. Barbara Windsor's keenness was a major problem. She saw herself as a reincarnation of Marie Lloyd, which was not hard considering her cockney background, her volatile character and her turbulent private life. As the opening drew nearer she rehearsed more and more strenuously, recording her songs, taking them home and singing them through the night. Her voice, though pleasant and practised, was not elaborately trained and during the dress rehearsals and previews signs of strain were beginning to show.

We opened on a Thursday, 18 February, and she was fine. Friday morning brought a crop of good notices. Bookings, which were already good, shot up, so Greenwich could be fairly certain that the theatre would be full for the run. On Friday night Harold Hobson was in for the *Sunday Times* and Barbara did her best, but the voice was going. By the end of the evening it had gone. Because of the short-handedness of suburban companies her understudy, Pat Ashton, was not adequately rehearsed, and after curtain-fall Robin Phillips and I tried to prepare her for two performances on Saturday. Both were fully booked and Greenwich, which had only been open a few months, could ill afford to give the money back. At three in the morning we gave up: Pat was too tired and nothing was going in. We decided to sleep on it and prayed that Barbara's doctor would work a miracle.

We had called the company for eleven the next morning and they straggled in, cold, damp and apprehensive. The verdict from Barbara's doctor was depressing – in no circumstances could she sing until next week. We were not sure on which day. Pat Ashton was not nearly ready to go on alone so we worked out a compromise. I had told the story to so many managements over the years that I was to stand at a lectern at the side of the stage and ad-lib my potted history of Marie Lloyd, leading into scenes and numbers which did not include Marie and could be played as staged. The snag was that she was in virtually everything. Robin, the director, wearing black sweater and black trousers, would read her scenes; the choreographer would dance her dances; and Pat Ashton would sing the songs. And so this extraordinary hybrid with a narrator and three Marie Lloyds was launched. I shall never forget the look of puzzled horror in Denis Quilley's eyes as I explained the plan, but there was no alternative and everyone agreed to give it a try.

It worked like magic. Indeed Irving Wardle, in the *Christian Science Monitor*, suggested it was the most perfect Brechtian approach to a musical that he had ever seen. No one asked for their money back and our only anxiety was that this was a trick that could only work once. Luck and nerves had got us through the matinée. Would we get our comeuppance in the evening?

No, it worked even better now that the actors were emboldened by seeing that their scenes played just as well. An extended season at Greenwich was followed by an anticlimax. We had to wait weeks to get a suitable theatre, and when we did move into the Garrick in May 1970 the excitement that surrounded the run at Greenwich had disappeared. The opening coincided with an election, a World Cup, a Test match, a heatwave and Wimbledon. We were not short of alibis, but the trouble with alibis is that some shows do not need them. There were seventy-one performances.

Two years later we wrote another musical for Greenwich, with a book by Dick Vosburgh and music by John Cameron; Gillian Lynne directed and choreographed. Once again we were trying for a recognisable style of popular music, in this case country and western. We used Goldsmith's *She Stoops to Conquer* as a basis and it proved a perfect vehicle for Vosburgh's twin skills – scholarly analysis of the virtues of the original and an impeccable ear for pastiching the clichés of movie Westerns. Instead of riding out from London to the countryside around Bath, Marlowe and Hastings set off from Boston for the Wild West of the 1890s. Tony Lumpkin became Tommy Hawk, an irresponsible Indian speaking only in Hiawatha-ese. The explanation? His mother, Mrs Hardcastle, had been raped by a Native American. Kate, when she stooped to conquer, became a saloon bar queen instead of a serving-girl. Derek Griffiths's Tommy was his first theatrical breakthrough. But the show failed to find a West End home.

It came at an interesting time when the 'miking' of musical shows was about to become universal. We opened in Greenwich at roughly the same time as *Jesus Christ Superstar* – another

Stigwood triumph – was opening at the Palace with the entire cast yelling into their microphones over a big orchestra sound. For *Liberty Ranch* we had the odd mix of an amplified band and acoustic singers. Never again!

For a saga to match the length of time it took to get *Sing a Rude Song* to a stage we have *Nickleby and Me*. This dramatisation of *Nicholas Nickleby* we first undertook for Giles Havergal for his opening season at the Glasgow Citizens' Theatre, where the roof was leaking and there were buckets in the aisles to collect the rainwater. Again we were working against time and had no clear idea how we could condense eight-hundred-odd pages into two and a half hours of stage time. The solution came in our first conversation with Giles. We were most attracted to the Crummles family – the touring theatrical troupe with whom Nicholas and Smike find shelter and work in Portsmouth. Among Nicholas's duties is the translation of French plays. But instead of translating we had him write an original play and like all beginning playwrights his first attempt was autobiographical. In this way we were able to have the Crummles company play the *Life and Adventures of Nicholas Nickleby* – in grand barn-storming style, with Mr and Mrs Crummles claiming plum roles like Mr and Mrs Wackford Squeers and Sir Mulberry Hawk. As an additional device we invented a miser for whom the company is giving a dress rehearsal of the play in the hope that he will see the promise of a hit and leave his fifty-pound investment with Mr Crummles.

The play went well in Glasgow and had other provincial productions at Nottingham and Crewe. We began to see possibilities of making it into a musical. At one point, when the craze for inflated movie musical spectaculars was at its height, I talked to Columbia Pictures about it. Columbia suggested that with a score by Richard Rodgers they might be interested, so we set off to talk to Richard Rodgers. By that time he had had a stroke and spoke with some difficulty, but he was still due to write a couple more shows for Broadway. He was polite but unenthusiastic, and we retreated without the necessary trump card in our hand.

Back in England we started to think of the theatre again and talked to Arthur Schwartz, the redoubtable composer of 'Dancing in the Dark', 'By Myself', 'I Guess I'll Have to Change My Plan' and a string of other standard tunes. Arthur, though in his seventies, had bursts of tremendous activity and always kept several projects on the boil. With most of our other composer collaborators we worked separately – delivering a lyric or setting words to a tune and then improving and polishing the finished result together. With Arthur we worked far more closely, meeting at his house in Walton Street, where he proved a witty and receptive collaborator, delighting in a felicitous phrase, lavish in his encouragement and boyish in his enthusiasm.

As the score progressed and the book was pruned down we started looking for a star and a management. We went to America on a forty-eight-hour trip and played to Alfred Drake one evening and to one of the producers of *Man of La Mancha*, Al Selden, the next morning. Caryl's usual vivacity at the second audition was replaced by jet-lagged sleep. The response was polite but lukewarm. Returning to England, we played to Harry Secombe, and in spite of my urgent setting up of the songs and Arthur's pounding at the piano and his vivacious attack on the lyrics, this time it was the turn of Johnny Franz, the music publisher who came with Secombe, to snore and whistle in contented fashion throughout. After Harry's memorial service at Westminster Abbey his widow and his son told me that Harry was still laughing at the embarrassment until nearly the day he died. Harry did not see himself in the role, so we attacked Harold Fielding, one of the few managers who mounted large-scale musicals. He was enthusiastic and suggested Ken Dodd as a possible star. The idea appealed to us and we drove Arthur and his wife Mary to Nottingham to see a Dodd pantomime. His command of the audience and his effervescent humour appealed to them and we arranged to go to Liverpool to play to the man himself. Ken Dodd was a lively audience, especially for one of the novelty songs in the play. All seemed to be going well.

At this time Harold Fielding went off to America to oversee the production of Harold Rome's musical version of *Gone with the Wind* which had already played in Tokyo and London. The London production spawned one of those glorious first-night disasters when a horse comprehensively fouled the stage. It was also the first time Bonnie Langford burst on the British public. The two phenomena prompted Noel Coward's famous cracks: 'If they'd stuffed the child's head up the horse's arse, they would have solved two problems at once', and 'Two things should be cut: the second act and the child's throat.' We have heard no more of the horse, but Bonnie Langford has developed into an ambitious and talented actress and singer. (She told me recently that she never heard these two remarks until some twenty years later.)

Fielding set off for California (and another first-night mishap when his Rhett Butler wandered off stage muttering oaths, not realising that his radio microphone was still switched on). Arthur Schwartz was travelling to and fro across the Atlantic and it was our understanding that we should start work together when Fielding was back in England at the end of the summer. I wrote to him to ask if he was ready to start discussions and received a puzzling letter to say that surely there was the question of which book we were going to use to be settled. It was the first we had heard of a second version.

It appeared that Arthur had submitted his own text, written with his wife Mary, under the impression that chances of production were being prejudiced by ours. We have never been able to work out if this was on information from Fielding or simply borne of frustration caused by waiting around for the manager's return. Arthur was impetuous and given to third-person pronouncements like 'Arthur Schwartz cannot be treated like this'. It also transpired, in a long letter that he wrote in response to mine asking what he was up to, that he had been keeping a diary of any disagreements we had had while working, including one memorable phrase documenting my bad behaviour. I had been reluctant to accept one suggestion and, heinous crime, '. . . Ned looked at the ceiling'.

Arthur kept custody of his tunes and Caryl and I hung on to our book and lyrics and reworked the whole play with Ron Grainer. Backed by his manager, Deke Arlon, who later became mine, we put our new version on at the Theatre Royal, Stratford, for Christmas 1975. In rehearsal some fine character performances began to emerge but disaster struck again when we moved to the theatre. Arriving to light the show on the weekend before we opened, I found very little of the scenery we were expecting had actually been built, let alone painted. 'I'm sorry,' said the man responsible, 'I have let you down; there is no scenery.' He had not liked to disappoint us by relaying the news before. Nor were there many costumes, and for three days scenery cloths and clothes were chased up and found from stores all over London. Moonlighting crews from West End theatres worked through the night to get the sets up and working. For the first preview, a free performance for old-age pensioners, very little had arrived and once again I had to do my Marie Lloyd act filling in the details from the side of the stage. By the press night two days later most of it was in place, and we got a remarkably good press in the circumstances. But once again the show was in no shape to justify a transfer.

We got it more or less right in 1981–2 in a Christmas season at Chichester. Meanwhile in 1975–6, I at last had a solid theatre success, directing, compering and writing the linking narrative for *Side By Side By Sondheim*.

CHAPTER 10

Side By Side . . .

The genesis of *Side By Side By Sondheim* was a series of fund-raising shows I did with the Dankworths for their tiny Stables Theatre at Wavendon. (The Wavendon All Music Plan grew out of a dream shared by John Dankworth and Cleo Laine. They wanted to bring an education in the best of *all* types of music to children interested in *any* kind of music.) The first show that we did together was a Gershwin concert in 1970. It established a pattern for others, including *Side By Side*. The setting was simple – four stools (Elisabeth Welch's idea: she thought she would like to sit down now and again), three singers and one narrator. On that first show Denis Quilley joined Cleo Laine and Lis as the singers, and Larry Adler was a guest. Later David Kernan replaced Quilley.

When, some years later in 1975, Kernan was playing in a long run of *A Little Night Music*, he thought it would be pleasant to sing something else on Sundays. In neighbouring theatres Millicent Martin and Julia McKenzie were also in long runs – in plays by Alan Ayckbourn. (Kernan had spotted McKenzie's special versatility long before, when she seemed condemned to life as an understudy and a takeover artist.) The girls welcomed his suggestion that they might care to keep their voices in trim. David asked if I would organise and link a Sondheim night on the lines of my Wavendon formula. The clouds had gathered over Virgin Films and were about to burst. I jumped at the chance. We had vague hopes that a short late-night theatre engagement might develop out of it. As I was at the end of my career as a film producer it could not have come at a better time. I was still clinging on to 19 Wellington Square and it was convenient and inexpensive to rehearse there.

Kernan enlisted the musical director of *Night Music*, Ray Cook, and with Sondheim's puzzled agreement and the Dankworths' enthusiastic offer of a couple of Sundays at Wavendon we set about devising the programme. Julia McKenzie knew exactly what she wanted to sing and suggested tearfully that she would probably kill herself if she did not do 'Broadway Baby' and 'Losing My Mind'. Millicent Martin, on the other hand, was less well briefed. She had to be shoehorned into 'I'm Still Here' and reminded that Sondheim wrote the lyric for 'The Boy From' which had been in her cabaret programme for several years. Finally we agreed on a two-hour selection and they set to, rehearsing it and working with exemplary discipline. They had a fortnight to get that formidable body of material under their belts. For once in building a revue there was no room for the usual arguments about the running order. All three performers were of course in every trio, and duets just gave the third time to get breath back from a solo. The general shape of the programme hardly changed from the first performance.

It was an extraordinary evening. It was billed as a dress rehearsal and tickets were sold at half the usual prices, which, at Wavendon, were low anyway. Even so, many of them were unsold and a busload of pensioners was brought in to fill the empty seats. The girls had been out to Oxford Street and bought little green dresses. Kernan and I had our dinner jackets. The entire set consisted of a platform, the four bar stools and two pianos played by Ray Cook and his assistant on *Night Music*, Stuart Pedlar, who also contributed to the final, show-stopping medley of Sondheim songs which I arranged for Caryl Brahms to put together. As her involvement was only peripheral Caryl had doubts about the whole project and flew off to Canada for the Stratford Shakespeare Festival before we got to Wavendon.

Ray Cook's great contribution was to insist on the accompaniment of two pianos. The rest of us tacitly assumed that at least the bass and drums of a rhythm section would be added if the show was ever staged on a more ambitious scale. Cook alone realised that Sondheim's music was best served by two pianos – especially as all his scores were very fully written for piano as a guide for his orchestrators.

We wandered into the small, oddly shaped Stables Theatre that morning, fussed over by Cleo, but not John, who was poleaxed by a violent migraine. Millicent Martin looked puzzled by the presence of a fourth stool – she had not realised that I was going to narrate the show, but conceded that it would help them to remember the running order. We went slowly through the songs and finished with time for make-up and a short break before the audience arrived. It was a quiet, methodical day with three professionals tucking their notes and effects into place in a businesslike fashion.

I watched the audience arrive – very few show-business people, mainly the hard core of Wavendon's local supporters and that busload of OAPs. Suddenly it seemed impossible that we could hold them with a body of material that was likely to be so unfamiliar. Only 'Send in the Clowns' was universally known, and many of the numbers from *Company*, *Follies* and *Night Music* were quite strange, let alone some of the obscure songs which I had turned up from odd sources.

I had reckoned without Sondheim's craftsmanship. In presenting evenings like the Gershwin compilation we had been capitalising on the frisson of recognition, the glow of nostalgia which the famous melodies inspired. In *Side By Side By Sondheim* – which at that time was called *The Sondheim Songbook* – we found as the evening went on that the effect was of sharply observed sketches set to artfully appropriate music: monologues, dialogues, conversations, usually planned so that each item told its separate story. The simple presentation allowed the audience to go straight to the nub of the situation, to follow the skeletal plot without the sugaring assistance of a familiar tune. Of course, they could relax when they got one, as in 'Send in the Clowns'; but they could be held equally firmly by Julia McKenzie's interpretation of 'Broadway Baby', which she had explored entirely by herself.

In Boston I had seen the artist who originally sang this in *Follies*, Ethel Shutta, a fine, feisty old lady, well into her seventies. She brought the house down by her energy and the convention that this was an old star recreating one of her long-ago triumphs. Julia chose to interpret it as a piece of realistic acting for a young hopeful pounding the streets and climbing the stairs to the dusty offices, cold rehearsal rooms and echoing stages around Broadway.

Halfway through the second act there was a disturbance on one side of the audience. The room is long and narrow and the stage was in the middle of one side. I realised that the OAPs were going home as a body. Had we lost them completely? They had seemed to be enjoying it. Later it transpired that their exit was determined by the arrival of the bus to take them away. The rest of the house was happy and we reached the climax with no further deserters.

I soon learned to look forward to the three great songs which complete the main part of the entertainment. They always reminded me of Robert Browning's *Dramatic Monologues* but the comparison eventually embarrassed Sondheim: 'I mean, I admire Browning, but doesn't it sound pretentious?' Julia

McKenzie found another powerful acting piece in 'Losing My Mind', a Gershwinesque tune for a lament by a bored housewife regretting a marriage which might have been. She was followed by David Kernan, who chose to sing a song, 'Leave You', written for another embittered wife, but to deliver it as a contemptuous kept man might have done. It was a daring idea, again entirely his own, and especially risky because Sondheim's approach to his songs is so specific in the delineation of character that to tamper with them to the extent of a sex change is playing with fire. We learned that it inflamed the audience rather than destroyed the material.

'I'm Still Here', Millicent Martin's last number, is a great cry of a survivor. The references are all to the thirties and forties in America but the defiant message is universal; and Millie, who has had her ups and downs, had no trouble in identifying proudly and passionately with the sentiment. I had first played her Yvonne de Carlo's original cast recording and she thought it too slight for her big spot. However, after a week I let her hear Nancy Walker's superb recording made at a benefit in Sondheim's honour in New York, and this time she realised its potential. 'Oh, yes. I think I can do something with that,' she murmured absently.

I found something splendid and cathartic in these three songs. The tight team of three singers had juggled the numbers brilliantly from one to another all through the evening, staying on stage for virtually the whole night, relishing one another's skills and loyally laughing when they judged that I had hoped to make a joke. Although, as the performances got into the several hundred count, I used to change the jokes quite a lot, there were still a load of asides which they had heard to distraction. But they still managed to crack a smile, which helps the audience share the illusion that the remark is new-minted.

For the last three songs they came up on stage separately, rather like weightlifters taking the spotlight for a tremendous effort. The three exhibition bouts over, the final medley was a perfect chance for them to resume their former partnership and appear to relax and let their hair down with the audience. The complexity of the medley ensured that this had to be an illusion, but it was always convincing as they mined the text to cap one another's laughs. The evening finished with 'Side By Side By Side', that charming pastiche from *Company*, which was eventually to provide us with our title.

One impresario came to Wavendon and was full of enthusiasm; another, Cameron Mackintosh, drove up the wrong motorway and did not arrive at all. As the weeks went by we found enormous reluctance on the part of managers to consider presenting the show, but from that first dress rehearsal none of us had any doubts that it could work.

The generally expressed doubt was whether this tiny gem, perfectly set in a mini-theatre, could grow to fill a West End house. We tried the Gardner Theatre at Brighton: it was a couple of hundred seats bigger and we thought we could lay the 'too small' rumour once and for all. No chance. Again we were considered too small, except by one fledgling impresario who thought it was a wonderful body of material but could I not replace the performers with sixteen- or seventeen-year-olds because the critics loved welcoming young talent. I relayed this to the rest with some relish because we were in fact a self-administering group under the title 'In Comes Company' (a pun on the money we hoped to make from it and also Stephen's title song for *Company*). A return visit to Wavendon brought us no sponsors and we were beginning to find Sunday dates hard to come by. Chichester turned us down but we found a home at Bury St Edmunds to which we could invite Michael Codron, one of the shrewdest managers, and at that time the employer of Julia and Millie. On this visit we were also being looked over by Burt Shevelove, one of Stephen's closest friends, and one of mine. He had written the book for *A Funny Thing Happened on the*

Way to the Forum with Larry Gelbart, and on the way up to Bury suggested our title – *Side By Side By Sondheim*.

The theatre at Bury St Edmunds is a beautiful early nineteenth-century hall in warm terracotta shades and we admired its exquisite proportions until we became aware of a keen, cold, Fenland breeze sweeping across the stage and through the house. The hall was not full, but the drive of the programme worked its magic by the end. Perhaps the biggest laugh came during the sentimental encore when the frozen audience saw the shivering singers link arms and sing, 'Isn't it warm, isn't it cosy, side by side by side?'

We were all sharing a dressing room and we waited anxiously for Michael Codron to come round. I am always fascinated by watching tact exercised in dressing rooms after performances. No one did it better than Noel Coward, but Michael's performance was masterly. However, it left me in no doubt that he was not going to present us in London. He came a couple of steps into the dressing room and opened his arms expansively. 'Show me,' he enthused, 'show me three more talented performers in the whole country!' This was high praise, sincerely offered, and it was exactly judged to hearten the performers. Through the glow of approbation I heard the sinister words 'Let's talk on Monday morning' to the business manager and I wrote off Michael there and then as a potential impresario. It seemed heartless to pass on this instinct to the others as they all had high hopes and Burt Shevelove said he would give the thumbs-up to Sondheim.

Stephen had heard a tape already – not sent by us (we wanted to be sure that as many rough edges as possible were rubbed off before recording), but by two musical 'buffs' who had sat in the audience with a tape-recorder and got it all down. This was perhaps lucky because their seats were in the centre of all the applause, giving a very favourable perspective of cheering in relation to performance.

Monday produced the expected rejection and we were running out of possibilities. We found one further date at the Greenwood Theatre, a versatile but rarely busy auditorium in Guy's Hospital which doubles as a theatre and a conference hall. The charming rumour is that a benefactor left money to the hospital for 'a theatre' and a theatrical theatre was built instead of the operating theatre he had hoped to provide. Again we were a sell-out, and again a gaggle of managers made their excuses like Sunday newspaper reporters and left. However, one backer, George Borwick, a modest investor in many West End productions, was loud in his praises. We went to dinner with him and he insisted that he would call Cameron Mackintosh – the man who mixed up his motorways and who had not, as yet, had a success – in New York next morning. He joined forces with Helen Montagu, an energetic and enthusiastic Australian who was working with H. M. Tennent, one of the senior West End managements. They were by now about the only two impresarios who had not seen the show and they had only the evidence of some tapes recorded at the Greenwood. The problem of a theatre arose. Julia McKenzie heard that the Mermaid was suddenly desperate for an attraction. A deal was struck with Bernard Miles for a limited engagement.

It was an odd nostalgic trip to talk to Bernard again about a musical. He listened to a few minutes of the tape, appallingly garbled on a machine that was malfunctioning, but appeared keen to take us on board sight unseen. We agonised a little about the set and it became simpler. We did some rehearsals and then broke for a short holiday preparatory to a concentrated bout with Sondheim before previews.

The two days of rehearsals with Stephen were critical to the final polish of the piece. Millie, Julia and David ran through the whole programme for him song by song, and his mixture of enthusiasm and instruction – the first generous, the second precise – was compulsively interesting. He is an instinctive teacher, certain, lucid and concentrated. He had doubts about David Kernan's choice of 'Leave You', but realised that there was not an equally powerful alternative and accepted it. He worked on Julia McKenzie's 'Broadway Baby' and then retreated, sensing quickly that she had found her own way of singing it – an interpretation which was faithful to every line he had written. He was a lesson in how to intensify an actor's performance by illuminating any moments of uncertainty with a reasoned explanation of the effects he had written for and which they were hoping to achieve. Most of this he achieved in a day and a half and very soon we were at dress-rehearsal time.

The dress rehearsal will remain a treasured moment. Not being a professional comedian, I hate to risk jokes before a few colleagues. Millie, Julia and David were used to hearing my commentary only when the audience was in. Stephen had heard the tape and knew roughly what was coming – he also turned out to be a bad barometer, rarely laughing at a joke which was tried out on him, but seeing the humour when he heard a positive audience response. When we ran through before a gaggle of colleagues at the Mermaid I did my usual trick of saying a few words loudly for sound balance and then gabbling through the rest no louder than a mutter and getting back to full strength at the final cue for song. As the evening wore on I became aware of a shadowy figure flitting in some agitation through the stalls. It was Bernard, now Sir but not yet Lord, Miles conveying his anxiety to Caryl and Stephen. I was inaudible. They failed to reassure him. As the rehearsal ended he came bustling up on the stage expressing his heartfelt thanks and deep admiration to the singers. He then bore down on me with a lump in the throat and moist eyes. 'How can you do it?' he said. 'Those bloody kids are working their guts out and every time you open your mouth you put the show on the bloody floor.' I tried to explain, but to no avail. 'Disaster,' he prophesied. 'Sorry,' I said, 'that's what happens if you hire amateurs.'

The picture of the first night is evoked for me more vividly by the diary I was asked to concoct for the *Sunday Times* than by memory. (I was also finishing off a disastrous television series called *Terra Firma* for BBC 2 at the time and had, on the previous Sunday, arranged for a profile of Millicent Martin and presided over Stephen Sondheim's first meeting with Christopher Bond, the writer of the version of *Sweeney Todd* on which Sondheim was to base his Broadway musical. It was a prickly encounter, with the Marxist Bond treating Stephen as a Broadway lightweight, a role to which he was unused and which he found difficulty in accepting.)

Monday
Final rehearsals for *Side by Side by Sondheim.* We are supposed to have fixed the running order on Saturday night, but Sondheim still has a reservation about cutting one of the Japanese numbers from *Pacific Overtures.* We put them in after the out of town try-outs.

I am fascinated by the way my three colleagues warm themselves up and create diversions in face of nerves. Millicent Martin bangs around a great deal and shouts at her dresser. Her dressing room is next door and her adrenalin can be heard being built up as she usually finds some minor irritation about which to be shrilly vocal. Julia McKenzie arranges a lot of flowers and swishes about purposefully in a green housecoat. David Kernan is exercised over his suits.

Sondheim is an expert at word games. Tonight I try a new pun on the first preview audience. 'A cunning linguist'. No response from the audience. It's out for tomorrow. We call the cast at five o'clock the next day for notes. Stephen has decided to put the Japanese number back for the first night and we opt to tell the company just before the first night.

Tuesday

Present-buying. Find Sondheim, who is a puzzles fanatic, a Victorian musical game at John Hall's shop in South Kensington. Have lunch alone at Alexander's in the King's Road and see an old friend, Paul Dehn, looking very ill. I wondered if it would be for the last time.

Slowly to the theatre, which is very quiet and dark and cool in the auditorium. Sit there with Stephen and David discussing nervousness. David admits to an uncontrollable desire to weep on first nights, Stephen on last nights. The girls come down. There is a suggestion of sleepwalking. We drop the bombshell about restoring the Japanese number. It fails to explode. Very quietly and very professionally they rehearse it twice and get back to unpacking presents, sticking up telegrams. The time gets nearer. Millie begins to bang about. To a novice the call 'Beginners please' still sounds self-conscious, but here it comes.

The best fun of the show is to be sitting so near three splendid artists performing such demanding material.

Fascinating to watch the Critical Brethren from the stage – to wonder why heads bow and pens begin to scribble at particular moments.

Emotion takes over as Stephen bounds down the aisle emerging from a dark cavern of clapping forms, loping slowly like an action replay. His speech is choked and simple. The evening ends at the Double Dutch in York Street with a lot of food, a lot of drink and the first papers, fetched by Alan Ayres of the Mermaid. *Telegraph*, Barber, favourable . . . Caryl drives me home. For some reason I am convinced the time is 1.30. Checking on arrival that it's 4.30 I wisely have two alka seltzers . . .

Wednesday

0900: Woken by Miss Godfrey who used to be my housekeeper. I take none of it in and go back to bed convinced that I have a first night tonight and must conserve my energy.

0905: Come to and go down to the papers which leave very little to be desired. Struck by the way in which Stephen's writing seems to have challenged all the critics to write more considered, more elegant, more important prose.

Thursday
Trying to pick up other threads. Going to the theatre each night plays hell with the balance of a daily routine. Off to the theatre . . . How long, O Lord, how long?

'How long?' turned out to be an extended season at the Mermaid followed by the rest of the year at Wyndham's and then a trip to America.

Our original idea of a series of one-night stands went out of the window with the success of the Mermaid and West End runs. The morning after the Mermaid opening at least four pairs of eyes were firmly set on Broadway. An encouraging number of American producers made enthusiastic approaches, but we were well aware that Stephen controlled the property and that his first loyalty would be to Hal Prince, who had produced most of his shows. Hal was at the first night and made canny but hopeful noises. As negotiations for New York started, the main obstacle was the perennial problem of the exchange of actors between England and America. Usually the factors which encourage the unions on both sides of the Atlantic to allow such an exchange are the stellar status of the performer in question and the indigenous quality of the material. Our singers were expert but not international names and the material was not essentially British. I was luckier because the convention that I was giving a largely improvised critique of Sondheim's work was soon accepted as an individual contribution.

Prince lobbied American Actors' Equity cleverly and

persistently, and eventually they agreed that if Julia McKenzie stayed three months, David Kernan four, Millie Martin five, and I six, they would let us all in. There were some demonstrations from rank-and-file members of Equity, but it was a compromise that suited us. There was one snag: Millie had agreed to extend her West End contract while we were awaiting the good news from America. The theatre owner refused to release her and our Broadway opening was postponed by a month. As a result, although we had gratifying notices and an exciting first night, we opened in April 1977, the same week as two other musicals – *Annie* and *I Love My Wife* – which were also hits. Had we opened on the earlier date we would have had a clear month of capacity houses. Broadway had been starved of a single musical success that season. As it was, we slogged it out with the other two shows and were not the blockbuster we might have been.

There were no changes to the Sondheim material for New York but I had to revise my contribution comprehensively. Although the spine of biographical information about Sondheim and my evaluation of his work survived, the narrator of the show has to fulfil other functions. Sondheim's is a highly idio-syncratic point of view. In many songs he deals with a specialised set of Manhattan characters, and the narrator has to help the audience to understand and sympathise with that rarefied world. He also has to supply light relief and remind the audience that Sondheim's people exist in the centre of contemporary society.

In London topical local references were a reassurance for British audiences picking their way gingerly through Stephen's thickly stacked American allusions. The size of the Liberal Party, the Slater–Walker debacle, Marcia Falkender's notorious hon-ours list, followed by Lew Grade's *Life of Our Lord* . . . 'which turned out to be autobiographical', and the ever-present Mary Whitehouse were recurring themes. Arriving in America, it was clear that new references would have to be found. I would have to 'translate' a lot of my material.

Hal and Stephen were anxious that I should find a romantic paragraph suggesting the genesis of the show – on the lines of a group of kids getting together in a barn and doing the show right there. This sort of American sentimentality was foreign to our instincts, so I had to find a way of accommodating the idea inside my own vocabulary. Eventually I produced a mocking paragraph in which I explained that the show was borne out of two ideas held by three English entertainers. One was to provide themselves with gainful employment, the other was to do missionary work in England on behalf of Sondheim's songs. Accusations of tunelessness are often (unfairly) levelled at his music and *Pacific Overtures*, then his most recent work, was, at that time, perhaps his hardest score to assimilate. I got a ready response from sophisticated early audiences by saying that I knew it might be difficult to believe that Sondheim needed any introduction in London when, in New York, 'on every street corner you can hear newsboys whistling the love theme from *Pacific Overtures*'.

The first lines of the narration were the most important because if they could be seen to have been a specific reference to that day's news the audience assumed that the rest of the narrator's contribution was ad-lib and new-minted. In England the opening line was an apology for the size of the company, usually 'roughly half the number of Liberal MPs in the House of Commons'. In America I had to find alternatives and there was no reference which was similarly perennial. I tried a wide variety: 'half the size of the Saudi Arabian Olympic ski-team'; 'half the size of the Idi Amin Fan Club'; after the Koreagate scandal in Washington, 'half the number of people in Washington who admit to knowing Tongsun Park'; and most effective of all for a few weeks after Polanski's arrest on a morals charge, 'half the American Mothers' Committee for the Defence of Roman Polanski'.

There followed another convenient device for a topical joke –

an apology in advance for any verbal slip on account of being an Englishman in a foreign country: 'Please remember, if I do say something wrong, so, from time to time, does—.' The name could be switched to suit whoever had made the most recent gaffe. Andrew Young worked for months; but when he was switched from his job at the UN others had to be found. Hermione Gingold, who understudied me in New York and then took over for the end of the run and the national tour, came regularly to see the first six months of the show and record the lines which got the biggest laughs. Once she had heard a solid response it was hard to persuade her that the joke was losing its topicality and potency. She clung to Andrew Young for months after I had let him go and indeed until the show arrived in Los Angeles, by which time he failed to raise a smile. Mercifully Vanessa Redgrave made her notorious Oscar speech the night before our opening in LA, and by various subterfuges I was able to inveigle Hermione into introducing the new reference, which brought a monster laugh that she then flogged with professional persistence long after its topicality had gone.

With a view to Americanising the text, I tracked down an American writer, Tony Geis, a man of wide interests, great sensibility and a bubbling wit who has a facility for spotting the pertinent topical target and encapsulating his trenchant comment in a one-liner. Nothing dates more quickly than humour from the headlines, but it was a vintage time in America with Carter as President, Andrew Young at the UN, Bert Lance in trouble, John Mitchell, and Dean, Ehrlichman and Haldeman in custody, 'the first person to be sentenced to three to seven years in jail and a hundred-thousand-dollar advance'. Kissinger was on the sidelines, 'admitting that his German accent was a plea for sympathy' and that 'the bombing of Cambodia was an error of the heart'.

Nixon and Frost were doing their interviews, Nixon supposedly replying to Frost's overworked question 'What is your definition of love?' with 'Love is never having to say you're sorry', and describing living the simple life in California as 'leaving his house only once a week in order to take his money to the laundry'. Barbara Walters, Pierre and Margaret Trudeau, Truman Capote, Studio 54 and Farrah Fawcett Majors were suitably frivolous names which could always be relied on to trigger an instant reaction. There was a convenient week when the election for Mayor of New York coincided with the election for Miss World. As Tony pointed out, the two elections were similar except that the questions asked of Miss World candidates were harder. We all know where we stand on capital punishment, but how would we answer 'Would you kiss on your first date?'

He also found a perfect comparison to illuminate the mystery of the monarchy at the time of the Queen's Silver Jubilee: 'The Queen of England reigns but she does not rule – like the Mayor of New York.' By great good luck America produced its own equivalent of Mary Whitehouse in time for our opening. Anita Bryant, a singer who appeared in orange juice commercials, mounted a ferocious anti-gay campaign and inspired the slogan 'Squeeze a fruit for Anita'. After Anita I was particularly fond of Tony's disclaimer about *Pacific Overtures* – 'This is not a story about foreplay in a Californian beachhouse.'

It was exciting to open at the Music Box in *Side By Side*. After a couple of previews, as I gained confidence in Tony's jokes, I began to think of a celebration. I promised myself a night of relaxation at the Everard Baths – a notorious cruising ground at 28 West Twenty-Eighth Street in New York. Fortunately some nervous hesitation restrained me. I decided not to challenge fortune but to wait until after our first night. I awoke next morning at the Algonquin hotel – where I had arranged to stay for the first few nights, sharing a suite with David Kernan – and opened the *New York Times*. On the front page was a huge picture of a burnt-out building. The Everard

Baths had been razed to the ground the previous night with many deaths. Such was its magnitude the event became a feature of gay fiction for years afterwards until the greater tragedy of the Aids epidemic took its place as a cornerstone of that body of literature.

Our first night climaxed at Sardi's. Hal had avoided that restaurant for first-night parties for some years because of the legendary risk of disapproval, disappointment and dispersal which attends a flop. However, he argued generously that for an English cast a Sardi's reception would be something to which to look forward. He also felt that for once the risk was minimal.

The Sardi experience is splendidly routine. There is no English equivalent. On ordinary nights a third of the room is held for regulars and celebrities – the rest of the restaurant is packed with rubbernecking out-of-towners. When a first night takes over, most of the room, depending on the generosity of the producer or the amount of optimism which attends the production, is occupied by cast, creators and hangers-on. The writers, directors and performers usually manage to linger until their supporters are seated. Then they enter as their loved ones or agents keep an eye on the door and start the required ovation. It would be idle to pretend that, however obvious the artifice, the moment is not a powerful, emotional, theatrical boost after the tensions of the evening.

There is a famous story of the near-identical Shaffer twins. Peter, having had a success (and a Sardi's ovation) a couple of times, turned up to support his brother Tony on the first night of *Sleuth*. Appearing accidentally before Tony at Sardi's, he garnered the applause which was rightfully Tony's from a roomful who had wrongly identified him. The proud author of the evening's hit arrived later to total silence from a group who thought that they had already applauded him quite enough.

We had no such mishap. We enjoyed our cheers, and the notices – telephoned before the papers were on the streets –

were good enough to make everyone happy. The party was spiced by an unlooked-for note of romance in that one of my guests, Marc Alexander, cornered Millicent Martin and, in no time at all, married her. And there was one of those dramatic, shallow 'incidents' which spout so readily from the fertile soil of Broadway hysteria.

For over a year on stage I had quoted an old Broadway joke about one of Sondheim's less successful shows, *Do I Hear a Waltz*. Owing to a reluctance to buy seats, this joint work of Sondheim, Richard Rodgers and Arthur Laurents, based on Laurents's charming play *The Time of the Cuckoo*, was frivolously nicknamed *Dearth in Venice*, the town in which the story was set. My reference to the joke had been on the tape which Stephen had heard before giving final permission to stage the show – and Arthur had listened to that tape before urging Stephen to give us the go-ahead. However, on that first night it struck a wrong chord for him and he assailed Stephen bitterly for this betrayal of their long collaboration and friendship. Oblivious to all this, I sailed into the storm just as the evening was coming to a mellow conclusion and collected my share of invective. He apologised ruefully when he came on to *Loose Ends* many years later.

Nothing happens bigger in the theatre than it happens in New York. Success, failure, envy, bitterness, triumph, betrayal, congratulations, recrimination – the hothouse of theatrical Manhattan is a powerful forcing ground for every emotion, and in retrospect I realised that I was privileged to be an extra in a wonderful row which had no business being a row at all.

Once we began our performance routine David Kernan and I decided to find somewhere to live on a more reasonable basis than the Algonquin. Eventually, through the columns of the *New York Times*, we happened upon a delightful house in Washington Mews in Greenwich Village, roughly the place whence Henry James's heroine in *Washington Square* expected her lover to spirit her away. The house divided itself conveniently. The living room was a high studio giving on to a small garden at the back where the grey squirrels from Washington Square played and marauded and sometimes scampered across the roof. Of all the happy memories at that house and other premises in New York, my abiding joy is the lady whom we inherited with Washington Mews and who looked after us. A joyous eccentric, Amy was handsome, statuesque and eminently quotable. After David left the cast, I moved to a smaller apartment and Amy followed me to its roach-infested, scraped pine and open-brick walls on the Upper West Side. You get quite fond of roaches in New York. Then we moved together to two other premises in the more fashionable Sutton Place area. The first looked like an off-Broadway set for a revival of Noel Coward's *Fumed Oak* and was owned by an elderly scoundrel who migrated to Miami each winter where he had a handbag-shop concession in a large hotel.

To all these desirable residences Amy would journey from the Bronx once or twice a week. She arrived at about eight o'clock after two changes of train and a bus which brought her to within a couple of blocks of her destination. She cleaned and washed and laundered from eight until three with a very short break for lunch. She wanted little: a pickle, a couple of slices of garlic-laden processed meat and a thimbleful of juice. She was very thorough and very talkative. Twenty minutes at least, preferably at the beginning of the day, had to be devoted to news of her family and her other employers. Ten minutes at the end were spent in admiring the miracle of transformation she had wrought around the premises.

Amy had two other regular places of work until one of her ladies 'passed on'. After the tragedy we spent many mornings trying to decide whether Amy should enter the old apartment at the behest of one surviving daughter in the face of the opposition of the other. A *Dallas* family power struggle was building up and Amy wanted to be sure of her rights to take away 'what I bin left'.

She had dire forebodings about another employer who refused to buy her an upstairs vacuum cleaner, insisting that she carry the heavy downstairs one up a flight of some twenty steps to the bedroom. This, coupled with the fact that she was only allowed either paper towels or dishcloths, but not both, plainly presaged immediate financial ruin. Amy's husband was a Jehovah's Witness, which took him out most evenings. Her daughter married a ne'er-do-well who led his wife a terrible life and habitually left his shirts to dry over a naked flame, invariably setting light to them and to the apartment.

In the *Fumed Oak* flat Amy took a dim view of an indelicately disrobed lady, artwork vintage 1940, whose sharp, naked breasts pointed out aggressively from their gilt frame. Amy dismissed her as 'unnecessary'. She was much happier when I covered her over with green tinsel at Christmas. After Twelfth Night the complaints started again.

She had an individual way with the English language. One of her blind spots was the plural of the word 'actor'. She had no idea that actors multiply by the addition of the letter 's'. When Kernan and I were in Washington Mews she could never quite understand why we went out on Wednesday afternoons. 'Where you going?' she would say. 'To the theatre, Amy.' She heaved a heavy sigh. 'Always enjoying yourself, you actresses!'

David's friend Basil Poole stayed with us for a time. A professional chef, he was a black mark in Amy's book. 'Mr Dazzle', as she used to mispronounce him, 'does leave a lot of dirty plates – but that's that chef-type cooking he do.' Dazzle also gave her an exaggerated idea of my importance. 'Mr Sherrin,' she asked one day after they had gone, 'do you control *all* the television?' And on another occasion, 'Does Diana Ross work for you?'

Amy had her own view of England, which she had never visited. It was based on the certainty that everyone lived in a spacious mansion. 'I expect you'll be looking forward to getting back to your spacious mansion' was a phrase often on her lips. On one occasion there was a variation.

'What is Miss Caryl Brahms's spacious mansion like?'

'It's more of an apartment, Amy.'

'Oh, that can be nice.'

'Yes, it's a very nice apartment. She has lots of antiques.'

Amy frowned. 'I don't like antiques. Sometimes they just junk!'

After leaving the cast of *Side By Side* in New York, I stayed on to direct the replacement casts and the national and Chicago companies. An extraordinary range of performers have done my narrator's chore. Gingold, Cyril Ritchard, Arlene Francis, the puppeteer Burr Tillstrom and, I am reliably informed, Dorothy Lamour are among the Americans. In England they include Michael Parkinson, Robin Ray, Russell Harty, Michael Aspel and Sheridan Morley, a more conventional list.

When I rehearsed the Chicago company Cyril Ritchard's understudy was the English actress Brenda Forbes, long resident in America, where she originally arrived to understudy Edith Evans as the Nurse to Katherine Cornell's Juliet. Cyril had asked for some songs to be added when he played my role and Brenda was anxious to get hold of all her material on the first day of rehearsal. I went off to get scripts duplicated and brought back the pages to her – she was thrilled.

'Oh, how wonderful,' she said. 'Everything is here, the script, the jokes – even the songs . . .' She leant forward conspiratorially. 'I'm told', she confided, 'that the poor boy who did it in New York wasn't allowed to sing them.'

Cyril Ritchard performed with apparent relish and was a charming survivor of an older tradition. He hated much of the material and could not bear any skittish religious reference. He relished a long-ago row with Noel Coward, with whom he had queried a line in Coward's song 'I Wonder What Happened to Him?':

Whatever became of old Keeling?
I hear that he got back from France
And frightened three nuns in a train in Darjeeling
By stripping and waving his lance!

Cyril wanted the three nuns out. Coward wanted to know why. Cyril explained that it was offensive to him because he had a cousin who was a nun. 'Oh, very well,' said Coward. 'Make it four nuns.'

When we opened in Chicago, Cyril had his last success in a long career but a couple of weeks into the run he had a heart attack on stage. He had to be helped off and never regained consciousness. The company manager, an old dancer, long starved of applause, grabbed the script and went on to read the one remaining announcement. Poor Brenda never got on. Her place was taken by the puppeteer.

The Chicago cast contained two of our New York understudies, Carol Swarbrick and Bonnie Schonn. With Jack Blackton, who understudied Kernan, they had done a special Equity matinée performance of *Side By Side By Sondheim* a few days after our opening. The show was free and an enormous line of Equity members stretched around the block. I had to narrate the piece as Gingold declined to go on so soon. It was an eerie experience which I enjoyed enormously. The audience was hanging from the rafters, determined to cheer the local performers home and prove that it had been unnecessary to let in an English cast in the first place. When the English stars took round collecting boxes for Equity charities during the interval they faced a deal of hostility. It gave me great pleasure to watch the understudy cast have individual successes, but also to have a chance to point out bluntly to the partisan audience that the show would not exist but for the imagination, skill, sacrifice, faith and talent of the three English performers who had made it. There is no feeling quite as exhilarating as saying something you know to be true and relevant to a very large audience who do not want to hear it. 'You do like to let them have it straight, don't you?' said Sondheim, looking puzzled.

Looking back on a subsequent career of showing off, I suppose that *Side By Side By Sondheim* provided my first *prolonged* exposure to audiences, my baptism of fire. A year and a half at the Mermaid, at Wyndham's Theatre in London and at the Music Box on Broadway gave me a chance to observe them. Sybil Thorndike used to say that there was nothing you could do to predict an audience. They bring their own varied and corporate life into each theatre. 'Some nights,' Dame Sybil confided, 'they're porridge; some nights – electricity!'

It came as a shock to discover just how much I could see from the stage. In the stalls I could pick out a face as far back as Row J. I could spot a sleeping head in Row M or N. In the circle, or mezzanine as they call it in America, only the front row is clearly visible but that was enough to witness one death in New York, completed by the removal of body and return of companions to see the rest of the show. You pay too much to waste a ticket in New York.

It is the front rows of the stalls which provide most entertainment for the alert performer. There were couples whose roving hands suggested that they believed in a mysterious insulating wall between them and the stage. Sometimes they talked animatedly as they might in front of the television. Hands reassured, hands massaged, hands set off on ambitious voyages of discovery around the body of a partner. I watched with fascination as one old gentleman, I should guess about eighty, sat down in the front row flanked by two 'girls' of around sixty each holding one of his hands throughout both acts. At the end of one of David Kernan's quieter, more lyrical songs I saw an old lady nudge her neighbour and point at his trouser legs. 'Look,' she said brightly, '"turn-ups" are coming back.'

It is easier to understand the unselfconscious behaviour of the middle rows in New York. One night I spotted Gregory Peck sitting bolt upright in an aisle seat, roughly Row F, concentrating with impeccable courtesy on the entertainment. Beside him sat a young girl, perhaps his daughter, equally engrossed. Next to her I could see a lady I identified as Veronique, Mrs Peck, a dark, attractive Frenchwoman, going through all the agonies of trying to stay awake. Jet lag, I assumed, judging by some of my own theatregoing experiences. I was happy in the belief that the family had just flown in from the West Coast. My report of her sleep and jet lag got into the *New York* magazine. Many years later, I met the Pecks at a BAFTA reception. They remembered the incident. 'Ah, yes,' I said, 'the jet lag.' 'No,' said Veronique Peck simply, 'it wasn't jet lag!'

Most celebrities arrange to buy their seats through the management, so they can usually be spotted in the house seats in the centre stalls. Robert Redford spoiled the game by lurking in the back row. In England the presence of a royal person always makes a theatre audience slightly self-conscious. We had Princess Margaret and Princess Alexandra on separate occasions, and although both enjoyed the show and took pains to show their enthusiasm, half the house inevitably spent the evening craning necks to check on the royal reaction. This divided attention diminishes audience response dramatically. The only Americans whom I have seen have a similar effect are Henry Kissinger and Jackie Onassis. Kissinger came round afterwards to check the text of a joke about the Democrat Andrew Young, in case he could use it.

In England, three Germans spent half of the first half in the front row about five feet away from me loudly discussing their bewilderment – in German. Finally they stomped off up the aisle. I saw Bob West, the company manager, pursuing them to pin down the nature of their displeasure. 'Ve don't understandt it,' they told him, 'and ve don't understandt vy three must sing and not talk and one must talk and not sing?' Had they heard me sing, that part of the mystery would have been solved.

After the show rituals like 'coming round' can be an enjoyable nightmare. At a time when I thought I was on a successful diet Alexis Smith came back one night and said that I reminded her of Orson Welles. She was followed the next night by Carol Channing, who told me I was 'the spirit of Robert Morley'. Sammy Davis wanted me to get Sondheim to rewrite 'I'm Still Here' to personalise it for him. 'Tell him I could make it as big as "Mr Bojangles",' he said, 'and if he can't, I'll get Sammy Cahn to do it.' That did not go down very well.

On the night that Leonard Bernstein was coming it was Sondheim who was apprehensive. 'He'll say something like, "Of course his early work is much the best."' In fact Bernstein was enthusiastic about the work and the performance. Apart from expressing amazement that David Kernan had never sung Pelleas at the Metropolitan Opera he was most interested in exploring the possibility of our mounting a *Bit By Bit By Bernstein* show. Finally I had to remind him that the two girls knew he was in the theatre. Conscience-stricken he rushed to their dressing rooms. They had already left so he lipsticked their mirrors with generous praise against which they were photographed the next day: 'Jesus, Julia!' 'Magnificent Millicent!' Still guilty, he wanted to know where they would be dining – guessing correctly, we took him to the nearby Backstage restaurant where he showered them with compliments and then spoilt it by pointing to Kernan and saying, 'And how lucky you are to be singing on the same stage as this man!'

After a Mermaid show I dined one night at Luigi's in Covent Garden a couple of tables away from Millicent Martin and an American friend, a girl who had been to see the show and at whom I had been talking for some two hours from the stage. I joined them for coffee. After half an hour of conversation a dim light began to shine in the lady's eyes. 'Wait a minute,' she said, 'are you the guy who reads out the announcements?' So much for charisma. On another occasion a London ticket agency sent in a number of the staff to see the show. They had a drink with the cast afterwards. I worked hard for twenty minutes with a young woman who had a ticket booth somewhere along the Strand. At the end of it she asked what I did.

'I work here at the moment,' I said.

'What as?'

'Sort of on the stage.'

'Oh,' she said, accepting the evidence. 'You look more sophisticated up there.'

One night on leaving the Music Box (quite sober), I slipped on the sidewalk and fell into the gutter on Forty-fifth Street. The *Side By Side By Sondheim* audience was still emerging from the theatre. Two precious young men, who had clearly been in our audience, and whom I can only describe in retrospect as vicious queens, surveyed me with no enthusiasm. 'Well,' one of them said, considering the fallen spectacle, 'it's funnier than anything she did in the show.'

CHAPTER 11

I Hear Music . . .

I flew Caryl out to New York a few times while I was doing *Side By Side* and in the later months when I was sorting the tours or doing a Public Broadcasting television series. She became adept at exploiting the invalid-wheelchair method of travel – she *was* seventy-six or more. Her manipulations climaxed triumphantly at Kennedy Airport. On her last trip I met her with a limo, and her airline 'minder', having seen her through the carousel and wheeled her out of the exit, suggested that she might care to walk the final ten yards to the car. 'No, no!' she said firmly. 'I don't think my doctor would like that.'

She stayed in whichever apartment I was renting at the time. I moved on to a couch. Caryl relished New York, bizarrely comparing it to Brussels. We managed to do some work. A project doomed to failure was a suggestion by the actor Roddy McDowall that we should devise a one-man show for him as Noel Coward. We did; but Graham Payn and the Coward Estate wisely laughed the idea out of court. However, Caryl and I did do useful work on another solo project which had started off with a chance breakfast meeting in Manchester a few years earlier.

One Sunday in 1976 when I was recording *Terra Firma*, that

unfortunate magazine programme for BBC 2, I ran into Arthur Lowe at the Midland hotel – much put out because his boiled egg kept arriving at the breakfast table too hard. Three eggs later one came along in a satisfactory condition and we talked of his recent success as Louis Pasteur in a drama documentary on television. He mentioned that it had drawn a letter from the accountant who managed many of Sir Thomas Beecham's affairs towards the end of his life. In his eye Arthur was the epitome of Sir Thomas. Arthur was interested in playing the old boy. I talked to Caryl about it and we became enthusiastic about devising what would be virtually a one-man show. However, Beecham was so inclined to score off people that we reckoned there must be a second actor to set up some of his memorable cracks.

I have always found one-man shows rather decorous, quiet affairs, though some exert a special magic, like Roy Dotrice's *Brief Lives*, Max Adrian's *Shaw*, Gielgud's *Ages of Man* and Michael MacLiammoir's *Wilde*. The attraction of the Beecham idea was the extra dimension the music would bring. We started to work on the material while I was in the Sondheim show in London. We went in the first place to Beecham's own autobiography and to Neville Cardus's warm and witty account of his conversations with Beecham. Helen Montagu, who was co-presenting *Side By Side* with Cameron Mackintosh, encouraged the enterprise and we produced a very long script. It got even longer when we worked on it in New York. I asked Leonard Bernstein if he had any Beecham memories. 'I only met him once,' he said. 'We shared a dressing room at the Met. We were both conducting ballets. He was very nice to me – but that's not what you want to hear, is it?'

Discussions carried on for the best part of two years. Indeed they were not resolved until after my return to England in 1980. Arthur thought there was too much musical material and not enough about Beecham – man and especially lover. Beecham had romanced many women and Arthur thought his wife should play them all. It turned out after their deaths that she demanded to play in any show in which he was involved. We were not to know this. Eventually he passed on it, and with his defection we lost Helen Montagu, too. However, by now we had persuaded Patrick Garland to interest himself in directing the play and with him we cut and reshaped the material and began to choose the music passages which were to give us a special bonus.

Patrick suggested Roy Dotrice as Beecham and we took Roy to see Shirley, Lady Beecham, the conductor's widow. We seemed set to go ahead in time for Beecham's centenary when Roy was offered a lucrative West End job in *Oliver!* Again we were without a star. By a great stroke of luck Patrick was talking to Toby Robertson, who was then running the Old Vic Theatre. Toby mentioned that his ex-wife had been pondering a play on the same subject and had discovered that Timothy West, whom we had always known to be a fine actor, was also a frustrated conductor. By now the form of the play was a Beecham rehearsal, and a great deal of credible conducting, even to the playback of Beecham recordings, was required. Tim West leapt at the chance and Patrick Garland found a theatre at Salisbury where we could try the play out. It was a success and we were in the unfamiliar position of being courted by half a dozen managers. Finally three of them united to bring the play to the West End. The impresarios outnumbered the cast by one. (There is a charming story of an American impresario, Arthur Cantor, who had two one-man shows following each other into the same theatre – Alec McCowen followed by Emlyn Williams. He gave a 'joint cast party'.)

Our three brave managers presented *Beecham* at the Apollo Theatre, where Beecham aficionados and old colleagues gave it enthusiastic receptions, but we were never able to persuade a large public to attend. However, whenever Timothy West and Terry Wale took the show out for a Sunday-night performance in the provinces the houses were packed and enthusiastic. Much later Yorkshire Television recorded a performance with Timothy and his 'supporting cast'. He conducted the Hallé Orchestra for real in the musical excerpts.

A more melancholy episode was an adaptation of a thriller which we called *Hush and Hide*. Caryl and I admired the novel on which we based it. We started work on it in New York. We liked our adaptation – so did the managers, the director and the cast. We liked the rehearsals and had high hopes for the play. We opened at the Forum Theatre, Billingham, planning a twelve-week tour and a triumphant London season. It was a sober experience to see the curtain rise for the first time on the play and to watch each cast-iron scene, each exciting twist of the plot, each great dramatic moment dwindle into decorous boredom. The cast were committed to tour the 'turkey' around England and we could find no way of enlivening it. It was dull and worthy and when it finally died in Richmond there was nothing to do but try to learn a lesson. Unfortunately I still have not decided what the lesson is so I cannot even take that satisfaction from the enterprise.

While I was in America I was approached to devise a revue. I flailed around for a theme and eventually picked up on an obsession with language among literate New Yorkers. Two books by Edwin Newman, *Strictly Speaking* and *A Civil Tongue*, were starting points. Newman, whose main bugbear was the word 'hopefully', was sympathetic. I also approached William Safire (*On Languages*) but when he heard that Newman was involved he withdrew. In spite of getting some interest from Ed Kleban, who wrote the songs for *Chorus Line*, and Maury Yeston, who was to go on to write *NINE* and work on *Grand Hotel*, the material was intractable.

However, the venture led to a meeting with Jerry Lieber and Mike Stoller, doyens of rock music. I approached Lieber thinking that his command of vivid street vernacular, in songs like

'Hound Dog', 'Charlie Brown', 'Jailhouse Rock', 'Love Potion No. 9', 'Poison Ivy', 'Searchin", 'Kansas City', 'Along Came Jones', 'Yakety Yak', 'On Broadway' and 'Black Denim Trousers and Motor Cycle Boots', might yield something for the languages revue. No luck. However, it became clear that Lieber and Stoller would not be averse to my devising another compilation show on the lines of *Side By Side*. I could not see a way of sitting on the side of a stage plumply pontificating with jokes while this street-smart, raunchy, gyrating youth music punctuated my observations. On the other hand the sharp observation of inner-city life in East Coast America that coloured the songs lent itself to a raucous 'day in the life' picture of young urban Americans which I found irresistible. I called it after another of their songs, *Only in America*.

I developed the idea with two young Americans, my friend David Yakir and Susan Crawford. The vivid narrative immediacy of the songs made extra dialogue unnecessary. Both David and Susan had grown up in the sort of streets where we were setting the musical. We flogged the idea around New York to no avail. When I came back to England after *Side By Side* prospects looked brighter. It was a false dawn. The record company, Chrysalis, came on board. We made a deal with the Roundhouse and assembled a talented company led by Bertice Reading. Bertice, that explosive, funny, powerful, sleep-prone singer from the original radio production of *Cindy-Ella*, had exiled herself to the continent for many years and it was good to have her back in triumph singing, 'Hound Dog', 'I'm a Woman, W-O-M-A-N', and 'Stand by Me'. However, the production was financially undernourished and the wacky world of rock 'n' roll was a rude awakening for me. The band of established rock musicians had a wonderful time taking session after session to work out their arrangements rather than a couple of band calls to play what was written. Jerry and Mike arrived late to indulge in even longer exploratory creative sessions on the set, with the cast, as the opening night drew nearer. Any regular theatrical routine went out of the window. Getting the set built was a nightmare. The Roundhouse had just discovered cocaine and it did not help their work rate. Several nights I sat in the stalls until the early hours to make sure that work proceeded. We opened to good notices. For Bertice it was a spectacular success but that failed to keep the show alive. The failure of *Only in America* is a major regret. Certainly older and perhaps a little wiser, it would be good to stage it again with adequate resources. Sadly it can no longer be with Bertice.

There was an absurd footnote. Jerry and Mike were invited to join the Bolcoms – two American purveyors of art songs – in a concert of Lieber and Stoller numbers in Paris. They asked me to compere it. The small hall was full of leathery, hard-core French rockers who had come to pay homage to Lieber and Stoller and were baffled by the concert arrangements that Mr and Mrs Bolcom were fluting away at their baby grand.

Only in America had received the full force of Caryl's cold shoulder and it made life quieter to confine my directing to a West End revival of *Cindy-Ella* or *I Gotta Shoe* and the Chichester production of *Nickleby and Me*.

The too-tempting exception was a visit to America to mount a production of a Noel Coward revue. An American producer had acquired the rights to *Cowardy Custard*, a Coward compilation of songs and sketches which Wendy Toye made into a success at the Mermaid long before *Side By Side By Sondheim* began its London run there. For some undisclosed reason the producer wanted to junk the title, the running order and the architect of the earlier success. I should have been warned. As I tried to assemble a cast in New York it became harder and harder to pin the producer down to theatres and dates. Eventually I passed on with no enthusiasm an enquiry from the little jewel box Goodspeed Theatre in Connecticut.

Goodspeed has a reputation as a successful summer theatre in idyllic surroundings. It specialises in revivals of between-the-wars musicals, giving them a fresh, young look. I was thinking of a spanking, Rolls-Royce Broadway vehicle. It was not to be. We starred Millicent Martin and Jeremy Brett with a willing cast of young American singers and dancers, somewhat at sea in the sketches. Millie managed a wide range of funny characters. Jeremy was in the middle of some sort of crisis and at one point in rehearsals became obsessed by the idea that I was keen to replace him with myself. I finally had a tearful encounter with him (his tears) in which I tried to explain that narrating *Side By Side By Sondheim* did not mean that I wanted to play the lead in *Noel*. (We had been through several uninviting title changes. That was the final choice.) I explained that I could not sing, could not dance or even move to music, was reluctant to speak lines while moving on stage, could not learn and remember them anyway and was a non-starter. Half convinced, Jeremy stayed.

The Goodspeed policy was to sell by subscription and the theatre was full of puzzled people throughout the run. The notices were lukewarm and there was no possibility of moving *Noel* to Broadway. Local reaction was summed up by one Connecticut matron. I heard her leaving the theatre after a matinée saying to her companion, 'Who was this Noel Coward guy anyway? Was he the one who collaborated with Hitler?' She had mixed him up with P. G. Wodehouse and got it wrong on both counts.

Another musical, *The Mitford Girls*, was an altogether happier experience. Choosing a subject for a musical is a lottery, especially a British musical, a much maligned art form. We picked the Mitfords as a subject because they were quintessentially English, and we enjoyed the exercise of attacking a story in which any spurious, second-hand, American energy would be out of place. The Mitford daughters had their own vitality, which was urgent and all-embracing.

Part of the excitement for us lay in the apparent problems – a mass of material but hardly a plot – although we were also aware that stories that seem to cry out to be set to music must be viewed with grave mistrust. The classic example is the irresistible temptation which *The Importance of Being Earnest* offers to every generation of songwriters; once they tamper with its delicate, impeccable clockwork, they sabotage their songs in the process. Hal Prince and Stephen Sondheim were being watched over by a particularly discerning Good Fairy when they failed to persuade Jean Anouilh to allow them to make a musical around the obvious charms of *Ring Round the Moon* until it was too late. They had to make do with the challenge offered by Bergman's *Smiles of a Summer Night* for their *A Little Night Music*, and how lucky (as well as clever) they were.

In 1980, back from America, I was bucketed around rented flats in Cadogan Square and opposite Brompton Oratory. Then I pitched myself down in a small house in Pimlico. This became the starting point for the Mitfords. An American house-guest with a highly developed sense of snobbery asked me to tape Julian Jebb's television memoir of Nancy Mitford, remembered by four surviving sisters. He could not see the programme when it was transmitted and could not bear to miss a duchess, a real lady and two Hon. missuses all in one show. As Caryl and I watched the programme, the idea of six leading ladies telling the story of their public and private lives and slipping in and out of character and in and out of song began to form.

We talked to Julian Jebb and he explained that the Duchess of Devonshire (née Deborah Mitford) was the key to securing the rights, the whipper-in. It was our intention to make a collage of the memoirs of Diana and Jessica, the novels, essays and letters of Nancy, and some of the reminiscences added on television by Pamela and Deborah. The Duchess (Debo) is Nancy Mitford's literary executor and controls the copyright in all her material. She also maintained easy contact with her right- and left-wing

sisters, Diana and Jessica, who did not communicate with each
other. I wrote to her at Chatsworth and got an immediate reply,
which I soon learned was characteristic, suggesting 'lunch at
Chatsworth on the 6th, 7th, 8th, 9th October or 13th, 14th,
15th October', enclosing detailed train arrangements from St
Pancras to Chesterfield, where I could be collected, and a postscript: 'You don't think the poor old British public have had
enough of our ugly mugs?' By the time I made the journey Caryl
and I had done most of the initial reading and had a fair idea of
the shape we wanted the show to take. We arranged with Peter
Greenwell to compose the new music and arrange the evocative
standard songs which we felt would add to the nostalgic period
flavour.

I arrived at Chatsworth in time for lunch and was butlered
into a small sitting room which I recognised from the television
documentary. I turned to find the Duchess and Mrs Jackson
(Pamela) prowling in, both with blue eyes wide open, rather
like very well-mannered, welcoming big cats. The beam of
Mitford charm is bright and direct, but the aspect remains formidable and the suggestion of a claw, however deeply sheathed,
is ever present. They laugh a lot and the laughter is infectious,
not empty. The importance of 'jokes' is paramount, and the passion for nicknames, well documented, has not been dissipated.
Mrs Jackson, as I knew from Jessica's *Hons and Rebels,* was
immediately 'Woman'; the two other guests at lunch had their
labels; and within a few weeks Peter Greenwell, our composer,
became 'Perfect'. In the course of two letters Debo called his
piano playing 'marvellous' and 'wonderful'. He was a little
dimmed by 'wonderful', thinking the phrase was not quite as
extravagant as 'marvellous'. I told Debo that she must be consistent or it would breed insecurity, so she plumped for 'Perfect'
and adopted it as a nickname – 'Perf'. When her husband went
on record as finding the show 'plotless', I had a letter starting
'Dear Plotless', which has not stuck.

After lunch we settled down to discuss the project. The question of over-exposure was aired, and Debo produced a fat file labelled, 'The Industry' (the Mitford industry). My own theory was that people enjoy the ingenious retelling of a well-known tale. In *Cinderella* everyone knows the heroine is going to get to the ball, the interest lies in the attractive and inventive manner with which her progress is plotted. Familiarity with Mitford myths – which have reached folklore status – would be an asset if we could be sufficiently beguiling in our presentation. The two sisters thought about that and labelled it the 'Cinderella Theory'. Debo wrote later detailing the amount of Mitford lore due to hit the screens, including an eight-episode family history, inspired by Diana's book, with three actresses playing each sister, 'older and older. I suppose I end up as a furious old woman permanently wearing a tiara! Oh well . . . I can hear the groans of our friends and the switching off nightly of many a telly.'

However, the Cinderella Theory carried the day and I went on to explain our idea of mixing new and old songs, and found an immediate response from both sisters. Pamela Jackson in particular launched into a repertoire of twenties and thirties numbers, some of which the family had sung in their original form, others elaborately parodied. 'You must have "Ukulele Lady",' she pleaded. 'Nancy always sang that. She learned the ukulele specially.' 'Write to Decca [Jessica] straight away', Debo advised; and indeed we had already approached her English agent. 'Dear Mr Sherrin . . . Sounds like a marvellously comic caper . . .'

Back in London we talked to Patrick Garland, who had taken over the Chichester Festival and was looking for some Sunday-night programmes. We thought our Mitford anthology could perhaps be tried out at one of those and, if successful, it might be specially mounted the following summer.

We finished a first draft in November 1980 and arranged to play it to Debo, who was by now referring to it as 'the high-kicking musical', and was coming to London for 'the Dairy

Show'. It took about three hours. I read all the parts and Peter Greenwell sang all the songs, with which she was much taken. She had very few complaints apart from correcting a few inaccuracies and pointing out a few sore points which might upset one sister or another. She was rather caustic about Decca's suggestion in *Hons and Rebels* that 'Debo always wanted to marry a duke', pointing out that Andrew Devonshire had been a second son when she married him. She followed up with a letter the next day:

> Thank you very much indeed for yesterday's memorable afternoon . . . I've no idea what Decca will make of it, I never have . . . I've had another thought, my mother never said 'Do admit', it was us who started that – silly fools. Oh dear, I did love the music.
>
> > I'm in an urching mood . . .
> > An anti-churching mood
> > That's the mood I'm in!
> > I'm urching, not churching,
> > I'm in a researching mood . . .
>
> [At that time we were including 'I'm in a Dancing Mood', which we later cut; it had been a Mitford house parody.]
>
> Get marvellous Mr Greenwell to sing that. THANKS again,
>
> > > > > > > > > Debo.

I sent copies of the text-so-far to all the sisters. ('Woman won't open it. Too busy feeding those chickens.') By this time we had agreement in principle from Jessica, subject to a television option on her books, which looked like lapsing at any moment. We took a chance on that. At about this time we played to Patrick, who had lost one play and decided to put ours on as a full production at the Chichester Festival for the main season. Things were moving almost too fast for us. Together, Caryl and I had spent years trying to get musicals written and staged. We had started on this one in October and by Christmas it seemed we had a production scheduled for that summer.

We arranged another play-through for the European sisters just before Christmas. Diana Mosley was coming to London and letters arrived from her and Debo on the same day. 'I think Diana might be able to snatch the time to see and hear *The Girls* on December 10th, latish afternoon if you could put it on again? [I love 'put it on'.] And Pam says if Diana comes she will . . . if wonderful Mr Greenwell and you have got the time?' Lady Mosley was due in London because she had promised to do a TV interview on Henry Williamson. I pointed out that we had used a phrase of hers from the television documentary as a song title. 'I laughed at the idea of a sequence of songs . . . "Why *do* people fall in love?" Did I really say that? It must have been in connection with Nancy, who did fall in love with rather strange people: at least so I thought.'

Two or three days before the day appointed Oswald Mosley died. I was interviewing Pamela Jackson about the television version of *Love in a Cold Climate* on a radio programme that morning and we heard the news after the broadcast. She was an enchanting guest, treating the BBC studio like a dinner table, oblivious of the microphone and engaging guests on her right and left in polite succession, showing equal interest in the odd range, A. L. Rowse to Clive Powell, a young footballer, and his manager. Rowse had a reputation for being 'naughty' in interviews. On this occasion he behaved beautifully, impressed by a Mitford on one side and thrilled by the sturdy, good-looking footballer on the other. Pamela Jackson told an unexpected story of trying to introduce her obscure Swiss breed of hens, Alpenzellers, to this country. The Ministry of Agriculture refused an import permit so, she explained with a wicked smile, 'In the end I just brought in a dozen eggs and hatched them!'

Mosley's death meant a postponement of our audition until well after Christmas. I went to America for a few days to set

up the Coward revue I was directing in Connecticut –
Christmas dinner at Sardi's, half empty, and no special menu
until Anthony Hopkins at the next table insisted on plum pudding and we shared it. When I came back we prepared for the
final test.

It was an uncanny feeling reading all six Mitford sisters aloud
to three of the survivors and braying like six demented impersonations of Edith Evans in a hopeful approximation of the 'Mitford
Voice'. They followed their scripts carefully and only really
relaxed when 'Perfect' Peter Greenwell launched into their
favourite songs. It was not made easier by the fact that Lady
Mosley and Mrs Jackson were, in one case very and in the other
quite, deaf. But they laughed at the familiar jokes and it became
clear as we ploughed on that we were winning. Lady Mosley
wanted a stronger case made for her parents. Mrs Jackson wanted
a reference to John Betjeman corrected. Basically they were happy
with it. Debo marshalled them out with, 'Come on, Mrs Nozel
Wurzle,' another nickname, 'they're bored with us, let's bugger
off.' She insisted that we got pretty girls to play them. 'We may
have been dull, but we certainly weren't dowdy!' We taped the
entire afternoon for Jessica and sent it off for her approval, which
came back smartly. By the time I left for rehearsals of the Noel
Coward revue in America we had everything but a cast.

I heard from Lady Mosley just before leaving:

> It is so kind of you to think of ways round, so that Muv gets
> anyway part of her due . . . Last night my son Alexander, who
> has seen *Love in a C.C.* which I have not, made a rather good
> point. He says that in Nancy's novels Uncle M. is eccentric
> and funny but he is not a buffoon. He says the whole tension
> in the novels, which makes them something a bit more than
> simply 'funny', is a result of the fact that the children were in
> fact quite afraid of him, as well as being amused by him.
> Decca of course makes him a buffoon and rather a nasty one

Caryl Brahms, an inspirational writing partner. We worked together for almost thirty years. *(Topix)*

Side By Side By Sondheim's first cast, 1976. From left, Millicent Martin, David Kernan and Julia McKenzie. I await my moment. *(Zoe Dominic)*

David Yakir (right) and me working on *Only in America*. *(John Oliver)*

'You didn't give her two points! She was right and you didn't give her two points!' A publicity shot for *We Interrupt This Week* – my American current affairs quiz show that started in October 1978. Initially not all viewers admired its irreverence.

The six leading ladies of 1981's *The Mitford Girls*. Seated from left: Patricia Michael, Colette Gleeson, Lucy Fenwick and Gay Soper. Standing are Patricia Hodge (left) and Julia Sutton (centre). *(Reg Wilson)*

Brighton races, 1989. *Jeffrey Bernard is Unwell* had just opened at the Theatre Royal. With me from left, Gary Fairhall, Royce Mills, Keith Waterhouse (light suit), Annabel Leventon (sunglasses), Sarah Berger, Jeffrey Bernard, Michael Redington, Timothy Ackroyd and Peter O'Toole. *(Alan Davidson)*

The three actors who first played Jeff – Peter O'Toole, Tom Conti and James Bolam – raise a glass, along with writer Keith Waterhouse, producer Michael Redington, me and the prose poet himself. *(Author's collection)*

In defence of tripe. Dennis Waterman and Keith Waterhouse sample my tripe and Chardonnay cuisine, celebrating the Australian preview of *Jeffrey Bernard is Unwell*. *(Simon Grosset)*

LONDON AND SOUTH EAST (BBC Local Radio London, Kent, Sussex: page 72)
20-26 August 1988   Price 37p

COMPLETE 7-DAY GUIDE TO BBCtv and Radio

RAID OUR HOLIDAY BOX!
Theme park discount – and 'murder weekends' to be won. p82

Radio Times

St Ned's school for scandal

It's not what you know, it's who you know!
Ned 'the Head' Sherrin teaches a lesson in shameless ambition
as a new term of 'Loose Ends' begins, Saturday Radio 4.
Star pupils' shock report, page 83

The cover of the *Radio Times*, August 1988. *Loose Ends* gathered steam after winning a Sony award for Best Magazine Programme in its first year. With me are, from left, Victoria Mather, Richard Jobson, Robert Elms, John Walters, Craig Charles, Victor Lewis-Smith and Emma Freud. *(Radio Times)*

With the marvellous
Elisabeth Welch.
(Author's collection)

The BBC's fortieth anniversary party for *That Was The Week That Was* in November 2002. From left, Sir Antony Jay, Bernard Levin, Herbert Kretzmer and Christopher Booker, all stalwart contributors to the show. *(Author's collection)*

At home, World's End, Chelsea. *(Author's collection)*

at that . . . I remember Alexander was asked to stay with him up at Redesdale and I asked him, 'How did you know which was Farve on Newcastle Station?' And Alexander, aged about twelve, replied, 'Well, I looked and then I saw a noble old gentleman and I knew it must be Farve.' I told Andrew Devonshire this . . . and he said, 'A perfect description of your father.'

I felt such a fraud the other day, poor old black crow [she was in deep mourning], at the idea of being 'beautiful' [the text made constant reference] . . . It made me laugh and cry. The song 'Some enchanted evening, you will see a stranger across a crowded room' [the song is not in *The Mitford Girls*] . . . always reminds me of Oswald Mosley. It was at a ball at Philip Sassoon's house.

With so many thanks for Muv.

I collected a fourth surviving Mitford sister, Jessica, in New York. Like all Mitfords she was exactly on time. Indeed she had arrived at 1 Fifth Avenue before the one o'clock date on which we had agreed, and I was further delayed as I got out of my taxi by seeing an elderly man knocked down by a car. He was dazed rather than hurt and had only walked a few steps from his doctor's office, so I pushed him back inside and hurried to the restaurant. Once again the Mitford obsession with the popular songs of their adolescence surfaced over lunch. I was treated to a spirited 'Brother Can You Spare a Dime?'; and Decca's greatest enthusiasm was reserved for my suggestion that her voice was marginally better than Debo's (not difficult). 'Compared to Debo you are Callas,' I said rashly. The news winged its way to Chatsworth by the next post as though a childhood argument were being carried to victory fifty years on. Decca often signed herself 'Your loving Callas' in letters to Debo.

The clockwork of *The Mitford Girls* was a delicate piece of machinery involving long musical rehearsals because of the number of songs which were treated to intricate harmonies for the six girls' voices. We were lucky to find six actresses all of whom were potential or actual leading ladies. Patricia Hodge was Nancy; Julia Sutton, Pamela; Patricia Michael, Diana; Colette Gleeson, Unity; Liz Robertson, Decca; and Gay Soper, Deborah. Oz Clarke, actor and wine expert, played most of the men, sprinkling the season with wine tastings and inspiring the girls to hurry to order the house wine on arrival at any after-show restaurant table, lest his constant search for expensive vintages should ruin their bank balances.

The six leading ladies, so used to competing for a single role, relished working together and produced a unique sound, beautifully choreographed by Lindsay Dolan with Sir Anton Dolin adding occasionally genuine period flavour.

The play opened at the beginning of June 1981, and was a perfect Chichester choice. West Sussex enjoys its summer theatre: black ties and long gowns parade in the parklands surrounding the theatre. Mitfords came in stages. Jessica planned to bring a large party of 'country relatives' in the second week. Debo was on parade for the first preview. The Duke of Devonshire had announced his intention of staying away: he preferred *Anyone for Denis?*, in which he was mentioned, to an evening of Mitfordolatry. Interviewing him once when I was doing a stint on *Midweek*, I managed to get through a whole hour without mentioning the Mitfords, a record which pleased him enormously. Later he dismissed the play as *La Triviata*. However, in one interview he confessed to a great liking for Decca and her books – which surprised her: 'I could scarcely believe it – always thought he loathed me . . . I have long yearned to review his book *Parktop: A Romance of the Turf*. It is up amongst my favourite books such as *Modern Pigsticking*, published in 1913, which begins, "It is now some twenty years since Baden-Powell published his charming brochure on pigsticking . . ." and goes on from there. Dedication: "To my Mother".'

I had had special badges made for the cast: 'I am a Mitford Girl', they proclaimed, and we distributed them without regard to sex. Four special ones were created for the surviving sisters, saying, 'I Really am a Mitford Girl'. They wore them loyally, to my surprise, on their visits to the theatre. (Diana: 'I wore my "badge" which made my companions shun me (shyness) but nobody noticed it because my clothes were black and white so my bold gesture was wasted.') For Devonshire and Bob Treuhaft, Decca's husband, two more badges announced, 'I'm Married to a *Real* Mitford Girl'. I don't think the Duke wore his, even in the intimacy of Chatsworth.

Debo categorised the first preview audience – almost entirely local – as 'her people': largely Women's Institute. She was more suspicious of the first-night crowd two nights later, which included a generous sprinkling of Londoners and critics. On this occasion she came with Pamela, who was still happily reliving the old songs.

With Decca's visit the element of controversy which surrounded the show came into focus. What we had attempted was an essay in style. The essay was designed to chart in their own words the development of a rich, eccentric English country family in the twenties and thirties – six girls who had wilfully, and often wittily, gone their very different ways. It had seemed to us unnecessary to editorialise or to judge the girls and the events in which their lives became entangled. Our main focus was on the characters of Nancy and Jessica. Patricia Hodge lent exquisite elegance and wit to her Nancy: beautiful, sharp, poised and precise, switching effortlessly to suggest the heavier step of her mother.

The real Decca shared the doubts felt by those who wanted us to make a more political statement of values which we assumed were obvious. To the *Sunday Times*' readers she confided her doubts. She characterised the Chichester audience, borrowing her mother's words, as a 'youngish crowd in their early seventies', and went on to say that she found the lack of dimension in our sketch of her first husband, Esmond Romilly, troubling. She objected to what she saw as a romanticisation of Hitler in his brief moment on stage, and she was critical of our bare statement of her sister Diana's marriage to Oswald Mosley.

I had a three-hour session with her at my hotel in Chichester, during which it was interesting to watch the technique of a self-proclaimed 'muck-raker'. I had noticed that in all her best pieces she found a dramatic structure, a hook on which to hang her investigations, a persuasive way of presenting her argument. In this interview she deputed the job of questioning me to Polly Toynbee, a young cub reporter and long-time family friend, rather more critical of the play than Decca herself. Decca took no notes and, I think, recorded nothing. She listened with great concentration and hardly intervened except on occasions when she sensed that little Polly was overplaying her hand. The technique lent an objectivity to the article which was very effective. Caryl and I happily conceded her point about Esmond Romilly, and we included a paragraph from the peroration at the end of *Boadilla* – his account of his experiences in the Spanish Civil War – at the climax of our play which added greatly to its poignancy.

I am still surprised by the need to underline the revulsion against fascism which most critics who disliked the play have expressed. It struck me as naive and superfluous. The play filled Chichester and moved to London. At the Globe it had a rapturous first night, a divided press and an uncomfortable rumour that it was 'that musical about Hitler'. Two sentences spoken by a supporting character who was on the stage for less than a minute evoked that label. However, I suppose that if you embark on an exercise in style and your pyrotechnics allow the audience time to look elsewhere, then you must accept that you have not lavished enough craft on the piece to justify your original hopes.

The impresario who controlled the theatre was troubled by the Hitler association and hardly supported the play. Then he became worried about the play that was following us in. His 'talent scout' had seen it out of town. 'What's it like?' the manager asked. 'Oh, it's another of those "black comedies",' said the scout. The impresario frowned. 'They don't all have to be niggers, do they?' he said.

There was a farcical footnote to the West End transfer. Caryl and I dined at Joe Allen after seeing a play and bumped into Michael Stewart (book writer) and David Merrick (producer), who had been to Nottingham to monitor Denis Quilley and Imelda Staunton in the first British attempt to stage their Mack Sennett musical *Mack and Mabel*. Michael said, 'We just saw your play up in lights outside the Globe.' Caryl couldn't wait to drive round to Shaftesbury Avenue. Having viewed the spectacle together, I got a cab home and she drove off up the Charing Cross and Tottenham Court roads towards Regent's Park. Back in Pimlico I got a call from her – somewhere between laughter and tears. She had failed to notice some roadworks and drove her Mini straight into a deep pit. Worse, she saw a posse of Teddy boys (a bit out of period) and feared a mugging. Instead the leader said, 'Let's get you out of this, lady.' They had heaved her out of the hole and back on to the highway. She was able to drive, limping home.

Caryl and I wrote three novels together, two collections of short stories, some fifteen radio plays, five plays, several television pieces and six musicals in the twenty-eight years of our collaboration, none of which matched the success of her great years with S. J. Simon.

The Mitford Girls was the last show we wrote together, although we revived *Nickleby and Me* at Chichester for the Christmas season 1981–2. It is worth pointing out – though Caryl preferred not to dwell on the fact – that she was nearly seventy when she collaborated on *Sing a Rude Song*; in her seventies when we wrote *Liberty Ranch* and *Nickleby and Me*; and nearly eighty when we worked on *The Mitford Girls*. Her friend Dorothy Fields, the great American lyricist, who died in 1974 at the age of seventy after her writing two last shows, *Sweet Charity* and *See-Saw*, is the nearest comparison I can think of in terms of longevity. I suggested once, when the London box-office returns from *The Mitford Girls* were dwindling, that we should advertise, 'Lyrics by the oldest, living, lady lyricist in captivity.' The suggestion was not welcomed.

When I met Caryl I was lucky to find a perfect launch pad for a half-hearted writing career and a very steadfast friend. She could, of course, like most of us, be jealous, possessive and obstructive – indeed her ability to make waves was probably greater than that in most of us. However, she had a unique ability to draw things out of a collaborator which were his own, but would not have surfaced without her husbandry. In addition, it would be foolish to deny that as she grew older I felt a responsibility for her. I believe that she, in her turn, found someone whom she trusted, as far as she trusted anyone, whose company she could enjoy, and who challenged her into new fields which otherwise she would not have entered.

She looked suddenly older and more tired during the last year of her life, her eighty-second. However, she continued to go regularly to the theatre, to add and subtract passages from her memoirs which she chose to present as a wilful stream of consciousness. At eighty-one she was still hunting for new projects. The failure of *The Mitford Girls* and *Beecham* to have long and lucrative runs in the West End was a keen disappointment, both financially and because she loved the involvement with a backstage theatre family. During the couple of weeks before her death she seemed to gather a new energy and, perhaps with an unconscious insight into the future, to put her house in order. Her handwriting was, by now, disconcertingly frail and spidery but batches of letters and postcards continued to wing out from her flat in Cambridge Gate. In several cases she wrote to people with whom she had had some real or imagined difference, making her peace, as it were, with a considered compliment. On the first Saturday in December 1982 we went to a matinée of *Babes in Arms* at the Arts Educational School. She had always had a particular fondness for the school and its links to the ballet. She decided that she would give a small annual prize for the best acting performance in a musical. She gave a similar prize at RADA.

She wanted an early night. The next day, Sunday, we had agreed to start on yet another stage version of *No Bed for Bacon*, this time without music. I left her after a cup of tea. We agreed to meet at my house in Pimlico at 11.30 a.m. She called me later to complain that she could not get Channel 4, on which she wanted to watch a repeat of *Upstairs Downstairs*. She died early in the morning. Having started to boil a kettle, she returned to her bedroom and collapsed across her bed, felled by a stroke. Her non-appearance and her failure to answer the telephone alarmed me. I got help from the local police station to enter the flat. The kettle had boiled through. The police took over.

On Monday *The Times* published Caryl's obituary. She would have been pleased that it was 'above the fold', which she always thought very important, and furious that it gave her age as eighty-two, which she thought no one knew and which she would not in any case have been until the next day.

When I registered her death, the official who took down the particulars raised an eyebrow as he noted the number of years. 'A very good age,' he said. 'What did she do when she was working?'

I did not like to tell him that she had never stopped.

CHAPTER 12

That's Entertainment

When I first saw Peter O'Toole he was a eunuch. This was back in the fifties. It said he was a eunuch in the programme of *Ali Baba and the Forty Thieves* at the Bristol Old Vic. I remember nothing of O'Toole's eunuch however much this bit of character-acting stretched him. I only remember the performances of Eric Porter as a ripe, fruity dame and Lally Bowers as a coy Good Fairy. I was next aware of O'Toole after he had written to Caryl Brahms asking her to come down to Bristol to see his Hamlet. 'I can't go chasing round the country to see every young man's Hamlet,' she had said. She always regretted it.

O'Toole came to London soon after as a Chekhovian uncle in the musical *Oh My Papa!* which starred Rachel Roberts and languished briefly at the Garrick Theatre in 1957. However, by the 1960s he was a star and I had launched *That Was The Week That Was*. Orson Welles was in London, staying at the Ritz. The playwright Peter Shaffer had already written some powerful pieces for *TW3*, one prompted by the Vassal scandal. 'The only way to stop a homosexual being blackmailed is to stop him being a homosexual. And the only way to do that is to lock him up in a prison with five hundred other men. That way he can see how unattractive they really are . . .'

Now Shaffer wrote a brilliant monologue satirising the pretensions of General de Gaulle, imagining him still alive in 1990, supreme spokesman of the European Community making a speech of acceptance – a piece of sustained invective which culminated in a resounding peroration, 'With God's blessing I crown myself King of Europe! Seigneur of Brussels! Suzerain of the Hague, Feudal Overlord of West Berlin! Warden in Chief of the Vatican! Long live French Catholic Europe!'

I sent it round to Welles who said, 'No' with alarming speed. O'Toole was in the West End doing a marathon stint in Brecht's *Baal* at the time. I whizzed the monologue off to him and his 'Yes' came back as quickly as Welles's 'No'. Looking back some forty years on, the logistics seem impossible. He played his enormous role twice that day in the theatre, stepped into a car and was driven to the Television Centre to deliver a long, live speech to a single camera within minutes of arriving. The performance was impeccable, the script powerful. The only problem was that it wasn't funny. It was over twenty-five years before we were to work together again. This time the script *was* funny.

I hardly knew Jeffrey Bernard before Keith Waterhouse wrote *Jeffrey Bernard is Unwell* in 1989. Certainly I did not think of him as an entertainment. Bernard was many things in his messy life. Boxer, stagehand, actor, barman, bookie, five times a husband, always a boozer. Yet somehow most weeks he managed to recall his degradations in and around Soho in immaculate, elegant prose in the *Spectator* magazine under the title 'Low Life'. On weeks when irresponsibility or incapacity prevented him from submitting his column the legend 'Jeffrey Bernard is Unwell' would appear in its place. On one occasion the exasperated editor inserted a variant – 'Jeffrey Bernard's column does not appear this week as it bears a remarkable resemblance to the one we published last week.'

Keith Waterhouse had been broody with a play about the death of Soho for years and it was Jeff, prose poet to the parish, who unlocked for him the mystery of how to write it. Sitting through a performance of *Tosca* at the London Coliseum the Waterhouse mind, when it was not asleep, wandered. In its travels it landed on Soho and, more particularly, on a little drinking club off Shaftesbury Avenue called Gerry's. Waterhouse often landed up there himself when he was *not* dreaming. The owner was an actor, Gerry Campion, best known on television in the schoolboy role of Billy Bunter. Gerry's was a favourite meeting place for entertainers and theatrical hangers-on. Many of the here-today-gone-tomorrow bar staff were out-of-work actors. Part of the lore of Gerry's was the regular appearance of Granada Television's senior casting director, John Murphy, who, after a hard day's casting, would refresh himself at the bar. Looking up from his vodka one night he focused on the young actor who had just served him. 'I saw you in that thing at the RSC,' he slurred. 'You were brilliant!'

'But you can't have, Mr Murphy. I've never been at the RSC. I had one audition but I didn't even get a call back.'

'I've seen you somewhere. You were terrific. Must have been the National.'

'Mr Murphy, I can't even get an audition for the National.'

'I know I've seen you somewhere. You were—'

'Mr Murphy, I haven't worked for two years. For the last three months I've been on the cheese counter at Harrods.'

'That's where I saw you! You were terrific!'

Murphy's other contribution to the history of Gerry's was to go to sleep in the lavatory one night and not to wake until after closing time. The place was deserted and locked up. Having helped himself to a generous hair of the dog, he telephoned Campion to explain his predicament. The owner, mindful of how quickly his vodka stocks would be eroded, screamed, 'Don't move! Don't touch a thing! I'll be there in ten minutes!', leapt into his car and arrived at the club in record time.

It was this episode which Keith recalled when he should have been thinking of Tosca, Scarpia and Cavaradossi. By now wide awake he spent the rest of the opera switching the scene from Gerry's to Bernard's more regular drinking hole, the Coach and Horses, imagining Jeff locked in, devising reasons why he would not be able to get through to the truculent Norman Balon ('the rudest landlord in London') on the phone. Meanwhile, he peopled the pub with ghosts from Jeff's columns and his past.

Keith has written: 'It is not a play about Soho, although Soho figures. It isn't a play about drinking, although the protagonist is required to consume a good litre of water (fortunately vodka is colourless) in the course of an evening in which he is off stage for only three seconds. It is a play about friendship, about failure, about vulnerability, about coming to terms with life. It all rounds up to a portrait of man, warts, vodka bottle and all. There is no better subject.'

When the play was finished Keith sent copies to me and to Michael Redington, who produced his last play *Mr and Mrs Nobody* starring Judi Dench and Michael Williams. Why did he send it to me? Here we track back a couple of years to 1986 and my first theatre adventure with Keith.

His earlier play *Mr and Mrs Nobody* is based on the Grossmiths' *The Diary of a Nobody*, the classic account of the genteel pretensions of lower-middle-class Victorian life recorded in the diary of Charles Pooter, and Keith's reply, *Mrs Pooter's Diary*. This began life as a novel read as a *Woman's Hour* serial by Judi Dench. This was lucky. Judi can rarely be persuaded to read a script before she starts to rehearse it. She preferred to rely on the judgement of Michael, her late husband, or directors like Peter Hall or Trevor Nunn whom she trusts. She swears she had never read *Antony and Cleopatra* before putting herself in Hall's hands.

On this occasion, having been paid by the BBC for her pains, she confided to the *Radio Times* that she would love to play

Carrie Pooter on stage. Keith took this as an invitation to start adapting – using the spine of events described by Mr Pooter and constantly puncturing his self-regard with his wife's scornful asides.

Michael and Judi persuaded the trusted Trevor Nunn to direct but with his multitude of commitments he kept putting them off. When Keith's patience was exhausted he sent me a copy and we met at the Garrick to discuss it. I couldn't have been more enthusiastic – or more available, not having any productions in prospect, let alone Trevor Nunn's umpteen.

The play's single flaw was that it was greatly over length. In researching his original Keith had amused himself poring over old bound volumes of *Exchange and Mart* and inventing contemporary household necessities for the Pooters like Neave's Varnish Stain Remover, *Jepson's Sunday Newspaper*, and an indispensable magazine, *Lady Cartmell's Vade Mecum for the Bijou Household*. The Pooters' favourite champagne was bought from 'Jackson Frères', 'Importers of Fine Wines and Vintner's Sundrymen. Runner-up, Isle of Man Bottlers' Exposition Medal 1883, Lower Ground Floor, Paxley's Varnish Warehouse, 235–239 Female Penitentiary Road, N., to which all complaints should be addressed.'

To Keith and to me Jackson Frères soon became a synonym for cutting the text. In Keith's flat or mine we would settle down at about 11 a.m. with a bottle of champagne and savage the play. When we could cut no more we would leave it for a day and convene the next morning with another bottle of Bollinger/Jackson Frères. We found that with fresh minds swaths of dialogue could be culled. I remember *Mr and Mrs Nobody* as about a five-bottle job – in Jackson Frères terms.

There was another snag. Although Judi and Michael shared Keith's impatience to get on with the play, Judi had a major reservation. Early in her career she had been much wounded by Caryl Brahms's reviews of her first performances. Caryl had identified, and perhaps overemphasised, a schoolgirlish-jolly-hockeysticks quality in the young actress. She persisted in referring to Judi as 'Dench J.' This rankled over the years and although Caryl had died four years before, Judi was suspicious that I might have inherited her prejudice.

Ironically one of the last performances Caryl saw was Judi's in Harold Pinter's *A Kind of Alaska* at the National. She phoned me on getting home late that night to say that she thought it was perhaps the greatest piece of acting she had ever seen by a woman.

Judi's reservations did not reveal themselves to me at this stage or I might have been less keen to plunge in. However, there were other insecurities. *Mr and Mrs Nobody* is essentially a two-hander but I added a silent maid, and a factotum to ease the mechanics of staging and a string trio in a minstrel gallery to create the atmosphere of a Victorian soirée. Judi loves a company and hates a quiet, empty backstage. This gave her five more colleagues with which to socialise.

She was still professing doubt as to whether she and Michael could hold an audience alone for a whole evening. One thing which helped to persuade them was Julia Trevelyan Oman's revolutionary idea for the set. At a preliminary reading (the time it took having demanded another two-bottle cutting session of Jackson Frères) Michael and Judi were enchanted by Julia's idea of a revolving set. She wanted the audience to see in turn all four of the walls on which her impeccably chosen treasure chest of Victoriana was to hang. It seemed so simple and so fresh that it won the day. All reservations were swept away.

Sadly, we failed to find any machinery which could realise these unique theatrical effects and on the first day of rehearsal I had to confess to the cast that the revolve had been abandoned and we were left with a beautiful but static set. Fortunately it was now too late for the stars to pull out so they stayed to shine. Working with Judi and Michael was a joy and a liberal education. Their different approaches were fascinating. Michael had to din the lines into his memory by endless repetition. He spent hours doing his 'homework' while Judi effortlessly absorbed her part by a sort of osmosis. Once, after a timed run-through, we found that another Jackson Frères session was necessary. When the cuts were given Judi took her script and gleefully tore out the pages, making the maximum ripping noise. A wince of sudden bereavement crossed Keith's face. Michael, having worked so hard to master the lines, was also reluctant to see them consigned to the waste bin.

Different approaches to preparation did not produce a different intensity. *Mr and Mrs Nobody* is both a tour de force and a tightrope walk for the duettists. The Pooters have to people the stage with imaginary neighbours, friends, City colleagues, tradesmen and their wayward son, Lupin. Michael and Judi agonised over exactly where the people they were addressing or describing would be, magically conjuring life out of empty spaces. It was an attention to detail which gave a rock-solid reality to the fanciful convention.

In contrast to her iron concentration in performance Judi likes to talk about any and everything else until the moment that she steps on to the stage. Her favourite game, a sort of twenty questions played with the company manager, is to guess what 'names' are in the audience that night. This is stretched out if possible to a second before she makes her entrance.

At a charity evening at the Old Vic to celebrate Dame Peggy Ashcroft's eightieth birthday I watched Judi stand by a pillar in the stalls enjoying the actors on stage throughout the first half. She was appearing in the second. I was surprised to see that she returned to her post after the interval and there she stood until Eric Porter, the actor preceding her, began his soliloquy. Only then did she slip through the pass-door, arriving upstage with just time to enter and rip off one of Dame Peggy's famous speeches.

Of course, every actor has his or her own method of preparing before a performance. If Judi's seemed to be like jumping off a precipice and expecting to fly that belies the intense work which she did during painstaking rehearsals. However, her openness in her very social, chatty dressing room ill prepared Keith for a later Mr Pooter. When he called in to wish him luck, '*merde*' or 'break a leg' before his opening night in a provincial theatre he was greeted by a frosty actor. 'Don't you realise they've called the half? How would you like to be interrupted in the middle of writing a sentence?'

The only time I saw Judi less than completely in control was for an instant on the first night in London when Michael leapt in to cover the moment of hesitation. As he said proudly afterwards, 'If Jude goes I turn to steel.'

It was a joyous experience: the Garrick Theatre was full for the run and the two stars were irreplaceable. Two bonuses for Judi were her heavy Victorian costumes and her energetic time on stage. She lost pounds during the run, splendid preparation for her Cleopatra which followed at the National; continents and centuries away from Carrie Pooter – but an even greater triumph.

To get back to the importance of Jackson Frères in our lives: *Jeffrey Bernard is Unwell* was a six-bottle job. When Keith finished the script he had given it to me and to Michael Redington. All three of us were admirers of John Hurt and knew of his close friendship with Jeff. So the play went first to him.

Hurt was not impressed. He could not see it as a theatre piece though he agreed that it 'might make a nice little radio play'. The next Christmas when it was up and running with O'Toole and we were both staying at Hickstead he told me, generously, 'God, you were bloody lucky you didn't finish up with me!'

John's inability to 'see' the play echoed Jeffrey's own reaction.

He couldn't believe it would work and viewed Keith's handsome arrangement for the division of royalties as pie in the sky. Putting the play together had been no easy task. Keith not only plundered published collections of Jeff's *Spectator* pieces but chased up other obscure columns he had contributed. It was a patchwork quilt he assembled. A sentence from the seventies was matched to a 'Low Life' paragraph from the eighties, seamlessly combined. Keith is an accomplished pasticheur and many of his own memories of Soho and its more celebrated incidents and characters hold the whole thing together. The final script was probably at least a third original Waterhouse – most particularly the notorious 'egg trick' which occurs early in Act Two.

Keith remembered this audience-pleaser from an encounter long ago with the religious correspondent of a Sunday newspaper – it involves a biscuit-tin lid, a matchbox, a pint mug of water, a shoe, a raw egg and a hand, preferably unsteady. The object is to hit the biscuit-tin lid, which is placed on the pint mug, with the shoe, dislodging the tin lid and the matchbox which has been supporting the raw egg so that the egg falls harmlessly into the water. Jeff, who had no part in the creation of the egg trick, disowned it until it proved one of the high spots of the evening – when he happily acknowledged it as his own.

Dimmed by John Hurt's rejection, it was without much optimism that Keith called a motorcycle messenger service and dispatched a copy to Peter O'Toole the day after he got the bad news. We were not encouraged by a rumour that O'Toole was planning a season of three plays at the Playhouse. However, that evening Keith returned home from a meeting to find a light flashing on his answerphone and this message: 'Keith, you bastard, you have screwed up my fucking life. I had this whole year mapped out and now I have to change all my fucking plans. I hate you. Love, Peter.' He kept it.

John Gunter the designer and I did a recce at the Coach and Horses and he sketched a faithful replica for our set. I asked if he could come up with something a little more eccentric and he responded with a mad variation in which everything tilted at a crazy angle. O'Toole was filming in France. We sent him a photograph and back came his delighted response: 'A pissed pub!'

Before leaving for the film Peter recorded the entire script on tape so that he could learn it before we started rehearsals. In this practice he follows Noel Coward, who always aimed to arrive word perfect on the first day and expected the rest of his actors to do the same. While he was away we cast our protean supporting actors – Royce Mills, Sarah Berger, Annabel Leventon and Timothy Ackroyd – who were to play the host of poets, hacks, wives, girlfriends, actors, scene hands, policemen, waiters, trainers, bores, publicans and sinners. (When we revived the play for the second time in 1999 at the Old Vic the cast was exactly the same.)

The reunion between interpreter and subject was touching. We met at the Coach and Horses for some publicity photographs. Peter did a little research.

'Cigarette in left hand; vodka glass, right. Correct, Jeff?'

'Correct.'

'I want you to know, Jeff, that I have no intention of doing an impersonation of you.'

'Just as well. I've been doing an impersonation of you since we met thirty-odd years ago.'

Their acquaintance had begun at the Old Vic when Jeff was a scene hand there. It turned out that back then there was some rivalry between them over a girl who used to rhapsodise to Jeff about somebody called Peter and to Peter about somebody called Jeff. They tried to remember who won.

'You won,' said Peter.

'No, you won,' said Jeff finally. 'I married her.'

It was told of Jeff that once when he was asked in the Salisbury pub whom he was citing in one of his divorce cases he said simply, if unfairly, '*Spotlight*' – the actors' casting directory.

A highlight of the three-week rehearsal period was a visit to the workshop where the 'pissed pub' was being built. It is the scene-maker's custom to label the back of pieces of set so that they can be more quickly assembled at the theatre. In view of Bernard's constant complaint of impotence in the text it was appropriate to find one such description which read, 'Jeff, Middle leg. Extra stiffening.'

We opened in Brighton at the Theatre Royal on 26 September 1989. It was race week and the town was packed with the raffish – Jeff's people. To make it overflow, the Labour Party was holding its annual conference. The first night was one of the few times Jeff watched the play. After all, he had lived two-thirds of it. He could not have seen it in happier circumstances. Among the bursting house were a coachload of Soho piss-artists, many of his racing friends and hacks from the papers who were supposed to be covering the conference. I doubt if we ever had such an informed audience. The crowds broke the theatre's record for bar sales – especially champagne. I further doubt if we ever performed to a more euphoric crowd.

After much deliberation – 'Do I have to have a dinner jacket?' – Jeff bought himself a new suit for the Brighton opening and turned up next morning for a radio interview with a gaping hole burnt in the pocket where he had stuffed a lit cigarette the night before while collapsing on his hotel bed. His life and the text of the play are full of similar incendiary incidents.

As with *Mr and Mrs Nobody* we found ourselves with an overrunning hit. O'Toole has a lethal eye for a paragraph which has outstayed its welcome. He loves a hefty cut. When we agreed that a chunk should go he delighted in whispering to other members of the cast as they played a scene, 'This one's a corpse!' We cut about thirty minutes in Brighton. The result was that the laughs doubled. When we opened in Bath, the next tour date, the timing was the same. More cuts finally made it manageable.

Jeff followed us to Bath – looking even more frail than usual as a result of living it up in Brighton. On the Monday morning we were called for a modest press conference in the little bar of the Garrick's Head, the pub which is attached to the Theatre Royal. There were half a dozen local journalists there. One was very young and, we later discovered, was on his first assignment. He left the questioning to his senior colleagues and dutifully took notes. As we were about to wrap up the meeting he raised a nervous arm and spoke in a tiny voice, mingling awe and dread. 'If I stay another forty years in journalism,' he whispered, pointing at Jeff, 'will I end up looking like that?' I haven't seen him since. Perhaps we warned him off.

The Theatre Royal in Bath is stuffed with legends of ghosts. There is a Grey Lady who haunts the top left-hand box facing the stage and the corridor behind it. She smells of jasmine and frightens dogs. There is a Phantom Doorman, another eighteenth-century apparition, who lurks only in the foyer. He is seen exclusively by visiting actors. Recently, soon after her death, an elderly cleaner, although invisible, spoke sharply to a stage technician. Bar staff have arrived to find the surface of her bar as damp and disordered as it was in the days when she was supposed to clean and tidy it. Her death was presaged by the theatre's best-known psychic phenomenon – the butterfly. Three dead butterflies were found in the building three days before her death.

The legend of the butterfly was waiting for us in Bath. The annual Reg Maddox pantomime used to be a feature of the Theatre Royal season. A pantomime still is. However, in 1948 Mr Maddox arranged a spectacular effect. There was to be a butterfly ballet. The girls were dressed in scanty tortoiseshell costumes and Mr Maddox had a large butterfly set built which would be lowered to applause as the ballet began. One day, as the ballet rehearsal started, a dead butterfly was found on the stage. Within hours Reg Maddox was dead. His son, Frank, took over and abandoned the butterfly ballet. The guilty piece of scenery was put to one side until some time in midwinter a live butterfly arrived and everybody cheered up. The scenic butterfly was hoisted into the flies where it hangs to this day undusted and untouched by the staff unless they explain to it reverentially what they are up to.

So the theatre legend has grown up that a live appearance of the insect – on stage – especially on the first night of the pantomime, when all good butterflies should have disappeared for the winter, is a benign omen. A dead butterfly presages a death.

Leslie Crowther, playing Wishee Washee in *Aladdin* in the 1979–80 season, remembered one fluttering happily on to his shoulder and resting there. The run was a triumph. However, some years earlier during *Little Red Riding Hood* a dead butterfly was found outside dressing room no. 6. Within hours the actor who dressed there was dead. Another insect fatality had heralded the suicide of a conjuror during the run of the 1952 pantomime.

In *Phantom Performances* the theatre's historian and fireman, M. L. Cadey, reports that a stagehand bet a large sum on a seven-horse accumulator at Bath races. First he went up into the flies and asked the butterfly's blessing. Six horses came up for him. Then he lost all on the seventh. Back at the theatre he cursed the butterfly. When the stage crew next moved the heavy set, a massive moulding broke his neck.

Perhaps the oddest incident occurred on a cold winter morning in 1981. A long-abandoned property box was discovered and the curious crew wondered what lay inside. They prised it open and released a cloud of tortoiseshell butterflies who vanished through the loading bay into the theatre. The only other object inside the box was a dusty photograph of Reg Maddox. Scribbled on the back was '*Follies 1932*'. Forty-nine years is a long hibernation. The favoured explanation is that Reg Maddox returns to his theatre and uses the butterflies to bless or warn.

When we opened the play in Bath I knew the legend. Keith

Waterhouse knew the legend: as far as we knew, Peter O'Toole did not know the legend. And we forgot to tell him. Everything was going well when he came to a speech about tortoiseshell hairbrushes. As he looks at them he wonders how he acquired them. Then he remembers that it was in settlement of a debt by an actor who suffered a severe case of alopecia. As if on cue down from the flies fluttered a tortoiseshell butterfly. There are many dramatic moments in *Jeffrey Bernard is Unwell* but none has ever gripped me quite as that. The actor was in full rhetorical flight when the butterfly started to dance playfully around his head. I was terrified that, unaware of the curse, Peter would lose patience with it and swat it.

He is, of course, much cleverer than that. Apart from realising that such a gesture would not endear him to the audience, he likes butterflies. He smiled on its hoverings, offered it a drink and addressed the rest of his soliloquy to it. Eventually it took it into its head to fly away. He bade it farewell and continued with the play.

Theatre buffs in Bath predicted a hit. They were not wrong.

A note of scepticism about the legend of the butterfly is sounded these days. For years there was a garden centre next door to the Theatre Royal with a large greenhouse. It has now been replaced by shops. Butterflies are thinner in the air now during the winter months of the pantomime season.

We had only one preview before opening at the Apollo in October. The show was in such good shape. We wanted to get on with it. Big mistake! It was made a 'free night'. No one paid for their seat. If you want a proper reaction, people must pay. The response was OK but no more. By now we were used to euphoria.

The bar was an interesting spectacle at half-time. The hardened drinkers who had been sitting thirstily for almost an hour while O'Toole appeared to be sinking pints of vodka on stage were besieging one end of the room. At the other, by the coffee station, a group of Alcoholics Anonymous graduates, led by Lionel Bart, were circled together in a massive support group.

We left the theatre chastened but optimistic. The first-night audience behaved as paying people should. Keith and I had a drink at the Groucho with Jeffrey Bernard's brother Bruce and Francis Bacon, whom he was taking to the show. Bacon had only been to a theatre once in years. That visit was commanded by his sister who arrived in England from abroad and insisted he take her to *Cats*. He hated that and didn't enjoy our entertainment much. He appears in a cameo which Royce Mills camped up to extreme effect. Jeff says, 'I once foolishly suggested to Francis Bacon that he could solve all his tax headaches by moving to Switzerland.'

In reply a limp-wristed Bacon lisps, 'Are you crazy? All those fucking views? They'd drive me mad!' This occurs in Act One and Francis left at the interval.

Nothing fascinates a journalist as much as another journalist, and Jeff was notorious along the recently dismembered 'Fleet Street'. Add to that Keith's popularity in the same area and O'Toole's return in triumph to the stage where he belongs, and from which he had been absent for some time after a commercially successful, critically savaged *Macbeth* at the Old Vic, and we were assured an unusual focus.

The play held a particular fascination for cartoonists' captions and headline writers. One or two of these are included here: Newman and Woolley's conversation outside the Apollo; that of the late JAK – one of Jeffrey's drinking buddies – in the *Standard*.

Michael Heath drew a crowd emerging from the theatre. *He* says, 'That was wonderful – a sort of two-hour suicide note,' to which *She* replies, 'I never thought I'd enjoy watching a guy drinking himself to death.' The third vignette reveals the auditorium: 'Snuff Theatre presents *Jeffrey Bernard is Unwell*.'

Trog's picture was a corner of the Apollo where a little man is

"It looks like Jeffrey Bernard can afford a new car now!"

looking at a poster with the title. He speculates in a balloon, 'If he's waiting for an NHS bed, it could run and run.' Jensen drew a line of hopeless drunks, slumped over a bar: 'For some reason or other they all want to meet Keith Waterhouse.'

Later the phrase slipped into general use: 'Boris Yeltsin is Unwell', 'John Major is Unwell', '*Bernardette* [the title of a monstrous musical flop at the Dominion – 'The People's Musical'] is Unwell'. And when Jeffrey Archer wrote a disastrous play about journalism Heath in *Private Eye* headlined 'Peter O'Toole* in *Jeffrey Archer is Unbelievably Bad*'. The asterisk referred to the unfortunate actual star of Archer's play: '*Shurely Paul Scofield? Ed.'

The reviews were ecstatic: 'With this performance [O'Toole] comes home and takes command,' wrote Michael Coveney in the *Financial Times*. 'Waterhouse and O'Toole present one of the greatest comic creations of our day.'

Jeff had to hire an accountant for the first time in his life to look after his royalties. The show became a magnet for a bizarre range of celebrities from the King of Norway to Cliff Richard, from Placido Domingo to Rupert Murdoch and Jim Callaghan. Jeffrey rarely watched the play – maybe three or four times in its various incarnations – but he became a regular in the stalls' bar at the Apollo. The bar ladies were a cosy, welcoming, vanishing breed. In the eighties Mrs Mac presided. Her other job was doing the same thing at race meetings. Jeff was already a friend. Suddenly he found this third congenial watering hole to add to his Soho favourites, the Coach and Horses and the French Pub. He used to arrive through the stage- and pass-doors halfway into Act One, take his favourite tipple, vodka and soda, from Mrs Mac and settle down for a snooze until the bell rang for the interval. Then he was pointed out as a tourist attraction and often treated to a drink by fans.

Some way into the run our front-of-house manager took a night off. His temporary replacement correctly checked that all was well in the bars before the interval. When he got down to the stalls' bar he was confronted by a comatose, white-haired derelict slumped over his table. He panicked to Mrs Mac, 'Get that drunk out of here!'

'You can't do that,' she protested, 'that's Jeffrey Bernard.'

He was having none of that. 'Don't tell me that, Mrs Mac. Jeffrey Bernard's up on the fucking stage!'

Perhaps our most unexpected distinction was to be featured on the front page of the *War Cry*, the Salvation Army newspaper. (We had another odd newspaper 'first'. Michael Redington rang the *Sporting Life* (or was it the *Racing Post*?) to ask if he could advertise the play. 'Certainly,' they said, 'on which page would you like it?' Michael plumped for the front page and for a modest sum achieved a unique spread.) The *War Cry* was not amused. Its front-page leader was headed 'Jeffrey Could Do Better'; and a contributor to the magazine *Hospital Doctor* under the headline 'Alcoholism is No Laughing Matter' demanded a theatre equivalent of the Press Council so that people like the Salvation Army could complain officially.

O'Toole played his advertised run – three months. He was beginning to think of the play the same way that Irving regarded *The Bells*. It was his part. He could take it out and dust it down when he felt like it. However, he also had a substantial investment in the piece and was not keen to see it close when he left. He was followed by Tom Conti, who continued to fill the Apollo with what – since he rarely touches alcohol – was a bravura piece of character-acting. Jeff was not so keen on Tom's performance – 'He doesn't know how to hold a glass' – but we suspected this was because, unlike Peter, Tom didn't stock vodka and soda in his dressing-room fridge.

Finally James Bolam brought back an average, if not legendary, drinker's shading to the role, learning the enormous part in two weeks' rehearsal, a Herculean task, and restoring a supply of vodka backstage.

It was about three years before Peter felt like taking it out again. This time he wanted a bigger stage. Or rather, a bigger auditorium. Michael Redington did a deal with the enormous Shaftesbury Theatre – large enough to accommodate big musicals like *Oklahoma* or *Follies*, or the whole of the Royal Opera while the House was being reconstructed.

How would we fare with our chamber piece, a big star and four clever character actors? Keith and I were surprised to read in the *Sunday Mirror* (where Jeff also had a column) that he'd gone to a preview and, contrary to his misgivings, he found 'House Full' signs, and people rolling in the aisles and hanging from the rafters. To cap it, O'Toole was waiting with a vodka and soda.

Keith bumped into him the next Tuesday at the Groucho Club. 'What was that rubbish you wrote in the *Mirror* on Sunday, Jeff?'

'It was amazing, Keith! I never thought we'd fill the Shaftesbury – "House Full" signs, rolling in the aisles, hanging from the rafters, O'Toole with the vodka and soda . . .'

'Jeffrey, we don't open for another three weeks.'

Shocked silence.

'Christ. You mean I dreamt it?'

Plainly Jeff had gone to bed pissed, dreamed that the generous royalties Keith handed out were flowing in again, woken up, remembered his deadline, tottered to the typewriter and banged out his dream. Then he sent it to the *Mirror*, where no one checked if the play had opened.

This revival spawned a plan to take the play to Australia. O'Toole was not keen to go, but Dennis Waterman, whose television shows had made him hugely popular down under and who had enjoyed the experience, especially the golf courses, when he played there in *Same Time Next Year* and *The Real Thing*, was another actor who understood the subtext of the role.

Auditions for the four supporting actors were over quickly –

not so the journey to Australia to interview them. A late start from Heathrow meant missing the connection at Changi Airport in Singapore. Then there was a solitary place in first class with all the time in the world for me to finish the stock of caviar as we bumped to Adelaide, then Melbourne and finally to Sydney, where, after a sleepless night and day, auditions were due to start in an hour – at 11 a.m.

Auditioning in a strange country is intriguing. Suddenly, after working in a town where you know or half know the back histories of 75 per cent of the people you are seeing, you are confronted with CVs and flattering photographs of actors slightly younger than the faces that follow their particulars through the door. Then there is the embarrassing need to say – possibly to the annoyance of an auditionee conscious of his or her status in the profession – 'I'm afraid I don't know your work.'

In *Jeffrey Bernard is Unwell* the process was made easier because the actors we were looking for had to make a host of very brief appearances in a multitude of roles. It is akin to revue acting. Pull on the skin of a character, especially the right accent, walk across the stage, confront Jeff, deliver the line or lines, get your laugh or more likely pause and stand still while he gets his, and then exit, pulling off the swiftly assumed exterior, a hat, a sheepskin coat, a policeman's helmet, a waiter's soup and fish, as quickly as you put them on, and grab costume, props and accent ready for the next brief incarnation.

Australia is awash with good actors and after two days in Sydney and a quick trip to Melbourne we had hooked four excellent specimens. Margot McLennan worked in revue and musicals in Britain before marrying the Australian actor/singer Rod McLennan, and emigrating. Peter Rowley, who played Royce Mills's parts, although an Australian, has spent a lifetime playing Englishmen. Tristan Gemmill, whom we collected in Melbourne, left England about ten years before aged fifteen. He retained an impeccable armoury of received and provincial

British accents. Gabrielle Adkins was the one Tasmanian member of the company, a ravishing brunette who had to work a little harder on her voice than the others, but did.

I rehearsed with Dennis in England for a week in early December. Then we set off for Perth where we were due to open on 7 January 1992. It was an indulgent schedule as Dennis was well up on his words before we left our Chelsea rehearsal room. We stretched rehearsals out for the two weeks before Christmas, taking advantage of long lunches at a very social new wine bar, 44 King Street, which specialised in its own Chardonnay from a local Margaret River winery.

My BBC Radio 4 series, *Loose Ends*, had been running for five years and the BBC arranged for me to fit in a couple of live broadcasts from Perth – 6 p.m. in Western Australia made for a convenient 10 a.m. transmission in Britain. Bill ('I've only got four minutes') Kerr lives nearby, so does Hank Marvin, the ex-Shadow, who played a virtuoso guitar duet down the line to Adelaide with Australia's leading guitarist. Kevin 'Bloody' Wilson is an Australian phenomenon. Dennis and I went to see his show in Perth and puzzled over how I could feature such a scatalogical and politically incorrect act on the wireless. He makes occasional sorties to Britain, filling the Palladium and large halls around the country with homesick young Australians. To give some idea of how rough his material can be I took Keith Waterhouse and his fellow journalist Jaci Stephens to see Kevin at the Palladium the next year and the not-easily-shocked Ms Stephens insisted on leaving in disgust at the interval.

On *Loose Ends* he managed to be both funny and broad-castable. However, we did leave out his lament of a lonely, sex-starved bushman trapped in the outback: 'My dick just dialled your number on his own.' Or rather, simply mentioned the title.

Jeffrey Bernard is Unwell opens in darkness. Once the interior of the Coach and Horses is revealed the lighting stays more or less the same. A bright stage was the one aspect of playing which always concerned O'Toole, who, like all actors, knows that it is hard to play comedy successfully if the audience can't see clearly what it is supposed to laugh at.

On our first tour Peter used to slip little handwritten lectures on 'chiaroscuro' under the doors of my hotel rooms. At one lighting call in Perth Roger Barrat, who interpreted the London lighting plot for the Australian tour, recorded the first lighting change, looked at the now bright stage and said sardonically, 'I guess that's the end of the operatic lighting.'

An Australian Christmas is happily disconcerting. In Perth the blazing heat, the golden beaches and the tempting Indian Ocean sent me daily to the English papers hunting for photographs of frozen snowdrifts, dangling icicles and shivering natives as I lay back on a lounger and took another sip of something cool.

Dennis and I were blessed by the hospitality of the Bond family, who were friends of Helen Montagu, one of our producers. It cannot have been an easy time for them. Alan Bond's billionaire financial empire was in disarray. There was talk of a break-up in the marriage; but on Christmas Day Alan and his wife 'Red' presented a united front and invited Dennis and me to join their large family for lunch. The Australian members of the cast had taken advantage of the break to fly east to their homes courtesy of a new cut-price airline. Dennis and I arrived from our hotel by taxi. As we approached the impressive spread I was touched to see that a little crowd had assembled around the gates. 'How sweet!' I said to Dennis – 'Carol singers.' Wrong! It was a mixed bunch of paparazzi and process servers trying to establish Alan's presence in his home.

We were smuggled in and given a boisterous family welcome. Drinks appeared from a bar in the pool; we were shown the unfaded spot of wallpaper where the notorious Van Gogh *Irises* once hung; introduced to the latest grandson, Banjo Bond, named after Banjo Patterson, the Australian poet; and treated, on the sunniest afternoon imaginable, to the full spread of an English Christmas lunch. Alan, we learnt later, was spirited out of the stockade a day or so afterwards in the boot of one of his large cars.

There was a hiccup before we could restart rehearsals. Our actors were able to afford to fly home to the East Coast thanks to the new cut-price airline. Over Christmas the airline went bust and the cast, now westward bound, were faced with large bills to replace their invalid tickets. Finally they were all rounded up and we were back in rehearsal at 'the Maj' – unlike Her Majesty's in the Haymarket, His Majesty's Theatre, Perth, does not change sex with a change of monarch. We were also back on long lunches at 44 King Street when one day Red Bond burst in to announce, 'They've got the bugger! They've got him!' Apparently Alan had been arrested at the airport in Sydney returning from a quick holiday on a Pacific island.

Our single preview was on Monday 6 January. A first-night party was planned for the 7th but I thought we needed a celebration after the preview to avoid a feeling of anticlimax. I had installed two electric plates in my hotel suite so that I could cook for myself, and coming across shelves stocked with fine Australian tripe in a supermarket decided to throw a tripe and wine party – for guests not keen on tripe there was crusty bread with cheese and paté. My crusade for a better understanding of tripe carried a few converts and of thirty or so people more than half attacked it enthusiastically. My last memory of the party is standing on the balcony with Keith at about two o'clock in the morning. A worried young waiter came out to us. 'Excuse me, Mr Sherrin, we've run out of water.' I waved him away grandly, 'Let them drink Chardonnay.'

Dennis was to lead the company to Brisbane and Sydney. Keith and I left soon after reading the good notices. We changed planes in Singapore and had a chance to go into town to see just how much Raffles had changed since I was last there on the recce for *The Virgin Soldiers*.

Dennis later took *Jeffrey Bernard is Unwell* on a long tour of England and a disappointingly brief run in Dublin – the one city which did not enjoy the show. I suspected because they reckoned they had enough witty drunks of their own and didn't need us to import another.

I had to catch an early plane the morning after the first night. Reaction at the party seemed good. I put in a six o'clock wake-up call and got to sleep by two. At three I was woken by one of the oddest calls I've ever taken. One of the cast had the papers and insisted on reading every word of the bad notices.

After 'the play' Jeff's health declined. He lost a leg to diabetes and his column was filled with complaints about health, hospitals, doctors, nurses, fellow patients, his accommodation, changing his accommodation, being pushed in a wheelchair and sometimes spilt out of it on the journey from his flat to the Groucho or the Coach. Here he famously conquered his hatred of mobile phones to grab one and ring the bar staff to yell, 'How long do I have to wait to get a fucking drink?'

His funeral, when he finally failed the universal prediction, 'He'll outlive us all', was another full house. In a passage in his 'Low Life' column which Keith extracted for the play he reflects,

Needless to say, in this situation one's thoughts tend to drift towards the Grim Reaper. There's a dreadful fellow in the French Pub who once tried to make a book on who would be the next in Soho for the last jump and he made me five to four favourite, so he was pleased to tell me. But the long shots keep coming in and although I'm only too delighted to survive, it's a long race to have been entered for . . . I do worry about my own wretched mortality, though. Shuffling off this mortal coil it seems as though we're in a queue that shuffles along towards a sort of bus stop. 'Who's next?' 'No, sorry chum. You were before me.' Maybe the party could go on, though. Different premises and no closing time. A kind of celestial and sterilized Colony Room Club.

Jeff's party could not go on. The host, who had a keen sense of his own importance, would have been furious at the unfortunate timing of his death – between those of the Princess of Wales and Mother Teresa, who grabbed his headlines.

His funeral was at Kensal Green Crematorium. Two memories stand out. O'Toole read the Chesterton poem in the most fitting setting:

For there is good news yet to hear and fine things to be seen.
Before we go to Paradise by way of Kensal Green.

The funeral preceding Jeff's was a bookmaker's. The floral display in the ante-room took some beating. The centrepiece was an enormous picture drawn in carnations of a horse and jockey passing the winning post. We hoped Jeff had money on it.

The Irving in O'Toole demanded one more revival – at the Old Vic in 1999. We fielded the entire original cast. The theatre was sold out before the six-week run began. Somehow the performance had become even richer. Peter seemed happier to investigate the darker, more sardonic side of Jeff than he had been when he was alive and might drop in. Once again it became a celebrity scrum (Peter Mandelson to Kevin Spacey) and at last we got a record of the play, preserved on a video which shot up the charts.

I doubt O'Toole will unpack it again. I wonder.

My directing life was becoming dominated by Keith Waterhouse. Having done *Mr and Mrs Nobody*, I had staged *Jeffrey Bernard* no fewer than nine times. *Bookends* was Keith's 1990 stage adaptation of Craig Brown's book *The Marsh Marlowe Letters*,

a very funny parody of the literary Lyttleton–Hart-Davis correspondence which I had come upon when I reviewed it in 1984.
It worked well as a two-handed theatre piece with a third off-
stage character, a wife, laughing or weeping maniacally.
However, Craig has since written that he did not feel the ironies
of his original transferred from page to stage. Michael
Redington sent it to Sir Alec Guinness. He replied immediately
and suggested a meeting. We lunched at the old Moulin D'Or,
which was about to disappear from Soho, taking its familiar
flambeaux with it. The atmosphere was euphoric. Sir Alec's
enthusiasm contagious. He wanted me to ask Tom Courtenay to
play the other part and he warned us about a drunk scene at the
end of the first act. 'I'm afraid I might go vulgarly too far at the
end of Act One. I've got a few ideas up my sleeve.' We were
happy to be shocked.

The anticlimax came about a week later in a letter. He had
tried every way to learn the text, writing it out, recording it,
ploughing through it again and again, but he could not make it
stick and must decline. He added a poignant postscript: 'Do you
think Dr Alzheimer is knocking on my door?' He never acted on
stage again.

Buoyed by the thought that our first knight liked the part, we
sent it off to our second – Sir Michael Hordern. ('Very dangerous!') Sir Michael was equally quick to take up the challenge.
This time we dined him at Bibendum. Once again the enthusiasm was there. No fears about learning the large part were
expressed. My abiding memory of the evening is of dropping
Michael in Old Church Street and watching that ancient figure
waving his stick and shouting angrily at a motorist who was
hooting at us to get a move on.

Dinsdale Landen was cast opposite Michael. An old friend of
mine, Magdalena Buznea, a Romanian émigré who had been a
fine leading actress in her homeland until the Securitate forced
her out, agreed to play the off-stage wife. Five weeks were

allocated for rehearsals. Here the nightmare began. Sir Michael found learning the part as hard as Sir Alec had feared *he* would. At the first reading Michael and Dinsdale played beautifully together and Michael's rich range of comic effects made the character leap into life. The moment we tried to put the play on its feet it was a different story. Day after day we hoped the words would begin to stick but they didn't. Dinsdale had to pretend that he was having similar difficulties so that Michael's problems were not overemphasised. Worst of all, if I stopped either of them to make any point Michael lost his way entirely and we had to go back to the beginning. Any hope of helpful direction had to be abandoned. Of course, as the five weeks proceeded some sequences began to work but one could never be sure on the day which ones. We approached Bath and the Theatre Royal with trepidation. We were not wrong. On the first night Dinsdale was a rock. Michael took thirty-five prompts. During the interval one angry woman accused me of 'subjecting a wonderful old man to unpardonable unkindness'. Useless to explain to her that he was a lonely old actor who felt more at home in a theatre doing what he had done all his life than sitting at home in solitary confinement. The notices in the local papers were surprisingly kind and one critic wrote of Magdalena's off-stage performance, 'A star is born!' Perhaps a record for an unseen actress.

Drastic steps had to be taken. By the third performance we had the whole play typed up as if we were doing a television production with autocue. It was fortunate that the action was couched as a correspondence. Both actors moved around their desks writing their letters and slipping into direct conversation. It was not hard to put an autocue screen into Michael's desk so that he began to have some idea of where he was in the play. Usually, as long as he was launched on the right speech, he would get through it to the end. Better, but not foolproof. At Brighton we built in another screen. This one was downstage, concealed by a potted plant. A third appeared in the wings when we opened in the West End at the Apollo. Now Michael could look across the desk at Dinsdale, downstage to the audience when he was soliloquising and out into the wings for the drunk scene. In each case one of the screens was more or less in his eye line. It must have been a nightmare for his fellow actor. Michael seemed to take it in his stride. With critics and audiences we just about got by; but the uncertain pace ruled out the explosion of comic fireworks we had hoped for and heard at the reading.

About three months into the run Dinsdale phoned me one morning, hardly able to talk through laughter. He reported that he had had a drink with Michael after the show the night before as they often did. Sipping his Scotch Michael said, 'You know, Dinsdale, I've got a feeling we've been seriously under-directed in this show.'

One of Keith's best novels is *Our Song*, a moving and often funny dissection of a love affair between a successful middle-aged, married advertising man and a destructive young woman in her twenties who describes herself as 'a freelance factotum' to whom he is in thrall. The theme is by no means new but the passion, the understanding and the detail the author brings to the relationship are remarkable. I persuaded Keith to adapt it for the stage. Since it had started as a novel, it arrived on my desk a good deal over length. A dozen-bottle job. After we had drunk the Jackson Frères and removed the necessary pages the slimmed-down version went off to the obvious choice, O'Toole.

Once again his reply was immediate and enthusiastic. We saw every available young actress and settled happily for Tara Fitzgerald as the freelance factotum. After a successful week in Bath in 1992 Peter's principal eccentricity manifested itself in his decision that Tara's wardrobe was too dowdy.

He bought her a more lavish one himself from Ricci Burns. (Shades of *Up the Front* and Zsa Zsa Gabor.) Back at the Apollo again we had a successful opening. At least, so I was told over the phone by Keith. I had to honour a long-time contract to give an after-dinner speech in Yorkshire and had infuriatingly to miss my own first night. The papers confirmed Keith's instinct and on the weekend we flew off happily to Rome to see an Italian production of *Jeffrey Bernard is Unwell*. It starred a leading Italian television comic. Melodrama followed us. A message from Michael Redington awaited us at the hotel. Tara Fitzgerald had been mugged and could not play the first Saturday matinée. Her understudy, Cara Konig, went on successfully – not easy so early in the run.

Keith and I were helpless at that distance. We trudged off to the theatre to see *Jeffrey* played in total silence to an audience who plainly regarded it as a gritty, realistic indictment of life in Thatcher's Britain. There was one laugh in Act Two. Unable to place it amid the torrent of Italian dialogue we asked the star what prompted this solitary outburst. 'Ah,' he said, conspiratorially, 'that is my television catchphrase.' Keith had better luck many years later with a production which toured France and Belgium. It starred another local favourite, Jacques Vilaret, and was called *Jeffrey Bernard est Souffrant*.

One of the joys of working with Waterhouse is the language. There are few playwrights to whose work I would be so keen to return after the excitement and discovery of the first outing. Keith's prose always reveals a new felicity, even after the umpteenth reading. After all the *Jeffreys* I was more than happy in 2003 to revive *Our Song*, this time with Peter Bowles in an irresistible partnership with a fine young actress, Charlotte Emerson, straight from her success starring in *Baby Doll* in Birmingham and at the National Theatre.

Bing Bong, a dark comedy which remorselessly exposed the friction between a pair of comedy writers, brought two excellent, complementary performances out of Dennis Waterman and Patrick Mower. *Good Grief,* which Keith wrote virtually simultaneously as a novel and a play, is triggered by a memorial service. A widow has been encouraged by her late husband to keep a diary. 'Got up, grieved. Is that what you had in mind, pet?' Throughout the play she discovers more and more layers of his deceit. It gave Penelope Keith a wonderful first-act curtain line when she suddenly, incongruously, says to a potential suitor, 'I suppose a fuck's out of the question?' It was hard to know if the bigger laugh came from her magisterial, surprise delivery or from Christopher Godwin's astonished reaction.

Each night it reminded me of the Broadway wit and playwright George S. Kaufman's plaintive enquiry as he followed his second wife, Leueen McGrath, on an extended and expensive shopping trip around Bloomingdales. As they passed through 'furnishings' he asked, 'Have you got any good first-act curtains?'

As I write, a new Waterhouse play, *The Final Page*, about the last days of Fleet Street, is somewhere along the production line.

Two excellent plays by women which I directed had different fortunes. Geraldine Aron's funny, delicate memory play *Same Old Moon* languished in Southampton after excellent notices and a 'producer malfunction', while Kay Mellor's *A Passionate Woman*, starring the splendid Stephanie Cole, had a triumphant tour and a long West End run.

Early in the 1980s the scourge of Aids began to kill friends and acquaintances. In 1986 a group assembled at John Schlesinger's house to plan what was to be the first of many charity concerts to raise money for one of the Aids relief charities. Liz David of the Terence Higgins Trust and the designer Peter Docherty were prime movers. I remembered with shame a joke I used to use at the beginning of the epidemic when we were not sure of the nature of what was being called 'the Gay Plague' – which 'turns fruits into vegetables'. I see from my files that Dickie Attenborough, John Drummond, Pamela Harlech, Esther

Rantzen and Schlesinger were the names that headed the writing paper for Action Against Aids. The group that John assembled was determined to stage something but could not decide on what. There was excitement at the speculation that Elizabeth Taylor would fly in to glamorise the project and some dismay at the thought of how much it would cost to ship her over. She didn't come. Taking advantage of the uncertainty, I suggested a play, legendary in its awfulness, which had a huge cast, giving ample opportunities for starry walk-ons and cameos. *Young England* was a freak hit for all the wrong reasons in 1934. Written and backed by its author, the eighty-three-year-old Walter Reynolds, a businessman steeped in Victorian melodrama, it aspired to be a modern morality. 'In *Young England*,' he wrote,

> I have aimed at providing a solid three hours of clean and wholesome entertainment – to put before you a theatrical bill of fare made up of the joys, the sorrows, the tears, the laughter and the hard realities of our work-a-day existence ... I have tried to re-introduce to the living stage some of its lost *virility* and its old-time attraction ... In addition I have *most respectfully* woven into my play as an extra pleasurable feature some threads of material of one of the most beneficent movements that have ever been instituted in the history of mankind, viz. the creation of the picturesque and practical *Boy Scouts and Girl Guides movement* by the indomitable defender of Mafeking ... a veritable army of youth that has disseminated not war but peace and brotherhood to the uttermost end of the earth.

He put this now-forgotten sensation on at the Victoria Palace. Two survivors of the original production, Patrick Ludlow and John England, advised us on its impact. On the first night Beatrice Lillie started the laughter early on in the stalls. As the hilarity spread the author raced up and down the aisles shouting that the play was serious. As the plot about a Scoutmaster framed by a conscientious objector and starving widows being ejected from their cottages rolled on hysteria set in. The author refused to withdraw his play and attended nightly to address the audience. It ran for a year in four theatres, after the Victoria Palace, one in Leicester Square, the Piccadilly and finally the Kingsway. Young men organised parties to boo and cheer. Many went several times, joining in with the more corny lines: 'You, marry my sister? Why, one of Lady Mary's ancestors was the Queen of Scotland' and 'I have a right and duty to protect my sister from any association that may tarnish her honour.'

The action starts during the early days of the 1914–18 war in the East End in the middle of an air raid. Here is a hint of dialogue which hoped to get by in 1934 in a West End dominated by the plays of Coward, Lonsdale and Maugham:

MRS R: What? Are you then Frank Inglehurst?

RONALD: That's the captain's name, madam. I recognised him the moment he stooped over that poor girl.

DR: You recognise me?

RONALD: We were in the same trench together – over there.

DR: Surely, you are not Ronald Spencer?

RONALD: All that's left of him.

DR: But you were an athlete.

RONALD: The fortune of war.

DR: Poor old Ron – and there, but for the grace of God, go I.

MRS R: And so at last I meet the man who tried to save my husband's life.

DR: It was just in my day's duty.

Nobody had a better idea, so *Young England* it was.

We hoped to persuade Lindsay Anderson to direct. Linsday felt that it was not for him but agreed to play a small part and sent a generous note after the event: 'I'm sorry I couldn't contribute more. Truth to tell I'd only have fucked things up: I'd have been hopeless, my every instinct going the wrong way.'

We rehearsed the nucleus of principals who were involved throughout the play in a crumbling ward at the old St Stephen's hospital. They gave two weeks of their lives and learnt a lot of lines for a play of over three hours – all for one night. They were Julia Foster, Royce Mills, Gaye Brown, David Firth, Ian Ogilvy, valiant in the longest role, replacing Kenneth Branagh, called away to film in Greece, and Patrick Ryecart as the manly hero, 'Hope Ravenscroft' ('Hope! Hope! The very name brings new comfort to me!').

Anthony Hopkins spoke the prologue – Reynolds's explanation for the play. The first scene involved Alan Bates (disabled soldier), Millicent Martin (Salvation Army lass), Miriam Karlin (Irish policewoman), Bonnie Langford and Daniel Day Lewis (two guttersnipes) and Jane Asher (second Salvation Army lass). They were followed by Barry Cryer and Harry Towb (Ikey and Izzy – two Jews. 'Vot, you been to the war?' 'Of course, where you ought to ha' been long ago.' 'Vot, me go, and me only nineteen and me got to 'elp Favver in his tailor business?' 'I joined the Jews brigade to let 'em see us Jews were good English citizens'), John Hurt (Chinese dope pedlar, making a lot of one line, 'Mlissy, mlissy, white powder?'), Simon Callow (well-dressed gentleman), Doris Hare (a feeble old woman caught stealing milk), Fenella Fielding, Niall Buggy, Geraldine Jameson, Alec McCowen, Nickolas Grace (a Yorkshire Tyke and Tenderfoot Scout), Marti Caine (low comedy), Amanda Redman, Christopher Fairbank, Frank Finlay, Felicity Kendal (a lady Guider), Maria Aitken and Miriam Margolyes (first and second Guides), Joss Ackland, Derek Fowlds and Judy Campbell (Duchess of Troisent). There was a star walk-down, compered by Nigel Hawthorne, Esther Rantzen as a 'Guider with a fine voice', Victor Spinetti (Chief of Police), Derek Deane arranged a

Scout dance around the camp fire, and Eileen Atkins and Jean Marsh threw in an expert Girl Guides tap dance. When the grasping villains had been routed the apotheosis was Sarah Walker as Britannia in her magnificent Union Jack evening dress, singing 'Land of Hope and Glory' escorted by Ronnie Barker as John Bull.

There were seventy-odd people on stage. The entire band in the pit under Mike Haslam and John Owen Edwards put their obligatory union fees into the charity bucket. There were more dancers staged by Lindsay Dolan. The four singers of Cantabile provided music. We had only one day on the stage at the Adelphi Theatre to fit the show into bits of the existing scenery for *Me and My Girl*, which had played there on Saturday night and would play again on the Monday.

In order to make sense of the limited scenery I gave a scene-setting commentary – at its best when culled from Walter Reynolds's stage directions. 'The road to the Scout camp. An idyll of English Spring Beauty, Apple Blossoms, Primroses, Violets, Tulips, Cowslips. A river meanders through the landscape.' (No wonder that the excess scenery Reynolds ordered for the original production had to be abandoned outside the scene dock of the Victoria Palace.) 'Enter Hope Ravenscroft in Captain's uniform, always natural and unaffected, pleasantly familiar and with gay light comedy.'

Sadly Martin Hoyle in the *Financial Times* did not enjoy the 'unremitting waggishness with which Ned Sherrin introduced each scene, waggishness which, whatever it does to him, certainly tires me'. However, he enjoyed everyone else and the moral conflict of 'Fresh air and exercise versus drink and nightclubs'. Like Nicholas de Jongh in the *Standard* ('sheer adorable spoofery'), he had to leave before the end to meet his deadline. Jack Tinker for the *Daily Mail* managed both to appear (as a Scout) and to review the 'wickedly courageous production . . . lines of hilarious vintage chauvinism and moral naïvety'.

The evening raised fifty thousand pounds for Action Against AIDS. Sir Peter Saunders wrote, 'I saw *Young England* about twelve times in the '30s . . .' He pleaded with Bernard Delfont to stage it again for a Royal Variety show without any luck. There was an odd epilogue. Derek Deane, the choreographer, flew off to sun himself in St Tropez. Next day on the beach he met two American friends who had come through London. 'We saw a wonderful show on Sunday,' they said. 'It was all about Boy Scouts saving the world. How long has it been running?'

There were many more AIDS concerts to come and Sundays were full of them. We celebrated Noel Coward, Cole Porter, Elisabeth Welch, Stephen Sondheim more than once, and at Sadler's Wells we staged an evening of Shakespeare. For the first half David Kernan put together a programme of Shakespeare sketches, songs and poems. For the second half I found an eighteenth-century musical burlesque version of *Hamlet*. Patrick Ryecart was again called upon to play the lead. His wife gave birth to a boy on the morning of the performance – second name Hamlet, of course. The climax stays most vividly in my mind. As the stage Elsinore filled with dead bodies I asked Dame Vera Lynn to pick her way through them, flicking a microphone cord away from the corpses as she floated, 'We'll meet again, Don't know where, Don't know when . . .' There was a sudden shout from Princess Margaret, who was sitting next to me in the circle, 'Oh, my God! It's Vera!'

A simpler delight, removed from charitable fund-raising, was staging Victor Spinetti's one-man show, *A Very Private Diary*. Initially this involved sitting in a rehearsal room with Victor, listening to his outrageous fund of anecdotes told with a sure instinct for inhabiting the real-life characters. He conjured up Attenborough, Olivier, Plowright, Brendan Behan, Joan Littlewood, The Beatles, Coward, Dietrich, Burton, Salvador Dali, Tennessee Williams, Peter Shaffer and a hundred others. He peopled the dull rehearsal room off the Tottenham Court

Road. At lunchtimes we would go to a spaghetti house near by. Gradually we found a shape on which to hang the stories. To balance the humour frenzy I was delighted to find that Victor had written several evocative poems – one about a wet Welsh Sunday, another about a solitary bather on a beach – which added invaluable moments of stillness and respite.

We opened at the Donmar Warehouse in 1989. The fine reviews and full houses justified a move to the Apollo, where, like so many one-man shows in the West End, the competition proved too strong. I wanted to quote one review outside the theatre. It read, 'Hilarious and totally absorbing despite Ned Sherrin's direction.' Victor rightly thought it would divert attention from the main body of raves so we binned it.

I am still at a loss to know why we couldn't get it staged in America, where Victor had earlier great successes with *The Hostage* and *Oh, What a Lovely War!*, won a Tony Award and achieved cult status from his appearance in The Beatles' films. We did take it to Australia, where it was a big hit after an initial hiccup. We were due to open in the theatre at the Sydney Opera House early in the New Year, 1990. Victor and his friend, the late Graham Curnow, flew out early to spend Christmas with Graham's relations in Queensland. When I arrived in Sydney I found Victor despondent. His confidence was shattered. Graham's family, many of whom appeared to be 'Garbos' – Australian for garbage gatherers – barely registered the battery of anecdotes that Victor, a compulsive conversationalist, volleyed over the Christmas table. They recognised none of his references, none of his characters. He was desperately thinking of substituting names of Australians like Googie Withers and Rolf Harris for Marlene Dietrich and Noel Coward. The solution was simple – ship him up to a gay beach resort some miles up the coast where a huge table of happy queens listened enthralled for several hours. From a negligible advance before the first preview the theatre filled to capacity for all the other performances. He went on to Adelaide and then returned to Sydney for another successful season.

It was a surprise to discover the GLC (Greater London Council) as a potential impresario. In the mid-eighties Ken Livingstone was embattled with Mrs Thatcher over the council's very existence. Some bright official had the idea of mounting musical propaganda in the Queen Elizabeth Hall in the GLC's South Bank complex. In league with the concert impresario Raymond Gubbay they wanted to put on a version of *Iolanthe*. Gubbay had already staged a traditional *HMS Pinafore* for them the year before. He asked me if I could tinker with *Iolanthe*.

With Alistair Beaton I started to play with the plot. A pseudo Fairy Queen – born 'metallic', the Thatcher figure (Gaye Brown) – has imprisoned the real Queen (Gaye Brown switching at the denouement from Mrs T to HM) in the Tower. She is conspiring to neutralise Red Strephon (David Kernan) into Parliament where he can prattle harmlessly of his dream of a London with 'a gay adventure playground on every street corner, discos for the disabled and wardens to help old, black, lesbian ladies across the street'. The Iron Lady is abetted by the Brothers Saatchi and Saatchi (David Firth and Dudley Sutton) planting stories in the *Sun*, 'a newspaper in the loosest sense of the word', and singing an Italianate duet imported from *The Gondoliers*. A chorus of City men replaces Gilbert's peers, 'Rise, rise we're upward and we're mobile'; Nigel Lawson, Chancellor of the Exchequer not Lord Chancellor (Doug Fisher), wants to marry Phyllis (Gay Soper), heiress to the Estate of Greater London, to balance his books. We gave him one of Alistair's sparkiest lyrics to accompany his nightmare fear of failure. Sgt. Willis (Michael Robbins), now a Special Branch phone-tapper, muses on how every Social Democrat born in a world alive is both a little Socialist and a little Conservative. Finally the real Queen is revealed. The false one is defeated by Red Strephon. He and Phyllis are free to live happily in an 'open and non-hierarchical relationship' ever after.

Having written it, we called it *The Ratepayers' Iolanthe* but we had to sell it to a meeting of Gubbay with Peter Pitt and his GLC committee of arts and education before they set aside £76,000 for the budget. This required a surreal morning when Alistair and I were paraded before the committee and I read and sang (unaccompanied) the entire operetta with various approximations to the tunes, watched by an increasingly distressed Alistair. 'Oh, Zola Budd . . .!' to the tune of 'Oh, Captain Shaw . . .!' was the bit I enjoyed most.

The GLC said, 'Yes.' We had a happy two weeks in which to rehearse. The cast and the orchestra were splendid. John Owen Edwards, who was to go on to the D'Oyly Carte, takes his Sullivan seriously. The first night – in the hothouse atmosphere engendered by the increasingly acrimonious Thatcher–Livingstone debate – was electric. MPs sneaked across the Thames in increasing numbers; some, it was rumoured, in heavy disguises. We transferred briefly to the Phoenix Theatre but the Queen Elizabeth Hall was the true home. The next year we did the same thing with *The Metropolitan Mikado*. The subtitle, *The Town of Mitsubishi*, gives an idea of the takeover plot, with the Rising Sun flying above the Union Jack. This time Mrs T was Katisha; Ken, Nanki Poo; Ko Ko, Sir Kenneth Newman; the Mikado, Michael Heseltine; and Pish and Tush, Robin Day and Alastair Burnet, 'Media Front-persons'. The Three Little Maids were Page Three girls. Again we interpolated some patter songs. Alistair's brilliant first verse to 'I am the very model . . .' from *Pinafore* for the Neil Kinnock-inspired Pooh-Bah is the only one I shall quote:

I am the very master of the multipurpose metaphor,
I put them into speeches which I always feel the better for,
The speed of my delivery is totally vehicular,
I'm burning with a passion about nothing in particular,
I'm well acquainted too with matters technological,
I'm able to explain myself in phrases tautological,

My language is poetical and full of hidden promises . . .
It's like the raging torrent of a thousand Dylan Thomases.

For the end of the GLC we experimented with a Dickensian tale, *Small Expectations*. In spite of lively music by Gerard Kenny it didn't really work but I got a song out of it, 'Not Funny', for Maria Friedman. It was beautifully recorded later by Marian Montgomery. There was a stirring climax in the Festival Hall on the GLC's final Sunday when we reprised both Gilbert and Sullivan shows in shorter concert form: *The Ratepayers' Iolanthe* for Act One and then *The Metropolitan Mikado*.

In 1985–6 I tried reviving intimate revue, so popular in the forties and fifties and so famously killed off by *Beyond the Fringe* in the early sixties. When I had the idea for *The Sloane Ranger Revue* the Sloane craze was at its height. By the time I got the show to the Duchess Theatre after a successful try-out at Windsor Rep it was past its peak. My theory was that if one could find a big enough theme as a talking point it would divert critical attention to the subject matter and away from the antique form. In a sense *Side By Side By Sondheim* was an intimate revue but the quality of the writing, the consistency and power of the single voice disguised the fact. However, in 1977 Sondheim was just arriving in people's consciousness. By 1986 the Sloane Rangers were already past their sell-by date. What could be written had already been printed.

A Saint She Ain't is a delightful small musical by Dick Vosburgh and Denis King. Vosburgh, who doesn't like plotting, based it on a little-known one-act play by Molière, *Sganarelle ou le Cocu imaginaire*. The show is an inspired attempt to recreate an MGM wartime musical designed to raise the nation's spirits. It features roles for Mae West, W. C. Fields, Jimmy Durante, Abbott and Costello, Gene Kelly, Rita Hayworth and Betty Hutton.

I first heard it at a showcase presentation in the bar of the

Prince of Wales Theatre back in 1995. It is an immaculate and very funny piece of parody-writing with a brilliant joke for the W. C. Fields character, played by Barry Cryer, 'I haven't been so happy since *Reader's Digest* lost my address.' When we staged it at the King's Head six years later it delighted Islington and had a unanimous welcome from the critics. We moved to the Apollo, where the notices were even better. Somehow the public could not be persuaded to enter the theatre. To paraphrase Yogi Berra, the great baseball player: 'If people don't want to come to the theatre, nobody's going to stop 'em.'

It was a similar story with a revival of *Salad Days*. The producer, Edward Snape, who often produces Kit and the Widow's shows, wanted to put them into something splashier. They suggested *Salad Days*, which was coming up to its fortieth anniversary. I loved it in 1955 but I wondered if the innocence which made it so attractive would work forty years on. It did for those who came but once again they were too few. The pre-London tour did well. Kit and the Widow were charming and funny. The surviving writer/composer, Julian Slade, was delighted. In 1955 the reviews ranged from the abusive to the condescending. It ran for five years. When we came to the same theatre, the Vaudeville, forty years later, the notices were terrific. It ran for five months.

The oddest saga was a musical which I *nearly* directed, for about two days in 1987. Traditionally these things start with a telephone call. My call came, quite late at night, from New York. Ian Bevan, right-hand man to the impresario Harold Fielding, told me that they were discussing a big Palladium show based on the life of the great American impresario Florenz Ziegfeld. The director was Joe Layton, whose successes included *No Strings*, *Sail Away* and, spectacularly, *Barnum*. To Fielding's surprise, Joe suggested that I should write the book. I agreed immediately – as long as I could co-opt Alistair Beaton, if he wanted to be co-opted. He did.

Ziegfeld was to be a record-breaking disaster at the Palladium, losing the best part of four million pounds. One problem was the marriage of producer and subject. Fielding's reputation was built on family shows, with *Charlie Girl* the prime example. Ziegfeld was not a family man. For all his gifts as a mounter of spectacle, for discovering artists, for lavish spending, for telegrams running through pages, he was a bastard. To bring any authenticity to the character would have offended every instinct Fielding possessed. He wanted the biggest, splashiest, most dressed-up show he could mount; but if we were to cover Ziegfeld's life the confection would have to be threaded through with a man behaving very badly.

Neither Alistair nor I could see an easy solution. When Joe Layton arrived to talk about the project we had one idea to offer. It was not a difficult concept at which to arrive. Layton's *Barnum* told the showman's story using the circus show as a metaphor for his life. Barnum was the star performer in all the circus tricks. Highwire, trapeze, juggling and plate-spinning were all called into service to chart his progress. He was played with enormous energy and charm in New York by Jim Dale and at the Palladium by Michael Crawford (Crawford's version was actually directed by Peter Coe, but the convention was the same). It seemed clear that we should tell the story of a big revue producer as a revue. We suggested songs, monologues, vaudeville acts and sketches. We were not surprised when Layton welcomed the conceit. Alistair and I went off to Spain to a little village above Malaga to write, with occasional visits from Joe. Another discipline was to construct the show around the various hit songs that, in most cases, had featured in Ziegfeld shows. 'Shine on Harvest Moon', 'My Man', 'Half-Caste Woman', 'I'm Always Chasing Rainbows', 'Make Believe' and 'I'll Build a Stairway to Paradise' were some. Negotiating the rights to 'A Pretty Girl is Like a Melody' with Irving Berlin's estate took Fielding months and was only resolved just before rehearsals started.

Fielding assembled an impeccable team around Joe. Two great Tony-winning ladies of American musical theatre had worked with Joe before. Theoni Aldridge designed hundreds of extravagant costumes which were to be magically lit by Tharon Musser. The young scenic designer Robin Don created enough lavish spectacle to have satisfied Ziegfeld himself. This presented another problem. Joe was determined to stage the show as Ziegfeld would have done, with giant pieces of built scenery. Scorning modern developments, Robin followed Joe's instructions. The Palladium is designed as a variety box with very little wing space. Flying scenery, or helicopters or magic cars, is about the only spectacle it can easily accommodate. When we got to production, scenes had to be punctuated by a song or a monologue downstage in front of a cloth, while huge chunks of scenery were hauled down from the walls on which they hung, and manhandled into place. Meanwhile, a quiet sentimental song was accompanied by an amplified orchestration of 'Bang!' 'Crash!' 'Thump!' 'Fuck!'

But we haven't cast the piece yet. The girls were easy, including Haydn Gwynne as Ziegfeld's second wife, Billie Barnes, and Fabienne Guyon, an enchanting ingénue from the original French production of *Les Miserables*, as his first wife, Anna Held. Alistair and I lobbied successfully for Louise Gold, Katisha Thatcher in *The Metropolitan Mikado*, as 'Goldie', Ziegfeld's faithful secretary. Geoffrey Hutchings was tirelessly inventive as a composite of Ziegfeld's comics.

The problem was casting Ziegfeld himself. We were within days of starting rehearsals when Harold – having been turned down by most of *Spotlight* – made a dash to New York. He signed Len Cariou, the Canadian star of *A Little Night Music*, *Sweeney Todd* and, at the time, an American musical about Teddy Roosevelt. He is a fine, classical actor and an excellent singer who is perhaps too committed a performer to exude the flashy charm and charisma which Ziegfeld would need to paper over the unpleasant cracks in our attempts to clean up his unsympathetic character. Faced with a similar problem in *Jolson*, the producers were wise to cast the personality plus, Brian Conley.

We rehearsed at Sadler's Wells. The final run through in the large room went surprisingly well as the pianist banged out the tunes so that the huge cast could hear him. The book scenes, new to the chorus, got laughs and, with no scenery changes to hold up the action, songs and sketches dovetailed and sped along. Alistair and I breathed a qualified sigh of relief. At the end Alistair ventured a 'that went quite well' to Harold Fielding, who was sitting next to the piano. This produced a mammoth explosion. Fielding, a small man, seemed to leap into the air. 'No, it didn't! It was a disaster! It was awful!' he shouted. Then he added, 'The music's too loud!' 'But, Harold, it's such a big room. He's got to bang it out so that the cast can hear.' 'Don't you tell me about music! I was an infant prodigy on the violin! Don't tell me about music!'

During the long days of technical rehearsal in the Palladium the strain began to tell on Joe. Denied energising cocaine he took to vodka, ending most evenings more tired and impatient than was helpful. Previews were dull and the opening night an anticlimax. With the exception of the *Times* critic, Benedict Nightingale, who saw some merit in the revue device, the notices were dismissive. The first casualty was Joe, who was packed off back to New York while Fielding wondered what to do. For a couple of days I was asked to 'save the show' with Derek Deane, who had taken a sidestep from ballet to work as Joe's associate choreographer. We decided on some drastic cuts and changes, agreed them with Fielding and announced them to the cast. A few hours later Harold cancelled them and appointed Tommy Steele to 'save the show'. Len Cariou was the next of 'the disappeared'. Tommy titivated and Len's understudy, Mark Urquhart, 'saved the show' again as Ziegfeld. There were two more saviours waiting in the wings. Fielding engaged Chaim Topol, who had a personality success behind the beard of Tevye in *Fiddler on the Roof*, to play Flo. Without the beard his personality evaporated and there was nothing poor Wendy Toye, who had had successes for Fielding in the past, could do to manufacture one. She was the last recruit brought in to replace Tommy and 'save the show'.

I crept in to one performance to see Topol emerge in Flo Ziegfeld's white tie and tails spouting some new dialogue which went roughly, 'Good evening, I am Chaim Topol; but sometimes I shall be Fleow. When I am Fleow you will kneow because this reows will appears in my button-heowl!' Here a yellow rose appeared magically where he suggested. 'When the reows geows you will kneow that I am Chaim again.' With that it went. Quite soon I left too and not many weeks later the notices went up.

Apparently the long-suffering Geoffrey Hutchings, who, like Louise Gold, had done a fine job of salvaging some comedy from the wreck, took to wandering around backstage muttering, 'Sometimes I am Geoffrey. Sometimes I am a comic. When I am a comic you will "kneow" because I shall stick a cabbage up my arse.'

CHAPTER 13

I Talk to the Trees . . .

Noel Coward once started a speech, 'Accustomed as I am to public speaking . . .' Since emerging from behind television cameras the custom has grown on me, too. Which comes first in this 'chicken and egg' cliché? If I hadn't done a bit of after-dinner speaking, would I have been happy or trusted to perform on radio or television? If I hadn't become visible on television, would I have been asked to address a hotel room of TV-impressed diners?

I made my first after-dinner speech at a gaudy at Exeter College in the late fifties. This reunion of graduates who matriculated in my year pitchforked me into an address. Having gone to ATV, I was the only person from that year on whom television had bestowed some notoriety so soon after coming down. I found myself isolated from my contemporaries, sitting on high table between two senior dons, Professor Neville Coghill and Professor Sir Salvador da Madariaga. I turned first to Neville, whom I had known well at Oxford. 'I wonder who is speaking tonight?' he said. 'I've heard some terrible speeches in this hall.' I switched my attention to da Madariaga. 'I wonder who is speaking tonight,' he opened. 'I have heard some *wonderful* speeches in this hall. I

don't suppose anything will live up to them tonight.' At least it
gave me an opening. The bigger bonus was that, having done it
once, I was confident I would never have to do it again.

However, in 2004 I got a panic call from the new rector of
Exeter, Frances Cairncross, a week before a gaudy I was due to
attend. She had hoped to persuade Alan Bennett. She had
failed – so I had to supply the anticlimax. At least I had an
opening – Neville and da Madariaga.

The meal before a speech is often a nightmare; but it is as
well to get a feel of the room. Willy Rushton encountered the
chairman of some company who said fiercely to him, 'I hope
you're going to be amusing, Rushton, we're paying you enough.'
'Yes,' said Willy, 'but most of that's because I have to sit through
dinner with you.'

I was speaking once at the hotel attached to the Conference
Centre at Birmingham. The Associated Boilermakers or some
such group were exhibiting in the nearby halls and enjoying
their annual dinner. I sat next to the president. Halfway through
the meal, having established that I had some connection with
radio and television, he said, 'We 'ad a bloke from television a
couple of years ago. Turned out to be a 'omosexual. Bloke called
Russell 'Arty. I think 'ee must have brought 'is Wimmin's
Institute speech. Blokes started chi-iking 'im after five minutes.
Had to sit down after ten.' It was not the most encouraging
news just before getting up to speak – redeemed, perhaps, by
hearing the period expression 'chi-ike' for the only time outside
the music-hall songs of Marie Lloyd.

I started speaking fairly regularly in the early eighties. At first
it was a casual response to an invitation with the occasional
five hundred pounds slipped in notes with no tax to pay, or perhaps a case of wine. After-dinner speaking boomed into an
industry at about then. More money was demanded by agents,
paid and declared. Gone were the gentlemanly days of Arthur
Dickson Wright and Lord Birkett – 'I do not object to people

looking at their watches when I am speaking. But I strongly object when they start striking them to make sure that they are still going.'

Early on, when I had just launched into a speech, I was interrupted by a guest at a nearby table: 'Hold on? Would you mind not going so fast, I'm trying to write these down.' Theft is not the big fear for an after-dinner speaker. There is always the possibility of a disaster. On one occasion a friend asked me to speak at a charity dinner at the Royal Lancaster hotel. Although it was a 'favour', he generously offered a fee to go to a chosen charity. My old collaborator, Caryl, had died recently. She was always on the lookout for deserving young artists who needed help. At Chichester she had come across a brilliant young musician and had been helping to put him through a school programme which was outside his parents' range. A few thousand pounds was still needed to complete his education. It seemed the ideal solution. However, it was a very liquored-up evening. They were something to do with haulage and long-distance lorries. By the time I got to my feet it was about half past eleven. I was following Barry Cryer. A few weeks earlier I had preceded Barry at a lunch which had gone so well from my point of view that he had recourse to his fail-safe emergency opening line: 'Owing to some confusion before lunch Ned Sherrin picked up my speech so I am speaking from his notes.' This night was a different matter. The all-male audience had heard more than enough talk and thought – incorrectly – that they had not had nearly enough to drink. I have never ploughed my way through a noisier room. The only thing to do was get my head down and carry on, remembering the boy's education. So I did. And I'm happy to say that he went on to be the highly successful, professional soloist musician whom Caryl had prophesied.

It is no fun to hear a preceding speaker losing his audience. I have seen a toastmaster roaming the Lancaster Room at the Savoy hotel hushing a crowd who had stopped listening altogether and were talking happily among themselves. The speaker, a junior minister, sat down at the end, smiled at the chairman and said, 'That went rather well, I thought.'

In the same room some years later I followed a similar debacle. I thought it wise to ignore what had gone before and try to recapture the room. I had forgotten that my opening words were to be, 'It comes as a great relief to be among friends.' I got no further than, 'It comes as a great relief . . .' when there was a great roar of laughter which sounded horribly ungenerous.

Perhaps the most potent and polished after-dinner speaker I have heard was the late Robert Runcie – the former Archbishop of Canterbury. I first heard him more than twenty years ago at a farewell dinner for Bishop Stockwood when Mervyn retired from Southwark. He proved impossible to follow. The luckless next speaker was poor Frankie Howerd, who had not done his homework or tailored his script to the occasion. I retain a vivid image of Francis, sweat pouring down his face as he stuttered his way to a near-silent conclusion.

By the time I was 'outed' as an occasional performer after dinner I had also started to make a few appearances on the television. A bonus of appearing there was that journalists stopped feeling the need to give descriptions of my appearance. When I was involved in *TW3* I was variously described as a 'fat, fair, yoghurt-eating West Countryman'; 'tall, with the shoulders of a rugby forward'; 'blond and bulky'; and, most puzzling, 'small, dark and darting'. Putting your face on the screen stops all this, although at one point a couple of radio series reactivated the urge. Ms Lynn Barber thus: 'Actually he is not *bad* looking – tall and rather gangling with a wicked Cheshire cat grin – though he does wear strangely hideous clothes'; and Ms Maureen Cleave thus: 'He is a very tall man with a barrel-chest that looks good in a waistcoat and watch and chain. Got up in three-piece suits, he looks the last word in suavity.'

Occasional appearances on television do as much to confuse as to inform the viewer. Taxi drivers don't find it easy to pin one down. 'Weren't you something on the antiques show?' was one attempt. Another picked me up outside Broadcasting House. 'You want the Barbican, don't you?' 'No, World's End, Chelsea.' 'Oh, I thought you was that bald-headed Australian bugger what lives in the Barbican.' He thought I was Clive James. Dropped off at World's End by another cab, after I tipped the driver he demanded, 'Go on, tell us your name.' 'Ned Sherrin.' 'Thank Christ! I was going to tell the wife I had that Patrick Moore in the back of me cab.'

At a literary lunch in Cleethorpes the mayor announced me. 'One person who needs no introduction from me – Mr Nick Sheridan.' The next day a receptionist at a Birmingham local radio station chose, 'You can go through to the studio now, Mr Ned Sheridan Morley.' Approaching Broadcasting House a few years ago I was greeted by an enthusiastic despatch rider as he emerged. 'How are your two sons?' 'I don't have any sons.' Accusingly: 'You are Desmond Wilcox, aren't you?' I explained that it was sufficient honour to have 'discovered' Esther Rantzen without being accused of marrying her. She had been slaving away in radio as a studio manager, making coconut shells sound like horses hooves, when I engaged her to work as a PA on *Not So Much a Programme*, her entrée to the small screen. Immediately after my encounter with Desmond's fan I lunched with the editor of a glossy mag. Halfway through the meal she asked, 'How's your very clever daughter?' She thought I was Alan Coren. According to Coren's 'very clever daughter', Victoria, it happens to Alan in reverse. Introduced to the great black actor Sidney Poitier at a BAFTA gathering, he enthused about Poitier's films, adding, '. . . and the "Banana Boat" song is still my favourite'. Perhaps the oddest meeting was late at night on Gatwick Station, where I was standing with Keith Waterhouse. A little man came out of the shadows and said,

'Excuse me, I don't wish to be rude, but are you Loyd Grossman?'

Entering a lift at the Hilton in 2001 I was joined by the late Lord Westbury, whom I hadn't seen for many years. 'I'm very annoyed that you've taken your play off before I could see it,' he said. I wondered which play this could be. 'That one with four old opera singers locked up in a home.' He thought I was Sir Donald Sinden.

At a time when we were having a summer break on Radio 4's *Loose Ends* I appeared on a lunchtime television programme to plug a book. Soon a letter arrived at the BBC. A mother wrote to say that she had been listening to *Loose Ends* since the very beginning of the series when she was in hospital giving birth to her daughter, Emily. Emily now seven or eight had grown up listening with her. On the day of my television appearance mother was in the kitchen while Emily, in the sitting room, was glued to the TV screen. Suddenly there was a yell and Emily rushed into the kitchen, tears flowing. Mother asked what was wrong: 'Mummy! Mummy! You didn't tell me Ned Sherrin was white!'

The blame for these mis-identifications can be traced directly, a few decades earlier, to a BBC producer, Tony Smith. Tony brought about my change of life. (He has gone on to be director of the BFI and president of Magdalen College, Oxford.) In 1968 Tony devised a series called *Your Witness* for BBC 1 in which well-known lawyers debated topics of public concern, calling and cross-examining witnesses in front of a studio jury under the presidency of Ludovic Kennedy. Knowing that the tiniest vestige of a barrister lingered in me, he invited me to debate censorship with Sir John Hobson, who was an immediately previous Tory attorney general.

My witnesses included Michael Foot, Ben Levy, Mervyn Stockwood, Anthony Storr (the psychiatrist), and Ben Daniel, a ten-year-old whose parents (Dad was a parson) had allowed him to read *Lady Chatterley's Lover*. Ben was happy to give evidence that he had not been corrupted. He knew what he meant and was very cool, collected and lucid. Sir John wisely did not cross-examine him. Sir John's own witnesses included the romantic novelist Denise Robbins and Donald Wolfit. It was exhilarating to sense the partisanship generated on both sides in the couple of hours of preparation, and to feel the needle which the brief confrontations produced. We won, but the triumph was obliterated in a very British way. Sir John smiled generously in defeat and I kept what I thought was a becomingly modest straight face. Most viewers who had not attended to the announcement of the score assumed that I was a glum loser and Sir John a gloating victor. Sadly, he suffered a brain haemorrhage and died a few weeks later.

Tony Smith then set about finding another vehicle for his discovery. We embarked on a Saturday-night series in the old late-night spot. He called it *Quiz of the Week*. A team of *Private Eye* regulars, groupies or sympathisers was pitted against various generic groups. On the pilot, the 'visiting team' was Lena Jeger MP, Antonia Fraser and Margaret Thatcher, in acid lime-green. She distinguished herself by getting the most correct answers and by making the smallest number of jokes.

At that time she was shadow minister for education. She brought her twins, Mark and Carol. (According to Carol, it was their first visit to a television studio.) Twenty years later we were both speaking at the Hilton at a 'Man of the Year' luncheon. The morning papers carried a report of some trouble in the Balkans. As we met for the first time since the pilot she said, 'Did you see that report in *The Times*? Do you remember the question you asked me on that quiz programme twenty years ago? You see, I was right all along.'

At the subsequent lunch Mrs Thatcher played a wonderful upstaging card. She – the reason most people had bought their tickets – was speaking first. Towards the end of her speech she paused and surveyed the room. 'I must hurry up,' she said, 'I'm only warming up for the principal speaker.' *Quiz of the Week* was very much the prototype for Radio 4's *News Quiz* and later the television programme *Have I Got News For You* – except that it was live with no editing safety-net like the generous recording time with which the modern shows are blessed. It was a much more dangerous exercise, as we found when we came back for a second series after the happy first run. Our return coincided with the declaration of a Conservative victory in the General Election of 1970, which put Ted Heath in power. As a result the *Private Eye* team, capitalising on his musical prowess, paid innumerable compliments to the prime minister's organ, and although Norman St John Stevas, who was on the other team, strove manfully to keep a straight face, and mostly succeeded, his ill-fated appearance on a frivolous programme in the very middle of the Cabinet-making process set back his hopes of promotion into Government by several years. In 1981 on *Friday Night, Saturday Morning*, in one of the most enjoyable interviews I have ever done, I reminded Norman of the previous debacle. He expressed the hope that the return engagement would not have a similar effect. Mrs Thatcher sacked him a week later.

Back on *Quiz of the Week*, on the second show Ted Heath's organ was forgotten in favour of Lord Hill's wife. Lord Hill was then pretender to the chairmanship of the governors of the BBC. We were abruptly withdrawn.

Jumping forward seven or eight years, when I stayed on in New York after I ceded the narration of the Sondheim show to Hermione Gingold, I spent some time setting up tours; but it seemed sensible to drum up alternative work. *Quiz of the Week* was an obvious vehicle, and Alasdair Milne arranged for me to acquire the North American rights to the programme, which I set up with Channel 13, the New York public broadcasting station. Tony Geis, who had worked with me on 'translating' the Sondheim commentary, invented the new title, *We Interrupt*

This Week. I was lucky to be produced by John Gilroy, a droll Irish-American who had at various times the responsibility of working on both Johnny Carson's and Dick Cavett's shows and who brought with him an experienced team.

The PBS executives went out on a limb to promote the pilot. My English friend John Heyman largely backed it. We were anxious to find new faces for the show, and we did. In the *New York Times* I came across a profile of Marshall Brickman, a writer and director who has directed his own films and collaborated on many of Woody Allen's most successful movies. He had worked with Gilroy before, and one lunch at Sardi's was enough to convince us that if we could persuade him we had found our first panellist. He has a whimsical, comprehensive grasp of current affairs and a mysterious sense of humour.

I saw my second target, Jeff Greenfield, cross-examining distinguished adversaries on a PBS programme hosted by William Buckley. A prodigal wit, Jeff slipped most easily into the new convention. Encyclopedic in knowledge and salting his debating finesse with street-smart wisecracks delivered from the face of an irresponsible schoolboy, he was at home at once. Nora Ephron, having been sensationally successful on the pilot, asked not to be considered for the series because, she said, it took away all the pleasure she had hitherto derived from reading the newspapers. Jimmy Breslin, the New York columnist, Pat Buchanan, previously a Republican journalist and speechwriter for Agnew who coined the phrase, 'Nattering nabobs of non-conformity', and Richard Reeves, national editor of *Esquire* magazine, completed the teams. Buchanan was to decline to appear when we went to series. He considered the programme too subversive.

Once Channel 13 had a tape of the pilot they had to place it with the rest of the PBS network. Public broadcasting grew up in America in a haphazard way. Funding comes from membership subscriptions, from auctions, from on-air marathons and from substantial underwriting by major companies – notably the oil giants. Many local stations cling desperately to their autonomy, either to preserve their identity or more frequently to protect the vanity of some big fish in one of those small pools. The larger stations, particularly Channel 13 in New York, are aware of the need to unite the network. In the first run of *We Interrupt*, Channel 13 shouldered the main burden and offered the programme to those stations which were prepared to take it. We taped the shows as live in an old CBS studio on Ninth Avenue on Friday afternoon between 2 p.m. and 2.30 p.m. and they were beamed to the other stations at that time. They could then choose whether they wanted to transmit at all and at what time they would put out the programme. In New York it had a peak spot on Fridays and was repeated at 11 p.m. on Sundays. This was a particularly good time for New Yorkers, who caught it on their return from weekends spent out of Manhattan when there was no enjoyable alternative on the other channels.

To confirm that it was a success in the major cities, I'd better quote a few reviews of the first series. In the *Washington Post* Tom Shales wrote, 'The merriest and most pleasingly snide weekly brawl in all of television . . . the zest of tennis, liquid protein and the inescapable Perrier . . . the snappiest and crackliest smug amusement show to hit television since the inception of *Saturday Night Live*.' In *Newsday* Marvin Kitman said, 'The answers are as witty and smart as the contestants can make them on the spur of the moment . . . it means a resurgence of comedy on public TV.'

Even in the Tallahassee *Democrat* Brian Richardson found things to enjoy. 'Fast paced irreverent . . . like no quiz show you have ever seen. Through a biting opening monologue and a series of loaded questions Sherrin (like no quiz show host you've ever seen) lampoons not only the Quiz Show format but American political life as well . . . The panellists can't win, it seems, but you can't lose.'

The reference to 'lampooning the Quiz Show format' is inter-esting. Of the three great original American art forms – the Western movie, the Broadway musical and the quiz show – the quiz show format is perhaps the most dangerous to meddle with. Playing the game in America, our 'irresponsible' attitude towards scoring caused a shockwave. I introduced each programme with the statement, 'I shall award points to those who give correct answers as well as to those who are evasive in an inventive, charming or provocative manner. Those are all the rules, except to say that my decisions will be arbitrary, prejudiced and final.' Nobody noticed, probably nobody heard this in England. In a country where spectacular prizes are the stock-in-trade of game shows, where the competitive spirit is a religion, it took time for audiences to get hooked on arbitrary irresponsibility. At first it looked like spitting on the flag. On one occasion a woman erupted in the small studio audience, yelling, 'You didn't give her two points! She was right and you didn't give her two points!' One critic took some weeks to surrender and then confessed that the scoring was 'a delicious un-American concept'.

In middle America the programme was hit and miss. Local stations clung to their right to choose the time to screen it or not to screen it at all. It was irritating to hear station managers saying proudly that they taped the show every week and showed it at private parties for friends. At the same time they decided that it was, of course, far too sophisticated for their viewers. More farcically when I went to Tallahassee to do one promotion I found that they were transmitting each show for its first airing on the Sunday lunchtime nine days after it had been recorded. Then they repeated it early the next Tuesday evening. It made fair nonsense of the title *We Interrupt This Week*; but America is so conditioned to repeats ad nauseam that they were surprised to learn that topicality played a part in the show.

The first series ran from October until just before Christmas. It ended with a final *Week* and a special hour-long *We Interrupt*

This Year, both recorded on the same marathon day. The result was extraordinary. First the press created an unprecedented fuss about the show's demise. Tom Shales, returning to the subject for the *Washington Post*, led off: '1978 was a no-frills year, but it did have its little luxuries and compensations. One of them was *We Interrupt This Week*, a lovably malicious current events quiz featuring media cut-ups waxing wary, wry and witty about people and events of the day. This made for a lively, funny, and infernally informative show.'

Jack O'Brien in New York wrote, 'This gleeful, witty, inform-ative show . . . capsules the week in uproariously amusing fashion . . . a minor miracle in itself.' Another: 'Channel 13 should sign it for Ned Sherrin's life. It is one of TV's rare exer-cises in intellectualism – almost its only spontaneously and dependably witty cavalcade of knowledge, observation in com-munications in risible depth.' Again: 'This chaotic satire represents the most stimulating television available.'

Terence O'Flaherty in San Francisco found it 'the most amus-ing and intelligent game-show on the air' and characterised the chairman as 'keeping the thing moving with all the dictatorial authority of an English nanny refereeing a neighbourhood cro-quet match'. The 'chairman of Cinema Studies' at NYU, Robert Sklar, spent 'several afternoons at the studio observing the show . . . [Sherrin] is playing not merely himself, or appearing as a British Television Personality: he is portraying the American fantasy of the urbane British intellectual – quick-witted, sharp-tongued, imperturbable and ineffably superior. He performs not only as host and quizmaster but as our image of the British schoolmaster.'

I bumped into one moment of history when I visited San Francisco and Los Angeles on a promotion tour with David Yakir, one of the show's producers. Our visit to San Francisco coincided with the morning assassination of Mayor Mosconi and Harvey Milk, one of the city's leading officials, famous in

San Francisco as a leader of the large homosexual community. As we watched a local morning television magazine before our press conference, the young woman who was hosting it was interviewing an overpowering lady novelist when suddenly a studio manager stepped into shot and handed her a note. She read it, looked shocked and read it again. Then she stared up at the camera, somewhere between alarm and tears, and said in an incredulous voice, 'The mayor's been shot – and so has Harvey Milk!' There was a pause and then she added, fighting back a sob, 'This is terrible!' There followed a triumph of opportunism as the lady novelist leaned forward and slapped a brusque hand on her shoulder. 'Terrible, dear', she said in a gruff voice. 'Let's get back to my book.'

Undoubtedly the most sinister guest on *We Interrupt* was Roy Cohn, who has been reinvented as a monster by Tony Kushner's play *Angels in America*. At the National he was played by Henry Goodman; in Mike Nichols's television film by Al Pacino. Neither performance was as scary as the real thing. Cohn and David Shine were Senator Joe McCarthy's sidekicks in the persecution of liberals and former 'communist' suspects. After the collapse of McCarthy, Cohn established himself as a power broker in New York and a particular enemy of the crusading left-wing lawyer William Kunstler – accusations of murder flew back and forth and they vowed publicly never to speak to one another.

On *We Interrupt This Week* we sometimes fielded a team of contestants from the same profession. We tried lawyers. We landed Kunstler and Cohn. Still determined not to speak to one another but unable to resist the chance of being on television. The third member was to have been Melvin Belli or Marvin Mitchelson. I cannot remember which, but at the last minute number three dropped out; he was fighting a case in Washington – defending himself.

I visited Cohn at his town house to brief him. He asked me to breakfast. He was dressed in a stained brocade dressing gown. Butlers and acolytes came and went. The most chilling moment involved the arrival of a letter borne on a salver. Cohn ripped it open, glanced at it and then said to the messenger, 'Oh, by the way, did you mail the cheque to the judge?'

Satisfied that this had been done, we returned to our discussion of the programme. We had to recruit one of our regulars, Jeff Greenfield, to make up the team of three. Jeff was technically a lawyer. He agreed reluctantly. The programme itself was something of an anticlimax but the aftermath was ironic. A naive young PBS photographer rushed forward to Cohn and Kunstler and asked, 'Could I photograph you gentlemen together, maybe shaking hands?' I've never seen the stage direction 'They turn on their heels' carried out more vigorously as they found separate studio doors by which to leave.

The volume of press support for *We Interrupt This Week* was underlined by an extraordinary response on the part of viewers. After I announced the demise of the show on the last transmission I came back to England. The show's staff arrived next week to clear up the office and were much dimmed when there were no letters in the in-trays: we had anticipated a trickle of public support. Some hours later it transpired that there were so many bags of mail for the shop that they had been diverted to a special sorting office. An 'enormous response from viewers' usually means a few hundred letters. We got about fifteen thousand, many including cheques, dollar bills and touching messages. Our favourite, from one George Diskant in LA, pointed out that he had been watching the show for five years and could not bear to lose it. As we had not run a year we wrote back to ask him what he was smoking.

As a result of this extraordinarily large demonstration, the Corporation for Public Broadcasting came up with a subvention of a hundred thousand dollars to produce five more shows; and I set off to New Orleans with the Channel 13 executives to lobby the heads of the other PBS stations for the future. There were three hectic days of blandishing in 'smoke-filled rooms'. It was a losing battle which continued to be lost as the year wore on. We were fighting for a return in the autumn season, but as the Middle West failed to come through we started to hunt for sponsors: if you can give PBS a show for free the chances are that they will take it. The programme had two built-in problems. It was recorded virtually as live, so it was spontaneous and could be controversial. The big firms prefer to back decorous, pre-filmed, 'classy' costume drama. Imagine the embarrassment if the ad-lib panel poked fun at the expense of a sponsoring petro-leum company's oil slick. Moreover, it was intensely topical, and repeats and residuals, shown again to infinity, which help to balance the budgets of most series, could not apply to us – even with a Tallahasseean lack of concern for topicality.

As Tony Geis used to say, the distinguishing feature of American television is that by turning a switch around a myriad of channels you can see Lucille Ball at any age. Tony and I were together in the office when we heard the announcement of the confirmation of the Polish Pope. 'Ah,' said Tony, 'the first thing he'll do is give the Sistine Chapel a second coat.'

He invented a routine about the Popemobile which I've heard quoted and mangled many times since. The Pope is in the Popemobile and the sun comes out. The Pope presses a button and the roof slides back. Then it starts to rain. The Pope presses another button and . . . it stops raining.

In self-indulgent mood I include a few echoes of *We Interrupt This Week* – because they evoke a happy period for me. As I no longer collect scrapbooks, they will be fixed between covers as memory grows dim. We saw the heyday and the busting of the socially impregnable club, Studio 54: 'How to get in?' 'Get a warrant.' Gore Vidal, assured as usual, but woefully unbriefed after having flown in from Rome, answered only one question – 'Who said this week, "The possibilities of heterosexuality are soon exhausted"?' The correct answer was a prominent pornographer, but Gore saw his moment. Optimistically he enquired, 'Did I?' He got two points on the grounds that though he had not said it that week he had probably said it most weeks down the preceding two decades.

Barbara Howar was one of the sharpest contestants. I had seen her on a Johnny Carson show decimating Robert Blake, an actor who was boring away on a chauvinist trip. On one of our programmes she was sitting next to Ron Nessen, who had been Gerald Ford's beleaguered press secretary. Helpfully he attempted to rephrase Barbara's answer. Jeff Greenfield leant across with a nostalgic smile, 'It's wonderful, Ron, once again to hear you explaining what someone *meant* to say.'

The tragic death in 1983 of a popular newsreader on a big network, Jessica Savitch, reminded me of her one appearance on *We Interrupt This Week*. The next day she was in a Gristedes supermarket. An old woman buttonholed her, saying, 'I enjoyed you on *We Interrupt* last night. Tell me, do you ever do any other television?' My own Gristedes moment came when another old lady stopped me. 'Hi!' she said. 'You're so much taller when you're standing up than when you're sitting down.' Peter Stone, the playwright and another panellist, ruefully mourned the end of the series: 'I completely abandoned a very lucrative career to work for $186 a show . . . I spend all my time reading newspapers . . . It was worth it.'

We failed to get the money we needed and the week before we finished, my work permit ran out. Coming through Kennedy Airport for the penultimate show, I wondered whether I should risk the last trip and not bother to get it renewed, relying on my non-working visitor's visa. Fortunately I renewed it. As I went through immigration the officer said, 'Who's on the show this week?' The customs man asked, 'Got a good one tomorrow?' And as I gave the taxi driver my address in Manhattan he said, 'You sound like that guy on *We Interrupt This Week*.' I began to believe that it was not quite the elitist excursion the Middle West would have had us believe. And it was fun.

Much later I had a go back in Britain at restoring the quiz to its original form. Bill Cotton at the BBC set me on to Alan Yentob. I proposed the idea over lunch. Yentob assured me that 'the time for joky news quizzes is past' and I thought no more about it until *Have I Got News For You* was launched some months later.

CHAPTER 14

Any Place I Hang My Hat . . .?

New York had been fun; but it was time to leave. I had a wonderful time there. I made many friends. I lived in and felt at home in the Village, on the Upper West Side, the midtown East Side and in what used to be Hell's Kitchen. But it was not the place to hang my hat. I knew that I would always look forward to returning but, back in London, *Beecham* was getting itself together, there was a Yorkshire Television series, *Song by Song*, to complete and various other television and radio series to consider. It was home addiction rather than home sickness. I succumbed to it.

My first venture on my return was BBC 2's *Friday Night, Saturday Morning*, based on the premise that there should be no regular host but a series of guest hosts who would do stints of two weeks each. The convention was that the guests should be very much the host's individual choices. It was recorded as live at the Greenwood Theatre in Guy's Hospital, which held happy memories after that last try-out of *Side By Side By Sondheim*. The original producer was Ian Johnstone. We settled very quickly into the formula. I was sorry to finish my stint after two weeks. Ian was excited. His next host was Harold Wilson. The consequent drama was not what he had bargained for. It has to be easier to host a chat show than to run a country but Wilson underestimated the challenge. When Ian called at his house in Lord North Street to take him to the studio, he said he'd come on later and told his driver to take the producer ahead and come back for him. On the way to the Greenwood Ian expressed some fears that the ex-prime minister might not be adequately prepared. The driver was reassuring: 'He grasps a brief in no time.' The programme was a disaster. Wilson was unsure when to talk, where to look, how to start and when to stop. Some of his guests – Tony Benn, for example – managed to cover for him. To introduce him, Wilson pinched a joke Neil Shand had written for me: 'Tony Benn, the incredible shrinking name.' However, even the usually ebullient Harry Secombe looked lost and alarmed.

However, Wilson was booked for two shows. On the second occasion he travelled to the studio with Ian Johnstone. He confessed on the journey that he had had seven sleepless nights since the first programme – and that he hadn't had one during his two terms as prime minister. He did not improve.

As a safety measure I was brought back to host six shows while they sorted out some new guest hosts. On one I was given a reluctant Christopher Walken to interview. He was on a long promotional tour for an action adventure movie that he seemed bored with – *Dogs of War*. I remembered that he'd been a chorus boy off Broadway with Liza Minelli in the musical *Best Foot Forward* and *on* Broadway with Beatrice Lillie in *High Spirits*, directed by Noel Coward. I asked him what it was like to be directed by Coward. I've never seen anyone switch from bored disinterest to animation quite so quickly. He had bought a brand-new, bright red dance suit for the first day of rehearsals of *High Spirits*. The cast were lined up to be presented, as if to visiting royalty. Coward progressed down the line and was introduced to each member. When he got to Walken he said, 'That's a very bright dance suit.' The tongue-tied young walloper couldn't think of anything significant to say so he blurted out, 'It's red!' 'Yes,' said Coward. 'It's been a very exciting day for us all,' and moved on.

While I was in America my manager, Deke Arlon, made an arrangement with Yorkshire Television to do a series on distinguished lyricists using the same formula as the Wavendon Gershwin programme and *Side By Side By Sondheim*. We called it *Song by Song*. We had already had a preliminary canter for the BBC, examining Ira Gershwin's work. The series provided two seasons of happy television directed by Vernon Lawrence. We worked on lyricists as varied as Alan Lerner, Lorenz Hart, Oscar Hammerstein, Dorothy Fields, Sheldon Harnick, Johnny Mercer, E. Y. Harburg, Irving Berlin, Cole Porter and Noel Coward. There were many old friends and American guests like Lena Horne, Barbara Cook and Howard Keel.

Lena Horne appeared first on the Johnny Mercer show. I suggested that she should join David Kernan, Millicent Martin and Julia McKenzie in 'The Waiter, the Porter and the Upstairs Maid'. She thought she was being asked to play 'the maid'. She answered with a very firm 'No.' Persuaded that she was to play a grand lady and the other three were her staff she quickly changed her mind. She made a brilliant, witty choice for one of her solos in the Alan Lerner show, Maurice Chevalier's 'I'm Glad I'm Not Young Any More'. She recorded it in one take with a slight error in the lyric. I asked her if she wanted to do it again. She thought not. It was the only time she ever performed it. Some months later I saw an edition of the impersonator show *Who Do You Do?* Faith Brown announced that she was going to sing Lena Horne's most famous song, 'I'm Glad I'm Not Young Any More'. She sang it with exactly the same mistake in the lyric – proof that the video-recorder had arrived.

My happiest single memory of the series is playing to 'Yip' Harburg in the programme we devoted to his work. He is one of my favourite lyric-writers and he was then, some three years before his death, already into his eighties. His enthusiasm was matched by his eagle-eared attention to see if any of his words had been rearranged. The occasion also had its wry side. There are those terrifying times when you know that certain subjects are taboo with a person. With Yip it was *The Wiz*. Without doubt, Yip's best-known score is the one he wrote with Harold Arlen which provided the springboard for Judy Garland's success in *The Wizard of Oz*. Among the colleagues in the viewing theatre was my friend David Yakir, who made a vow not to mention the black version of the Frank Baum classic, *The Wiz*, which he had enjoyed, but which we both knew Harburg hated. After Yip had enjoyed the celebration of his work we chatted happily until David and I took him home in a cab. He lived where so many songwriters hang out in style on Central Park West. Suddenly, out of nowhere came the 'brick' which David was determined not to drop. 'Mr Harburg, how did you like *The Wiz*?' The old man was civilly dismissive; David bit his tongue off.

Among other things, *Song by Song* led to an appearance on the Royal Variety Show. In addition to Millie, David and Julia, we added six guests to a segment of standard songs. They were Elisabeth Welch, Marti Caine, Hinge and Brackett, and Carol Channing, who finished the first half with the title song of *Hello Dolly*, and a forthright Welsh chorus silent in Jon Scoffield's television version because no microphones got near them. They looked like geriatric chorus boys gone to fat.

The two rehearsal days were attended by heavy security. Passes were demanded. Performers were denied entry. It was all very clandestine. Our dressing room was a wonderful cross-section. James Galway, accustomed to flying into a town and carrying a whole concert, was bemused by having to perform no more than three items and hang around a great deal. Noel Edmonds was not entirely sure whether hosting a pop-music section would prove the most popular part of the show, which has a notoriously unpredictable audience. Bernie Clifton, who was to score one of his big successes, came surrounded by a little family of woolly ostriches and camels inhabited by an army of assistants; or was it just one? I could never quite discover. Poor Jim Davidson had the traditional comic's Royal Variety dilemma – which of his best jokes could he possibly get away with in front of the Queen?

Just before the performance was due to get under way I was standing in the wings with the group of artists who had assembled to watch the Queen's progress from Buckingham Palace on television monitors. Suddenly I was aware of a small Indian man at my side carrying a piece of paper. 'Mr Sherrin?' he enquired.

'How nice,' I thought, 'an autograph hunter.' I smiled in agreement.

'Mr E. G. Sherrin,' he continued.

This sounded less like an autograph hunter. Those are indeed my initials, but few people know them and fewer use them. However, I could not deny it. 'Yes,' I said lamely.

'Will you please accept this?' He put the writ firmly in my hand, thanked me politely and left through the elaborate security precautions which he had breached so easily on behalf, it turned out, of Her Majesty's Inspector of Taxes.

I took the writ up to the dressing room the better to read it and was immediately struck by the archaic form of address. It purported to be a directive from the Queen herself. Her Britannic Majesty was instructing me in no uncertain terms to pay a sizeable chunk of surtax or be clapped in irons. It was hard not to see the funny side. After all, I was due to be presented to her in about three hours' time. I began to ponder possible approaches. Rather than answering the writ, it would surely be more sensible to have a word with her personally – something like, 'I got your note . . .'

I stuck it in my briefcase and we did the show. Sitting around through Act Two, waiting for the walk down, discretion banished such fantasies. When the Queen did her rounds I bowed low, listened politely as she said, 'Very enjoyable', and watched her pass on to the late Bill Haley, to whom she talked with great animation. The impresario Louis Benjamin sent me a picture of my bow. My eyes are closed tight. Under it he added a caption: '. . . And when you woke up she was still there.'

My accountant sorted out the writ the next morning. They were very apologetic, but they did not shave anything off the total.

Two modest radio programmes provided a spine for my subsequent performing life. I had served wireless apprenticeships before *Side By Side By Sondheim*, hosting Radio 4's *Midweek* for some months. Henry Kelly was a regular supporting interviewer. Then there was a group of shorter outings with easy punning names, *Dry Sherrin*, *Medium Dry Sherrin*, *Extra Dry Sherrin*. The first bizarre concoction took place late at night on the dance floor of the old Quaglinos. It was an attempt to recreate for Radio 2 the style of pre-war American shows evocative of the opening sequence of *The War of the Worlds* from the Waldorf Astoria: chat from the tables surrounding the ballroom floor. Elegant couples dancing by. A smattering of cabaret. It worked quite well in the early weeks when Quaglinos, restaurant and dance floor, was more or less deserted. Unfortunately our last programme was just before Christmas. Suddenly the room was full of office parties who had no intention of keeping quiet while a radio programme they couldn't hear was being broadcast live to listeners at home. Two of my guests were octogenarians – the old actor Richard Goolden, the inevitable Mole in annual revivals of *Toad of Toad Hole*, and Arthur Marshall. Diners grew more frustrated at being hushed and not being able to hear what they were missing, which wasn't much. They began to bombard the elderly broadcasters with bread rolls. Sadly the scene of chaos and confusion couldn't come across in the broadcast.

The other *Medium* and *Extra Dry* shows were more decorous affairs for Radio 4. One programme was going out during the Falklands War. Roy Hudd and the Oxford don and comedy fanatic Anthony Quinton were discussing music-hall routines. The conversation hadn't really caught fire when Radio 4 switched to the House of Commons and the announcement of the sinking of HMS *Sheffield*. The network did not return to our studio but played solemn music. 'Ah,' said Quinton, 'I know that tune. It is Sibelius's "You can't win 'em all".'

There is nothing like a good mismatching of minds in a chat show. One night the producer, Ian Gardhouse, booked Sir Robert Helpman and the small, noisy 'singer' Pia Zadora. I talked first to Helpman but Miss Zadora was itching to get in and make her mark. Sir Robert was in the middle of a long story about Lord Berners, his exotic lifestyle, the doves whose feathers he dyed all the colours of the rainbow and a horse that wandered into the drawing room through French windows and was fed a teacake. Miss Zadora leapt in.

'What is a teacake?' she enunciated.

As a conversation stopper it took some beating.

An anecdote is often told of Miss Zadora's disastrous appearance off Broadway in the title role in *The Diary of Anne Frank*. As the story goes she was so bad that on the first night when the German soldiers entered the flat the entire audience rose as one man and yelled, 'She's in the attic!' I subsequently appeared on breakfast television with Miss Zadora. I asked her if the 'Anne Frank' story was true. 'What is that story?' she said. So I had to tell her to her face this tale which did not reflect well on her acting ability. She was very brave and said, 'No, that story cannot be true. I have never enacted the role of Anne Frank and I have never enacted off Broadway.' So now you know.

Counterpoint, an annual thirteen-programme series of music quizzes is a delight to do with very sporting lay competitors answering questions on musical subjects. For years the *Radio Times* billing characterised them as ranging 'from Bach to The Beatles'. It started in 1986 and was scheduled to go out at lunchtime on Mondays and at 6.30 p.m. on Wednesdays – the more popular spot. Sadly, during James Boyle's largely beneficial reorganisation of Radio 4 a few years ago, the programme was confined to Monday lunchtime along with a slew of ghastly new quiz flops; their only virtue, cheapness. The Wednesday drive-time slot went to depressing would-be comedy programmes. We still await a decision by an enlightened head of Radio 4 to revert to the status quo, and make do with a late-night Saturday repeat.

Loose Ends, my other regular long-running series, was the brain-child of Ian Gardhouse, then a highly imaginative, senior talks producer. He cut his teeth on all the staples of Radio 4 – *Start the Week*, *Stop the Week*, *Midweek* – and he tinkered with two experiments in 'rolling radio' which didn't work. One was an attempt to bind together all the shows on Radio 4 on a Thursday morning, with a single overall presenter. It seemed an arch and unnecessary development and was soon dropped. The BBC then experimented with a similar idea on Sunday mornings called *Sunday Supplement*. In effect it was a long magazine programme without the punch or the personality to establish itself. However, during its run Ian discovered several unfamiliar broadcasters whom he was able to draft in when we started to assemble *Loose Ends*.

At the end of 1985 he was asked to tailor a programme to run for an hour on Saturday mornings. It had been the home of *Pick of the Week*, magisterially hosted by Margaret Howard. Her breathtaking segues between unlikely subjects were a thing of wonder. Ian's idea was to surround an 'old fart' (me) with bright, pushy younger interviewers and correspondents who would keep me on my toes. Starting at the beginning of January 1986, he recruited an impressive range of voices and minds,

many of whom were not familiar to Radio 4 listeners. Among
them in the first few years were Stephen Fry, Robert Elms, John
Walters, Emma Freud, Victoria Mather, Carol Thatcher, Craig
Charles, Jonathan Ross and David Quantick.

Stephen Fry and Robert Elms were on the first programme. In
the early days the formula was more varied than it is now. There
was a monologue, brilliantly written for the initial two seasons
by Alistair Beaton, followed by interviews, musical breaks and
brief glimpses of stand-up comedians. These items were inter-
spersed with reports taped on location by the bright-
young-things.

Nowadays these excursions are too expensive for the budget
so the pattern of the programme is more predictable. The initial
response to *Loose Ends* was qualified. It was slagged off by several papers in a way that most new programmes which contain
a glimmer of a new idea are received. Gillian Reynolds, the
doyenne of radio critics, penned a personal letter to the effect
that with Ian Gardhouse, she felt, I had fallen among thieves and
should repent, resign or generally keep as far away as I could
from his evil influence. I got the impression that he was a disaster who had the worst interests of me, the BBC and Radio 4 in
particular at heart. A destroyer of all that was sacred and probably a usurer, a mass murderer and child molester to boot. In her
column she confined herself to writing of *Loose Ends* as
'putrid . . . a sad disappointment'. It was all good rough and
tumble. Fortunately we won a Sony award for Best Magazine
Programme that first year. Gillian was on the panel of judges but
not, thankfully, in our section.

We settled down to build up a large, happier audience.
Alistair's topical monologue, an elegant essay, gave us a good
start. He sustained it for two years. The best example was
unbroadcastable and unprintable. Several weeks into the series
Ian Gardhouse took a Saturday off. His young second-in-
command, Simon Shaw, had to 'hear' the monologue. Alistair

always wrote it late on Friday night, working into the early hours. He brought it into the office on Saturday morning and there was a ritual reading for timing, libel and laughs. He played a wicked practical joke on Simon and wrote two versions. It was the end of the week that a fish bone got stuck in the Queen Mother's throat up at the Castle of Mey. The first page which I read out contained every conceivable sexual double entendre that could be wrenched from the subject of what the Queen Mother had swallowed. I watched Simon, who had started by concentrating only on his stopwatch, as the filthy litany unfolded. Agonies of embarrassment flicked across his face. Faces do go white. I saw it happen. Over a minute into the story Alistair resolved the joke but it was a poignant drama in which to take part.

Confrontational spats are rare on *Loose Ends*. The general purpose of the conversation is to be informative and anecdotal rather than controversial. However, Alistair did provide a couple of off-air shouting matches. He stormed into the studio after the novelist and photographer Pat Booth had loudly sung the praises of Baby Doc Duvalier, the deposed dictator of Haiti: 'Such a nice host.' No meeting of minds there. With his impeccable left-wing principles he still managed to bring a balance to the monologue, realising that both left and right should be equally subject to criticism. This did not suit Stephen Wells, a more extreme left-wing journalist. He rose from the studio table during some jibe about Sinead O'Connor's loony-left convictions in the monologue and rushed into the control room, ranting, 'Who wrote this fascist rubbish?' I'm sorry I missed the row which apparently rambled on through the programme.

The topical jokes of yesteryear do not wear well but after Alistair retired there were sparky contributions from Andrew Nickolds, Steve Punt, Mike Coleman and others, especially Neil Shand. At least two of Neil's best, bitchiest lines have found their way into anthologies – 'John Selwyn Gummer, living proof that the weak are a long time in politics' and 'Jeffrey Archer, the only seaside peer on which Danny La Rue has not performed.'

Debbie Barham was an extraordinary, precocious recruit to the team. She sent jokes and sketches to the Radio 4 sketch show *Weekending* when she was fourteen – many were accepted, her age unknown and unqueried. She started to write for *Loose Ends* when she was still in her teens, coming to join us via a programme called *The Treatment* on Radio Five Live. For a very young woman she had the sharpest tongue, the raunchiest sense of humour and the bravest attitude to extreme thinness and dangerous eating disorders – which were the crosses that bore her to an early grave in 2003. She always submitted at least ten pages of gags, leaving you to pick your own. Here are a few which might survive the curse of immediate topicality.

'A man is beginning a six-month sentence for picking up lost golf balls from a lake. The judge defended his stiff sentence, saying, "If there's one thing guaranteed to stop him wanting to jump into the water, bend over and start looking for balls, it's a day in the showers at Belmarsh".' She welcomed a Gordon Brown Budget with some other sectors of the population. 'Particularly pleased will be mothers, the over-sixty-fives, people who drink a lot, and keen gamblers. The tragedy is that the Queen Mother isn't around to enjoy it.'

During the Queen's jubilee, when in the north-east a male streaker ran alongside the royal Roller: 'Her Majesty uttered a disdainful, "We are not aroused". Explaining his actions to the police the exhibitionist said that he was "just trying to measure his tackle against a ruler".' She had a healthy contempt for 'reality TV'. '*Big Brother 3* features a flight of stairs for the first time. It'll be nice for the contestants to have an intellectual challenge to deal with.' She was well up on the World Cup. 'Sven Goran Eriksson has been slipping out of his dug-out to enjoy ninety minutes of gripping end-to-end stuff with a woman young enough to be in his team.'

Debbie must have written for Angus Deayton but that did not inhibit her reaction to his disgrace. 'The young hooker claimed she was shocked when Angus started doing coke – but at least he wasn't doing jokes.' The Spice Girls were a regular target. 'Geri Halliwell has started work on her second autobiography. Let's hope she finds a more interesting subject than she did for her first.' The target she hit most frequently – incredible considering her own illness, which was to kill her in her mid-twenties – was the stick-like frame of Victoria Beckham. For David Beckham's birthday, 'Posh gave him a special treat. He'd expected a girl jumping out of a cake, but she surprised him by sticking her fingers down her throat and making a cake jump out of a girl.'

There was a sad/triumphant combined funeral and memorial service for her at St Paul's, Covent Garden, organised by her proud father. Several of us who had worked with her were asked to recall her and her jokes. Clive Anderson, Bruce Hyman, John Langdon, John McVicar and I remembered her with admiration and affection. Usually there is a gap between the mourning ceremony of funeral and the celebration of a life in a memorial service. It was curious to find myself firing off her quips while standing beside her ominously light, wicker coffin. With her relentlessly macabre sense of humour, I have no doubt that she would have enjoyed the irony.

Initially Ian Gardhouse rounded up a bizarre variety of guests. A retrospective roll-call would pall but I remember one guest early on who professed to have invented a computer game. In order to while away the hours he spent at NASA on the space programme he used their equipment to come up with a kind of electronic ping-pong. He went on to invent several early arcade games before selling out to the games giant Atari for several million dollars. Part of the deal was that he could not market any other electronic device for a fixed period. The necessary time having elapsed, he was flogging his latest creation – a couple of large teddy bears which, when activated, said banal things in childish American English. Having demonstrated these, he couldn't deactivate their speech mechanism. John Walters, who was next on, had then to deliver a five-minute essay with a four-foot-high furry bear intermittently uttering words of endearment to him. Distanced, it went chuntering on through the programme until it was finally banished beyond the studio doors.

We took a perverse delight in broadcasting essentially visual items: the juggler Paul Morocco spitting out table-tennis balls in time to accompanying music; tightrope walking; the Oxford and Cambridge bid for a Half Blue for ballroom dancing, demonstrated by a spinning couple with a commentary by the Royal Ballet *premier danseur*, Wayne Eagling; the inevitable Uri Geller bending spoons; the conjurer Fay Presto performing tricks with listeners over a telephone link.

Musically the producers always cast a wide net. We accommodated a range from Ozzy Osbourne to Ian Bostridge. As Blur and Pulp arrived on the scene, Damon Albarn and Jarvis Cocker arrived in Studio B13. So did Placebo, Gomez, Divine Comedy, Yoko Ono, then her son Sean Lennon and her stepson Julian. For a visit from the New York Gay Men's Choir, eighty-strong and not a looker among them, we had to move into a much larger studio. They coincided with the New York writer Jay McInerney, in whose new novel I found a homophobic sentence. Reading it aloud initiated some good-natured hissing and booing from the choir and brought a blush to the speechless novelist's face.

A regular collecting point for singers and especially piano acts was the cabaret room at the Pizza on the Park, now renamed Larry's Room after Larry Adler. Michael Feinstein, Steve Ross and the Coward specialist Peter Greenwell were the most regular guests.

Elaine Stritch is always a lively visitor. One Saturday she told a story of the London first night of Noel Coward's musical *Sail Away*. It opened at a time when Elaine was having a rough time with alcohol. There was to be a smart party after the show and Coward warned her to behave herself. Accordingly she dressed conservatively and drank nothing, before going up to the party in the same lift as Vivien Leigh and Kenneth More. Both were 'pissed'. As Elaine stepped out into the room she was greeted by Coward's wagging finger. 'Elaine, I told you to behave yourself. I didn't tell you to come dressed as a fucking nun!'

Here Elaine stopped and gave me a half-guilty look. 'You can cut that out of the tape,' she said helpfully.

'It's live, Elaine.'

'Live television?'

'No, Elaine, live radio.'

'Live *radio*! Christ! I didn't need to make up my face.'

A look at the guest list over a few months taken at random in 1995 gives some idea of the variety of people we entertained: Leslie Nielsen (who brought a tiresome farting machine with him), Gary Glitter, Rhodes Boyson, Kate Winslet, undecided then if her career was to be as an actress or as a children's TV presenter, Frederick Forsyth, Russ Meyer, the soft-porn film-maker who characterised one of his leading ladies, Anoushka Hempel, as 'insufficiently cantilevered', Ariel Dorfman, Art Malik, George Melly, Alistair McAlpine, Beryl Bainbridge, Dale Winton, touchingly grateful that I remembered his mother, Sheree, who appeared in one of the *Up* films just before her suicide.

That very year I see that the astronomer Patrick Moore and Tony Benn turned up on the same show. Politically they are poles apart but they relished each other's enthusiasm. Poor Patrick was on the last legs of a book tour. We had strict instructions from his agent not to reveal that his home in Selsey had been broken into. She feared it might sap his enthusiasm for plugging the *Guinness Book of Astronomy* (fifth edition), which is crammed with facts. His effortless answering of all my questions was in sharp contrast to some interviewees. When I interviewed Hunter Davies over his book about the Orient Express I fished for a splendid story about Sir Basil Zaharoff, the arms magnate. Hunter couldn't remember it. 'After all,' he said, 'I did finish the book three years ago.' I was left to tell his story. There was none of that with Patrick, who rattled off information about intriguing minutiae like 'the Sombrero Hat Galaxy', 'Bode's Nebula' and 'the Coat Hanger Constellation' as though they were old friends. They probably were. It sounded as if I was trying to catch him out. I wasn't. Questions about impenetrable phrases like, 'What was the Dirty Ice Ball Theory proposed by F. L. Whipple in 1950?' triggered beautifully clear and simple answers. Patrick is a born teacher and an irresistible enthusiast. I did try to surprise him by asking him ('on information received') if it was true that he possessed a bootleg copy of the notorious pirate recording of the BBC children's exercise coach, Ann Driver. Ms Driver broadcast a 'Music and Movement' keep-fit class for schools in the forties. 'Now, children, toss your balls in the air . . .!' etc. He owned up gleefully. Meanwhile, Tony Benn joined in, claiming that he too had acquired the Driver classic during his term as a BBC producer. Ah, the pornography of innocence if not the innocence of pornography.

The next week I interviewed the American film actor Billy Crystal on tape. His new film, *Forget Paris*, was about a baseball referee who falls in love on a quick jaunt to Paris. I risked quoting one review at him. It suggested that he increasingly represented 'Mr Menopausal Manhattan', which threw him for a moment into a rare, wordless puzzlement. Indeed, after we'd finished the interview and he was being led out down the labyrinthine corridors of Broadcasting House I could still hear him muttering to himself, 'Mr Menopausal Manhattan . . . Mr Meno . . .' He was interesting about his grandfather, a Yiddish Hamlet who toured America in the role; and his father, a concert promoter who as a child got him into Louis Armstrong's box to watch his first baseball game and on to Billie Holiday's lap to watch his first movie, *Shane*.

We've had most of the chefs: the Roux brothers together, Marco Pierre White long ago when he started his own restaurant in Wandsworth, Rick Stein when we were in Exeter, Antony Worrall Thompson, Gary Rhodes, Ainslie Harriott, whose father I remembered as a part of the musical double act Harriott and Evans, Jamie Oliver, Marcus Wareing when he revamped the Savoy Grill and both Fat Ladies. Jennifer Paterson poached two perfect eggs in the studio to refute A. N. Wilson's accusation that her method was rubbish. Hugh Montgomery-Massingberd (as he then was) ate them both on toast.

The birth of *Loose Ends* coincided with an explosion of young comedians. I only made the mistake of using the word 'alternative' once – to Robbie Coltrane, who looked at me pityingly. Stephen Fry was with us from the beginning, sometimes as a character comedian with his donnish character Dr Trefusis, sometimes simply as a conversationalist. He was a little upset one Saturday in the George, the pub that hosts a short 'winding down' session for people who feel like it after the programme. It has always been a BBC pub. I tell Americans that it is the pub where Dylan Thomas threw up most frequently. There is always a gaggle of autograph hunters outside Broadcasting House. They are usually considerate and leave the guests alone in the George. On this occasion a young girl penetrated the circle and hovered. She could have been after the signature of any of three or four guests. Finally she said, 'Could I have an autograph . . . [my pause] . . . Mr Fry?' The table erupted with laughter. Stephen signed and had a few words with her. Then he reproached us, pointing out how much courage it must have taken, 'public, our lifeblood', etc. He quite missed the point that we were laughing at ourselves. She could have been addressing anyone at the table and indeed everyone had probably expected that it was them she was after. Rhona Cameron, Sandi Toksvig and Hattie Hayridge all became 'regulars' for a while.

Graham Norton first appeared in his character, 'Mother Teresa' on her 'final tour'. He was working as a waiter and occasional stand-up disguised with a tea-towel on his head at the time. He soon became a regular interviewer and still returns on occasion. He confided to me that, as a drama student at the Central School of Speech and Drama, he had been in a production of *Macbeth*. He had been directed by Judi Dench – the part was small, either Ross or Lennox. In the middle of Judi's interview I asked her if she'd enjoyed her first steps into direction. 'Yes,' she said, 'very much.' 'Who played Ross in your production?' I asked. She looked puzzled, thought for a moment and then said firmly, 'Surely it's usually cut?' 'Well, it wasn't this time. And he's sitting next to you!'

Craig Charles was another guest who became a regular interviewer. He was initially invited to contribute performance poetry. He had an endearing habit of failing to turn up and then explaining that his father had died the previous day. It was perhaps unwise to use this excuse more than once. When the programme visited his native Liverpool he compounded the mistake by saying that he didn't need a hotel room. He would stay with his father. As I write Craig's father is healthily approaching his eightieth birthday. When Craig was in prison on a rape charge – summarily dismissed when it came to court – I had a melodramatic call from a concerned colleague, Victoria Mather, saying, 'Do you think we should try to "spring" him?' Fortunately he was soon released.

French and Saunders arrived as comics while they were doing very funny stand-up in Battersea; Lenny Henry soon after he abandoned *The Black and White Minstrel Show*. *Loose Ends* was probably the first time that Jack Dee told a wireless audience of his experiences as a trainee chef in the Fulham Road and at the Ritz. At his lowest point he sent supper up on a tray to the night porter. It was returned with a twenty-pence tip. Eddie Izzard discussed his transvestism for the first time on *Loose Ends* and Derek Jarman revealed that he was HIV positive. It was not discussed on air then. When I bumped into him and Tilda Swinton two nights later, they were still triumphant that he had perhaps raised public consciousness a little.

Eddie Izzard, who has been wise about limiting his television appearances, was initially reluctant to make jokes on air. He adopted a serious conversational approach. However, when I talked to him before a large audience in Edinburgh he couldn't resist being funny. After he said, 'I suppose it would work better if I was funny in the studio interviews, too?' I didn't try to dissuade him.

Lily Savage, Paul Merton, Pete McCarthy, Tony Hawks, Lee Evans and Scott Capurro (the provocative gay San Franciscan comic) swelled the ranks. Sadly it was on *Pebble Mill* not on *Loose Ends* that Alan Titchmarsh asked Scott, 'How do you go down in America?' Scott threatened him with a demonstration. We met Garth Marenghi; and the League of Gentlemen when they were graduating in comedy in Edinburgh. Barry Humphries phoned in as Dame Edna Everage from Hampstead. To play her in the studio he would have had to dress up. At ten o'clock in the morning that was beyond the call of duty. Arthur Smith, the grand old man of compering 'on the circuit', became a regular early on. He has survived, along with Emma Freud, as the two most frequent guest interviewers.

Rich Hall, the American comedian, brought his funny paperback *Self-Help for the Bleak*, an effective antidote to all those optimistic American self-help books. Two Geordie comics, Richard Morton and more recently Ross Noble, have been regular visitors. Ross and Arthur Smith provided one memorable improvisation. Arthur's guest was to be Engelbert Humperdinck. When Gerry Dorsey, as he originally was, arrived at Broadcasting House he found he was to be interviewed not by Emma

Freud, whom he had expected, but by Arthur. Worse, there was a studio audience. He promptly left, leaving a seven- or eight-minute gap in the programme, so Arthur interviewed Ross Noble – as an Engelbert who had developed a very broad Geordie accent and had no useful information about himself. It was one of the funniest bits of nonsense over nineteen years. Of the older comics, Bob Monkhouse, Frankie Howerd, Eric Sykes, Ken Dodd and Ernie Wise turned up. So did pensionable Hollywood stars – usually flogging a book – like Tony Curtis and Kirk Douglas. Celeste Holm came courtesy of the Pizza on the Park where she had a sort of cabaret act.

Peter Ustinov, Elaine Stritch and Victor Spinetti would feature on any shortlist of favourite guests. Impersonators suit the programme, bringing fleeting hints of a variety of characters. Phil Cornwell, Rob Brydon, Jan Ravens, John Culshaw, Ronni Ancona, Alistair McGowan and Rory Bremner have all run through their repertoires. One 1 April in the early nineties fell on a Saturday. Ian Gardhouse decided to people the entire show with impersonators. Partly with scripting, partly through improvisation, they managed to sustain the hour. Rory Bremner played me. I listened at home. I had two phone calls. One was from my Romanian actress friend Magdalena Buznea, who said, 'Are you all right? You didn't sound very well on the programme today.' The other was from the late Lorna Bunn, who asked, 'Who was that old queen who was trying to imitate you this morning?'

For one anniversary we broadcast from the roof of Broadcasting House; for another from the crowded bar of the George. Most bizarrely we mounted one show from my flat; I had Diana Rigg and Rory Bremner in the sitting room along with two comedy pairs, The Men Who Know and Dan (Freedman) and Nick (Romero). Arthur Smith talked to Kate Adie in the bath and the chef and food-writer Simon Hopkinson cooked a lavish breakfast with Victoria Mather in the crowded kitchen – bacon, eggs, fried bread, sausages, mushrooms, tomatoes and best of all chitterlings, which he knew was a favourite. He sourced them from a shop near Bath. I still have some safely in the deep freeze.

It was on *Loose Ends* that Jeffrey Archer confessed that when he sent his first play to the actor Frank Finlay, Acts One and Two were in reverse order. Finlay suggested that they should play Act Two first and then Act One. That is what they did. However, it didn't stop the Irish playwright Hugh Leonard saying that *Beyond a Reasonable Doubt* was a terrible play. He was told not to be hard on Jeffrey, 'After all he wrote the whole thing on a Friday.'

'Precisely,' said Leonard, 'but I'd like to know at exactly what time on a Friday.'

No one else seems to have remarked a footnote in Simon Sebag Montefiore's fine biography of Stalin, *The Court of the Red Tsar* (p. 260). 'President Vladimir Putin's grandfather was a chef who cooked for Rasputin, Lenin and finally Stalin.' A new dimension of 'celebrity chef'. One of the most bizarre recent incidents on *Loose Ends* was a conversation in which the subject of the Singing Nun came up. Suddenly two extrovert guests, Jerry Springer and Michael Barrymore, who were sitting side by side, burst into song with 'Dominique, Domenique' and having had one success with it reprised it a few moments later.

Early in 2000 James Boyle, the director of Radio 4, asked me to lunch at the Caprice after a live broadcast of *Loose Ends*. He had decided to move the programme from its morning spot to 6.15 p.m. In many ways it made sense. When John Peel's 'people' show, *Home Truths*, preceded us our figures went down. The audience which was happy to stay with us after Cliff Morgan's excellent sports programme and a travel show, *Breakaway*, were not the same people who switched on in large numbers for Peel's very popular new programme. Many people wrote to say that, switching off at 9 a.m., they often forgot to switch on again at ten. Moreover, the 6.15 slot had never captured a following since the BBC axed Robert Robinson's *Stop the Week* many years before. It meant recording the programme, which lost some of the spontaneity. We record in the morning. Many of our theatre guests would be unavailable between 6.15 p.m. and 7.00 p.m. I mourned the loss of immediacy but we record 'as live'. I still get moans from many listeners who miss the 10 a.m. transmission but the new timing has apparently trebled the audience for that time on a Saturday evening.

James Boyle was anxious to start with a bang. For the first programme he commissioned a seventy-five-minute show which we did broadcast live from the Radio Theatre with a starry cast that included Robert Runcie, Diana Rigg, John Dankworth and Cleo Laine, and Simon Callow.

I had written to Robert Runcie to ask if he would appear. He replied that he would love to but at the time his illness made it a day-to-day decision. We agreed to wait. About a week before the broadcast he wrote again to say that he was allowing himself 'certain little treats'. This would be one.

He arrived in good time and must have taken his painkillers exactly. He was enchanting with the other guests. He sparkled on the programme, including with his stories a wicked impression of Ian Paisley. A few days later he sent a message: 'Being hugged by Diana Rigg was better than three sessions of chemotherapy.' A couple of months later he died in great peace, with his family around him and praying that death would come quickly so that he could be reunited with his old friend Cardinal Basil Hume.

I had long before accepted an invitation from Sir Don Gosling and his business partner, Ron Hobson, to go on a Mediterranean cruise. On Saturday 3 June we were due to be in Dubrovnik. James Boyle was keen not to ruffle the programme a couple of months into the new timing. He decreed that a team should drive to Croatia and we would broadcast from the ship. As Terry Wogan, Kit and the Widow, and Tim Rice were on board there was no problem recruiting a cast and a local band. We managed forty-five minutes – the only casualty the engineer who had to sit on top of the deck in blazing sun adjusting the transmitter so that it never lost contact with the satellite which was broadcasting back to Britain.

There were few upsets on the programme after Ian Gardhouse moved on to higher things. I have been fortunate with a succession of bright producers, but I did fly off the handle when we were in Amsterdam for one show. Neil Shand's monologue cited a French joke about women in London – 'What do you call a pretty woman in London?' 'A tourist.' Neil then riposted with three anti-French gags. I got back to London to find that these had been cut by the otherwise admirable producer, simply leaving the original insult to British womanhood to stand by itself. I fired off a pompous apology to *The Times*, which prompted a seven-day wonder of tabloid coverage on the same lines. When I bumped into Greg Dyke, the director general of the BBC, at a first night he said, 'Looks like Sherrin one, BBC nil.'

CHAPTER 15

Life Upon the Wicked Stage ...

I am occasionally asked by people if I am an actor. I am not. However, I have on three occasions been paid to pretend to be. In 1976 Alan Gibson was directing a television play about Michael Arlen, the rich, controversial author of the decadent twenties novel *The Green Hat*. Arlen rescued Coward's first hit, *The Vortex*, by writing a large cheque which enabled the rehearsals of the play to continue after a hiccup at the Everyman Theatre in Hampstead. In the television play Coward and Arlen meet in New York in the forties and enjoy a brief nostalgic reunion. Gibson rang me to say that he wanted me to play Noel Coward in the three-minute scene, 'rather than a proper actor'. It sounded like a lark and I unwisely said, 'Yes.' I enjoyed the experience and Alan Badel, who was playing Arlen, could not have been more encouraging. By the time of the transmission I was in America with *Side By Side* – so I didn't see it until the 1980s. I was in a retrospective programme hosted by Emma Freud. I was curious to see what it was like. I foolishly asked for the clip to be included. Although I was warned by Emma that I was appalling, I could not believe how bad it was. The terrible attempt at the voice was made worse by a remorseless wagging finger. The art of coarse acting ran riot. I was reminded of Coward's criticism of Daniel Massey, who played him in the film *Star*: 'Too many "dear boys", dear boy.'

Once bitten; but then I was asked to play Alexander Pope in the film of Virginia Woolf's *Orlando*. Pope was short, thin, hunchbacked and bald. I could only manage one of those qualities. I declined – besides that there were quite a lot of lines and I do not learn easily. However, the essayist Addison was in the same scene. Nobody knows what Addison looks like and he had far fewer lines, so I asked to play him. It is the scene where eighteenth-century wits test Orlando, who – as Tilda Swinton – has just metamorphosed into a woman. Directed within an inch of my life by the very detailed Sally Potter I didn't feel too bad about the final result in a scene which, apart from Tilda, also included stylists like John Wood, Roger Hammond and Peter Eyre. I was secretly delighted to get a few good notices.

My third venture into drama was on *Kavanagh, QC*. Again the star, John Thaw, could not have been more accommodating. I played a stern judge – an advantage for the hard-of-learning because you can refer to notes while delivering your summing up. I can report honestly but vaingloriously that one critic wrote that I should be given a series. Stephen Sondheim is a *Kavanagh, QC* fan. He tapes the shows and views them for the hour he labours on his exercise bike. He told me that he was so surprised by my forbidding first entrance to the court that he fell off it.

I think I should let my acting career rest there. Other actors have always fascinated me. A fringe benefit of *Loose Ends* was a high-enough profile to embark on a series of 'solo' performances based on my book *Theatrical Anecdotes* and frequent invitations to chair Foyle's literary luncheons. The *Theatrical Anecdotes* tour began in 1992 when I was asked to do a charity evening one Sunday at the Yvonne Arnaud Theatre at Guildford. It went well and Duncan Weldon, a theatre producer who was in the house and who was, at the time, running the Chichester

Festival Theatre, said bluntly, 'Do you want to come to Chichester one night and do for money what you're doing here for nothing?'

The result was a merry few years of one-night stands sometimes speaking to a few hundred people in some vast civic hall or sometimes filling a more suitable arts centre which could only hold five or six hundred anyway. I was lucky to persuade Nick Romero, part of the occasional *Loose Ends* comedy duo 'Dan and Nick', to drive me to the venue, deal with the front and back of the house, organise the sale of books after the show and then drive me home through the night on one of those journeys which John Mortimer describes so vividly: 'swilling warm champagne and eating service station sandwiches'.

You have to lead people gently into anecdotes about the theatre. They are not the homely tales of disaster beloved of amateur theatricals: 'Then all the scenery fell down! My! How we laughed.' The best tales are those borne out of the tensions, excitement and bitching of rehearsals and first nights, rivalries and jealousies. So many stories are handed down from generation to generation of actors. If it's a story about drunken actors it will be dumped on the current hellraiser. It is a matter of honour to try to get as near the truth of the story and to identify as accurately as possible the protagonists. For example, perhaps the most told 'drunk' anecdote has two Shakespearean actors appearing in *Richard III*. One plays the King, the other the Duke of Buckingham. After a heavy liquid lunch they totter to the theatre for their matinée. Richard III staggers downstage and begins, 'Now is the winter . . . hic! . . . of our discontent . . .' A voice from the gallery shouts, 'You're drunk!' Richard replies, 'You think I'm drunk? Wait till you see the Duke of Buckingham!'

One tends to believe instinctively in the authenticity of the story in the form in which one first hears it. I first heard that one about two fine tippling actors, Robert Newton and Wilfred

Lawson. After a little light research I discovered that neither Lawson nor Newton had ever appeared in *Richard III*, let alone in the relevant roles. In his autobiography Sir Cedric Hardwicke places it somewhere in the nineteenth century but names no names. Peter O'Toole, relying on W. MacQueen Pope, a dodgy authority, awards it to Edmund Kean and George Cook, great Shakespearean lushes. I suspect the truth lies somewhere earlier with a barnstorming touring band. Oddly, not long ago a young actor approached me saying, 'I don't know what all that fuss is about Richard III and the Duke of Buckingham. Everybody knows it was Peter O'Toole and Richard Harris.' Needless to say, neither of those fine, drinking actors ever appeared in any role in this particular play.

Witty remarks tend to be handed down, too. Often they are awarded to acknowledged wits. Prefacing a remark with 'as Noel Coward/Bernard Shaw/Oscar Wilde/Evelyn Waugh said . . .' creates a promise of humour for the listener. Long ago I was told that the vocally orchidaceous Edith Evans had said of her near contemporary Isabel Jeans, 'Such a good actress, pity she's got such an affected voice.' The next time it was reported she was saying it of Kenneth Williams, 'Such a good actor, pity he's got such an affected voice.' Finally it was awarded to Maggie Smith considering Geraldine McEwen, who was taking over from her in *Lettice and Lovage*.

I recorded one of Dame Edith's famous lines in a collection. She lived in Albany, almost opposite Fortnum and Mason. During the war when exotic fruits were in short supply thanks to the U-boat blockade she was delighted to spot a pineapple on display in Fortnum. 'I'll have that,' she cried, proffering a pound note. The pineapple changed hands and she was shocked to see that with it she was only given back two shillings and sixpence. 'Keep the change,' she said imperiously. 'I trod on a grape on the way in.' Very soon a letter arrived from Melbourne, Australia. 'Dear Mr Sherrin, I have always heard that story ascribed to

Lilian Braithwaite and the fruit was a peach. It is almost certainly apocryphal.'

I had a chance to check one of Maggie Smith's stories at source. When she opened on Broadway in *Lettice and Lovage* she had as big a triumph as she had in London. She and Margaret Tyzack were appearing at the Barrymore, or was it the Longacre? – anyway, they back on to each other. The Longacre, or the Barrymore, was dark for the first part of Maggie's run. Eventually a new, lively, all-singing, all-dancing, all-drumming black show arrived to fill the empty house. At the first matinée Dame Maggie could hear them loud and clear through the walls. She was not pleased. When stars are not pleased managements appear quickly and the directors of the Shubert Organisation, which owned both theatres, were soon on the case. They apologised and said they should have thought of it. It had happened before. They had a stock of heavy, black velour curtains which would deaden the sound. Not a whisper would come through. When Maggie returned for the evening performance the stage manager greeted her with 'I think you'll be very happy, Dame Maggie. We've hung the blacks.' 'There was no need to go that far,' she said. Or at least that's what I was told she said. When I checked, she showed some relief. 'Thank God you've cleaned it up. What I actually said was "I know who I'd start with".'

Noel Coward has been accused of the authorship of innumerable dirty limericks and half the extra verses to 'Eskimo Nell' without anything to back the accusations up. Even the classic Coward off-the-cuff remark at the Queen's Coronation is disputed. It was a wet day and the undoubted star of the royal procession (after the Queen) was Queen Salote of Tonga – an enormous, genial figure who, in spite of the cold and the rain, insisted on riding in an open carriage waving vigorously to the cheering crowds. This did not please the little Sultan of Kelantan, who was sitting opposite her. Although he had gone to Austin Reed and kitted himself out with long johns, he was still freezing. 'It's all right for her,' he said bitchily, 'she's dressed from head to foot in tree bark.'

As they passed the balcony on which Coward was standing someone asked him, 'Who's that little man sitting opposite Queen Salote?' He is supposed to have replied, 'Her lunch.' I suggested that it could not be true because Coward had denied it, saying that it was in very bad taste, that he was a personal friend of Queen Salote and that she would be very hurt if it got back to her.

Soon after that I heard from the stylish actor John Moffat. He was playing in Shaw's *The Apple Cart* at the Haymarket Theatre at the time. Coward was giving his King Magnus. As he arrived for the evening performance Moffat and Hugh Manning were standing at the stage door. 'Who was that little man with Queen Salote?' they chorused. 'Her lunch,' Coward replied. I moaned about this saga of verification to Graham Payn – Coward's life-long companion. 'Oh no,' he told me. 'It wasn't Noel at all. It was Noel who asked the question. It was David Niven who said, "Her Lunch."' A few years ago I was talking about *Theatrical Anecdotes* at a charity dinner for the Duke of Edinburgh's Award Scheme. When I got to Queen Salote I could see the Duke waving at me. Not wanting to be interrupted in full flow, I ploughed on. I waited until after the speech to ask him about the waving. 'It was extraordinary,' he said. 'A few years after the Coronation I took *Britannia* round the world. When we stopped off in Malaya, all the sultans came on board and we had a very jolly dinner. It was going so well that I asked the table, 'Now, come on, which of you was "her lunch". They all screamed with laughter and pointed to the Sultan of Kelantan and said, "Him! Him!" The Sultan beamed and said, "Me! Me! I was her lunch!"' So I'm still not absolutely sure who first said it; but it does appear to have gone round the world remarkably quickly.

It's not only with theatre stories that you have to be careful.

I've always enjoyed the account of George Brown, when foreign secretary, at a diplomatic reception in Brasilia, the modern inland capital of Brazil. Standing beside a tall, imposing figure in a purple dress the already 'tired and emotional' statesman heard the band strike up. Turning to the tall, imposing figure in the purple dress he offered, 'Madame, will you waltz?' To which the tall, imposing figure in the purple dress replied, 'No, Mr Brown, and for three reasons. One: it is not a waltz. Two: it is the national anthem of Peru. Three: I am the Cardinal Archbishop of Lima.'

I believed this story to be true until I read Peter Paterson's biography of George Brown in which he proves conclusively that the foreign secretary never visited South America before, during or after his time in office. However, Lord Chalfont comes to our aid here. He swears that he was with George in Vienna when it happened there. I cling to the version I first heard. 'Cardinal Archbishop of Lima' has a ring to it.

A sporting tale which may be apocryphal concerns Sebastian Coe, the former middle-distance running champion. My main reason for hoping it is true is that it takes place at Lord's cricket ground and the MCC are tight-lipped about it when I ask. Sebastian Coe arrives at Lord's to be a guest in a hospitality box for a Test match. He goes to the wrong gate. The club servants on the gate are as rude as those at Lord's usually are. They examine his ticket. 'Wrong gate. Go round the "other gate".'

'But you don't understand. I'm late. I've missed an over already. I'm a guest.'

'Wrong gate. Go round the other gate.'

Then the fatal mistake. 'Don't you know who I am?'

'No.'

'I am Sebastian Coe.'

'Right, then you'll be able to run round the other gate all the quicker!'

A small cloud of doubt has grown over this tale since I heard a similar story about Linford Christie being refused membership to an exclusive golf club.

An A to Z shape suits the programme of *Theatrical Anecdotes* – Jeffrey Archer to Pia Zadora. I've told most of them in various other books so I won't repeat myself. However, some of the stories are racy. I devised a litmus test to indicate what audiences are up for. Fortunately the test is applied early on under the letter A – for Eileen Atkins. Back in the 1960s, when young women were burning their bras enthusiastically, Dame Eileen went shopping in Harrods. She does, she admits, conform to Russ Meyer's classification, 'insufficiently cantilevered'. As she approached the store she was aware of workmen on scaffolding doing what they always do as young women pass, whistling and yelling compliments; or, in Eileen's case, criticism. She was particularly riled by one man who shouted, ''Ardly worth 'er burnin' 'er bra, was it?' Furious, she shot into Harrods. She bought everything on her list and as her anger festered several things that were not. Still fuming she left the store and marched across to the scaffolding, looked up at the labourers and yelled, 'I expect you've all got small cocks, but I don't go around shouting about it!' She turned on her heel and it wasn't until she rounded the next corner that she realised she had come out of a quite different door from the one through which she entered.

There is usually a faintly embarrassed laugh on the 'small cocks' line if people think that is that; but it seems to liberate the audience to laugh twice as hard at the twist which comes after it.

One Atkins story I haven't printed before is perhaps pushing it for delivery to a civilian audience. Some years ago Eileen was in New York. She went with an American friend to see the film *Nicholas and Alexandra*. When Julian Glover appeared, grandly robed as an Orthodox bishop, she nudged her friend and said, 'Oh, that's my first husband.' Soon another familiar face appeared on the screen as another grand Russian. She confided that she'd had a little fling with him. Finally, as Lenin entered she giggled and admitted that there had once been some chemistry there. It was too much for the woman in the seat behind who said in loud disbelief to her companion, 'Now she thinks she's fucked Lenin!'

The story that depends on the response to 'Eileen at Harrods' is about Sir John Gielgud – the everlasting source of stories, often gaffes or, as they are known, 'Gielgoodies'. This is Gielgud not as an actor but as a director. He was rehearsing a play bound for London. The leading actor had a long speech and one morning he decided to pause during it. Sir John was on him immediately: 'Don't pause! Don't pause!'

'But John, it's a long speech. It gives me a moment to think of what's coming and it gives the audience a chance to take in what I've just said. Besides, I think it's rather effective.'

'No. No. You mustn't pause. We're coming to the West End.'

'But John, why can't I pause in the West End?'

'Never! I paused once in the West End and in that awful silence I heard a voice in the gallery say, "Oh, you beast! You've *come* all over my umbrella." Never pause in the West End!'

I first went to a Foyle's literary lunch in 1963 with the *TW3* team. Of the earlier visits odd memories cling. Alvilde Lees Milne saying, 'I do enjoy your little previews of your wireless programme. I hear them in my bath. Of course, I never hear the actual programme.' A lunch – then at the Dorchester hotel – which launched Anton Mossiman's new cookery book. Was his new scheme *cuisine naturelle*? The meal cannot have been supervised by Mossiman himself. I sat between Elizabeth David and Marguerite Patten. They hardly touched their food. Nor did I. There are two sadder memories. One took place at the Dorchester. It was Malcolm Muggeridge's last appearance. The men's room in the space reserved for guests of honour was entirely faced by reflecting glass. As I entered, poor Malcolm was trying despairingly to feel his way out and couldn't solve the problem of the mirrored wall. I managed to guide him through the door but when he came to speak the biting orator who had so often set the room on a roar could manage nothing until he finally pulled a scrap of paper from his pocket and said, 'I think I'd better read a prayer . . .'

Equally heartbreaking was Michael Redgrave's last appearance at the Grosvenor House. Christina Foyle had been assured that Michael – a victim of Parkinson's – would be able to say a few words. His son Corin, who had written his autobiographical book with him, would make the main speech. When Michael rose – on a top table at which so many of his peers, Guinness, Robson, Ashcroft, Richardson, were sitting – he found it impossible to put the words together. Looking around in an agonised silence he finally mumbled, 'No, I think I'll just tell you the words . . . of a song I learnt in Portsmouth as a very small boy . . . I have never forgotten them . . .' Sadly, on this occasion, he had. He sat down to shocked, sympathetic silence.

Foyle's lunches declined in popularity towards the end of Christina Foyle's life. In the great days when she inaugurated them she coaxed Shaw, Churchill, Kipling and hundreds of legendary names to speak – people fought for tickets. In the nineties audiences shrank to a few tables. There was speculation that there was no Foyle heir to the empire. Christina told me that her nephews showed no interest. One weekend she advised her husband, who was to die before her, that she was considering putting the firm's future in the hands of a promising assistant she had spotted. She would call him in on Monday and suggest that he took on the challenge. On Monday morning she arrived at the office to find he had already asked for an appointment. Ushered in, he explained that he had received a good offer. He proffered his resignation. Christina said nothing. He never learnt of the fortune he had passed up. I like to think his name was Tim Waterstone.

After Christina's death two nephews came forward. They

have modernised the firm, the shop and the luncheons – which are Christopher Foyle's speciality. My most bizarre experience was chairing the 75th Anniversary Lunch in the Great Room at the Grosvenor House. There was an audience of more than a thousand. Half of them previous guests of honour. I had Lady Thatcher on my right and Denis Healey on my left. I used a grace which Mervyn Stockwood wrote for me for the first Foyle's lunch I chaired: 'For the food we eat and the books we read, we give thanks to God, the Author of Life.'

'Very good,' said the Baroness. 'Very short. Very appropriate.'

I fell short of her standards when it came to the loyal toast. I hurried it. It was a shambles. 'All wrong,' she said. 'First you should say, "My Lords, Ladies and Gentlemen, will you charge your glasses?" Then you say, "My Lords, Ladies and Gentlemen, will you rise?" When you've got them up, and only then, do you say, "My Lords, Ladies and Gentlemen, the Queen!"'

She was right, of course. However, there were five speeches to come after mine during which I regained some of her favour. One of the five speakers was to be Larry Adler. I worried a little as Larry had been known to go on. It was a matter of months before he died. Perhaps he was already anticipating it. Instead of a speech he drew his miniature mouth organ from a pocket and began to play 'If You Were the Only Girl in the World'. This is one of those tunes in which the whole room feels impelled softly to join. They did. I found myself looking into Baroness Thatcher's eyes and singing, 'If you were the only girl in the world . . .' and hearing her answer in a robust baritone, '. . . and you were the only boy . . .'. It is, I think, the most surreal moment of my life.

CHAPTER 16

I Get a Kick Out of You . . .

'You must have met everyone,' people say, happily unaware of how fleeting were most of the meetings. One paragraph of chance encounters conveys the idea of how little it takes to be able to drop a name.

Martin Amis, small and perched precariously on a stool in the old Zanzibar in Great Queen Street in the eighties. A nod. John McEnroe at the carousel at Heathrow after a flight from Los Angeles: another nod as we reached for our bags and politely stood back for each other to grab. With Salvador Dali the silent relationship lasted for a few floors in an upward elevator at the St Regis, New York. His moustache quivered but not in acknowledgement. Arnold Schwarzenegger, one ride *down* a lot of floors in another elevator at the Drury Lane hotel, Chicago. We exchanged 'good mornings'. Bob Dylan once in the BBC canteen at Television Centre in 1965. Guitar in hand and harmonica round his neck he was making a brief appearance in a play by Ian Dallas. 'Hello,' he said. Irek Mukhamedov, backstage at a charity ballet show in the Banqueting Hall in Whitehall. 'How shall I introduce you?' 'Just say, "vorld's greatest dancer".'

I had lunch with Princess Margaret in the same hall. This time the charity occasion was John Dankworth and Cleo Laine's Wavendon All Music Plan. 'That's the window poor King Charles had to walk out of to be executed.' She pointed to it. 'At Windsor we still have the shirt he was wearing.' Princess Margaret was often quotable. Once at a cocktail party of Derek Hart's she asked me to come on to dinner at the Ritz with David Westbury. I said I couldn't. I had promised to visit Caryl Brahms who was not well 'and is quite old'. 'How old *is* Caryl?' I told her. 'My God! She's nearly as old as Mummy! You'd better go straight away. You may never see her again.' After the Aids charity *Hamlet* at Sadler's Wells she spotted Maurice Denham, who played the gravedigger. 'Oh! It's the lift man!' she cried. In the early thirties, before Maurice became an actor, he was a lift engineer. He helped to install the lifts at Broadcasting House and at York House, where he used to give the two excited young princesses rides up and down.

One night I gave Princess Margaret a lift home from a Dankworth/Laine programme at Ronnie Scott's. As we sailed along the Fulham Road she pointed to a derelict shop. 'Fortunately that has closed,' she said. 'They used to sell dresses. It was called the Countess of Snowdon. People thought I was selling my old clothes. I was going to sue them; now they've gone bankrupt I don't have to.' 'It must have been very difficult for you,' I offered unwisely. 'After all, you've got that restaurant at the back of your house called the Maggie Jones.' 'Ned! I *am* the Countess of Snowdon. I have *never* been called Maggie Jones!'

Visiting Los Angeles, she wanted to know about hotels. 'In the last one where I stayed the beds were so uncomfortable. The lady-in-waiting and I had to drag all the cushions in from the sitting room and pile them up on the bed. When I climbed to the top I felt like the princess and the pea. While in LA she wanted to meet Starsky and Hutch – 'of Starsky and Hutch.

Not Hutch, Starsky. Can you arrange it?' I got Robert Stigwood to fix an introduction.

She came to *The Mitford Girls* and seemed to enjoy it. Anton Dolin tried to get the Queen Mother to come as well. He was a friend of her private secretary, Sir Martin Charteris. Charteris declined on her behalf. 'She says she met all the Mitford sisters in real life. She doesn't feel she needs to see them on the stage.'

I met her only once, at Fleur Cowles's set of rooms in Albany. I asked her if she would confirm a story. 'What is the story?'

Chips Channon, the diarist, was notorious for commissioning an entire dinner service in gold in the thirties, not long after the Coronation.

'It's about Chips Channon's gold dinner service.'

'How does it go?'

'Someone is said to have asked you if you'd seen it.'

'And what am I supposed to have said in reply?'

'"Oh no! We're not nearly grand enough to be asked there."'

She gave one of those silvery laughs old ladies are believed to use in fiction.

'Ah yes! I think I may very well have said that.'

She went on to discuss whether she should have a glass of champagne or a cup of tea when she got back to Clarence House. 'Tea, I think.'

Old ladies are often good value. Just after coming down from Oxford I was asked by a contemporary to a party in Paulton's Square. The host was Margaret Rutherford's not very rich nephew. The drink was scarce. What was there was Madeira. Dame Margaret circled the room holding her glass aloft, sipping occasionally and murmuring, 'Ambrosia! Ambrosia!'

She was believed to have been furious when she heard that Dame Edith Evans was to play Cleopatra. 'There! Edith has beaten me to a role again!' It did not do Dame Edith much good. She, the production and her Antony, Godfrey Tearle, were roundly criticised, partly for being too old. Another senior lady,

Margaret Harris, of the brilliant design team Motley, told me when she was in her nineties that Robert Helpmann renamed the production after Barrie's play, *The Old Lady Shows Her Medals*. He called it *The Old Lady Shows Her Nipples*. Margaret – always known as Percy – was watching a rehearsal from the stalls when a large black actor playing a Nubian suddenly pointed to Evans and Tearle up on the stage and whispered, 'Those two old people are going to lose somebody a lot of money.'

Edith had her rooms in Albany redecorated when she was out on tour. The interior designer was thrilled to find a famous Sickert painting of her hanging behind a wardrobe. It had been missing for years. He put it in pride of place above the chimney piece. 'Why', he asked when she admired the improvements, 'did you hang it behind the wardrobe?' 'I expect it was because there was a hook there.'

Starring in Enid Bagnold's play *The Chalk Garden*, Edith was attacked by constipation. Being a Christian Scientist, she refused treatment and would not see her impresario, 'Binkie' Beaumont. Box office dwindled as she stayed away. He considered replacing her with Gladys Cooper, who had played the part in New York. Edith called his partner, John Perry: 'Binkie is talking of replacing me with Gertrude Cooper,' she moaned – an old actor's trick, mixing up a name to demean a rival.

Finally, she took her medicine.

One day I collected Edith from Albany to take her to lunch at the Café Royal. I was guiding her downstairs when the door of a set on the ground floor opened and an elderly man emerged with a woman who looked up and spotted the formidable dame descending. 'Hello,' she cooed.

Edith looked at her with blank incomprehension as through a lorgnette.

'It's Lady Clark,' said Lady Clark helpfully.

Edith swung round to me in her best Lady Bracknell manner.

'Why is she telling me that?' she intoned. 'I know perfectly well who she is.'

I first met Alan Clark when I went to Saltwood Castle to film a later aborted sketch for an ITV series in the mid-seventies. He and Jane were affable and attended on the filming with keen lay interest. When his *Diaries* were first published in 1993 Alan came on *Loose Ends*. We had an entertaining discussion and he was amused by a story of a disastrous cheese-rolling competition which had been written up for me for the opening monologue.

'Richard Ryder [a Tory whip] says you're all right,' he offered as an accolade and as proof of friends whom he considered influential.

It wasn't until I saw a television profile of Alan that I realised how many of his contradictory characteristics I experienced in ten minutes or so. The willingness to flatter, the reckless pursuit of his own objectives, the easy charm and the wily instinct for survival. The flattery over, the monologue bore fruit when Bill Alexander and John Stalker of the Birmingham Repertory Theatre persuaded him to grant them the rights to stage a version of the *Diaries*. Asked who should bring these to the theatre, Alan suggested me. With Keith Waterhouse we concocted a formula in which the Alan character would be making a speech as the honoured guest at a Foyle's lunch. The actors surrounding him at the table, along with a Christina Foyle figure and a toastmaster, would play a multitude of roles as people in his life. For example, Christina would metamorphose into Maggie Thatcher and other senior ladies. The toastmaster would lose his red jacket to be various heavy Tories and so on. It was a technique which we had used to good effect in Keith's *Jeffrey Bernard is Unwell*.

There was a great deal of delay caused by Alan's literary agent. I was never sure how much stemmed from Alan himself. Whenever we spoke or corresponded he was full of enthusiasm and dismissed any suggestion of delaying tactics. Keith finished a fine first act and we were about to set a date with Birmingham when the atmosphere changed. News of the play emerged at the time that Alan saw his chance to get back into the House of Commons as Member for Kensington and Chelsea. The portcullis came down with a bang.

Jane had been alarmed by the recurrence of press interest when news of the play was leaked. Indeed, she told me at a David Frost party, 'I put my foot down.' However, it was the prospect of getting back into the House which swayed Alan. There was no way he was going to rock the boat with a theatrical sensation.

Quotes are often misremembered. In much the same way that Canute stands for arrogantly commanding the tides to go away when historically he was demonstrating to sycophantic courtiers that he had no such power, Alan will always be labelled as the person who fingered Michael Heseltine as 'a man who bought his own furniture'. He points out punctiliously in his diary that the phrase was Michael Joplin's. Somehow I don't think he objected to the misattribution in the long term.

I read after Alan's death that Bill Bryden had been licensed to do a stage adaptation. That moment also passed. Finally the BBC made the television series, which had many good points and a fine performance from John Hurt – edged, I thought, too much towards self-pity. It did not quite relish the 'bastard' side of Alan which was so manifestly there.

To get back to old ladies. The worst bit of dressing-room manners I witnessed was when the elderly Lotte Lenya went round to see Lila Kedrova, who was playing the part Lenya had created on Broadway in *Cabaret* in the West End. It was after the last matinée before the first night. Lila was taut with nerves. Lenya, who had been watching conspicuously from a box, swept into her dressing room and asked if she was enjoying London. Did she have good digs? Was the food agreeing with her? She did everything but mention the performance and then swept out again, leaving a shattered artist.

Between two old Diaghilev ballerinas there was a more civilised tingle. Dame Alicia Markova gave a small cocktail party in New York for Caryl Brahms. Among the guests was another great dancer, Alexandra Danilova. Dame Alicia mentioned that she was working on her autobiography. The competitive spirit had not died. 'Me, who am not dame,' said Danilova, 'have written two autobiographies.'

Bernard Levin invited me to appear with Alfred Hitchcock and Ian Fleming's widow, Anne, on a late-night interview show in the sixties. In a sycophantic moment I decided to tell a story which I thought flattered the star guest. An extremely nervous, claustrophobic friend of mine had gone to the cinema to see an innocuous film. Somehow he went into the wrong auditorium. The cinema was packed. He finally found a single empty seat in the centre of the stalls. When the censor's certificate revealed that the film was *Psycho* his instinct was to run for it – he knew the movie's and Hitchcock's reputation. The choice was between the terror of staying and the disturbance of a quick exit. As he was marginally more shy than scared he decided to sit it out. He lasted as long as the shower scene and the stabbing of Janet Leigh. He held on to the sides of his seat and thought he had withstood the worst when he heard the man who was sitting next to him chuckling appreciatively in a low and sinister register. 'Heh-heh-heh!' My friend was finished and fled the theatre. I offered this as a tribute to the master of suspense. Hitchcock was not impressed. He brushed it aside with a contemptuous sniff.

'You must have very naive friends, Mr Sherrin,' was all he said.

Gore Vidal is a friend who, sadly, I have lost. I first met him in John Bowen's Fulham flat soon after coming down from Oxford. It was a small drinks party: Stephen Runciman, Gore and his companion Howard Austen. When John was still at Oxford he reviewed one of Gore's early novels, *The City and the Pillar*, for *Isis*, under the title, *Kiss Me Hot Lips, I'm Asbestos*. That intrigued Gore and brought about their friendship.

After that I bumped into him off and on over the years. Once we were dining together in Rome. A precise bit of social fencing followed. The great film director Michelangelo Antonioni arrived at another table. According to Gore, this presented a tricky problem of etiquette. It was not proper for either maestro to come to the other's table – so they both got up, met in the middle, had a brief chat and then returned to their companions.

Sometimes we met at dinner at Maria St Just's house; often in radio and television studios. Thanks to Gore I can also add Bernardo Bertolucci – he came to Gore's Roman flat for a cocktail – and Muriel Spark (I walked her home after dinner, early seventies) to my list of glancing acquaintances. Then there was the occasion when I matched him against Peregrine Worsthorne on *BBC-3* in 1965.

One year Gore flew in to Edinburgh for the festival. He was put up at Drue Heinz's poets' retreat. 'I agreed to stay if the poets retreated before I arrived.' Then he came south to talk about his book, *Hollywood*. He had discovered that the Gores – whom he always assumed stemmed from some landed, aristocratic Irish family; perhaps the Earls of Aran or at least the Gore-somebodies – came of humble English stock, from the village of Nether Wallop. All this made mockery of his one unknowing visit to the ancestral inches some years earlier. As a *Sunday Times* literary joke Stephen Pile set up a Nether Wallop arts festival. Jessye Norman, Wayne Sleep and Peter Cook all went along with it. Gore was to sign and sell his new book at the local greengrocer's. I drove down with him and slipped in twelve remaindered copies of one of my own books and outsold the bestseller. We went on to lunch with Maria St Just at Wilbury, where he teased Taki, just out of jail on his cocaine conviction, unmercifully.

After his Edinburgh trip I was to record an interview with Gore for *Loose Ends*. I gave him and Howard lunch beforehand with my producer, Ian Gardhouse. As always he offered nuggets of good gossip. He had developed an interest in Margaret Thatcher's forebears. His well-researched theory was that she might be a second cousin, once or twice removed, of the late Lady Diana Cooper. Few people doubt that Lady Diana was the child of Harry Cust, nephew of the third and last Lord Brownlow. She was not therefore a fully fledged Manners, the family name of her official father, the Duke of Rutland.

Gore's theory was that her actual father, Harry Cust, was notorious for cutting a swath through ladies of all classes. Mrs Thatcher's grandmother had been in service at Belton, the Rutland seat. Since the overly romantic Harry had fathered many children in the area, why not with the servants? An Eton master who taught Cust reckoned that he had a brilliant future and a better prospect of being prime minister than his contemporaries, the Lords Rosebery and Curzon. How appropriate if his early promise was finally realised three generations later in Mrs T, his putative great-grandchild.

Gore raised the question with Lady Diana, who had acknowledged her own parentage. She thought the theory 'only too likely . . . but it is always important to check the precise dates'. A supporting coincidence was the fact that when Mrs Thatcher moved to No. 10 Downing Street she borrowed the Belton silver for the duration of her tenure as Prime Minister. Then it was sent back.

We laughed a great deal over lunch. I had a column in *The Times* then. I made copious notes under Gore's nose. When we had recorded the interview I went home and wrote up my jottings. They were duly published in the column that Saturday.

I was bewildered the next week to read a letter to the editor from Gore protesting that a confidence had been betrayed. He would never talk to 'a print journalist' again. As he knew about the column and had seen the note-taking, I was dismayed. It is hard to think of a more amusing and provocative companion. I wrote a letter of mystified apology to no effect. Then I wrote another at Maria St Just's suggestion. She tried to arrange a rapprochement. No luck. I regret the loss of a prized acquaintance. I have tried to think of a rational explanation for his decision. Could it go back to outselling him in Nether Wallop? Was it delayed revenge for a piece picking up an error of his? In another article he had poked fun at the pair of ballet shoes which an anonymous balletomane placed on Diaghilev's tomb in Venice. Gore mocked them, both were for left feet. I queried this with the ballerina Nadia Nerina. 'Gore should know better,' she said. 'He wrote a good ballet novel. Ballet shoes don't have a left or a right – they mould in practice to the feet of the dancer.' Perhaps Gore simply loves a feud. I wish that this time he hadn't chosen me. Maybe he just got bored. It's a very efficient way to end a friendship.

Now, whenever he brings out a book, a *Loose Ends* producer tells me, 'We've been offered Gore Vidal.' I say, 'He won't come.' Sure enough, they later get a call from his publishers, who have by now checked with their author. No Gore. A pity. I would like to have written to him on the recent death of Howard, his long-time companion, but I do not think the gesture would have been welcomed.

His last *Loose Ends* interview was well up to Vidal standard. There was an echo of his career as a playwright. He once described that, in a paraphrase of Emerson, as 'From failure to classic with no intervening success.' He had recently been approached by the flamboyant Broadway producer David Merrick, who wanted to turn his play *A Visitor to a Small Planet* into a musical. Merrick sent the script to Jerry Herman, the composer and lyric-writer of *Hello Dolly* and *Mame*. Herman told Gore that he had passed as it was 'too old-fashioned'. 'Yes, Jerry,' Gore said, without blinking, 'that's why we thought of you.'

His *Hollywood* book was full of out of the way sidelights on American history. Where else would you find the origin of the phrases 'a schoolgirl complexion' and 'a smoke-filled room'? Or the inventor of 'puffed wheat'? An early appearance by Elsa Maxwell and a late one by Proust's male brothel-keeper (researched by Vidal after the Second World War)? The revelation that Woodrow Wilson had 'vaudevillian comic timing'? And the news that one of Douglas Fairbanks Senior's gym buddies, a former flying ace, had three testicles?

I queried this last claim. I was rewarded with a forthright, 'I knew because he was my father.' Eugene Vidal, later an aeroplane tycoon and an admirer of Amelia Earhart, had, his son insists, this strange pawnbroker's packet. It is not, I understand, inherited.

I met Salman Rushdie at a *South Bank Show* annual review. We met for lunch beforehand. The place name next to me said, 'Harold Pinter'. It was the name which always stood in for Rushdie to confuse potential assassins immediately after the *fatwa*. During lunch we got on to the subject of old-style first-night theatre rows. I gave an account of the uproar at John Osborne's musical *The World of Paul Slickey*. Innocently Melvyn Bragg turned to Rushdie and said, 'Nobody ever makes a fuss like that when we bring out a book, do they, Salman?'

Philip Roth came with Claire Bloom to Patrick Garland's wedding to Alexandra Bastedo in the Chichester Cathedral and to the reception afterwards in Bishop Kemp's quarters in the cathedral grounds. Edward Kemp, the young teenage son of the bishop approached him. 'Mr Roth,' he asked, 'may I shake you by the hand?' After his wish had been granted and he slipped away (to become in time an excellent writer/director), Philip Roth whispered, 'Women at literary luncheons across America have run a mile rather than shake the hand of the man who wrote *Portnoy's Complaint*.'

J. B. Priestley? Going back to the stalls on the first night of Peter Brook's revolutionary production of *A Midsummer Night's Dream* at Stratford.

'What d'ye think?' he asked.

'It's extraordinary.'

'It's rubbish!'

It was at Ken Follett's old house in Cheyne Walk that I met Erica Jong. I am ashamed to say that I have never read Ms Jong's work. Ignorantly I thought that the only title of hers that I knew, *Fear of Flying*, was a trendy self-help book. So when I asked her if she had ever written a novel, she turned to her companion on her other side for the rest of the dinner.

Having talked to A. L. Rowse on *Midweek*, I met him again while I was recording *Ninety Not Out*, an occasional series for Radio 4, featuring nonagenarians. We went down to see him in Cornwall. At the door the housekeeper said suspiciously, 'Have you brought your wife?' I said, 'No, I don't have one. I've come with my producer.' 'He'll be pleased to hear that,' she confided. He couldn't have been more affable. I confess to buttering him up with fulsome praise for his identification of the Dark Lady of the Sonnets as Emilia Bassano. It led to a flow of confessions, including naming the great love of his life as Adam von Trott. A few weeks later he was interviewed by Naim Attallah for the *Oldie* magazine. I was delighted to read that while many fools denied his find of the true Dark Lady, 'really intelligent people, like Ned Sherrin', accepted it immediately.

The most startling remark on the *Ninety Not Out* series came from the late Anthony Havelock Allan, then aged ninety-two, the producer of films from *Brief Encounter* to *Ryan's Daughter*. I asked him what his earliest memory was. He thought for a few seconds. 'I suppose it was my circumcision.' It happened in Yorkshire when he was two years old. He could still remember, and feel, the pain.

I met Hammond Innes and his wife at Christina Foyles's

country home, Beeleigh Abbey in Essex. Sir Arthur Bryant, clearly bored by our conversation and frantically looking for someone more august with whom to talk, escaped as Mr and Mrs Hammond Innes came into the room. Mrs Innes made a bee-line for me. 'Ralph recorded the most extraordinary radio programme last night,' she said proudly. 'He had to think of all his favourite bits of literature and then he and some actors read them out to an audience.' 'Ah, yes,' I said. '*With Great Pleasure* – it's a very good programme. I did it myself a few years ago.'

'Nonsense, you couldn't possibly have! They only ask very well-known people!'

With playwrights, I'd better begin with Noel Coward. He was a casual friend of Caryl Brahms. Only on one occasion did I feel that I had engaged his attention. He was always concerned and interested in very young theatre practitioners. I followed him round backstage at the Streatham Hill Empire where a revue was limping its way hopefully towards the West End. It did not arrive at its destination, but Coward's combination of tactful compliments to the cast without offering a certainty of the big time was a lesson in 'going round'. He was also, of course, sparkling with big names. I fell into a no man's land in between.

I did catch one off-the-cuff Coward crack. I went to see Arthur Miller's autobiographical play *After the Fall* in New York on the same night that Coward went – escorting Claudette Colbert. As we all left the theatre I could see Claudette trying to distance herself from Coward and the remark he had been saving up. This was a bad mistake. It meant that he had to shout what he might have whispered, 'D'you know, Claudette. I think', he shouted, 'I preferred *This Is Your Life* when it was a television programme.'

My friend Burt Shevelove was driving through Hyde Park with Claudette when she began to ask him the names of trees and flowers as they passed them. 'What's that, Burtie?' 'That's an oak.' 'What's that, Burtie?' 'That's an ash.' 'And what are those little white things, Burtie?' 'Those, Claudette, are Englishmen.'

Burt was famously once in the Everard Baths, the gay bath-house in New York, when his advances were furiously declined by a handsome, much younger man. His rebuff was so over the top that Burt summoned all his dignity and said, 'A simple rejection would have sufficed.'

Returning for a second time to see the London production of Sondheim's *Company*, Burt arrived at the bar at Her Majesty's Theatre in time to hear a woman ask in clipped terms, 'How long is the second act?' The barmaid said, 'About an hour, I think.' 'Oh!' The woman pondered a moment and then came to a decision: 'I think I'll go home and watch the King of Denmark's funeral on television.'

To get back to Coward. The only time we communicated was at a party which Julian Pettifer gave in the late sixties. Caryl Brahms and I were rehearsing and writing our musical about Marie Lloyd. I asked Coward if he had ever seen her. I assumed that he must have. He was an inveterate theatrical enthusiast. It was unthinkable that he had not seen the great British music-hall performer. He was twenty-two when she died. However, he had not. He was fascinated and slightly guilty. For half an hour I told him as much as I had been able to ferret out from the various old music-hall stars who had known her well. It was interesting to catch the conversational lion in a listening mode. I once interviewed another great talker, Peter Ustinov. Halfway through I found that I was doing all the talking and Peter was proving a great listener. I swapped roles quickly.

I shared a doctor, Patrick Woodcock, with Coward. Patrick told me that one day when he was seeing Coward he talked, as doctors often do, a lot about his own ills. He complained that his memory was not what it was: 'I get these lacunae.' Ever afterwards when they met Coward would say, 'Ah! Here comes the Lily of Lacunae.'

Since his appearance long ago in 1957 on *Tonight*, Jonathan Miller and I have only crossed paths occasionally. In the seventies he produced Chekhov's *The Three Sisters* at the Cambridge Theatre. I came out behind two American matinée matrons. One mourned sadly to her companion, 'More a play than a show, wasn't it?' On another occasion Jonathan was directing the late Denis Quilley as Sir Benjamin Backbite in *The School for Scandal* at the National Theatre. Quilley was a fine actor and a generous, forthright man. He later told me that he found the role of the archetypal, bitchy gossip hard to fathom. Eventually he took his troubles to his director. Jonathan considered the problem for a moment and then said, 'Do you know Ned Sherrin?' 'Yes!' cried Denis. All was explained and Denis was very good in the part.

Whenever I meet Harold Pinter he is polite, expansive and genial. I particularly admire his monographs on Arthur Wellard and Anew McMaster. It is perhaps unfair to collect stories that emphasise his solemn side. But, go on . . . Rehearsing at Chichester one morning during the Balkan wars he was greeted with a cheery 'Good morning, how are you?' 'Good morning? What's good about it? How am I? What sort of question is that when people are dying in Bosnia?' Nigel Williams swears that when Harold was running through a play at the Royal Court he heard a rumbling noise. 'What's that noise?' 'It's the underground, Harold.' The Circle Line runs under the theatre. 'The trains must be stopped.' When my friends Neil and Anne Benson took their thirteen-year-old son Mark to audition for a child's part in a Pinter play at the National Theatre with Peggy Ashcroft, no less, starring, Mark was given a script to read. After one sentence Pinter piped up, 'That's a *funny* line.' Mark looked straight at him. 'I don't think so.' He failed to get the role.

There is a story – apocryphal, I suspect – that Pinter once canvassed Tom Stoppard in the cause of changing the name of the Comedy Theatre, where many of his successes have been staged, to The Pinter. Stoppard is said to have replied, 'Wouldn't it be much simpler to change your name to "Comedy", Harold?'

Alistair Beaton and I were commissioned in the late eighties to write a twentieth-century version of George Villiers's 1671 play *The Rehearsal*. Sheridan, of course, came up with an eighteenth-century version in *The Critic, or A Trajedy Rehears'd*. We called ours *The Rehearsal, or The Emperor's New Play*. Terry Hands, who was running the Royal Shakespeare Company at the time, had asked us to provide a vehicle for Derek Jacobi. He suggested *The Rehearsal*. We had a wonderful time devising a play starring, written and directed by a monomaniac 'man of the theatre' for the Royal Shavian Company, sponsored by Welsh Widows Insurance and known as the RSWWC.

The pretentious, banal author we created was fatally addicted to plagiarism but in denial. We told the story of Tolstoy as a musical, backwards from his death, parodying David Hare, Howard Brenton, Pinter and many other avant-garde playwrights. My favourite scene was Alistair's brilliant pastiche of a Stoppard version of Tolstoy's death at Astapovo railway station. It combines Tom's technique of gathering surprising people together in an incongruous time and place, throwing off puns, jokes and obscure scientific and political arguments:

CHERTKOV: Doctor, what are we going to do? His fever is worse.

DOCTOR: I suggest an enema.

TOLSTOY: Oh no, not that.

CHERTKOV: An enema will do you good, Leo. It is a treatment much favoured by the common people.

TOLSTOY: An enema of the people? Is Ibsen here? . . .

[*Enter Kipling*]

KIPLING: Oh it's Rudyard this, an' Rudyard that, and Rudyard go to hell . . .
[The bedclothes stir and we realise there is someone in bed with Tolstoy]
LENIN: Allow me to introduce myself. Vladimir Ilyich Lenin.
KIPLING: But it's thank you, Mr Kipling.
When my cakes begin to sell . . .
LENIN: I want that man shot.
TOLSTOY: I am an apostle of non-violence. I get letters from Gandhi. I will not have Reds in my bed. Get out!
LENIN: All life is thesis and antithesis. Through a dialectical process . . .
TOLSTOY: This man is taking dialectical liberties . . .

Mrs Tolstoy drops in for a quick word with her husband about the mystery of wave particle duality. Told to leave, she makes way for Isadora Duncan. Seeing a new phonograph sent to Tolstoy by Eddison himself, Isadora puts on a record and dances, trailing her scarf near the revolving phonograph.

[Enter Joe Orton]
ORTON: Sorry I'm late. I was at my mother's funeral. Christ, that gravedigger knew how to give head . . . There aren't any Arab boys around here, are there?
LENIN: Pushkin. He had Arab blood.
ORTON: Did he? Will he do it for fifty copecks? . . .

We delivered a draft and never heard another thing. Soon Terry Hands was replaced by Adrian Noble. However, looking at it again recently I wish we had been indulged. Perhaps a reading?

Tom Stoppard called me when he was invited to start work on the American screenplay for *Shakespeare in Love*. I gave him a copy of the Brahms–Simon classic novel *No Bed for Bacon* about which so many correspondents wrote to me alleging plagiarism when the film came out. In borrowing the book Tom had sought to avoid these charges by not duplicating the jokes. Indeed, apart from the central situation, only one moment pays direct homage to the novel – Shakespeare practising various ways of writing his name: 'Shaksper, Shakespere, Shickspob . . .' It is not surprising that three of the greatest humorists of the century, Tom Stoppard, Caryl Brahms and S. J. Simon, confronted by Shakespeare, Burbage and a young noblewoman (daughter of a nouveau riche in *Shakespeare in Love*) should come up with similar stories. I was happy to give Tom a written clearance when his studio producers worried that allegations of plagiarism might prejudice the Oscar for Original Screenplay which he eventually shared.

As the battle for the Oscars hotted up another American author of an Elizabethan bodice-ripper sought to bring an action for plagiarism against the film-makers. No more has been heard of that case.

The number of letters and phone calls I got from Brahms and Simon fans from all over the country testified to their protective affection for a book which, along with their *Don't, Mr Disraeli*, invented the idiom of anachronistic, historical humour which would lead to *Monty Python's Life of Brian*, *Blackadder* and *Shakespeare in Love*. The furore over the film created a demand for a reprint of the novel. It has gone through several new editions. I added a subtitle, *The Story of Shakespeare and Lady Viola in Love*. Had Simon not died suddenly in 1948 one of their possible projects was *The Brahms–Simon Bible*. Caryl had dearly hoped that *No Bed* might be filmed. Alec Guinness and Ealing came near to doing it: but if she had to choose a writer to tackle the subject after her death she would probably have asked for Tom Stoppard, for whom she had great admiration.

It is hard not to meet writers, actors and directors if you host the *Evening Standard* Awards for twelve or so years, as I did. It was easily the most congenial 'presenting' job. Each occasion was a happy reunion of people who enjoyed to catch up with one another's news. It ended for me when Max Hastings became editor of the *Evening Standard* and foolishly sacked Michael Owen, his invaluable showbiz editor. I lost out as part of the old, discredited regime. It has been small consolation that the replacement hosts have often been inappropriate and the 'star' presenters dumbed down to minor TV celebrities instead of the international stars whose arms Michael used to twist. His unique contacts book and his sympathetic manner gave him easy access. I can also corral the Shaffer twins, Christopher Hampton, Alan Bennett, Alan Ayckbourn, Stephen Poliakoff, Patrick Marber and a long list of 'Most Promising Playwrights' and 'Best Play' authors into my store of casual acquaintances. Add all the leading directors and any number of actors. Who to pick out? Dame Flora Robson on *Tonight* – 'If I have to cry I think of those seventy-one poor boys who went down in the submarine *Thetis* in the bay of Liverpool in 1939. The tears just flow.' Albert Finney in the Grill and Cheese, Coventry Street, asked about his first big West End success *Billy Liar* after the first preview – 'Well, it's not exactly epic.' The Grill and Cheese on the site of a Lyons Corner House now houses the ghastly Planet Hollywood. In the late fifties and early sixties it was an after-theatre oasis with a plain and practical menu used by everyone from Dame Edith to Georgia Brown, John Gielgud to Kenneth Williams, and Coral Browne long before her happy marriage to Vincent Price.

I was immediately on guard on seeing her in another restaurant – John Schlesinger and Geoffrey Sharp's Le Carosse in Chelsea in the seventies. I had been called up by the vice-president of Columbia Pictures, John Van Eyssen. A friend of his family, Jeremy Railton, had arrived from Johannesburg that day. John intended to entertain him. Suddenly he was called out of town. Would I look after Jeremy, who knew no one else in

London? He arrived on time in Wellington Square and I opened the door to a twenty-something who looked like a Walt Disney prince. At Le Carosse I was filling him in on the London theatrical scene when Coral arrived with another actress, Jill Melford. We would have to run the gauntlet when we left the restaurant, as seemed likely, before them. Sure enough, as we passed their table I stopped to say hello and introduce Jeremy. I was aware that they were looking him up and down. He was and is extraordinarily good looking. So I said, 'I don't think you know Mr Jeremy Railton. Miss Coral Browne, Miss Jill Melford' – still no word. As the silence became oppressive I thought I'd better break it, so to fill the awkward gap I added, 'He just arrived from South Africa this morning.' 'Ha!' Coral pounced. 'Got the trip wires at Waterloo Station again, have we?'

Long before Coral met Vincent Price I asked him to dinner at my house one night along with Kenneth Williams and Bishop Stockwood. Mervyn had come direct from a confirmation and was wearing the full purple. 'It's not fair,' said Vincent. 'If I'd known it was fancy dress . . . I've got much better drag than that at home.'

I have always wanted to interview Dennis Hopper, if only to ask my preferred first question: 'Did you ever see the whole of Edward Albee's *Who's Afraid of Virginia Woolf?*' It is a three-act play. When I saw the original production in New York with Uta Hagen and Arthur Hill, I sat next to a young woman who bit her nails throughout the first act. There was an empty seat beside her. Through the second act it was occupied by Dennis Hopper. For the third act both seats were empty. I would like to know.

I was in the line-up to meet the Queen and the Duke of Edinburgh at Cameron Mackintosh's charity celebration of his career at the Lyceum Theatre, *Hey, Mr Producer!* The programme opened with a little boy in a kilt listening to Julian

Slade play the *Salad Days* magic piano – the incident which triggered young Cameron's obsession with musical theatre. During the royal parade backstage the boy stood next to Cameron, both wearing kilts. I was near enough to hear the Queen ask, 'Is this your son, Sir Cameron?' and to see Stephen Sondheim and Julia McKenzie suppressing giggles at this unlikely parentage.

Although the Queen is usually well briefed, some bits of information elude her. After my second Royal Variety performance, where I introduced a sequence of songs, she did ask one question: 'Do you often get up on the stage and do this talking thing?' When she gave me my CBE she said, 'I expect it's for television, isn't it?' I said, 'Yes, Ma'am, and I think the citation mentions theatre.' 'Oh! How long have you been doing that?' 'About forty years, Ma'am.' 'Oh.'

My very first glimpse of a royal had been in the 1930s, from the roadside of the Fosse Way at Lydford. We were bussed up from Barton St David C of E School to line the damp route as King George VI and Queen Elizabeth made a royal progress down to the Duchy of Cornwall. We waved our little Union Jacks enthusiastically and a gloved hand waved back.

Speaking once before the Duke of Edinburgh at a luncheon I did a now long-forgotten joke about Prince Andrew – then in his romantic heyday. Prince Philip opened with 'If we're going to tell royal jokes . . . I was in Houston, Texas, a while ago to raise money for the World Wildlife Fund. They put me on the television and they obviously thought no one would know who I was. So they explained. They put up a picture of Diana and said, "That's *not* the one he married." Then they put up a picture of the Duchess of York and said, "That's not the one he married." Then they put up one of the Queen, on a wet day, looking sad at a funeral, and said, "*That's* the one he married!"'

The Princess of Wales was another 'line-up' acquaintance. There was one more intimate near miss. A friend had told me that one of his restaurants – he had several – was doing well in the evenings but languished at lunchtime. Some time later he rang to ask me to have lunch there, muttering in tones of heavily muffled secrecy that 'a royal person' would be there. From the vagueness of the invitation I understood that he wanted me to take a table and bring a few friends to dress the restaurant, which would impress his royal guest, whoever it might be. Something cropped up on the day appointed. It was impossible to get a group together. I left a message saying that, sadly, I couldn't make it. The next day I got a call from my would-be host: 'Princess Diana was very disappointed that you couldn't come. There were only to be the four of us.' As it happened, I sat next to her at a dinner at the Garrick a couple of Sundays later, a charity do, part of the Covent Garden Festival. I made my confession and my apologies and we laughed. That was the last time I saw her. In the way we know where we were when we heard of Kennedy's death, so it is with Diana. I woke in the early morning and thought it was a dream. When I woke again the radio was still telling the same story and I knew that it was not.

I met her brother at a party of Shusha Guppy's. He said he was interested in 'the media'. I arranged for him to do a recorded report for *Loose Ends*. He did quite well. We were arranging for him to do another when the first was transmitted. His friends told him we were sending him up – which was not the case – and he flounced out of the second recording.

Politicians pass like intercity trains. *Loose Ends* is a busy catchment area. Michael Portillo, Douglas Hurd, Iain Duncan Smith – usually they come along after they are out of office and bearing a book. Tony Benn was on *Loose Ends* and later, coming up to chat at a Westminster cocktail party, he offered, 'I saw you were talking to Hattersley, so I waited until he'd gone . . .' Enoch Powell on *Any Questions?* explained beforehand that he liked a full bladder. He debated with more vigour. Ronald Reagan at a lunch. I still have the photograph. He appears to be laughing. I do not remember how I provoked that. Oswald Mosley, a voice on the telephone and then footsteps on an echoing floor as he went to fetch his wife, whom I had telephoned at Temple de la Gloire when we were planning *The Mitford Girls*. My first *Any Questions?* was back in the post-*TW3* sixties. Other panellists included Dr Edith Summerskill and the playwright Alan Melville. The original chairman, Freddie Grisewood, still presided; physically very frail, vocally resonant. A question came up about marriage. He surveyed Melville and me. 'A question about marriage and we've got two bachelors. How queer!' Edith Summerskill nudged me and in a stentorian aside bellowed, 'Did he say "queer"?'

Through Caryl Brahms I met a lot of dancers. Notably, Ulanova, when she came to Covent Garden with the first visit of the Bolshoi Ballet. Nina Latta, Maria St Just's aunt, was an occasional interpreter for her. One day the ballerina was photographed by Cecil Beaton. When Beaton had finished he wanted a picture of himself with Ulanova. He handed the camera to Nina and showed her what to press. She was very proud of her effort, which she thought equalled Beaton's: 'Me, I ask myself, this photography – is it the man or is it the machine?'

Nureyev occasionally gatecrashed late-night parties I gave at Dover Street after *TW3*. He would grab a drink, circle the room, collect the man of his choice and disappear with him into the night. At the Ad-Lib club in Leicester Square I saw him approach Gordon Waller, the infinitely better-looking singer in the pop duo Peter and Gordon. After Gordon had let him work his wiles for a time he moved off to the exit, saying, 'Look 'ere, Nureyev, I'm not that way bent.' I long treasured the look of surprise on the dancer's face.

A few years ago Rita Moreno came on *Loose Ends*. She was in London to take over in Andrew Lloyd Webber's *Sunset Boulevard*. Drinking in the George afterwards the young comedian Tim Vine filled a silence by asking in reverential tones, 'Miss Moreno, did you ever meet Elvis?'

'Meet him?' she said. 'I dated him . . . but only to make Marlon jealous.'

This rates as the most concentrated name drop I have collected. Two real bouncers in eleven words.

Meeting someone well known for the first time, there is always the temptation to ask the one question that you know is out of bounds. I did it in spades with Judy Garland. She threw a party for a friend of mine, the American actress Marti Stevens, at a large house in the Boltons. It was a reasonable early 1960s mix. A lot of actors, half the Ad-Lib club, Danny La Rue, one or other of the Kray brothers. Miss Garland was accompanied by her newest husband, a tall, good-looking, dark young American called Mark. She arrived in London from the Far East. Australia was her forbidden subject. Her recent tour down under had been a nightmare. She was often late on stage. Her subsequent appearances were greeted with catcalls. Her performance had not always banished displeasure. She left in a hurry, grabbing the first plane out she could hop. In no circumstances was I going to mention Australia. I was introduced to her. 'How did you like Australia?' I said.

I need not have worried. She took a breath and launched herself into a vivid monologue. 'It was terrible! That country! They were so awful. I was a little late a couple of times. But they were so bad. I said to Mark, "Let's get out of here." We got a plane. I said, "Get any plane," and we got one . . . We got the last one out. We didn't even know where it was going until we touched down. It was the Philippines! When we got out there were all these little yellow men. And they all started shouting and asking questions and I couldn't hear what they were saying, and then I heard one say, "Miss Glaland" . . .'

She began to enjoy telling the story, mocking the Oriental accent using that infectious, comic quality which so often showed in her acting. '"Miss Glaland," he said, "is it tlue that you tlied to slit your lists thlity-thlee times?" Well, I didn't know what to say, and I looked at Mark there, so big and strong, and another one said, "Miss Glaland, is it tlue you slit your lists thlity-thlee times?" And Mark was so good and big and strong, and he said, "We don't give press conferences here. Let's go to the airline building."' Mark smiled modestly as Judy continued, 'And he took me along and there were all these little yellow men and cameras flashing, and we got to the building and they were all around us, and Mark was so big and good and calm and strong, and all these little men were saying, "Miss Glaland, is it tlue you slit your lists thlity-thlee times," and I still don't know what to say and I looked at Mark and he just looked right back and said, "What was the question?" "Miss Glaland, is it tlue you slit your lists thlity-thlee times?" And Mark just said, "Who counts."'

A friend of mine played piano for her on one of her visits to London. She took a fancy to him and installed him in her suite at the Dorchester. Thinking he'd hit the big time, he went out and bought a smart new sweater. Asked to admire it, Garland was furious: 'Don't you ever do that again!' She promptly shoplifted five for him.

CHAPTER 17

Thanks for the Memory . . .

Back in 1992 I received a letter from Richard Ingrams, the editor of the *Oldie*. 'Dear Ned,' he wrote, 'would you like to review memorial services for us? I am told that you go to nearly all of them.' Richard got his piece of not quite accurate information from Keith Waterhouse and Victoria Mather. However, it is true that I have made a habit of attending the memorial services of friends over the years and felt better for it.

A memorial service is not only a chance to pay respects and to celebrate a person's life. It is often a happy way to put a period to a time of mourning. Funerals arrive too soon. Even so, after arranging for Caryl Brahms's memorial service at St Paul's, Covent Garden, I had a recurring dream in which she would turn up to press a point. I would explain how inconvenient this was as there had been a full house for her send-off and how surprised everyone would be at her reappearance. Gradually the dream faded and it no longer comes to me, but there was something comforting in arranging the service.

I was happy to record these events for the magazine as I had so many rich memories of moving moments on earlier occasions: Barbara Windsor singing 'The Boy I Love is up in the

Gallery' for Kenneth Williams; Evelyn Laye gaily conjuring up the dancer John Gilpin from the pulpit of St Martin-in-the-Fields; and Dame Sybil Thorndike's service in Westminster Abbey. Sybil loved trumpets. Tremendous clarion calls blew her over to the other side.

Americans often have a more secular approach to remembrance. A theatre is taken and the stage is filled with the theatrical great and good, who bear testimony. When the leading American theatrical lawyer Arnold Weissburger died, his devoted companion, Milton Goldman, assembled a cast at the Golden Theatre which included Louise Rainer, Orson Welles and Martha Graham. Arnold's signature white carnation and silk evening scarf occupied a prominent position on the side of the stage. Then, with suitable changes of cast, Milton 'toured' the ceremony to Los Angeles and to the Haymarket Theatre in London, where he, in turn, was remembered in the fullness of time.

Milton was a gregarious New York agent. Arnold had also, at various times, represented Richard Burton and Elizabeth Taylor. Rumour had it that years earlier the rich lawyer, driving back into New York from Long Island one Sunday night, had stopped for petrol at a gas station where young Milton was minding the pumps. A romantic beginning to a relationship, but not one which anybody could get Milton to confirm.

The couple gave regular parties in their large apartment off Sutton Place and would visit London each summer and hold a week of pre-theatre parties at the Savoy. Here Milton could exercise his compulsive talent for introducing people, Arnold his equally compulsive desire to photograph his guests. On one occasion Milton introduced Robert Morley to his son, Sheridan, and both pretended to be delighted and to admire each other's work.

When Barry Norman was doing a TV feature on Broadway I arranged for him and his crew to join one of the parties. As it got into gear they emerged from a bedroom and Milton gave a bravura display introducing Barry five times to Alger Hiss and four times to

Sean O'Casey's widow. I once heard an English guest whisper in surprised tones, 'Is that Hermione Gingold over there? I thought she was dead.' To which an astringent New York voice replied, 'She is; but we don't want to spoil people's Christmas.'

At Milton's service at the Haymarket, Keith Baxter brilliantly caught his compulsive introducing style. 'This is Dame Wendy Hiller who is starring in such and such. This is Miss Martha Graham whose company opens next week. This is Keith Baxter who opened in a new play by Christopher Isherwood on Saturday and closed the same night. And this is Mrs X . . . [lost for words, obviously a civilian of no distinction] . . . who is a very devout Catholic.'

Their Savoy parties were at the height of summer. I once saw Vanessa Redgrave trapped on a sofa with Arnold's very old mother. Several attempts at conversation having fizzled out, Vanessa was beginning to sweat. It was before she had discovered contact lenses. I couldn't help overhearing her final desperate attempt to find a fruitful subject: 'Tell me, Mrs Weissburger, why did you and Arnold never have children?' Anna Weissburger had the distinction of once having called to her son across the Savoy suite, 'Arnold, Arnold, come over here. Mae West is leaving.' Only it happened to be Dame Rebecca West.

Milton's French was shaky – but he loved to exercise it. In Monte Carlo the pair called up Princess Grace. They were invited to the palace. They thought they were going to be given dinner but when the princess had shown them over the building she led them into a courtyard. Two large doors opened and before they knew it she was bidding them farewell. Stuck for dinner, they found a nearby restaurant, La Bonne Auberge. When they left Arnold thanked the proprietess in English. Milton was more ambitious. '*Madame, vous avez une Bonne Auberge et . . . et . . . et . . . vous êtes une bonne aubergine . . .* Oh my God, Arnold, I just called her a fucking egg plant.'

After Arnold's death and his theatrical memorial, Milton,

following a decent interval of mourning, started a new relationship. He told me of the first time he invited the beloved back to
the flat. As they entered the bedroom Arnold's picture fell off the
wall. Milton was a supreme optimist. 'I thought that was a gesture of confidence,' he said happily.

On occasion I find out things about a person at a memorial
service that a casual acquaintance has not revealed. At Hardy
Amies' memorial the programme quoted him, 'I expect to see
God in a five-button suit.' Selena Hastings remembered him
saying, 'Kim Philby was always pumping me for information.'
'Good God, what about?' 'My tailor, of course.' Did he fall in
love? 'Every week. With the milkman.'

Dame Thora Hird was eulogised by Victoria Wood and Alan
Bennett. Victoria felt that a stair-lift would have been appropriate to carry her up to the high pulpit. Alan gleaned a last glimpse
of a muddled Thora who called her daughter Janette to complain that she was filming with John Wayne and had been
abandoned on the set. Janette reassured her that she was in her
own flat. Thora doubted it. Janette asked her to look out of the
window. What did she see? 'It looks like the mews – but, you
know, they can do very clever things with scenery these days.'

At John Paul Getty Jnr's service at Westminster Cathedral
Cardinal Cormac Murphy-O'Connor found an ingenious way of
reconciling his text with the life that was celebrated. The text,
right on the nose, was, 'It is easier for a camel to go through the
eye of a needle than it is for a rich man to enter the Kingdom of
God. What is impossible for men', said the cardinal, 'is possible
with God.'

Robert Runcie's eulogies, like his sermons, were meticulously
researched. Regularly he called on his staff and others for
contributions. He was an excellent amateur mimic and a stylish
anecdotalist – no disadvantage. The careless spontaneity of his
speeches concealed conscientious enquiry and occasional ghosts.
He wrote around to Mervyn's friends before he eulogised Bishop

Stockwood in Southwark Cathedral. A half-sentence of what I supplied was woven seamlessly into the text. Although it did not appear in the printed text, he couldn't resist a concluding anecdote. Bishop Stockwood was 'outed' at a synod some months before his death. He had retired to Bath, and Jim Thompson, Bishop of Bath and Wells, rang him to warn him. Stockwood waved the worries away. 'And if the press get on to you, Jim, tell them I've had a lot of women, too!'

We learnt that when the great film director John Schlesinger received his CBE from the Queen she fiddled with the ribbon as she put it round his neck. 'Now, Mr Schlesinger, we must try to get this straight.' John took it as a tacit recognition of his homosexuality. Robert Runcie told us in Southwark Cathedral that the first question Mervyn Stockwood asked on arriving at the University Church in Cambridge was: 'Show me the relics; or are they already in their pews?' The *Evening Standard* film critic, Alexander Walker, was a fervent anti-smoker. At St Bride's Church the final touch was his recorded answerphone message: '. . . and remember, smoking is the slow way to suicide'.

So many theatrical memorial services are held at St Paul's, Covent Garden, that the rector, Canon Mark Oakley, is inclined to mutter, 'There's no business like holy show business,' after the more elaborate productions. When Canon Roger Royle announced the bidding at Bernard Braden's memorial Sir Clement Freud, a gambling man, whispered to Peter Cook, 'What's he starting at?' Gwen Frangçon Davies was over a hundred when Nigel Hawthorne arranged hers. He revealed that he had asked her if she was afraid of death. She replied, 'I'm always nervous of doing something for the first time.' When Dame Gwen heard that Dame Edith Evans was to be remembered in St Paul's she thought that meant the cathedral and hissed, 'She'll never fill it!' At the service for the theatre historian and museum collector Joe Mitchensen the actor Timothy West found a charming, obscure quotation from Victorian actor John

Coleman's diary: 'A *Tempest* in Glasgow. Ariel's flying rope snapped and she broke both legs. I was playing in Cardiff on the Monday – so never knew what happened to her.'

Alan Tagg was a busy stage designer from the moment he made the set for John Osborne's *Look Back in Anger*. Edward Fox saw him in a different context filling old footballs in his mother's garden with concrete and painting them pink. 'His soul is with God,' Edward told the congregation. 'But his balls are in Sussex.'

Brian Pringle, a much-loved character actor, was once arrested in charge of a tandem going the wrong way up a one-way street. His explanation? 'I'm looking for my passenger, Officer.' His favourite story concerned two old, needy actors. One reported that he had at last been offered a part. He was philosophical about it. 'Not much of a part. Not much of a play. But there's a cake in the third act.'

Michael Williams's favourite joke was revealed in the same church. The scene is Madame Tussauds. A man is asked to walk his wife up and down in the Chamber of Horrors. He asks why. 'Because we're stock-taking.' For many years Gerald Campion had played Billy Bunter on television. He resented being typecast. He was called to Broadcasting House for an interview. The producer spoilt his pleasure by asking him for 'a few "yaroos" to round it off'. Campion was incensed: 'I am happy to do the talk for ten pounds but if you want a performance, "yaroos" are fifty pounds each.'

The near excesses of the ballet critic Richard Buckle were beautifully summed up: 'He knew how far to go too far.' Paul Eddington's widow Patricia touchingly remembered that towards the very end of her husband's life the word 'oxygen' had been spoken by the bedside. He opened one eye and whispered, 'Did he say, "gin"?' When Paul was playing John Gielgud's old part in a revival of David Storey's play *Home* he was visited on the same night by Gielgud and by Storey's parents, resulting in 'mutual incomprehension never seen before or since'. At the elegant actor James Villiers' memorial Peter O'Toole quoted the Vicar of Arundel, who, conducting his funeral service, had taken for his text, 'In my father's house are many mansions.' He went on to point out that in the Aramaic this meant something different and more appropriate to Jimbo's lifestyle: 'It means "on my father's estate are many inns".' John Peter, dramatic critic of the *Sunday Times*, conjured up a mischievous vignette of his great predecessor, Sir Harold Hobson. He saw Hobson at a first night at the height of the Cuban Missile Crisis. Across the aisle sat his arch rival Kenneth Tynan. Peter observed Hobson, who was painfully lame, hobble across to Tynan and say, 'Kenneth, I gather we may never see tomorrow so I thought I would come over to tell you that I never really thought much of Brecht [Tynan's passion].' Tom Stoppard, eulogising Tynan, spoke to his children as he said, 'Your father was part of the luck of our generation.'

At Dorothy Tutin's farewell Patrick Garland quoted Tynan on her lovely, idiosyncratic voice, 'cooing like a turtle dove with laryngitis'. Often a quotation from the subject's writing hits the spot. You can hear Elizabeth David's dislike of powdered custard as she laments the passing of the syllabub: 'In 1846 Mr Alfred Bird brought forth custard and Mr Bird's brainchild grew and grew until the land was covered in custard.' Elizabeth sprang to my aid when I accused the biographer of the impresario Hugh 'Binkie' Beaumont, the eccentric actor and writer Richard Huggett, of inventing the menus which he claimed Beaumont lavished on visiting theatre stars when they played at the theatre he managed in Cardiff in 1923. He asserted that Binkie served avocados to his star players at the Royal hotel and invented deathless dialogue for the Welsh chef: 'How about a nice, little bit of vichyssoise to start off with, Mr Beaumont? Really nice when it is chilled, you will see, and they'll love it . . . or perhaps an avocado with prawns in a rich creamy sauce? You could serve champagne with it – always a good start to a meal.' A correspondence raged in *The Times* for weeks. No survivor of the twenties backed Huggett up. Although there had been occasional sightings in sophisticated surroundings the consensus was 'rubbish'. Elizabeth supplied a clincher: 'Notions of filling [avocados] with prawns, making them into a mousse with eggs and so on, were aberrations of the fifties and sixties, the sort of thing one found in Chelsea and Belgravia restaurants. I'm not sure the recipes weren't put about by the avocado growers themselves.' She was even more dismissive of Huggett's suggestion that Dame Marie Tempest might have served Binkie 'exquisite smoked mackerel with lemon mayonnaise'. Before the war mackerel was regarded as a scavenger and barely edible until the exhaustion of fish stocks in recent years. Elizabeth simply hoped that 'Dame Marie had better taste'. I had good reason to doubt Huggett's foodie expertise. When he understudied Timothy West for us in *Beecham* he invited Brian Kirk, the company manager, to dinner in his flat, which was above a prostitute's parlour in Old Compton Street. He served his 'vegetarian casserole'. His guest was disconcerted a couple of days later to see Huggett grubbing among the vegetable stalls in Berwick Street when the traders were packing up for the day. Enough had fallen from their carts into the gutters to provide an inexhaustible stock of 'vegetable casseroles'. It wouldn't have been so bad if he had bothered to learn Beecham's part.

Recently there has been a pocket-sized reaction against memorial services. Robert Morley dismissed them as 'cocktail parties for geriatrics', and John Gielgud, Alec Guinness and Elisabeth Welch all said they didn't want one – but they go on. Timing varies. Some choose the post-lunch period, around three o'clock – inconvenient. Lawyers – who are often celebrated in the Temple – tend towards the close of play in the courts. I go with Arthur Marshall: 'Nothing sharpens the appetite for lunch like a good funeral.'

Fleet Street, even after the journalists' diaspora, usually goes home to St Bride's. It boasts a versatile choir equally at home in traditional church music and Broadway show tunes. Dee Wells was remembered in a non-religious service there, happily received by the incumbent Canon David Meara. The highlight was Susan Crosland's memory of Dee staying at the Randolph in Oxford with the designer Hylan Booker. Her daughter had also booked a double room. When they were given their bills Dee noticed that she had been charged five pounds more than her daughter. She confronted the receptionist: 'I see you charge more for African-Americans – and, you know – they're worth it.'

Godfrey Talbot, long the BBC's royal correspondent and previously a war reporter, was fingered for a prodigious BBC expenses claim. 'For pulling vehicle out of mud . . . Drinks to King of Italy . . . Gratuity to nun for special services . . .' Michael Grade paid homage to the television sports editor John Bromley: 'He taught me all I know about journalism – unfortunately not all *he* knew.' More frivolously, there was a celebration in Blooms in Whitechapel and Bromley's order, 'Quick bacon and eggs, mate.'

St Margaret's, Westminster, hosts politicians and some political journalists, like Peter Jenkins, whose earlier period at the *Grauniad* was commemorated by a glaring misprint in the order of service, a reading from John Donne: 'No man is an inland.' Julian Mitchell picked out Peter's vitality: 'He was the only person I ever met who, when he was depressed, was depressed with gusto.' There was a Guinness Award for Delicate Tightrope Walking for the eulogist Lord Blakenham, talking of Arthur Guinness, Earl of Iveagh, soon after the Guinness/Saunders scandal. 'The introduction of professional management . . . had far-reaching consequences . . . not all of them good.'

Euan Graham's address for Alan Clark revealed that while Alan was at Oxford, 'He lost his driving licence for the relatively trivial offence of allowing a girl to drive his car sitting on his lap while he controlled the pedals with his feet.' In the same church we heard of Churchill's rebuke to Fitzroy Maclean, who was attempting to promote a cause: 'You have used the Mother of Parliaments as a private convenience.'

Warren Mitchell hymning the career of Sam Wanamaker at Southwark Cathedral, 'speaking as a non-practising Jewish atheist – thank God!' When John Osborne was remembered at St Giles-in-the-Fields a notice was pinned to the door 'forbidding entry to certain persons'. David Hare called Osborne, 'The English theatre's vital voice . . . he knocked down the door and a whole generation piled through.'

At a memorial mass for Coral Browne at Farm Street, Alan Bates represented her husband, Vincent Price, whose Parkinson's was too advanced for him to travel. Alan told the congregation that he had strict instructions from Vincent not to tell Coral Browne stories. Many in the church might feature in them. However, he said wickedly, he had not been told that he couldn't tell Vincent Price stories. He told two. Some months before her death he telephoned Coral in Los Angeles and got Vincent, who said, 'I'm sorry, Alan, she's out. She's gone to confession.' Pause. 'I think she'll be a very long time.' When Alan led a company at the Ahmanson Theatre in Hollywood in John Osborne's play *A Patriot for Me*, there was a nucleus of British actors in the cast. Coral and Vincent took them out to supper after a performance. Before they could order, a woman slapped an autograph book down in front of Vincent, said, 'Sign here,' and turned to engage Coral in conversation. Alan watched Vincent sign a bold 'Dolores Del Rio' across two pages and close the book. Dolores Del Rio was a Mexican film star – not long dead. When the woman had gone Alan remonstrated with his host. 'She'll be furious when she finds out!' 'No, Alan,' said Vincent, 'I have to do that. I saw Dolores just before she died and she said, "Vincent, don't ever let them forget me," so now I always sign "Dolores Del Rio".'

St Martin-in-the-Fields is as grand as you can get short of Westminster Abbey, Westminster Cathedral or St Paul's. Kevin

Whately revealed John Thaw's ability to mock himself when looking at a script: 'I can't say this rubbish. I'm a Commander of the British Empire!' And his speculation on how television programme planners might discuss casting him: 'Let's have that little, fat, white-haired one . . . that John Thaw.' At Peter Parker's celebration Professor Antony Giddens, director of the LSE, retrieved John Paul Getty's splendid recipe for success, 'Rise early, work hard and strike oil.' Here a trick was played on Spike Milligan. He once told Harry Secombe he hoped that Harry would die first so that he would not be able to sing at Spike's funeral. Harry obliged but the organisers of the service did not. They played a recording of the Welsh tenor and 'Guide Me, O Thou Great Redeemer'. Eric Sykes, one of Spike's oldest collaborators, told how long ago he had gone to lunch with Milligan in Shepherd's Bush. As they passed an undertaker's premises Spike threw himself down on the pavement in front of the door and shouted, 'Shop!' Eric reflected, 'It only took them fifty years to answer.'

Demonstrations are rare and distasteful at memorial services. There was a gay rights protest at the *Daily Mail*'s editorial policy when the life of Sir David English was celebrated at St Martin's. The faces of Lady Thatcher, Tony Blair and William Hague were frozen as the offenders and their placards were hustled away from the pulpit they had mounted. Bodyguards fingered the guns in their bulging pockets and let the church staff deal with the eviction. I witnessed one disturbance at Westminster Abbey. It was Bishop Trevor Huddleston's day. He would have taken it in his stride. So did the abbey staff. I could hear, but not see it. There were cries of 'Islam!' but whether they were for or against I could not tell. It was moving to see Hugh Masekela mount the pulpit. Back in Soweto, Huddleston got him his first trumpet, 'to the immediate discomfort of his neighbours'. To the lasting joy of the rest of us. Jimmy Tarbuck surveyed a full abbey from the same pulpit and remarked how pleased Harry Secombe would be to see the immense turnout. However, he added a Secombe caveat: 'Don't let Ken Dodd take the collection.' The abbey often combines theatricality with its inevitable grandeur. It serves cricket well. For Brian Johnston we had the 'Eton Boating Song', his regimental march and Richard Stilgoe in fine form with Johnners looking forward to angel cake while 'He talks to total strangers/Calls the Angel Gabriel "Angers".' Stilgoe saw Johnston's future as 'heavenly greeter': 'When St Peter's done the honours/He'll pass you on to Johnners.' Not to be outdone, Tim Rice wrote splendid Gilbert and Sullivan parodies for Colin Cowdrey. He had a little list, '. . . and then there is the batsman who will never walk, alas . . . unless at least three stumps have been uprooted from the grass . . . I think you've got the gist, he never would be missed.' Christopher Cowdrey recalled his father's flight to Perth to face Jeff Thomson at the age of forty-two: 'I think it'll be rather fun.' On arrival at the wicket he had greeted Thommo with an outstretched hand: 'I don't think we've met. My name is Cowdrey.' Was it after Johnston's or Cowdrey's service that someone said to Denis Compton, 'Can I get you a drink, Denis?' to hear Compton's magisterial reply – 'No, thanks, the prime minister's getting me one.'

A scatter of other memories. Alan Bennett – the laureate of eulogists – on the press after they had hounded his friend Russell Harty in his last illness, now furious because 'he died of the wrong disease'. Valerie Grove, speaking for Elizabeth Longford at Westminster Cathedral, recorded Evelyn Waugh's reaction when Longford's *The Pakenham Party Book* was presented to his wife: 'Laura has never given a party in her life. Pray God this book does not inspire her to do so.'

Frank Longford cropped up at the service for the agent and publisher Desmond Elliot at St James's Piccadilly. When Longford was on the committee to report on pornography he failed to see the funny side of Elliot's reply to a question about sex: 'I've only had two complaints. I gave them a refund.' It emerged that one of Elliot's basic tenets was, 'Have a few

influential enemies. They talk about one to all the right people.'
Leslie Thomas had dismissed the Irish institution in which Elliot
grew up as 'the only orphanage to have a Parents' Day'. When
Donald Reeves was the incumbent at St James's Piccadilly he
could never resist introducing the hymn 'Jerusalem' – one of the
top of the pops for memorials – by explaining the significance of
'dark, satanic mills'. Sadly, I have forgotten what it was.

Clement Freud queried the coat of arms engraved on the but-
tons of the cloak worn by Derek Nimmo's uniquely grand
chauffeur, 'Your coat of arms?' 'No, my chauffeur's.' Lord
Bingham recalled Lord Denning overturning a precedent estab-
lished by Lord Simon and six other Lords of Appeal, protesting,
'Lord Simon was very sorry he said that . . . he told me so.' At
Oxford David Pryce Jones sketched in a moment when the poet
Peter Levi taught his Stonyhurst pupils on a school outing to sing
'*Il est cocu le chef de gare*' out of the train windows as they drew
in to a railway station in the Auvergne. Peter Ustinov spoke as
an old friend of the playwright and speechwriter for Margaret
Thatcher, Sir Ronald Millar: 'I cannot remember how, or if, we
met . . .' Millar coined the notorious phrase, 'The lady's not for
turning.' Standing in the bar at the National Theatre one night
I heard a neighbour ask, 'Shall we go and see that play at the
Haymarket? It's bound to be good. It's by the man who writes
Mrs Thatcher's speeches.'

I cherish an invitation card which reads, 'John Warner sends
his apologies but requests the pleasure of your company at a
party, in his memory at the RAC Club Pall Mall, London SW1
on Thursday 11th September 2001 at 12 noon.' After raising a
few glasses to the original leading man of the musical *Salad
Days* we emerged to find that the significance of that date had
changed for ever.

The church next to Lord's cricket ground, St John's Wood, is
often favoured by cricketers. The great Warwickshire captain
R. E. S. Wyatt was remembered there. So was the comic writer

Barry Took. Barry and Alan Coren often picnicked in its grounds. Barry's sandwiches, bought at a nearby delicatessen, were always 'salt beef' so that he could add 'and make it lean' just to hear Sam, the server, say, 'Lean? Which way?' Geoffrey Durham told the congregation that the longest laugh recorded on *Round the Horne*, the show Took wrote with Marty Feldman, was instigated by creating a character as head of the Football Association and naming him 'Sweet' – so that when he answered the telephone he could say, 'Sweet, FA.' The late David Land, agent, impresario, manager of the Dagenham Girl Pipers, first bankroller of Tim Rice and Andrew Lloyd Webber, owner of the Brighton Theatre Royal, had a similar ploy. He called his company 'Hope and Glory' so that his telephone response was a simple, 'Land – of Hope and Glory.' We remembered him in his theatre. Jack Tinker had seen Land receive his doctorate of literature at Sussex University. Gazing at his black hat and yellow robes in a looking glass he muttered, 'They'll think I'm a rabbi with jaundice.' Tinker himself got a full matinée concert at the London Palladium.

My one-time doctor, Patrick Woodcock, had a lot of theatre patients – many of whom attended a mini-concert for him in Smith Square. Alec McCowen testified that Patrick was usually more interested in their productions than their medical problems. 'Who's in the play? Who wrote it? When does it open?' 'Patrick, I'm in pain!' 'Sorry, I forgot.' Chita Rivera could not resist the double double entendre in his surname. One of Patrick's *obiter dicta* has the ring of truth: 'A meeting between two oldies invariably degenerates into an organ recital.'

At St Luke's, Chelsea, where Dickens was married, Lt. Col. Harry Llewellyn, showjumper with 'Foxhunter' permanently attached to his name, was eulogised by the Master of Hickstead, Douglas Bunn. He gave an impeccable recital of Col. Harry's life and achievements but the address was memorable for a change of gear towards the end. There was a pause as Douglas weighed his message. 'There is one word which you don't usually hear at memorial services, but I've got to use it. And that word is "skinflint".' There was a marvellous murmur of affectionate collective recognition of Llewellyn's famous close-fistedness which rippled through the church.

Some of my happiest times have been at Hickstead with Douglas and his family. I have spent Christmas and Easter there most years since 1982. I am a director of the All England Jumping Course. Douglas likes a board who *know* nothing about his sport so that they can *do* nothing to ruin the way he runs it. I must have done a dozen or more addresses at memorial services. Easily the hardest was at the funeral of Lorna Bunn, Douglas's third wife, in 1995, a few days after she died by her own hand.

My friend Sharmini Tiruchelvam, who has a beautiful voice, is often asked to sing at funerals. It must be a strain as well as a very personal privilege.

I was relieved only to have to read at the funeral of my old Oxford friend Brian Brindley in 2001. Brian had come up from Stowe with a Wildean aura. His rooms were crammed with Victoriana, stuffed birds and glass cases full of exotic fruit. Walking down the High one day, carrying a glass walking stick, he was catcalled by Teddy boys. Studiously ignoring them, he also ignored a lamppost against which his glass stick shattered. Clutching the handle, all that survived, he carried on as if nothing had happened. After Oxford he became a priest. He was particularly successful in reviving Holy Trinity Church in Reading, transforming it into a gilded Anglo-Catholic confection. He followed three previous incumbents who had left under various clouds. Although he filled the pews, Brian, in time, fell victim to a piece of gutter journalism. As a result he left his parish and then the Church, transferring his allegiance to Rome. As he approached seventy he spent months planning an elaborate dinner party at the Athenaeum. He invited fourteen people 'who have played a significant part in my life'. I represented the

Oxford period. Lest one guest fall out, leaving a sinister thirteen, he arranged for a close friend to stand by at home, dinner jacket already donned. The eight-course menu he devised was prosciutto and figs; avgolemono; 'drest crab' with samphire; lime sorbet; *boeuf en daube*; summer pudding; angels on horseback; and fruit for dessert. I bounded in to find him in a white dinner jacket, a waistcoat reproducing the wallpaper of the Brighton Pavilion and a psychedelic bow tie. One stockinged foot rested on a gout stool and he seemed smaller, even than the last time I had seen him, a consequence of years of heart disease. I gave him a pot of caviar, saying, 'I thought I'd get you something perishable, Brian, because neither of us has long to go.' After the splendid 'drest' crab he looked distracted and excused himself. When he returned, propped up by the youngest guest, a fashionable jeweller, he sank on to a chair, his head lolling forward. The Jesuit historian Fr. Anthony Symondson, who had said the Latin grace, whispered absolution and when a doctor who was dining at the club appeared, he pronounced Brian dead. Fr. Symondson recited a beautiful formal prayer and a club servant asked the young jeweller, who had taken off his jacket while he tried to revive Brian, if he would put it on again. Brian would have approved the formality. We shared a chiropodist who told me that he had seen Brian during the afternoon. He warned him that if he did not go straight to hospital he would lose his toes. He told him, 'You could even die at your own dinner.' 'Then so be it,' Brian had said. 'I shall go down in flames.'

At the 'Solemn Mass of Requiem' offered for the repose of the soul of Brian Dominic Frederick Titus Brindley at St Etheldreda's, Ely Place, the oldest Catholic parish church in London, I read Romans, 8.1: 'Nothing can come between us and the love of Christ.' The passage of Isaiah which Alan Bennett read was inspired: 'On this mountain, Jahoveh Sabaoth will prepare for all peoples a banquet of rich food, a banquet of fine wines, of food rich and juicy, of fine strained wines.' Appropriately, Fr.

Symondson, who preached the homily, told mourners that they should look forward to meeting Brian in heaven, 'where some of us hope to resume our interrupted banquet'.

Of all the memorial eulogies I have written and spoken the hardest to prepare was for JAK, the fine cartoonist of the *Evening Standard*. Although I met him at a couple of luncheon clubs, I did not know him well. I was surprised when Claudie, his widow, asked me to give the address at St Bride's. I think he must have come home well inebriated from a lunch at which I had spoken and enthused about it to his wife.

What I did not know was just how riotous his life had been. Nor did I know that he had two families: one for whom he was legally responsible; another for which he accepted responsibility. Both families were at the service. The second could only be mentioned elliptically. I was allowed to say at the very end, 'Above all, he loved his children – *all* his children.'

I should like my own memorial service (if awarded) to come as a complete surprise. I would enjoy to speculate on the contents. One request: perhaps Maria Friedman might be persuaded to sing a song Gerard Kenny and I wrote for her, 'A Funny Thing to be Alone, Not Funny'. If not there is a lovely recording by Marian Montgomery.

And maybe someone among the singers with whom I have worked might offer Rodgers and Hart's ballad, 'I'm Talking to My Friend'. The rest? Jolly!

Until that day I shall continue to attend memorials of others and repeat Noel Coward's words to myself:

> It gives me comfort to dwell upon
> Remembered friends who are dead and gone
> And the jokes we had and the fun.

EPILOGUE

Soon after I moved to World's End in 1985 I interviewed myself for a magazine. 'People describe him as "a wit",' I told myself, 'and yet in private he rarely says anything funny. Indeed, he confesses that the things he says in public are usually written for him by someone else.' As my own interviewer I was able to describe my location – a flat on the first floor of a large mansion block built at the turn of the twentieth century. 'Pleasant gardens flank the macadam path that leads up to the front door. A patch of garden on the left is ablaze with cottage garden flowers – roses and hollyhocks predominate.' I greeted myself and found myself clad, to my surprise, in blue jeans and a pink denim shirt, 'though for his public appearances Mr Sherrin is usually seen in three-piece suits. The informal garb has the effect of making Mr Sherrin seem even taller,' I noticed, 'than he does on television, where we do not see him nearly as much as we once did.'

I observed that I lived alone. 'His flat is a sprawling affair. The long central corridor is hung with song covers of the "hits" of the music-hall star, Marie Lloyd. The master bedroom is decorated in dark green, the walls hung with costume designs from *Liberty Ranch*, one of his theatrical productions. The bed was unmade. The second bedroom has become a library with no room for a guest bed – to his relief. The passage opens out into a hall which doubles as a dining room. On the walls are hung glass walking sticks in many shapes and colours which Mr Sherrin inherited from his collaborator, Caryl Brahms.'

I then led my interrogator into the living room. 'Spacious, airy and light. Plainly this is the result of "knocking through". Scattered around the imitation "coal" fire are a comfortable sofa, a couple of armchairs and a baby grand piano. The room looks out over the gardens. French windows give on to two small balconies. We admired the gardens below. Mr Sherrin disclaimed any responsibility, giving the credit firmly to his neighbours.'

In fact, beside the 'good garden' there is an untended one immediately beneath me. The good garden is the fiefdom of Mr Munns, flat number one. Mr Munns likes to have a garden but not to work it. On the other hand, Mr Mount, who lives way up in number seven, loves to garden. He has the run of Mr Munns's turf. For producing an enchanting floral display, Mr Munns rewards Mr Mount with one excellent bottle of wine a week. Everyone is happy, especially me.

My interviewer didn't get much more out of me. 'Mr Sherrin had to change into a broadly striped blue suit to attend a first night.' There were some regrets. 'Although he had been unfailingly polite, I did not feel I had got to know much more about the man behind the ample façade – probably no more than Mr Sherrin knows himself.'

There is some dispute over my address. The Post Office insists I am in Ashburnham Road. The sign opposite clearly says Cremorne Road. Both names have their history. Cremorne Farm was at one end of Lots Road – which led to the house where the Lots family lived. As when people who visited a Dutch family at the top of Manhattan in the seventeenth century used to say they were going to see the Bronx, the name stuck. In 1785 Thomas Dawson, created Viscount Cremorne, converted his farm into gardens. They were opened to the public in the 1830s as 'the resort of a motley crowd of pleasure seekers' – just down the road from Crazy Larry's, which in the 1990s was a teenage bimbos' disco. The nineteenth-century passion for ballooning flourished in front of our as-yet-unbuilt mansions. A certain Charles Green made 526 flights from there. On one he was accompanied by a lady with a tame leopard. I have a print but it does not feature the leopard.

Cremorne was shut down on 5 October 1877. Terraces of workmen's cottages – now desirable residences – covered the greenery. Alf Brandon, a born-again tailor and Baptist minister, a 'prude on the prowl', had published verses on 'the Horrors of Cremorne . . . a nursery of every kind of vice'. The proprietor of the gardens, a man called Baum, sued him for libel. He won a farthing damages and no costs. He was too ill to renew his application for a licence so the area found respectability.

And it suits me. I have never had any problem with a solitary life. Thirty years of working a demanding schedule with Caryl, snatching every leisure moment to write, frustrated any desire I might have had to share a domestic life. It certainly made my two attempts at some sort of partnership difficult, but in any case neither would have worked out. Both were with men starting on their careers. One went on to be a very successful theatre director. The other, twenty years younger, I met in New York during *Side By Side By Sondheim*. In 1977 he was feckless and thirtyish with an obsession for a glossy model-driven clique in Manhattan, refusing to mature, although there was a very definite theatrical talent as a director which he never properly pursued. When we split up and I left for England, he spread his wings and applied himself for the first time, finding a niche in a big advertising firm in New York, developing and organising their computer systems. He has continued to work highly successfully in Internet advertising; his childlike inquisitiveness and enthusiasm, balanced by his new-found maturity, have prepared him perfectly for this rapidly expanding field. We have remained excellent friends. We meet when we are in each other's cities and take holidays together.

I published a diary for 1995 in 1996 (*Sherrin's Year*). It

contains enough further information about my private life to satisfy the very curious, but now, some ten years on, that is the stuff
of nostalgia.

My brother Alfred retired in 1990. Having a hip operation is
no good for a working farmer if he continues to work. Besides
that, he was past irritation with the increasingly complicated
European directives. He could not subscribe to the idea that you
should make more money out of *not* growing something on a
piece of land than if you did. I went down to collect a few bits
and pieces which lingered at the old farmhouse. It was the day
he was selling his farm implements.

A catalogue advertised, 'Highly attractive and genuine dispersal sale of three tractors, Toyota Land Cruiser, farm
machinery, implements and effects.' The implements and effects
were lined up in the Home field: harrows, cultivators, scythes
and sickles, rubbed blades with a sheep footbath, two of
Lampert's of Somerton's finest tipping trailers and several cider
barrels.

There was a group called 'Bygones', now good museum
fodder but mostly implements with which I can claim first-hand
acquaintance from childhood. There was the twin-screw cider
press complete with frame, a 'Day of Mark' apple mill, a winnowing machine, and the 'Long Single Twin-Furrow
Horse-Drawn Match Plough. With Press Wheel' – with which
Herbie Bown used to win ploughing matches, guiding Jolly, the
chestnut carthorse, or Captain, Bonny or Prince. They would
return festooned with rosettes attached to the shining brasses on
the polished harnesses.

The bean droppers, the bull tether and the hay sweep stood
alongside the hay elevator, which the farm men christened 'Ned'
when I was too young to lift the bales alone and had recourse to
it.

Alfred unearthed a copperplate inventory of the last Sherrin
sale on my grandfather's death in 1903. Same auctioneers. Some

of the bygone items appear in it. Bought in then by an uncle. The bean dropper fetched six shillings, the apple mill five and the winnowing machine three guineas. I hoped Alfred would do better. In fact, the winnowing machine went for a mere two quid. A few months later I was doing a *Loose Ends* programme from the Brewhouse Theatre in Taunton. A man in the audience told me he had bought the cider press and the apple mill. He was well pleased with his bargain.

Alfred retired to Lydford-on-Fosse, a few yards away from the spot where we waved our Union Jacks in the thirties as the brand-new king and queen made their progress to inspect their Duchy of Cornwall. From Lydford he indulges his hobby of giving expert on-course commentaries on West Country point-to-points.

I intend to stay in Chelsea until the big box arrives. Some years back – to be precise, it was Sunday, 20 March 1988, because it is recorded in the *Kenneth Williams Diary* for the day – Kenneth Williams wrote, 'I was dining at Joe Allen.' He was with his mother, Lou. 'I drank Fernet Branca, seemed to ease things. Had soup and then fish. Ned Sherrin was at the next table and we chatted.' In fact, Kenneth was 'working the room' energetically, leaving poor old Lou alone. I went across to keep her company until, after some ten minutes, he returned. However, I got my reward in his next sentence: 'He is a kind and courteous man.'

That is the epitaph I would like added on my parents' gravestone in Kingweston churchyard when my ashes are scattered around the Somerset soil. It would surprise a few people.

ACKNOWLEDGEMENTS

I would like to thank those who generously agreed to my sampling their material for this book: Peter Barham, for his daughter Debbie's sketch material (which she first submitted to *Loose Ends* at an even younger age than I thought), Alistair Beaton, John Bird, Christopher Booker, Eleanor Bron, Sir David Frost, Robert Gillespie, Gerald Kaufman, Herbert Kretzmer, the Right Honourable Lord Lang of Monkton, Peter Lewis, Charles Lewsen, Keith Waterhouse and Alan Watkins.

I am also extremely grateful to Deborah, Duchess of Devonshire, and Alexander Mosley, on behalf of his mother Lady Mosley, who both agreed to some of their spirited correspondence appearing in this volume.

My progress towards this milestone has been piloted by my literary agents, Rivers Scott and Gloria Ferris, while Deke Arlon and Alison Sloan tidied up the rest of my life, and Tom Erhardt at Casarotto Ramsay looked after the plays I wrote with Caryl Brahms. Christine Motley has successfully deciphered my unruly longhand, having computer skills at which I can only marvel.

Finally I must thank Antonia Hodgson and Iain Hunt at Little, Brown for guiding me through the narrows of publishing.

Ned Sherrin
Chelsea, 2005

INDEX